Ma, Your Son is CRAZY, Do Something!

JC Fabio

MA, YOUR SON IS CRAZY, DO SOMETHING! by James C. Fabio

Published by James Fabio

For permission requests, contact the publisher at:
James C. Fabio
jcfabio.com
jcfabioauthor@gmail.com

This publication is a work of nonfiction. Names, characters, places, and incidents are verified to the best of the author's ability. Pseudonyms have been used is some instances to protect the identity of certain individuals.

Edited by Salvatore Smiriglio
Book cover by Peter Selgin
Book cover photograph by Sae Hee Hong

First Edition: October 2025

ISBN: 979-8-9932660-1-5
ISBN: 979-8-9932660-2-2 (pbk)
ISBN: 979-8-9932660-0-8 (ebook)

Preface

I decided to write this book at the insistence of my cousin. He is a natural-born storyteller. His stories, outlandish tales of his life on the edge, always seem to be exaggerated to the point of hyperbole. He often says: *I had a crazy life; I should write a book.* When he asked me to help him write a book, I hesitated but then thought, why not? I never wrote a book, and this may be very interesting. We certainly had taken very different paths in our lives. Perhaps by revealing our shared experiences and contrasting our choices, readers could be entertained. Maybe the readers could learn from the consequences of our choices. Thus, the premise of the book was born.

This book is biographic and autobiographic. The people, places, and events are real and true. His experiences and my experiences are weaved together and contrasted. His words reflect the actual dialogue I recorded. Real names of the people referenced by my cousin are only used if they are deceased or have a third-party reference such as a newspaper article. Real names referenced by me are also used. Some are public figures; some are professional acquaintances. Many are family members.

I recorded my cousin's stories over a thirty-month period between 2022 and 2025. During our rides to his doctor appointments or drinking coffee in his apartment, I put my iPhone on video and let him share whatever came to his mind. He shared names and events in detail despite suffering from a stroke many years earlier. Most of the people he spoke about were referred to by a nickname. He did not remember dates very well. To understand a precise date or timeframe I was able to reference the event with who his girlfriend or wife was at the time. His stories were a puzzle that needed to be pieced together. Remarkably, what he told me has been substantiated as mostly factual. With either a nickname, name, or description of an event I was able to find references in newspaper articles and other sources from the internet.

My cousin's pronunciation is terrible. At first, I had trouble believing if anything he was saying was true. He kept taking about Butchy. *That Butchy was a terrible person.* Every time he said his last name it sounded like the first letter was V. I could not find any reference to anyone with the last name that sounded like Vitea. Nothing in ancestry.com, nothing in newspaper.com. I thought the stories were the made-up tales of a madman. Only when we were driving on Saw Mill River Road and passed a diner was I able to discover that Butchy was a real person. I found an article that described a murder. A murder in front of a diner in Yonkers. Butchy's last name was revealed. My cousin was telling the truth. I started to believe his outlandish tales. And I started to understand the extent of his sordid lifestyle.

Introduction

Ma, your son is crazy, Do something!

I have heard this statement so, so many times. It was my cousin who described his sister's plea to their mother, a plea to address his bad behavior. I have heard stories from my cousin who is only five years my senior, and who was an enigma to most of his family. His stories seemed so over the top, outrageously so, and detailed. It often left me amused, embarrassed, and even bewildered. It left me wondering whether any of it was true. How would anyone find out since he never gave complete details on anything? And when you asked clarifying questions for some more information on the subject, he became suspicious—even irritable—and eventually, he clammed up.

My cousin often hinted at making lots of money by running after-hours casinos in New York and by sharing bits and pieces of information about mafia figures who had run-ins with the law. Could any of it be true? How much was embellishment, or bravado, or just grabbing someone's ear for the sake of talking? I had no idea, and no one in the family did either. At best, family members would know only what he told them during conversational snippets at holiday gatherings. Most of the time, family members shook their head and just accused him of being crazy.

Don't listen to him, don't get involved.

They would say in a hushed tone.

This story involves two cousins whose lives intersected for decades; it is a story about whispered secrets, true and verified accounts; stories about how choices induce to good and evil, and how life takes sundry twists and turns that lead to either virtue or immorality.

Robert claims he should be dead by now, but someone is watching over him, he just doesn't know who. I know better and hope for him to understand. In God's time, not mine.

Chapter 1

> If you only notice human proceedings, you may observe that all who attain great power and riches, make use of either force or fraud; and what they have acquired either by deceit or violence, in order to conceal the disgraceful methods of attainment, they endeavor to sanctify with the false title of honest gains.
>
> —Niccolo Machiavelli

Monkey! Monkey! Monkey! Monkey!

Screaming rang out in rapid successions. The six of spades was dealt. There were murmurings, and disbelief, and intense expectations of a face card.

Monkey! Monkey! Monkey!

These Korean workers called face cards *Monkey*. Anticipation was palpable, and intense. The gamblers rubbed their sweaty hands and fixated their eyes as if frozen in time on the dealer's swift fling on the cards. Money was on the line, and the thrill to win spiraled the mind down a money pit. The heart thumped ever so hard that it sounded like a hammer on anvil. Every card dealt was an extra heartbeat.

Four of hearts! Aaah shit.

The room was crowded with five players that consisted of the dealer, a doorman, a waitress, and ten or so guys who were waiting for their turn at the 61st St. Club near 1st Ave. There was nothing fancy about this club. A ground-floor entrance led down five steps to an apartment focused on one activity, blackjack. The walls were dark grey, with three pendent lights shining brightly on the card table. All card players were singularly focused on what would be revealed from the dealer's quick hands. These were working men with labor-torn faces looking for action and for the big win. They came to play alright, but the club won every time. Tonight was reserved just for the working dogs. These beaten down riff raff were exhausted from their jobs as they delivered, lifted, carried, drove, and whatever else these wretched men routinely did. On Thursday, Friday, or Saturday, guys and girls showed up with their dates abreast to flash their money. The after-hours were reserved for those who wished to get lucky at cards, and maybe, if lucky, pleasures of the flesh. They gulped bountiful shots of hard liquors, snorted coke, and filled their lungs with weed. And while intoxicated, they gambled and gambled at a fever pitch until the wee hours of the morning.

Koreans love to gamble!

Dasi kadeuleul deonjinda, throw the card, Joker! Spade! Ahhhhh, Ssibal geulae, ssibal geulae, fuck yeah!

A crowd of Korean men were delirious seeing Ho-jun win with three jokers. *Don, don, don, keundon*: big money for this emaciated Korean delivery guy who reeked of cigarettes, smelled of whiskey, and stunk of foul fish. As he was elated in gathering more chips than he had ever seen, he boldly cried out:

Cash me, cash me out, hahaha, you Jesus Christ, JC, JC, you are my luck, you, you the best, you JC!

George *Kelly* Ambrosini, the doorman, and his friend Matty laughed, mocked and laughed harder.

JC, you are JC mothafucka.

And the nickname was instantly hatched, the dealer would be now known as JC. He laughed, downed another Heineken, and went in the back room. Bobby, a six-two dropout from Yonkers was tired, but so self-satisfied. He didn't care about his old man's drudgery, why would he? After all, he knew that he would be dealing again, and most importantly, he'd clear easy cash. He counted on easy cash to gamble, easy cash to play the horses, easy cash for craps, and lastly, easy cash for blackjack. He was greedy, and when he gambled his face changed to a pale-yellow tinge, as if he were stricken by the color of the second deadly sin. This is what got him excited, quick easy cash, no bullshit. During his first night on the job, he was nervous but totally focused throughout the eleven p.m. to four a.m. game. Breaks for the bathroom, breaks for coke, then back to action, and nothing else but total concentration. He loved it. His take-home pay was one-hundred and fifty dollars, Ho-jun won eight-hundred dollars, the club thirty-thousand dollars. Everybody was a winner.

Listen, Bobby, Johnny Mac has heard good things about you, he wants you to work the club, Don Key Park, 230th Street in the Bronx. Get there at midnight, we'll have two tables going, you'll be with Kimmy, she's got the other table, you understand?

Got it! Eddie patted him on the shoulder.

Ok, good.

Busy night, rowdy crowd, but no one got out of hand. Everyone is checked for guns and knives at the door. You are not getting in if you have either, no excuses. George was big and jovial to those he liked but he was mean, brutal, and violent to those who crossed the line and caused trouble. He didn't put up with any crap. When George was at the door, the dealers always had an easier time with drunken guys who fumed over their losses. Robert, known to his friends as Bobby and to everyone else as JC, was big, but wasn't going to start throwing people out in the middle of a game. That was George's main job. He was trustworthy and had the dealers' back, besides, what was five-foot five petite Kimmy going to do?

Money rained into Robert's coffers like manna from heaven. He raked in $150 a night, and a hundred or so more on tips from the Asian gamblers. Robert was a friendly guy to the Asians who were notorious gamblers, always polite, and made sure the waitress knew when they needed refills on the overpriced whiskey, or whatever food the gamblers requested. Robert, the smooth operator that he was, smiled at will, effortlessly and authentically. He converted cash to chips quickly, so a game would keep rolling. On his night off he would make his way to other clubs run by Johnny Mac, or head to Atlantic City, or stay local and head toward Yonkers Raceway. Blackjack excited him, but horses were always exhilarating; you could hear a thrill in his voice, see a glint in his eyes, and his arm gestures became wildly animated, as he shared the excitement he felt when he won a large amount of cash. He became effusive with his play-by-play analysis of winning hands. He, naturally, scrutinized every card, every decision, and every counter-move made by rival players. He loved it and would spend hours at OTB or any club with tables. He mostly lost, but like every gambler, winning enough times kept him feeding his thrill. After working the club, he would make his way back to the Hideaway Bar in the Bronx, have a few beers, smoke a joint, and answered Pop's questions about the state of business. Pops was Johnny Mac's father, an affable older gentleman with huge hands that were worn through manual labor, but now in retirement, gladly collected the news at the end of a night's hustle.

Bobby, how was it tonight?

Pops, stop saying Bobby, I don't want these people knowing who I am.

Bobby, how was 61st Street?

Pops, I always win, I try my best.

Oh, God Bless You, we love you!

The late seventies trudged along. Legitimate work was a thing of the past. His life was about gambling, partying, drug dealing, and womanizing. He always snorted the best coke and smoked the best pot; connections get you those things. Connections also get you to easy money and sanctioned violence. He was protected by the unknown, by unspoken rules of the clubs and by the constant flow of money. While working, he'd take breaks in the back. Eddie would say,

Go relax, take thirty minutes, tell me what girl you want, we'll send her back, remember, no rough stuff.

Easy women and prostitutes always were around the clubs ready to fulfill the lust of those who won quick money or comfort the poor bastard hanging on to his last hundred to ease the burden of losing three months' worth of wages. Coke, liquor, beer, and sex poured in between poker hands. He thought he had the life.

I don't give a fuck. Robert would say.

I believe in myself. I don't care about anybody.

Once, there was a Russian guy who was gambling at the 84th St. club. He was losing and getting loud, and Robert took notice. He was just yelling at the cards being dealt. There were low cards, no face cards; but nothing to win with. Five hands passed by, and he was losing fifty bucks a pop. Eight more hands and he made some of it back, but he was still down five-hundred dollars. As the night wore on, he started to curse, slammed the table, and soon agitated some of the other gamblers. Most players just ignored the hulking Russian and chose to continue to converse with their buddies, or simply concentrate on the game at hand. This churlish Russian with short hair sported a gold horseshoe on his ear lobe; perhaps thinking it was a good luck charm. He spoke with a raspy voice that accentuated his Slavic accent. His grand gestures displayed a distressed Soviet attitude, and an air of toughness to be reckoned with. Robert was visibly irritated, lost his patience, and confronted him:

Listen, this isn't fucking Russia, quiet down or I'm gonna throw you the fuck out.

The enraged Russian responded belligerently and growled: *Fuck you, you can't tell me what to do, just deal the fucking cards.*

He stared with hatred in his eyes. Robert reacted with a facial contortion and a snarl in his voice, barking;

Listen, you fuck, you're in America, we don't do that here, either you quiet down and play or get the fuck out.

The Russian mumbled to himself, repressed his rage, continued to play three more hands, ordered another whiskey, and finally erupted:

Fuck this, this table sucks, you're stealing from me, these cards suck, this is fixed, this is bullshit.

Now it was getting personal. Robert responded with a disbelieving tone:

Stealing, fixed, are you kidding me? I run a legitimate game, no one accuses me of that bullshit; listen, you're done, you fuck.

Robert stopped dealing to him. Twenty minutes earlier Robert made eye-contact with the doorman who understood what that glare meant. Now the Russian was seething, flaming darts shooting from his bulging eyes. He stood up from his seat and with an even raspier voice he growled again:

Deal the cards you fuck!

Like a bolt of lightning, ten guys rushed in and surrounded the out-of-control Russian:

Hey you, fuck head, over here.

Two guys each grabbed an arm, another guy put his hand on his shirt behind his neck and together they pulled him up. He was big, stocky, and ready to fight. They got him up, turned him around and another guy had a hand on his throat. The raging Russian gagged and stifled his words as his face reddened from the chokehold. The security enforcers loosened the hold, and the truculent Russian pled in a semi-choked voice:

Hey, what's going on, I just want to play, give me my chips, I just want to play. I didn't mean anything. This is bullshit.

As he struggled to get free, Robert triumphantly blurted:

I told you, you fuck, you're gone.

That's it, he was gone. The stupefied Russian was gone. He vanished like a bad dream as if swallowed by a casino down the depths of Hell. The ten guys who took the Russian got a call from the doorman to come and fix a problem, and they did. If they had to come out and solve a problem, they did so with purpose and speed. His game was over. If you interrupt the money flow, action will be taken. That is the rule. No tolerance for anything else.

On Thursdays, Fridays, and Saturdays, Robert would go from club to club. Sometimes he would be at the 26th St. storefront, other times in the basement of the 84th brownstone near Lexington Ave., other times at Don Key Park on Bailey Ave. in the Bronx. If one casino shut down, another popped up. Johnny Mac and family went back generation upon generation here in the Bronx. They had access to bars, apartments, back rooms of every kind of delis, dry cleaners, and small mom and pop business all over the Bronx and Manhattan.[1],[2] Eddie Ackerman was the number two man running the operation. Even the license plate on his green Cadillac displayed #2 in large blue digits on an orange background. He made sure that money flowed, and operations ran smoothly. Eddie stored cash in the trunk of his luxury car, but he took no chances, he made absolutely sure to have no weapons or cards, for police could practically smell their presence.

Others who knew Johnny Mac counted on their cut of the profits, and they sure as hell were going to get it. Others, the overseers of every illegal gambling operation, drugs, prostitution, theft, loansharking, and extortion reigned supreme in their realm. They had their turf well established before Johnny Mac's business mind kicked into high gear. Italian immigrants ran backroom gambling clubs throughout the Bronx, Westchester, and Manhattan. They operated with impunity. Johnny Mac saw a business venture and paid the Belmont "Capos" for protection.

Who the fuck are you, you guinea bastard? And who the fuck let you in here? We don't allow you fucks in here.

Robert was dealing at the 1081 Club on 79th and 10th Avenue. It was a run-down studio apartment with a couple of blackjack tables with flood lights centered on the tables and a bar off to the side. Guns drawn! Robert was approached by two big, boorish looking Irishmen: they were true sociopaths. They loved violence, and they were willing to give him some sort of beating just for pleasure. Robert cut a formidable figure with his long, brown hair with an eighteen-karat gold rope chain around his neck, and matching gold bracelet around his wrist. He was muscular, self-assured, and held his ground. Robert certainly didn't look Irish. He generated a visceral response because of it. These thugs were animal-like as they snarled and salivated like stray dogs with their eyes fixed on the prey, ready to attack. He was told to deal at the 79th St. club near 10th Ave., and that was what he was doing. This was Westie territory. They catered to their own, no undesirables were welcomed. If you weren't one of them, Irish that is, you were not welcome.

Who let you in here, why are you here?

Fuck you, I'm JC, I'm dealing. I'm the dealer.

Guns were in his face, as three more goons grabbed him, pulled him, and yelled,

Fuck you, you guinea, who let you in here?

I'm JC. Get out of my face.

Robert didn't back down to anyone, not even to those Micks who pranced around with total disdain for anybody, especially Italians. They loathed those interlopers, those Wops from Sicily. Robert was tough and didn't care about who faced him, nor did he care if he was beaten to a pulp, he understood survival and he was fearless, ready to throw punches if he could get his hands free and the guns out of his face.

Ask Johnny Mac. Ask him if he knows JC. Don't give me your shit, fuck you. Call this number, call Johnny Mac.

With guns aimed in his face, odds weren't good. At the very least, he was going the get a serious beating, maybe broken arms and legs, and probably dumped somewhere. At worst, he was history, gone and turned into mincemeat, or dog food. The leader was a guy named Jimmy C. who continued to berate him

Fuck you, who let you in here, we don't let guys like you in here.

I'm JC, I told you, call Johnny Mac, he sent me here.

Jimmy C nodded and one of the crew disappeared. A few minutes later he came back and leant in his ear.

Ok, he checks out.

How do you know Johnny Mac?

I work for him in the Bronx, and the clubs on the East Side.

Guns were put back behind their jeans, the stranglehold was released. Things calmed down. Robert was offered a whiskey. He downed it in one gulp.

Ok, finish the game, we'll talk afterwards, deal me in.

After a few hands, Jimmy said, *That's it, game over.* He watched him deal and appreciated his skills. He was cocky and he dealt fast, stood his ground, and showed no weaknesses.

You come here. Listen you now work for me and Johnny Mac, you get it?

Good, yes, good.

You need anything, you have any trouble, you call me, you got it?

Yes, I got it!

Robert just got a raise; he was now making four-hundred dollars a night to deal cards in Jimmy C's clubs on the West Side.

Money rolled in, and it was easy money. Robert dealt four, sometimes five nights a week. There were tips, there was coke, there were many types of women, there was flowing beer and powerful weed, there was, best of all, free money.

Robert bought a new custom Trans Am with the golden eagle painted on the hood and rented an apartment downtown. He oozed cockiness, money, and power. His hair was long, and his wrist sported a golden Rolex. A gold chain hung on his neck, and his fingers sported shiny, golden rings. The Korean women who hung out at the clubs liked his charm and his bravado. They were working-class girls, culturally submissive, and respected money, and as such, treated him like a god. Life was good. He was paid in cash and paid for everything in cash. He paid his rent in cash, stayed in hotels in cash, bought clothes in cash, rented cars in cash. He never had a bank account, never had a credit card and never had a driver's license. His fake license was acquired through friends that were proficient in forgery. He never paid taxes, and never filed a tax return. He was proud of what he did. He never gave a second thought about his life in the underworld. He loved the opportunity to work and amass wealth, no matter how. He never gave a second thought regarding the illegitimate world of gambling and extortion because ultimately, it would feed his appetite for wealth and a lavish life. The ends justified the means, once noted Machiavelli. He robbed people who won at the clubs, and who had lots of cash on hand. At times his losses were big. He liked the thrill of the big payoff, but this was a lean month, and that felt like a punch in the gut.

Down big! He owed people money, money that he lost at the track. But that wasn't all, he, the master of the trade, lost big playing blackjack. Jimmy C. always told him to come to him if he needed anything. He wasn't going to get cash, but he was going to get tip-offs as to where to get easy money.

Jimmy, I need some money, you have any extra work? Do you need a job done?

Jimmy C. liked Robert, as he had him on the payroll. He was a good kid, he worked when asked, dealt fast, and kept the blackjack table humming.

Listen there is a guy who is a bookie. He came to the 49th St. club last night. He's got $25K. Just pay him a visit where he works, it's easy money.

Robert automatically nodded as he was grateful for the tip. He staked out the delivery door at 11th and 45th at ten p.m. when the warehouse was closing. The last man out was the guy Jimmy C. pointed out to him that he, the guy that is, would be there. Robert entered, eyed the shaking man, shoved a gun to his face, and with a menacing voice demanded his money. The balding man was in his mid-fifties and displayed a prominent paunch and was not ready or able to put up any resistance,

Don't hurt me, I'll give you anything you want.

Give me the money and you'll be fine. Now do what I say, move. Ok, ok, over here.

And that was it. Easy money, Robert mused, as he disappeared into the night with twenty-five thousand dollars.

Jimmy C. gave Robert lots of tips over the next few months. Robert made Jimmy C. lots of money dealing cards for his illegal clubs, and Jimmy C. provided tip-offs where Robert could get easy money, one hand washed the other, a win-win for both men. Other times Robert earned money by collecting debts. Jimmy C. often played the part of loan shark. The rates for transactions were on the high side. Robert made a healthy percentage by doing collection duties, life was easy pickings, he loved his job.

Listen, this Serbian fuck owes me eighty-thousand dollars and has not paid a dime. Make sure he pays.

The deal was, Robert would get ten percent of what he collected. He had the juice, a certain confident fierceness to induce the Serbian to pay up. He and five other burly guys carrying axe handles were ready to do business, and off they went. Robert told me that axe handles were the best because bats broke too easily and are too bulky.

Axe handles do the job, will knock a guy right out if he resists.

The message to pay up was delivered with a half dozen swings of the axe handle on the Serbian's back, arms, and legs. Forty-thousand dollars was forked over, and he promised the rest the following week. JC hinted a smile as he turned in the take to Jimmy C. who then nodded in approval upon seeing the weighty cash. The men parted in silence as there was nothing further to communicate.

Chapter 2

Sangu du me Sangu, Blood of my Blood

—Richard Gambino

JC was my cousin, his actual name was Robert, a guy I hardly knew. In the late sixties and early seventies, we celebrated many family gatherings. We lived fourteen miles away from each other and there was an age difference of five years. Robert's behavior was so out there, so different from the rest of the family, that he had to be from a different planet. Actually, I really didn't know much about any of my cousins except bits and pieces when I listened to table-talk between my parents and my aunts and uncles. There were all kinds of conversations on many different topics; topics such as who's getting married, what grad school is he attending, or what's so and so's latest career. These conversations were both about joys, and sorrows.

Over the years I listened, I had no choice in the matter, since I had to be there. I listened to my parents' whispering about Robert, and Uncle Jack's boasting, and about Cousin Vinny's warnings. I listened to Aunt Margie talk about her fur coats, listened to stories about Uncle Jack's new cars, listened to stories of Robert's latest escapades and his beautiful Korean girlfriends. And I paid particular attention to what Robert didn't say.

What was really powerful in all this was my father's priceless expressions. You learn quite a bit if you read the faces of your parents, and you get to know their moods and their thoughts. I came now to understand my dad really well. I deciphered his enigmatic expressions and came to understand their true meanings. Expressions that were hidden in plain site until wisdom and experience helped me navigate the true meaning of this nonverbal form of communication. My high school grades aroused a distinct facial expression, a particular look. Bad grades elicited *the look*. Getting thrown off campus in college, that definitely elicited *the look*. My choices in girlfriends elicited *the look*. That unmistakable look was one of disappointment and contempt. He tilted his head, tightly pressed his lips, and swiveled his head left to right three times. Many times, the look was followed by an expression he heard his father Basilio utter so many times. A phrase that expressed an impossibility:

Quando sole facia sera!

This phrase expressed the impossibility in nature. The impossibility that the sun itself could make the evening.

The combination of the look and the phrase was reserved for endeavors Pops thought to be most impractical.

This time, the look and phrase were meant for Robert. Pops learned that he was a card dealer. His brother Jack bragged about how successful Robert was in his new endeavor. My father had no first-hand knowledge about private clubs, or illegal gambling. Those were the interests of the people with no education looking for fast, easy money. Those were the people my father escaped from growing up in the Fordham section of the Bronx. A peculiar world where wagging tongues whispered in the ears of the most powerful figures in the community. Patronage and corruption went hand in hand. This was the Bronx, the borough where the police precinct was named Fort Apache, the borough of broken dreams and dilapidated old buildings. A part of New York City where the vocalizations of derision and contempt was coined The Bronx Cheer.

It was the late 1970s and all I cared about was getting more at bats on the high school baseball team, scoring tickets to concerts in NYC, and getting a beer buzz with my friends at the local bars with my fake ID. At the same time, I had another cousin running a successful real estate business in Whitestone, as well as another cousin who was pursuing a master's in economics from Columbia University. But then, there was Robert.

Pops, what do you mean he's dealing cards? Like for an Atlantic City casino?

The conversation stopped, if it was a conversation at all. It was I who overheard a comment, not just any comment, but a consequential one. During a family party, my father attempted to learn more about Robert's nefarious activities. My father was not a skilled conversationalist, at times a dialogue with him was as futile as having a cogent conversation with a mad man. If he were seeking an answer, he reverted to his default position by asking some questions with a small commentary, and if he wasn't satisfied with the answers, the conversation turned into an interrogation. Robert's perturbed reaction at one Christmas gathering was:

Uncle Paul, you ask too many fucking questions!

He snapped back in annoyance at the increased attention to his career choice. Robert had a way of throwing out small pieces of information here and there, boasting for example, about winning big in Atlantic City. He bragged way too much about how to bet, and about the inner workings of a casino, and he droned on and on as if casinos were the center of gravity in a modern society. He shared details of the specific brand of cards, commenting that Bee are the best because they do not bend easily; or the discarding of decks when the dealers changed shifts; or when to double down, and what to look for when watching other players face cards.

These were small signs of his intimate knowledge of gambling, a knowledge available only to people in the inner circles of that venal world. Gambling represented a seedy world where addiction consumed the mind, and people lost their moral moorings. He abhorred the very idea that people treated life like a tenuous roll of the die where wealth and destitution were cause and effect of a random moment, and just like that, puff, you and your world could end in financial devastation. Games of chance were too much for my father, for he valued frugality, temperance, and probability. He never considered risks simply to satisfy an appetite, a thrilling urge. Pops was not a risk taker. He hated to lose his hard-earned money to worthless schemes, or to professional card sharks. He believed in a real career, a successful line of work. He was driven by curiosity, as he wanted to learn more: Why was his brother Jack always bragging about his son? Where was all this money coming from? How did he afford the new cars, the fancy fur coats, and trips to some Caribbean resort? His nephew did not even graduate high school. How does this happen? My father wanted details, but he wasn't able to get much, but the little he learned was enough for him to form an opinion. That opinion came in the form of an expression: the unmistakable look of disappointment and contempt, his head that tilted slightly down, his lips that were tightly pressed together, and the head that swiveled left to the right three times. Now this disappointment and contempt was aimed at Robert.

Robert grew up in the Seminary Heights neighborhood in Yonkers, just south of St. Joseph's Seminary. This area was predominantly comprised of second and third generation Italian and Irish families. According to the population census, Yonkers in the nineteen-seventies was the third largest city in New York, but it was the smallest in geographic area. It sits just north of the Bronx and could very well have been part of New York City except for a vote where the residents overwhelming favored the forming of their own city. Yonkers sits along the east side of the Hudson

River, opposite Bergen County, New Jersey. The Palisades, along the West Side of the Hudson River, is a stretch of cliffs that start south of the George Washington Bridge and continue north to Rockland County. Housing and development north of the bridge were shunned in favor of keeping its natural beauty. Yonkers has a beautiful view of the Palisades, yet its development takes no advantage of its natural beauty. The city of Yonkers was formed by glaciers with hills and ridges that run north to south. This city grew and developed into a jumble of apartment buildings, row of houses, warehouses, light industrial constructions that finally blended into the characteristics of the areas it bordered. Southeast and Southwest Yonkers bear a resemblance to apartment buildings and high density lots in the Bronx. Getty Square, an epicenter of municipal and industrial activity, was filled with highly clustered houses and factories, and main transportation arteries that converted from trollies to vehicular traffic. Northeast Yonkers looks more scattered, just like Hastings-on-Hudson, a town with a small business district surrounded by suburban housing development. The further north you go, the bigger the lots and the housing become. Backyard privacy was one of the assets. From these backyards the smell of cooking wafted in the air as children played. The buzzing of families arguing, and nosey neighbors gave way to upper middle class living. Yonkers became a rich tapestry for diversity, dynamic interactions and division, and a good neighbor policy accented by good fences to make it so.

As the demographics changed in immigrant communities, families migrated to Westchester County. Second generation immigrants from the Bronx now wanted to own a house in the suburbs, but still have reasonable access to New York City. Single family earners strove to educate their children while keeping up with the cost of living and insulate themselves from the changing demographic of Black and Hispanic residents clustered largely in the southeast and southwest neighborhoods. It was widely known that Yonkers was one of the most segregated cities in the United States.

Robert lived ten doors down from his Aunt Josie and Uncle Jack Schinasi and their three kids. Josie was Robert's aunt as well as Jack's sister. They were supportive of each other and had each other's back. When Jack Fabio was short of money, he would walk down the street and borrow twenty dollars to get him through until the next pay day. If Jack Schinasi needed a hammer or other tools, he would know where to get them. Every Easter the three Schinasi kids, Linda, Garry, and Richie, would walk down the street to their aunt and uncle Jack and Margie Fabio, to show off their new Easter outfits and take pictures. The three Fabio kids, Jackie, Patty, and Robert would then do the same and walk down to see Josie and Jack Schinasi. They were close growing up in post WWII Yonkers. They lived their lives with their friends on the streets.

I grew up in a small hamlet known as Pearl River, just seven miles west of the Hudson River. Pearl River is not actually a river, and doesn't have pearls, but rather small community traversed by a body of water called Muddy Brook. Someone with business sense attracted developers and businesses to invest in this area and Pearl River emerged as a vibrant community, and with its newly minted name, it certainly sounded more impressive than Muddy Brook. Pearl River is known for Central Avenue, a wide street that recalls the open, country roads of rural America. Perhaps the most unique downtown area in Rockland County, this double-wide street enabled large horse-pulled wagons enough turning radius to make U-turns. Julius Braunsdorf, inventor of the carbon-arc light bulb, and the first postmaster of Pearl River designed the street layout. Pearl River was also known for the now defunct Lederle Laboratories and its large campus. For decades, Lederle was the largest employer in Rockland County. Lederle was founded in 1903 by the former New York City Department of Health Commissioner

Ernest J. Lederle, who purchased a ninety-nine-acre farm to start a pharmaceutical company in order to produce diphtheria antitoxin.

My father Paul came to Pearl River in the nineteen-fifties when he received a job offer as a chemist at Lederle Laboratories. He was the only one in his family to finish high school, and more impressively, he earned a Masters in Organic Chemistry from Stevens Institute of Technology in Hoboken, New Jersey.[1] He also was the first to venture over to Rockland County, unlike his other brothers and sisters who moved to Yonkers or remained in the Bronx with their families. My father Paul and Robert's father, Jack, were hard-working men who embodied the old-world view of family life. They were the bread winners and the ones who controlled finances. The women were the anchors of family life. Housework, cleaning, and cooking were the domain of women. Robert and I were fortunate to have devoted mothers and to be raised in close-knit families. My father's generation was driven by different values, with a rigid moral code of *pater familias*. The male head of the family ruled the roost, while the women abided and deferred to the decisions of the men.

The Fabio family was a mystery to me for many years. We knew little about my grandfather, Basilio, and where he came from. Pops would often muse about his upbringing in the Bronx, and utter words like *Mannaggia*! (Damn it), *Mulignana*, (eggplant), *Cucuzza*, (zucchini), *Salsiccia*, (sausage), *Chooch* (idiot) and *Citrullo* (stupid) or phrases his father would say. The aforementioned

Quando sole facia sera,

or

A fa Napoli!

Literally, *Go to Naples*, which was akin to tell someone to Go to Hell! Or the ultimate put down of a slut,

Puttana du sceccu, (meaning, a donkey's whore).

Amused and bewildered we wanted to learn more of this mysterious language and of our ancestors who spoke it. We were left unfulfilled with his answers. We were curious about the events and circumstances that shaped his life and that of his siblings. Many times, after dinner, my brothers and I would linger around the dinner table waiting for dessert. This large, round, pine table, stained walnut, dominated the kitchen. It was our home's center for dining, discussion, debate, and discipline. Here we found ourselves asking:

Da, where did you your father and mother come from in Sicily?

His reply was always the same.

I really don't know. I think my father was from a town near Messina.

He would comment while deep in thought as he tried to enlist his memory banks to fill in the details. He knew his mother was from Corleone and that she had many brothers and sisters, but he lost track of who they were. He had a vague comprehension of how his cousins were related to him, and my knowledge of his extended family only came from those who sent him Christmas cards. We asked him to write down what he knew. His feeble attempt barely filled half of a post-it note.

A family reunion of the Crosbie clan, my mom's people, lighted a spark in my interest in genealogy. The central meeting place was at St. Juliana's Church in Rock Lake, PA. A church built in part by Mom's great-grandfather and grand uncles, as attested by the stained-glass windows in the church sanctuary, which displayed the donors, James Crosbie, and his two eldest sons, Daniel Crosbie and Cornelius Crosbie. Cousins of my grandfather, James Leo Crosbie, organized a gathering and tour of the homestead, cemetery and church in 1992. His father, James Edward Crosbie, was the youngest of eleven children borne to James Crosbie, originally from Kirkcudbright, County Balbrex in Scotland and Catherine Reilly, originally from Virginia, County Caven in Ireland. An old family Bible recorded a saying about James Crosbie, *GOD BE RIGHT AND JIM CROSBIE BE RIGHT*. Family lore stated that James Crosbie was recruited to keep peace amongst the Irish homesteaders. I met so many distant relatives from around the country and was fascinated to learn how we were related. I began to think why no one on my father's side of the family had not recorded their own family history and stories.

When *The Godfather* movie came out in 1972, I had little awareness of the stories of Sicilian immigrants, or organized crime. All I heard about the film was that the main character, Vito Corleone, was from the same town as my grandmother. My father would giggle at the dinner table about being teased by his friends that he was from a mafia town, Corleone. My father was so far removed from the old world. He was an educated, family man. A man of science. He shrugged his shoulders when asked by his children about his family background. He had no burning desire to research it, as genealogy was just a curiosity that had little practical application to earning a living and raising a family. He learned little about life in Sicily from his father, Basilio, a man who my father described as a tyrant. I grew tired of not knowing where my family name originated from or knowing any details of why my grandparents emigrated from Sicily to New York. I was partly inspired to research my father's genealogy by the television miniseries, *Roots.* This TV production was one of the few shows where the whole family was encouraged to watch together. My father tolerated sitcoms with my mother, but when an educational series interested him, he made sure the whole family was just as excited as he was. *Roots* was based on the book by Alex Haley of the same title. It allowed me to see the possibilities of discovering my own family history. The stories of Alex Haley's ancestors were fascinating and highly entertaining. Unfortunately, years later the authenticity of the stories came into question as accusations of plagiarism and historical accuracy tainted the author's declarations. It all seemed so true at the time. We had all also watched *I,* Claudius, a miniseries about the lives and political intrigues of the early Roman

Empire. My father would explain that this was Italian history, Roman history, and that we were somehow connected to the past. I was only a teenager at the time of these miniseries and had little discipline or resources available to undertake any serious research on my family background. Not until decades later did the burning desire to carefully research my family background become a reality. It flowed from the discipline I learned when studying the Bible and the desire to know more about what I would come to believe.

My father's family followed the traditional Sicilian convention of naming their children after relatives. The children were named after their grandparents, aunts, and uncles. Robert's father, Jack, was the eldest of five children born to Basilio Fabio and Antonia (Lina) Berlingeri and was named after Basilio's father Giacomo. Giacomo translates to James in Italian, yet everyone called him Jack. Joe, the second eldest, was given the birth name Giuseppe, named after Lina's father, Giuseppe Berlingeri. Agnes, the third child, was given the birth name Gioachina and was named after Basilio's mother Gioachina Odovardi. Josie, short for Josephine, was named after her maternal grandmother, Giuseppa De Luca. My father Paul was originally named Frank Paul Fabio. Frank was short for Francesco, Basilio's oldest brother. Francesco, a military police officer in WWI, never settled in America but moved to a town called Cividale del Friuli in northeast Italy. My grandmother seemed to like the name Paul, in honor of her own brother, Paolo, better. The hand that rocked the cradle made the final decision. My father officially changed his named from Frank Paul to Paul Frank. He never even knew he had a *Zio* Francesco until I discovered the vital records in Sicily.

Basilio Fabio was born in 1887 in a small hilltop town called Galati di Tortorici, now renamed Galati Mamertino. I poured over ship manifests of Italian immigrants stored on microfiche reels housed at the National Archives in New York. For hours I flipped through reels looking for anyone with the surname Fabio, trying to locate Basilio's date of arrival and any other information dutifully recorded at the town of embarkation. It was five p.m. and eureka, there it was. Basilio Fabio arrived in New York on the steamer, *The Sicilian Prince.* I knew it was him because he was accompanied by his sister Carmela Fabio, and uncle Carmelo Odovardi. Galati was recorded as Basilio's place of birth. Further research into Italian phone books revealed that there are more Fabio *cognome* (surname) in Galati Mamertino than any other town in Italy. This small town sat on the edge of the Nebrodi Mountains of Northeast Sicily. Throughout the centuries, the ancestral generations of Fabio's lived and died in that ancient parcel of land. Gioachina Odovardi, his mother, was from a nearby comune called San Marco D'Alunzio. She arrived in New York in 1902 to join her brother Salvatore Odovardi at his Elizabeth Street apartment in Manhattan. She died in 1903, two months after Basilio arrived in New York with his sister Carmela and uncle Carmelo Odovardi. With no money to cover her funeral expenses, Basilio's mother's body was transported from Columbus Hospital, later renamed Cabrini Hospital, and buried in an unmarked grave in Potter's Field. As a young man, Basilio settled in Brewster, New York. He worked and went to night school, which showed his resourcefulness and impetus to succeed in those early years of isolation from everything he knew as an Italian immigrant. He met Antonina "Lina" Berlingeri through mutual friends. Portrait cards were exchanged between the parties, which supplemented the introductions and courtship ritual. They married in 1915 at the Italian language store-front church named Chiesa di Nostra Signora del Carmelo, Our Lady of Mount Carmel, located on 187 St. and Belmont Ave. in the Bronx.[2] This church became a hub of activities as it was the focal center of the entire community. Basilio and Lina's kids spoke Italian, or rather some version of Sicilian, most likely the Corleone dialect that Lina, who never learned to read or write, spoke at home. Lina would tease Basilio's Galatesi accent saying he sounded like a rural mountain peasant, unlike her sophisticated accent from the cosmopolitan town of Corleone. Jack's uncles, Vincenzo, Biagio, and Libori Nicola (Benjamin) Berlingeri, were plasterers who settled in the Fordham section of the Bronx. Basilio acquired a peddling license to sell produce in New York City, and after getting married, ran a neighborhood grocery market in Ozone Park, Queens, and then finally settling in the Bronx near his brothers-in-law. Jack studied portraiture painting but was not accepted into the professional schools of the era, so he settled for painting houses with his brother Giuseppe, who everyone called Joe. Jack was a marine who proudly served in the H & S Battery, 1st Battalion, 11th Marines in the Pacific Theater in WWII. He bragged about, with a degree of patriotic pride, his war exploits, especially killing; *Them Japs.* He would dramatize his feats while squeezing his right-hand index-finger, extending his left hand and screeching Rat-Tat-Tat-Tat. He would then move his arms more emphatically, with a sudden crazed expression as if reliving the war drama: his eyes opened wide and gleefully as if he saw war-crazed Japanese soldiers charging us. It was entertaining to see his excitement, but little did we know of the real horrors of what he experienced. War scars your body, but it also scars your very mind. In a letter to his brother Joe, Chief Petty Officer, stationed in Portsmouth, RI on October 27, 1944, Jack shared the following: *"But brother Joe, the main thing is that I'm still in one piece. I thank the Lord for that. I'm fine & doing well. I gave & given Japs plenty of hell & how brother. In fact brother I made myself a popular Marine & name for myself & Fabio's Yep! Joe I have spotted early one morning in our area four Japs. I killed them with my B.A.R. Killed more Japs with my machine gun & so forth with my men in the sections...I was the first gunner on my 50 cal. machine gun."* Jack never forgot the bloody carnage left in the blood-soaked battle fields of Peleliu littered with brave US Marines and fanatical Japanese soldiers. Jack never forgot guarding Rev. Joseph T. Ryan, the future Archbishop of the Archdiocese for the Military Services, as he said last rites over the war dead at the Okinawa battlefield.

Jack Fabio never finished high school. Instead, he learned the trade of painting and plastering and wound up working for his uncle. He talked incessantly, rambling about anything that came to his mind. He had a soft heart with a tough streak. He never hesitated to share his opinion, no matter how offensive. He held his convictions strongly because he believed in his physical power. He was endowed with confidence and his physicality gave him power and fearlessness. Once, while driving in New York City with his bride Margie and Robert in the early '60s, he saw a guy slap a girl in the middle of the street. This man could have been married, they could have been boyfriend/girlfriend, could have been anything, didn't matter. Jack stopped the car, got out—despite Margie's screaming—and proceeded to throw punches at this brute who was pummeling a defenseless woman. Robert noticed!

On the other hand, Paul was more composed—thinkers usually are—not prone to use fists to settle a perceived injustice. As a kid, he was cautioned to take it easy with physical activity due to his heart murmur, a condition that could cause harm if not careful. Paul was a sophisticated man, and he enjoyed the pleasures of the mind. His likes were eclectic, as he enjoyed opera and classical music. Oh, how he loved those colossal symphonies of Beethoven and those grand operas of Verdi. His father Basilio, also a music lover, took him to Manhattan to experience live performances, to bask in the ambiance of arias, ensembles and chorus'.

As a married man, Pops pursued gardening and bowling as his preferred hobbies. He was proud of his dahlias, so proud in fact that he entered his prized flowers in garden shows. He prodded his sons to turn over the soil in early spring to prepare for planting. But he loved doing it himself because he felt something special about the sensation of the soil in his hands. He would dig some loose soil and put it in the cup of one of his hands and rub it and sniff it, appreciating that his composting efforts would provide the nutrition for the diversity of flowers, fruits, and vegetables in his prized garden. Throughout the summer, we enjoyed multiple varieties of tomatoes, peppers, cucumbers, lettuce, corn, string beans, eggplant, and zucchini. He loved the aroma of grilled eggplant and zucchini drifting out of the grill on the back porch. He was filled with pride as every ingredient in the salad came from the work of his hands. Lettuce, radish, cucumber, carrots, tomatoes, peppers, onions, and celery. He was pleased that the work from his sweat and toil was enjoyed by a grateful family. He was especially fulfilled that his toil saved the family money. Money which he hated to spend.

His passion for rhododendrons led him to become President of the Tappan Zee Chapter of the American Rhododendron Society.[3] He would teach us how to deadhead the fading flowers of his many varieties of plants after the May bloom and to be careful not to pinch away the new growth. Despite my father and Jack being complete opposites, they never interfered with the family reunions. These familial bonds could never be broken; they were bonds created by Sicilian immigrants forged over centuries that defined your identity. The bonds of family, and extended family, allowed you to thrive and prosper in a city of possibilities. Robert and I had the bonds of family, two fathers who were close brothers, who celebrated life triumphs and mourned each other's loses. But similarities stopped there. Jack divorced his first wife after WWII. He had a son, Basil James, whom he rarely saw. His first wife remarried and settled in San Francisco. Jack remarried and had three children, the youngest being Robert. Neither Jack nor Margie finished high school. Higher education was not a priority, as in their minds, hard work was the ultimate goal to achieving the America Dream. Jack owned a painting business, an honorable trade that provided a steady stream of income, especially with Jack who excelled in paint mixing and plastering. Robert apprenticed with his father from an early age. It was a tedious job with long, endless days. On the other hand, while I was taught how to paint correctly, with accuracy and speed, there was no option for me to learn this trade. On the other hand, while I was taught how to paint correctly, with accuracy and speed, there was no option for learning a trade. I once expressed an interest in carpentry, or being an electrician, in high school, but my father chuckled and said that I had no choice because, as he sternly said:

You're going to college!

Meanwhile, my mom was the only college graduate on her side of the family. She became an elementary school teacher who graduated from the University of Oneonta.[4] My parents were determined that my brothers and I all to go to college, no matter what. It was not open for debate.

During the summer I worked the packing lines at Lederle Laboratories. I either sat at the end of a conveyer belt and collected polio vaccine ampules in the chill room or grabbed Centrum multiple-vitamin bottles in the larger assembly line area to place them in a box. I earned eight dollars an hour for my effort, and it was a bonanza for a high school kid like me. It surely beat working as a paper boy. My summer job was mind numbing. I mean, it was a chore to pack and to collect polio ampules in paper trays, then quickly take four of those trays and place them in a ready supply of small boxes, and finally collect those boxes to place them yet in larger cardboard boxes. I labored eight hours a day, not to mention that I worked in a chilly room in the company of cranky old women, uneducated gossips, and a bunch of slackers whom my parents would label as unambitious. This was a tedious job where time ticked ever so slowly, so monotonously, hour after long hour, day after eternal day of soulless, repetitive work: work governed by a shrill whistle to start, and again a shrill whistle to signal time for the blessed breaks, and the final whistle to signal the end of the hard day. This could have been my future if I didn't study hard.

This job taught me a valuable lesson. If I did not study hard and focus, I may end up as a mindless automaton working in a vacuum. I chose to go to college and sit through lectures and science labs, as opposed to the drudgery of a packing line.

I hate painting! Work, work, work, work all day long. All Jack did was paint, and now that's what I was doing.

Robert had enough of painting. He started trailing around with his old man and uncle since he was nine years old. Jack would mix his own paint to create the colors that customers requested. He would make sure everything was clean before he would leave. Everything had to be done right. The Fabio Brothers Painting Company had a reputation to maintain. Long hours and sacrifice were part of the equation. The Fabio Bros. served the Bronx and lower Westchester. Business was steady and supported the needs of their growing families.

No little league game this Saturday, you're working with me and your Uncle Joe. We have a job in Pelham and you're coming.

Pops, they want me. I want to play. Why do I got to go with you on a Saturday?

I'm teaching you and you're coming and that's it. Get ready.

This is garbage. I never have any fun.

He attempted to go out the basement door and run to Mike's house down the street before Jack caught up with him and cracked him over the head with his knuckles. This was how Robert learned his ongoing lesson: the cracking of knuckles on his head knocked some sense into him, and thus he learned a trade. Painting was Jack's money stream, conversely for Robert it was drudgery and boredom. Robert had no choice, he was going to paint closets, listen to his father bark out commands or listen to the endless story-telling as Uncle Joe listened, and laughed.

Robert learned other lessons. He learned how to read the racing forms and to understand the odds and what they paid out. When Robert was ten years old, Jack would have him read the racing results published in the local paper, *The Herald Statesman*, or the *NY Post* or *NY Daily News*. Who won the third race? How much did it pay out?

Spiral Down won, Pops, two-hundred-fifty dollars on a five-dollar bet.

How about the fourth race?

Dixie Rose won, three-hundred dollars on a ten-dollar bet.

You see Robert, I don't have to work, I make free money!

Robert looked at him and remembered the long hours of painting and of cleaning-up. He wasn't sure what to believe, but he took notice: bet small, win small. Robert would rather take a risk and bet big. High risk, high reward, he thought. He studied the odds, and he learned which odds were more likely to pay big. He learned not to bet trifectas since they would be too risky. He mastered schemes and patterns early on, and he discovered that reticence was a paralyzing force that prevented a big payoff.

I fondly remember the family reunions during the Christmas holidays. Between Christmas and New Year's, we would go what we affectionately called *"visiting."* We would go off to the Bronx to see Uncle Joe and his family; we also visited Aunt Agnes and her family. Both families lived near Pelham Parkway. Uncle Jack and his family, and Aunt Josie and her family lived on Hayward Street in Yonkers, just north of Yonkers Avenue. I can never forget the ornate way my Aunt Margie, Robert's mom, had decorated her small cape cod style house. The house was decorated with lush, Italian landscape paintings on the wall, including an artwork Jack painted in art class. The painting featured an Italian girl filling a water jug at the fountain of the town piazza. My aunt's house showcased some interesting furniture as exemplified by wood-inlay end tables in a rococo style, as well as a sofa and chairs with gold trim covered in clear plastic that stuck to your legs when you stood up. This was quite a contrast to the sleek Danish modern furniture style my mom preferred. I always thought I was missing out on Italian style and culture whenever I visited my father's family in Yonkers.

The Fourth of July arrived with a morning electric storm that crackled all over New York City. The Bronx registered a temperature that climaxed to an unbearable ninety-five degrees. Fat raindrops pelted our windows. The storm rattled the china in the dining room, and the whole family was jolted out of sleep in a state of bewildered confusion.

We were well prepared for the Fourth of July celebrations, but mother nature delivered an early flash of lightning rumble, and we feared the thunder most of all, especially us kids, even though we love Fourth of July fireworks. But this was Saturday, the Fifth of July of 1969, and we planned for a party, a big one, one with Pop's side of the family. Late that afternoon, Dad's family was coming over to partake in this great American celebration. As a little kid, I looked up to my cousin Garry. And even though he was twelve years older than me, he treated his younger cousin with respect, not as some little kid to be ignored. When all the relatives started to arrive, Garry headed to the downstairs of our black, high ranch house with a brown shopping bag. He winked and smiled and for some reason he said: *Don't touch.* My brother Tim and I instantly knew this was something we had to see but we promised not to touch. We craved to see what was inside that mystery bag, and we schemed some stratagems. We kept on wondering about the brown paper shopping bag; we kept on looking at it. We just waited and hoped for the right time.

When no one was looking, we opened the closet door and peeked into the bag and saw it was loaded with fireworks. We fumbled through the bag and saw an assortment of large and small rockets, firecrackers, cherry bombs, and a gray cylindrical explosive we later discovered was called an ash can. There were different sizes and a rainbow of different colors. We looked at each other with hearts racing, for the excitement gripped us like a pair of pincers.

This bag of breathtaking possibilities was sitting there ready to be had, just sitting in the closet. We peeked at the bag for a second, and for a third time as well. Temptation is the devil's workshop, and our burning demons were urging us to pick up this pyrotechnic bag of tricks. We couldn't believe that our father was so liberal with this bag of magic. But my father, ever so cautious, distrusted our judgement in handling anything so potentially dangerous. We weren't even allowed to hold sparklers.

W... W... Watch out, it's too close to your eyes!

my father would scream before taking them away for good. They let us burn punks however, those sticks that burned slowly producing smoke and a hot glow. We were allowed to twirl that around. At eight-years old I thought,

Big deal, this isn't fun.

My father was a prudent man, and his careful nature would not allow him to spend money frivolously or would not allow him to be daring with fireworks. But this once he did; he did so without raising an eyebrow. He surrendered to the family dynamic where his brothers and his sisters and nephews and nieces expected a big show.

As night fell on this hot summer evening, the fireworks show began as the women and children kept a safe distance on the back porch and the patio underneath. The men, drinking beers, smoking cigars and cigarettes migrated to the far end of the backyard to light up the night sky. Even the house shingles stained in black creosote reflected the light and amplified the loud bangs of these wonderous explosives. My father kept a casual frown, for this type of amusement was against his nature.

Our house sat on a one-acre lot next to our neighbor Frank Fornabio who expressed concerns about rockets landing in his backyard, or worse, on his roof. My father allayed his concerns and assured him that things were under control.

The fireworks were set up in front of the vegetable garden. He warned everyone not to step on his precious vegetables as they were just starting to flourish from his careful springtime cultivation.

Be careful! Don't step on my bed of vegetables. I don't want the stems disturbed; they are delicate. Don't step in the soil and ruin the roots.

I wanted to get close, but a stern voice boomed:

You stay right there and watch from the patio.

He intoned with that rare moment of irascibility. I sulked for a while and yearned to be older and do away with this baby stuff, but I quickly recovered and went for dessert and soda to better enjoy the magic of fireworks. I didn't interact with Robert much, for after all, a thirteen-year-old wants nothing to do with an eight-year-old when his older sisters boyfriends showed him what a good time is like. I was jealous of my cousin, who acted with an indifferent attitude toward his younger cousins. Robert was allowed to light rockets. Why couldn't I? I burned inside. The answer, of course, was that he was older. I mocked him in my mind, oh, yes, he was old enough! Finally, a eureka moment blazed my mind: I realized that our respective families had different values. I could not quite describe it. I observed how careful and cautious my father was with his money, children, and hobbies. I contrasted that by my uncle's willingness to spend money for cheap entertainment and tolerate the unpredictability setting off explosives in a small backyard. Even though I was so young, I realized that there were differences between my father and his family, but at that tender age I could not articulate what the difference was. All I knew was that my uncle and cousins were fun to be around and conveyed a slightly different set of values. Such are the lessons of fireworks and pyrotechnic displays.

I liked Robert and clearly remember our horseplay together during our Christmas get-togethers at his home in Yonkers. My two brothers and I wrestled the now fourteen-year-old Robert who was somewhat big for his age. Tim, Paul, and I joined forces to bring down the maturing, tall Robert. He would swat us around like gnats. We tried to bring him down, but he stood firm like a massive bolder. We snuck to his parents" bedroom and started to grab and kick and punch. After all, boys will be boys, and wrestling and playfighting was how we got excitement and expended our wound-up energy. Robert tossed us around and around as if we were made of pillows. We jumped about as if circling a wrestling ring. We threw off our sweaters and shirts as sweat poured down our brows and underarms. The bedroom filled a blend of different scents of perfume and sweat as we threw our aunt's fur coats off the bedspread and onto the floor.

Grab his legs! Twist his arms!

I barked to my younger brothers while I jumped to grab his thick neck. He thrust us around like we were three rag dolls, and the impact on the bed-coils shook the lamp on top of the end table, nearly toppling over, and perfume bottles jostled, almost falling to the floor below. Aunt Margie heard the commotion and yelled,

Knock it off!

We froze for a moment, then continued to play-fight. Aunt Margie marched right in and screamed at us like our Catholic school nuns when irritated by a classroom of unruly school kids at the end of the day. We laughed in exhaustion. Aunt Margie screamed even louder,

Get back to the living room. Now!

We froze for a second, then soundlessly walked with our heads bowed in submission back to the living room, half-heartedly apologizing for not behaving. I remember feeling exhilarated from the expenditure of muscle energy as we strived to best Robert's strength and stamina. We grunted and laughed alternatively with each attempt to bring down this formidable opponent, this indomitable cousin who loomed in our minds as a mighty professional wrestler who tossed his opponents with ease.

Monetarily, our families were quite different. My father would have never handed me money to buy anything unless it was absolutely necessary and if was on sale. Placing bets on horses was not in our vocabulary.

Robert, do us a favor, walk to the raceway and place these bets. Remember, if I win, you'll get ten percent.

Meanwhile, Jack sagged on his ample kitchen seat and nonchalantly puffed cigar smoke across the kitchen table while Aunt Margie stirred her tomato sauce made of puree, sans skin and seeds. Jack was giving racing tips at will to anyone who would listen. He once gave a tip to his sister-in-law, Rose Fabio. Sure, why not, she mused, it's just a few dollars, no big deal. The following Sunday, Rose Fabio confronted him about his so-called tips and scornfully remarked,

Jack, your tips are no good, the horse you told me to bet on dropped dead while racing.

Everyone burst out laughing, except for Jack.

How in the world does a horse drop dead in the middle of a race?

Jack wasn't fazed and had nothing to say but offered another tip on an upcoming race.

Hey, hey, Robert, take this money, wait, wait, Robert's going to the track, I want in.

Everyone wanted in, Jack, Margie, Jackie, Vinnie, Patricia, and Lenny.

Pop, it's cold outside, can someone please drive me?

Hey, here's the list, it's not that far, one mile each way, give me a break, you're fifteen years-old for God's sake, Go!

Off he went with three-hundred bucks in hand and a list of bets. Jack's bets: Race 2, ten dollars to Win on horse 1, ten dollars to Place on horse 4. Race 3: ten dollars to Place on horse 1... and on it went. Everyone gave him money.

It was a windy, chilly Sunday afternoon in October. The cerulean skies opened up to a splendid array of tumbling clouds that were pierced by powerful sunbursts. There was a brisk wind that energized the spirit. It was one of those days that people felt alive and glad to retreat into the comfortable routine of Sunday dinner. Typical of every Sunday, they came over to read the papers, watch football, and wait for Margie to cook dinner. And finally, dessert, Italian pastries from Menger's Bakery on Yonkers Avenue. This Sunday they would eat when Robert came back. Robert got to the Raceway thirty minutes before the start of the first race, waited in line, handed the guy the list of bets for the first race, got the betting slips and went to watch the race. He repeated that for the seven races that afternoon. He stayed at Yonkers Raceway for two hours and lost every bet. He accumulated a heap of worthless slips and a pocketful of nothing.

Yonkers Raceway made lots of money! It's path to fortune started seventy years ago as a trotting club, and it later added thoroughbred races to the mile track, and then switched back to trotters. It became one on the most successful raceways in the country. When off-track betting was legalized, it grew exponentially and it flourished to this very day, and now remains a veritable gold mine.

Where the hell is Robert? What is taking him so long?

Lenny shouted, as he took a drag of his cigarette held between his index and middle finger, and thumb.

That dumb ass kid probably got lost.

Patty swatted him with the back of her hand across his right arm which inadvertently resulted in ashes dropping on the dinner plate. Just then, the front door opened, and Patty ran over.

How did we do? Did we win? How much? Show me the money!

Robert took off his shirt just before he got to the front door until Jackie saw him entering. She knew instantly that there was no money.

Patty, he has no shirt, he lost his shirt! Don't you get it? No money!

Everyone laughed! Losing was no big deal with small bets, besides, there was always tomorrow. There would be greater excitement when it was time for the next bet. But now the anticipation switched to Margie's cooking. *Let's eat*, Margie interjected, and off they went into the kitchen for ravioli, escarole, meatballs, and Italian bread to soak it all up.

Tomorrow could not come soon enough for Robert as he wasn't going to wait for family members who worked for their hard-earned cash to give him money to place bets. He was going to take matters into his own hands.

May I speak with Mrs. Fabio.

The branch manager from a local bank in Yonkers was calling Margie to inform her that her account was being suspended for unusual activity.

I don't understand. I did not write out any checks for cash for any amount of money ever.

Mrs. Fabio, we have had a series of checks being cashed at our branch for sums or $500, $800, $300, and $600 over the last six weeks. We thought that these withdrawals were suspicious and wanted to let you know and will suspend the account until further investigation.

Margie was dumbfounded. She shared this revelation with Jack when he returned home later that evening from a day of house painting. She was concerned that someone had stolen her checks and forged her name. She sobbed as she told Jack of the large amounts of money withdrawn and that there could even be more. Jack went into a rage. He also carefully observed Robert's aloofness and aggressively questioned him. He soon discovered that Robert had forged his mother's signature on all the checks that were made out to cash. These checks were used for transactions at Yonkers Raceway. No one laughed anymore about losing money.

Chapter 3

My object all sublime I shall achieve in time — To let the punishment fit the crime.

—William Schwenck Gilbert

Nineteen-seventy through nineteen-seventy-one saw most of America reeling over the tragedy of a seemingly endless and pointless war waged in Vietnam. News of protests filled the evening news and newspapers. Intellectuals and idealists voiced their opinions on talk shows and AM radio. Teenagers and college students raged against authority by taking to the streets. Individualism was prevailing over conformity. Rebellion against authority in all its forms manifested through personal liberation. And while Yonkers was a microcosm of America, many were too focused on the daily task of making ends meet, working hard pursuing the American dream. As in every age, a small percentage of people seek to circumvent the reward of hard work and education to advance their station in life. Lawlessness in all its forms seeks to satisfy the cravings of the self. Those looking for a quick buck tend to not worry about the larger societal unrest. Robert was unfazed about the loftier questions posed by his teachers and contemplated by his peers. He pursued interests that satisfied his other needs.

Robert cut classes and smoked cigarettes or weed with his

friends Matty and Dave to break up the monotony and doldrum of teenage life without money. They sat on Matty's stoop so as to evade his family's prying eyes. Other times, Robert would hang around Yonkers Raceway with his friend Buddy Kucharcyzk to sniff glue with kids that lived close to Yonkers Raceway. Patricia ratted out Robert to his parents saying,

Ma, Robert hangs out all day. He gets called down to the principal's office every day. He is embarrassing! He doesn't go inside! He fights everybody after school, and he hangs around smoking pot.

Jack heard this and took out a long, wide belt with a heavy belt buckle. He windmilled the belt as if it were a long string, no effort at all. Robert bobbed and weaved like a skilled boxer and managed to evade most of the whipping belt. Robert lifted his arms as a sign of resistance before the belt stung his bare arms. His arms reddened and his face tightened, but he remained silent to hide any sign of weakness. This belt was not an instrument of style, although it was pure thin, black leather, but it was a disciplinary tool: a symbol of beauty delivering lashes of torture. My father was like Jack, regarding fashion trends. Except for a professional meeting or evening with friends, his clothes lacked the aesthetics of popular fashion and the thin black leather belt with plain brass buckle was no exception. None of us would ever suspect its medieval application. My mother was hesitant about its utilization, for she was wary of her husband's motivation. She had witnessed his rage firsthand where physical punishment was doled out of frustration and not for instructive discipline. Even if the belt was used to stop boys from loud disruptive fighting, she preferred a loud admonition as the first option.

My father drove a pale blue Plymouth station wagon that was both practical and affordable. It was the quintessential family car of the time and was now transporting this rambunctious family of six to Cape Cod for a week away at a cabin near a lake. The four of us were buoyed by the excitement of the speed and the wind in our hair as the wide-open windows drowned out any conversation. At my father's request, Mom would occasionally open a butter-scotch drop and slip it on to his waiting lips. The four boys sat in the back on the bench seat without seatbelts dangling our arms out the windows to capture more of the swooshing air. My father turned around while driving with one hand and the car slightly swerved. We were boisterous, and as we got entangled more and more, arguing whose leg was encroaching on the others space, the screaming was followed by pushing and punching. We were told to quiet down, but the real reaction came when my father's seat was banged into by one of us pushing the another into it. Somehow, my father managed to unleash his belt and swung the instrument of discipline wildly and indiscriminately to the back seat. We screamed in pain as each one of us felt the sting of the belt across our faces, hands, and arms as we cowered and ducked to avoid the blows. Suddenly, the voice of our mother cried out in protest, breaking up our screams. She was not protesting the disciplinary methods of her husband but rather she was protesting that his random swings had hit her right across the face. The folded belt managed to break free from my father's grip and now that it was being swung at full length. She experienced the same wrath as we did. She yelled out of surprise and out of pain. My father was enraged at our behavior, but suddenly his screaming wife distracted his focus as she shrieked:

Paul, you hit my face!

Suddenly, the discipline stopped as we held in our laughter while rubbing our sore arms and cheeks from the sting of the belt. There were mixed feelings as anger and laughter blended into a confusing din of sounds of the wind and whimpering as the car sped down I-95.

The belt from Jack's waist didn't have any effect on Robert's behavior. Robert was wild and undisciplined as he managed to repeat the eighth grade. His friend Matty Dalton was a diminutive Irish kid whose father was confined to a wheelchair and his mother unfortunately died when he was younger and when he needed her most. Young Matty Dalton sometimes wandered aimlessly in the mean streets of Yonkers looking for thrills and any kind of company he could find. Another friend, Dave Stefanik was a fearless only child who sought attention and craved company like children without siblings often do. Robert referred to his friend as a psycho, not because he was giving Dave a psychological evaluation, but because his behaviors conflicted with social norms. Dave and Robert admired each other for different reasons. Dave taught him skills on gun handling and successful petty larceny. Robert taught him how to gamble, party, and have a good time. Dave was a wild-looking kid with long brown hair, sporting a tattoo of an eagle on his muscular right arm. Dave was so out there that he had the gumption to challenge a young cop to a fight. Surprisingly, Dave bested the youthful policeman. The fledgling youth gang smoked pot and drank beers. They became productive juvenile delinquents when they planned to make money to fill their empty pockets. They dealt weed for easy money and carried a pound or two to sell as loose joints or nickel bags in school or at the local parks. Aunt Margie once found two pounds of pot and she casually flushed it down the toilet in spite of many objections.

Brian Vigliotti was a few years older than the others and they got to know him because he always seemed to have stuff to sell cheap. His older brother Dan was involved in petty crimes, holding up convenience stores and whatever else he deemed as an easy target. Dan was a clean-cut, good-looking kid but wanted easy money and with a need for a lookout he would take Brian and one or two friends along. Armed with a fake gun, everyone turned over whatever cash they had within reach. Most robberies took less than two minutes. Breaking and entering businesses also proved profitable. Brian and Dave fenced the goods and soon earned the titles of Bargain Brian and Discount Dave. They parked their car in front of the local high school as students left for the day and they fenced the stolen goods. They were not too fussy as they would amass cigarettes, car parts, jewelry, jeans, sneakers, shirts, chains, joints, pills, whatever they could get their hands on to make a buck. Robert, Matt, Dave, and Brian figured they didn't need Dan and began pulling off their own robberies. They all would rob easy targets like gas stations in Mount Vernon, liquor stores down the street from Getty Square, and local hotels. One motel they robbed was a motor inn on Tuckahoe Road in Yonkers. Brian drove and Robert went in with a bandana around his face around three a.m. A gun in anyone's face is going got attention. Robert loved how easy it was to get a quick $1000. They were happier than pigs in shit. Gone in under a few minutes.

Petty crime was Butchy Futia's business too and soon he became aware of these Yonkers boys' extracurricular activities. They all knew each other from the local bars. Butchy and Joey Portanova were two big, tough guys who were involved in a local crime ring engaging in extortion and loan sharking in White Plains and Yonkers. The extortion involved cigarette machines which were placed in most local businesses. If they found out that some business had a vending machine that was not theirs, a simple message was sent: a smashed-up store front and broken windows. No warning, nothing! The next day a screaming, menacing, muscle-head would come in the store with a warning that only his machines were allowed and only his cigarettes. These business owners got the message. Now Robert and the others were recruited to go around to the stores, and collect the money, and replace the machines with stolen cigarettes. If there were any problems, they issued the owner a warning and said that trouble would be coming. Trouble always came to those who didn't oblige.

Dan is dead!

Dave says as he approached Robert and Matty at the CWP Bar. Robert and Matty couldn't believe it. What the hell happened? Dan and Brian were robbing a toy store in new Rochelle and as Brian was loading the goods into the car, a neighbor spotted them and called the cops. Dan took off, leaving Brian standing alone. Cops pursued Dan for three miles when suddenly he skidded around a curve and slammed into a storage garage. The car flipped, Dan was trapped and then the gas tank exploded. Dan was burned alive.[1]

Holy shit, that's fucked up.

How's Brian?

Brian is fucked up. We'll see him at the wake.

Weeks later, they consoled themselves with more partying and scheming. They still needed money and weren't going to let Dan's unfortunate mistake stop them. Dan died a senseless death over ninety-one dollars' worth of toys and games. The cops found them along the chase route. This twenty-year-old died, leaving behind his parents and three younger siblings. They would never be the same.

Chapter 4

> If you prick us, do we not bleed? If you tickle us, do we not laugh? If you poison us, do we not die? And if you wrong us, shall we not revenge?
>
> —William Shakespeare

Everyday life marched along, even in my family, until tragedy struck. Robert was returning home from a little league game, and he felt buoyed by his three-for-four hits game. He did nothing but talk about his inside the park homer that was determined by his dazzling speed that enabled him to slide safely at home plate in a cloud of dirt. He relived his feat as his uncle, Jack Schinasi, drove him home after to the game due to his father's typical late work schedule. The euphoria suddenly snapped when Robert heard and saw his uncle cough and spew blood.

Are you okay, Uncle Jack?

It's nothing, Rob. It's nothing, don't worry about it.

Retorted Uncle Jack, as more spasmodic, loud coughing mingled with a tinge of blood. Robert spotted the blood but said nothing. Later that night, Aunt Margie sobbed as news spread that her brother-in-law Jack Schinasi had died of a heart attack that night. He was just a few weeks shy of his fifty-third birthday.[1] It was his second heart attack in two years; the saddest day of

Robert's life. Elation and tragedy could soar and crash from one moment to the next.

Jack Schinasi was the son of Jews who emigrated from Turkey to settle In New York City. A distant relative named Moses Eskenazi established himself as a cigarette manufacturer in New York City after exhibiting his cigarette rolling invention at the 1893 World's Fair in Chicago. Upon emigrating to America, Moses changed his surname to Schinasi in honor of the Muslim doctor that treated him as a child, Sinasi Bey.[2,3] Together with his brother Solomon, their ready-made cigarettes and the Schinasi Bros. cigarette brand made them a fortune.[4,5] The Schinasi mansion dominated the landscape with its massive twelve thousand feet expanse that included thirty-five rooms sporting marble floors, luxuriously spread throughout the manor. This stately home on Riverside Drive on the Upper West Side of Manhattan was built for Morris Schinasi.[6] Many family members were in Morris' employ, and Jack's father Isaac was no different. When he emigrated to America in 1912, a job was already waiting for him at the Schinasi Bros. cigarette manufacturing building located at 32 W. 100th St. By 1925 and eight years after the business was sold to the American Tobacco Company, Isaac was on his own supporting his young family. His youngest son Jacob (Jack), a WWII veteran, became an insurance salesman experiencing none of the material riches his famous family had acquired. The riches he had were instead measured in the bond of love, devotion, and commitment from his loving wife, Josie, family, and friends.

There always was an Italo-Jewish social and business alliance in our country ranging from Las Vegas casinos, to Hollywood, to labor unions, to graphic novels, to cartoons, and naturally to migrant communities, and of course organized crime syndicates. The Fabio's and the Schinasi's were close and lived ten houses apart. Robert was very close to three of his cousins who were virtually his brothers and sisters. But yet another tragedy befell the family a year after the passing of Uncle Jack. This time, it was Richard Scholl, our cousin Linda's husband, who drowned while skin-diving in the Long Island Sound near New Rochelle.[7] While underwater he cramped up, came up too fast, and choppy waters swept his flailing body down-current beyond visible horizons. His bloated, flaccid body was found by a friend of his older brother Jerry. Linda was crushed for losing Richard at a time so early in their short marriage and barely a year after her father died. How sad it was that tragedy at times strikes when you reach the peak of happiness. Bob and Jerry were also devastated by the drowning of Richard, the youngest of the brothers.

Richard and Linda enjoyed seeing his brothers perform in local clubs. Bob and Jerry Scholl were founding members of the Doo-Wop group the Mello-Kings. They gained national prominence with their hit tune "Tonite, Tonite."[8] Robert was close to Aunt Josie and Linda. The loss of loved ones makes you feel vacuous, disoriented, and deeply mournful. Josie lost her dad and husband and son-in-law; Linda lost her dad and husband within one year.

On June 5th, 1968, Robert F. Kennedy, the 64th Attorney General, was shot. The fiery Kennedy died at Good Samaritan Hospital and his body lay buried at Arlington Cemetery. The Anti-Zionist Egyptian and pro-Palestinian activist stated that he abhorred Kennedy and testified in 1969 that he shot the Attorney General with twenty-years of malice aforethought. Earlier in the year on April 4th, 1968, Martin Luther King was shot dead while standing on a podium at the Lorraine Motel, Memphis, Tennessee. News of King's assassination spread like wild-fire and prompted riots throughout America.

This tumultuous era was punctuated by civil unrest and racial strife. Americans were beset by massive protests, sit-ins, and generational class conflicts. There was chaos in the neighborhoods, in the streets, on university campuses, and in the political arena. In this environment, Robert continued his life unperturbed by civil unrest. He was a pugnacious, ill-tempered young man who settled his arguments with iron fists instead of reasoned conciliation. His fists were louder than his voice. Force over logic was his overriding solution. He was impulsive, a force to be reckoned with. He cut classes at will. He rode his motor bike with cigarettes dangling on his lips and boldly sped around the hilly, grassy easements of the Sprain Brook Parkway following the electric power lines that formed a ready-made path for his afternoon adventures. Local police targeted this rebel and apprehended him on several occasions and let him stew in jail until his parents came to pick him up. The cops would often confiscate the bike. Jack had no empathy for the local law enforcement and frantically voiced his anger as he felt that cops were petty, corrupt, and power hungry. Robert managed to reclaim his beloved bike with a superficial slap on the wrist.

Ma, Robert was in detention again!

His older sister, Patty, would report to her mother as she made sure everyone knew how embarrassed she was. Margie would scream and Jack would discipline, but Robert was defiant, self-willed, unmanageable, and increasingly cynical.

Why the hell should I even go to school!

Robert thought,

The world is falling apart, Bobby Kennedy is dead, close family members are dead. Who the fuck cares about anything!

His mental machinery stewed, and stewed with anger, with disobedience, and with determination. He was on a path of his own making, and no man of the law was going to stop him.

Tragedies were as commonplace as breathing. Simply listening to the news, you'd be saturated with dreadful, tragic stories. Misfortune reared its ugly head once again in 1972. Richie Schinasi, Josie's son, died. Robert was close to Richie: they were inseparable, attached at the hip. They were three years apart and Robert tagged along, hanging out to watch drag racing on Central Park Ave. in Yonkers. The racing landmark was named The Bridge to Bridge—specifically the section of Central Park Avenue between Cross County Parkway and Midland Ave. This stretch of road provided an easy escape route if the cops made an unexpected appearance from the Thruway and Cross County Parkway. Car racing was the ritualistic entertainment for motorheads, gamblers, and the curious, as it involved souped-up muscle cars and their drivers competing for bragging rights, approval, and recognition. They caroused in the wee hours of the morning when law abiding citizens slept. Cars showed up precisely at two a.m. Robert was the flagger, starter and bleacher of tires for better traction. Local kids downed beers, smoked pot, and placed bets. Robert went to each driver and asked for the betting sum: Five hundred was proposed. Richie raced against '71 Impalas, '72 Corvettes, and '72 Rivieras. Richie's car was so fast it would *piss on them* because of his blazing speed. Richie won ninety percent of the time, with an occasional lapse when he missed a gear while shifting, or if the car did a wheely. A profitable take was as high as eight-hundred dollars, in those days a tidy sum. If Richie lost, Robert mockingly called out,

Hey, short shift, you're costing me money.

A screaming match ensued but eventually everyone calmed down until the next race. Richie was so confident in his car's speed and his racing ability. He often competed at the Dover Plains Drag Strip in Dutchess County. As a self-taught auto-mechanic, he ran an auto business on Nepperhan Ave and School Street where in his spare time he modified cars for high performance racing. He was excited that his older brother, Garry, was coming to watch. He had been racing for years, but this wasn't Garry's thing as he was pursuing his master's degree in economics at SUNY Albany. Richie was agitated, had nervous energy thinking about the race, thinking about how the Camaro would hold up, thinking about impressing his older brother. The quick monster was ready to perform. This '67 Camaro 396/375 hp was fast, 10.3 seconds in a quarter mile race. The car wasn't fancy and just had the words "Quarter Toll" painted on the side of this eggplant-colored monster of a car. He was ready to let it fly. Richie flat towed his Camaro with his two friends, Floyd and Al, following closely behind in their cars. Robert and his friend Paul were in the Camaro as it was being towed. They were followed by Garry in another car, and Vinnie Mastrullo and Lenny Cirino, Robert's brothers-in-law, in the last one. It would normally take ninety minutes to get to Dover Drag Strip, but with a race car in tow it took over two hours, and he was running late. As Richie got on the service road heading toward the drag strip, his front right tire got caught in a rut. The road was not well maintained, and it was a risky doing sixty miles per hour.

He's cutting it too close, what the hell is he doing?!

Robert yelled at Paul as Richie's car violently jumped over the curb into the service road several inches lower than the regular road. Richie could not get out of the rut; he tried several times but turned his wheel hard left. His car managed to get out of the rut but finally swerved into a tailspin snapping the v-bar attached to the Camaro. The Camaro t-boned the rear quarter panel and Richie's car flipped. There was a crash and shrill metallic crunch. Robert freaked out:

Richie's gonna kill me. His car is wrecked!

Robert got out and saw Richie lying on his back halfway out the window with the car on top of him.

Richie, get up, you alright?

No answer. He'd flown out the window, busted his head, and died instantly. Robert turned ashen and froze like an icicle hanging on an eave, and words could not escape his lips.[9]

No one understood how this happened. In a span of four years, Robert lost an uncle, a cousin's husband, and another cousin. Everyone was affected in different ways and handled it dissimilarly. Robert couldn't understand what in heaven's sake was happening, better yet, *why* it was happening. His parents could barely comfort him or provide perspective because they didn't understand the twists of fate and the randomness of life and death. They were wrapped in their daily vicissitudes supporting Josie, Linda, and Garry. They drowned in the depths of grief. Robert became disillusioned, unable to believe in anything. Although Catholic, the family eschewed the holy church as this religion did not speak to their soul, for the essence of religion could not provide comfort or explanation to their jaded inner spirit. They mechanically observed the rituals of Baptism, Communion, weddings and funerary solemnity. They never attended Sunday morning services, nor ever stepped in a confessional. In the end, Robert confessed to himself that he was now an avowed atheist, a godless man, and a solipsist: he believed in nothing but himself, and if there were any possibility of a god, he was unknowable and inaccessible.

Robert cut classes since he saw no merit in education. Disparate thoughts swam in the convoluted lobes of his brain:

What does biology, and boring, endless books on English and history have to do with life today? And who really cares about Old-England during the Industrial Revolution? And who cares about George Washington crossing the Delaware armed with his wooden teeth? And really who gives a rat's ass about those philosophers who complain about crap that no one can possibly relate to? I don't need any of this garbage!

He loved to sweat and toil with gym equipment in Vinny C's basement. The two of them worked out to total exhaustion. Not only did they do multiple weightlifting reps, but they also competed to outdo one another. Robert and Vinny developed some physical definition as they gained muscle mass advertising to the rest of the world that they were not to be messed with. They got strong and developed an attitude of invincibility.

Fabio, Fabio, why don't you cut your hair, be a real man, join the wrestling team.

Robert heard this and thought,

Who the hell is this guy bothering me?

He looked around and noticed that it was Mr. Mongarella, the wresting coach, goading him into joining the wrestling team.[10] He was a short man, hardly reaching five-foot six-inches tall but had a solid power. Mr. Mongarella wanted to motivate Robert. Unfortunately for him, it simply motivated a guy with a short fuse.

Listen, you cocksucka, I'm going to put you in the mail sack and mail you to the office.

Robert grabbed a mail sack, stuffed him in it and dragged him down the hall to the office. Those who saw it laughed. Mr. Mongarella was pissed off, but Robert took off and was later brought down to the principal's office.

Mr. Fabio, why did you do that?

Blah, blah, blah. Robert could care less what anybody had to say and had no explanation for why he did what he did, except to say the guy pissed him off. He was promptly suspended from school, but his smug arrogance refused to yield to the lessons of being disciplined.

Robert was a chip off the old block as he resembled his father in psychological as well as physical attributes. Robert itched for a good brawl. He wallowed in the possibility of a melee to build up a legendary status in the neighborhood. Big, tough, and cocky, Robert didn't take any guff from anybody, especially if it involved his public persona, which he guarded at all costs. He preferred to be feared than respected, for fear was primal, whereas respect was socially achieved. His reputation was now widespread, and thugs from other schools wanted to challenge the baddest ass in the neighborhood. Robert brazenly ventured into other territories to challenge other neighborhood toughs. Aggressive, young criminals often fought for utter pleasure. At times he would venture into other neighborhoods and ambush an unlucky, poor bastard.

Word spread like toxic rumors in a school hallway. The word got out that Robert Fabio would fight after school at the flagpole. Within thirty or so minutes dozens of bored kids seeking thrill and excitement showed up. Robert approached his target wearing his blue denim jacket with an emblazoned American flag stitched on the back. As the two fighters jawed each other with insults, threats, and mocking, Robert would hand his jacket to Matty and face his opponent with hands up, body shifted to the right so his left arm could jab as he would assess his opponent's distance. Three punches thrown, teenage boy lay on the ground, fight over. Robert mocked his opponent again and warned him with threats. The bystanders took notice as Robert's reputation for a hard fast right was not to be underestimated or dismissed. He battered the McDermott brothers outside of the local pizzeria, Raceway Pizza on Yonkers Ave. One of the McDermotts had a busted nose as a result of a hard right.

Fuck you! Fuck you!

The fight was over. The shrill curse pierced like a needle against one of the temples on the head. The abruptness of the brawl rang out all over Yonkers Ave.

Life in the streets teemed with marginal characters in search of mischief. People of all ages hung around streets for a number of reasons, most prominent of which was bored teenagers. Teenagers not seeking to improve themselves according to school standards but improved their stature within the universe of friends with the same interests of partying, stealing, flirting, and quick money.

Ma, Ma, your son is crazy, Do something!

Patty yelled out. The bellicose Robert, the protagonist of yet another bloody fisticuffs stood sternly at a Carvel ice cream parlor as cops arrived in force to quell down the mayhem. The turbulent teenagers turned on the cops as a general brawl broke out where cops and neighborhood toughs hammered blows. Margie was distraught over the unrest and was incredulous over the raucousness. Some thug named Pepe Rocco started to jam his right shoulder into Robert has he walked past, knocking him back a few steps,

So, you think you can fight, tough guy? I don't think you're so tough.

Everyone turned and eyed the two locked in a stare. Rocco looked fierce as his eyes widened as if in rage ready to pulverize anyone who stood in his way. Thirty or so high school kids armed with ice cream cones, milkshakes, and "Flying Saucer's" egged on the two snarling teenagers who were ready to maul each other to shreds. Robert was big for his age, lifted weights all the time, and earned the respect to hang out with kids a few years older. But Rocco was having none of that. Not everyone wanted younger guys hanging around and viewed them not as peers but as easy targets for abuse. Robert didn't back down and was quick with a verbal response of

Fuck you!

Followed by a volley of punches. Within a matter of minutes, an all-out brawl started as the two wrestled each other to the ground, got up, and threw more punches, only to be tackled again. The ice cream shop was in disarray. Tables and chairs were everywhere except where they should be. Sodas and ice cream spilled on the floor from those who stood too close to the brawl. Yonkers P.D. showed up and tried to break it up but the two were focused on tearing each other apart and the cops inadvertently got elbowed and punched and that made matters worse. The clubs came out and both got a beating from the cops, and once they were pulled apart, they were taken to the police station to cool off. They were released within an hour as their parents picked them up. The parents were totally silent, humiliated, raging on the inside.

Patty was so uncomfortable with Robert's vicious displays of violence. Even when she was personally harassed in the high school hallway by a pervert reaching out to grab her ass, she was dismayed at Robert's immediate defense of her honor. Patricia was walking up the stairwell in between classes at Lincoln High School just when Robert was coming down the stairs. Robert instantly recognized Patricia's screaming and went ballistic.

You touch my sister, you cocksucka!?

Robert yelled. Within seconds, fists were flying everywhere as this high school freshman began beating the piss out of the guy three years older.

Ma, he almost killed this guy, there was blood everywhere, he's crazy! I felt so bad for him!

Patty screamed when she got home from school. While Robert could not tolerate anyone harassing anyone in his family, he also would not back down from a confrontation. Reflecting on his reaction he shared his thoughts on the fight many years later:

Hey, you're touching my sister you cocksucka, give me a reason to beat you.

While Patty and her mother were exasperated of Robert's fighting, it eventually became a recreational activity for the family. At the dinner table Robert announced that he was going to be fighting some kid, and they were going to meet in front St. John's Episcopal Church near Getty Square. His sisters and their boyfriends left the house after dinner together for the evening's entertainment. Robert jumped out of Vinnie's car and approached the guy who wanted to fight. They cursed, mocked, and threatened each other, as is customary with street fights. Robert was the first to throw a punch and then grab the guy in a head lock as he pounded his face with his powerful right hand. The guy dropped and his brother-in-law Vinny revved up the engine of his Corvette displaying his approval. Robert confessed that,

I like to have my family there, it felt good.

Unfortunately, no other activities that Robert was involved with resulted in the positive attention he received when defending his sister or defending his own self-respect. Jack was not convinced or understanding of Robert's angst. He questioned him,

What are you fighting for?

To which Robert responded with his true motivation,

Pops, these guys think they're tough, I'll show them.

Robert was out to prove that he was the toughest of them all.

He was now in the eleventh grade and finally he was going to make the team,

All right, team, good practice today, take the playbook and study these.

The code of conduct was written with bold letters on the last pages of the playbook:

You must not have failing grades, nor substance abuse, nor gambling, no acts of vandalism, nor fighting, nor theft, and finally, no hair below the ears.

This football edict was serious, as the football coaches practiced their aspirations of team dominance through cohesiveness, discipline, and skill. Victory is won through collective effort and commitment to these rules. They were essential in the coach's mind to begin having individual team members morph into team mentality through self-discipline, to believe in a sound body with a sound mind, and above all, team spirit.

We have two more practices, and then our first game of the week.

The next day, Robert is running in fear down the school hallway.

Fabio, Fabio, I'll kill you! Get over here!

Coach Sal Milanese shouted as he ran after Robert a few days after sharing the code of conduct. Robert ran and beat him to the safest place he knew, the principal's office. Coach Milanese had been one of the high school football coaches for years.[11] He wanted dedicated kids who followed the rules.

You punk, who the hell do you think you are, you bastard!

Coach Milanese had to be restrained. He was furious. The principal pulled Coach into his office. Sal went off,

Get this degenerate out of her!, I'll kill him, this punk. I have had enough.

The reason for his fury would soon be known.

There was bad blood between Robert, Peter Bradley, and James

Joyce, the other two football coaches.[12] Robert was left back in the eighth grade because he cut gym classes. Robert looked like a hoodlum, wearing a guinea tee—his sleeveless cotton tank top—with hippy-like hair down to his shoulders. He smoked Marlboro's or weed, whichever was available, and prowled around the flagpole, itching to fight against any challenger. Now he was a high school junior, and he wanted to play football just like his friends did, so he figured he'd try out for the team. When he showed up with the rest of the prospects, he was scolded that his hair was not short enough. He recently cut his hair specifically for this try-out, but the coaches, with their closely cropped hair, blew a gasket. He just got this haircut, he mused, for no *fucking good reason!* Coach Bradley bellowed loudly with his raspy voice:

Fabio, out! No practice for you. You don't listen, you think this is a joke. You're a joke with that hair. Your hair is over your ears, come back when you get it shorter.

The team laughed. Robert was pissed off, embarrassed:

These coaches are a joke, fuck them. Who the hell cares? What difference does it make?

A few days later he was at the Polar Bear Bar, a local bar on the corner of Midland and Cerone Avenues frequented by working people getting a cocktail before the commute home, or others coming in for a bite to eat before heading out to a movie, or some simply hanging out for a few hours with groups of friends in their mid-twenties. Robert was seventeen years old and he proudly possessed a fake driver's license, and no one questioned him. Due to his six-two frame, he looked like every other patron, and so he slipped under the radar. He relished the situation and was having a good time chatting with Linda G., two years his senior, downing Heineken's, laughing, flirting, and stealing kisses at the bar.

Bradley and Joyce, the two Irish-American coaches, walked into the Polar Bear, and as they positioned themselves at the bar, Joyce motioned to Bradley:

Hey, get a look over there. It's Fabio, he ain't eighteen.

Joyce got the bartender's attention.

Mickey, don't serve that kid, he's not eighteen. Get him out of here.

Robert looked up and couldn't believe it.

These two coaches are always on my shit, this is bullshit.

He wracked his brain trying to figure out why these coaches had it in for him. What did he possibly do that was so bad? Mickey, the bartender, who had known the coaches for years, leant over the bar and asked Robert for his license. Robert recoiled in disbelief:

Why the hell is Mickey questioning me? I've been here a thousand times.

Mickey intoned with a pinch of gravity:

It's fake. Out! You can't drink here.

Robert jabbed that he wasn't bothering anyone, what was the big deal. He spotted the coaches pointing at him, and the bartender sententiously stated:

Fabio, you are outta here. You're underage, you can't be here.

Robert abruptly left, leaving Linda at the bar. Robert was pissed off, embarrassed, and the more he thought, the madder he got:

Those motherfuckers, I'll fuck them.

Robert found a phone booth down the street and called Joey Portanova, the muscle-head that he partnered with to lifted weights at a friend's basement gym. Joey was the son of a prominent past president of the Yonkers PBA as well as Robert's workout buddy. This friend boasted massive arms and an attitude to match them. Joey was also involved in loan sharking, and when people didn't pay up, Robert would make the rounds with him to intimidate, and bashed anyone who did not pay their debts. Robert also made a quick buck robbing gas stations, liquor stores, and other easy targets with a handy fake gun and a bandana over his mouth and nose: he made sure Joey got a cut of the take, knowing he had connections to more influential law breakers that could cause him trouble. Joey would help him out whenever he needed anything. Fifteen minutes passed after he placed the call and a new black El Dorado emerged in glistening from the streetlights reflecting off its polished exterior, and it stopped down the street and out came Joey P. and Butchy. The latter was just released from jail. Robert had met the con a while back when he was invited up to Butchy's apartment above the New Rochelle Fire Department building to smoke some weed, snort coke, and listen to Butchy's planned robberies. Butchy Futia was a massive, hulky guy standing at six-foot with mammoth arms like professional wrestler Antonino Rocca, Robert's childhood idol. He had a noticeable jagged scar dominating the face-scape of his left cheek; a scar which accentuated his nasty attitude, an attitude that was expressed in intimidation, violence, and worse.

Robert described the appearance of his coaches as they walked into the neighborhood pub and pointed them out as soon as he spotted them. Bradley and Joyce, engaged in friendly banter with Mickey, looked up apprehensively as this barbarian, just released from jail, trudged into their personal space and threatened:

Hey, you fucks, who do you think you are.

As soon as the words were blurted out, punches were unleashed, tables were upended, and people seated could not believe what was happening at the bar. As the fight escalated, both coaches were abruptly thrown out the window. They landed on their asses, and soon after, without hesitation, they were jumped on curbside. They were no match for Butchy and Joey. These two big, tough guys in their early-thirties and mid-twenties who liked to intimidate and beat up people bested these high school pillars of the football community. Both coaches were no push-overs. They could hold their own, and landed several good punches themselves, but they were beat so up badly that were taken to the emergency room. Bradley suffered a broken wrist and Joyce sustained a concussion. Coach

Sal had a reason to be furious. The principal wasted no time in confirming the story and Robert lost his chance for a high school diploma. His formal education ended at Lincoln High School at age seventeen. Robert confided to me about his high school years saying:

The years of sniffing glue, smoking pot all day, taking quaaludes, getting high for free, doing blow, cutting classes, and hanging out with drug dealers all day; crazy times, no education, it all came to an end: what a shame, it's really a shame. It's horrible, no education, a shit school, they didn't give a fuck.

Jack and Margie went crazy. Jack screaming, Margie crying:

What the hell are you doing, you have no future, you are an embarrassment!

This went on for weeks. Jack had enough,

You are not gonna lay around here all day, no way, you are now working with me.

Robert hated the drudgery. It was the same thing day after day.

Buddy Kucharcyzk was a buddy of his from Lincoln High. They practiced together on the football team until Robert got himself expelled. Buddy was an elite, popular athlete and was well liked. He excelled at basketball and football but was easily influenced by the idea of a quick buck to purchase drugs to get high. They robbed an elementary school off Yonkers Avenue across from Yonkers Raceway. The tandem stole microphones, tape recorders, and whatever else they could find and eventually sold it on the street. He, like so many of their friends, were opportunists and thought a stick-up at a Yonkers Ave. liquor store would be easy. They figured they could easily score five-hundred dollars each. With little planning, they both went into the store, pulled bandanas over their mouths and noses, and rushed to the counter where a man was unpacking bottles of liquor. They gruffly demanded money. The owner was not intimidated by a couple of high school punks. He alertly pulled out his Saturday Night Special and fired two rounds. Robert stood aside several feet behind Buddy. He luckily was on the move before the gun was even in full view. Buddy wasn't so lucky, and he was shot in his shoulder as he turned and was trying to make a quick exit. A shockwave circulated throughout the high school's sports community and even throughout Yonkers and surrounding towns. People could not believe that this star athlete was involved in a robbery. And now that bullet would be a personal scarlet letter for the rest of his life: all for nothing but cash. Besides the physical scar, the mental anguish followed him for the rest of his living days. Buddy would not be able to compete again. Robert remembered too, but he was a budding criminal and would also shirk this nefarious experience. He pronounced to himself that he would never do anything like that again. Not that he would not rob liquors stores, he would be much more methodical in his approach. Observation and surveillance trumped spontaneity.

Observation and surveillance didn't always result in success. Other variables were at play. He once held up a guy who was very frail who all of sudden claimed he wasn't feeling good and thought he was having a heart attack. He readily gave up the five thousand dollars in cold cash. After the victim called the police, he managed to give a good description of Robert. He drew an oral picture of a tall white man with long brown hair and a gold chain conspicuously hanging on the neck. The cops had an idea who it might be because they pulled him over for speeding later that night not far from the robbery. While the money had been stashed and the cops had no physical evidence, he was processed based on the witness's description. As he was locked up at the second precinct, he was issued a warning that if that man died, Robert would be charged with murder. That resonated with him. Murder is a serious charge, with life in prison. Luckily, the man survived, but Robert had to face robbery charges and go back and forth to the Yonkers Courthouse court for years to come and pay multiple fines. Yet somehow, he managed to stay out of jail. New opportunities presented themselves! He made money and the how didn't matter to Robert. Butchy, an ever-ready criminal mind, approached him and enticed Robert that he could make a quick two-thousand dollars. All he had to do was to grab the two body bags in the back of a truck located by such-and-such body shop and bury them. As far as Robert was concerned, he didn't murder anyone. Besides, it was easy money.

Dave, Matty, and Robert were told where to find a Chevy Blazer. With keys in the vizor and two body bags in the back of the vehicle, they hauled off to La Pier Park, which is what they called Untermyer Park on North Broadway. It was four a.m., Robert sat in the car smoking a joint while Dave and Matty dug holes four or five feet deep. They didn't know who was in these body bags or what had happened and didn't really care. When he asked if he had a problem with burying dead people, he was nonplussed:

We got rid of some bodies, they were already in body bags ... It was good money. You can't make money like that ... That's why I had a new caddy.

Shocked as I was to his indifference, it really didn't surprise me that he never expressed any concern for anything except getting easy money, and gambling at will. Those were his main ambitions, and everything else was a means to those ends.

These three brothers in crime each took their ill-gotten gains and started to buy themselves cars. Dave bought a 1970 Cadillac Coupe DeVille convertible, white with black interior and black top. Matty had a blue Buick Skylark and Robert had a 1972 Cadillac Coupe DeVille, green with beige top and interior to match. After tiring of the green color, he bought the same car in blue. His father, Jack, was driving a 1962 Chevy and in disbelief, grabbed him, demanding,

Where the hell did you get the money from?!

His mother Margie and his sisters protested,

You are up to no good!

His brother-in-law Vinny Mastrullo would constantly question how a seventeen-year-old kid could afford a brand-new Cadillac. He grumbled with skepticism,

How does this happen?

Robert defended himself saying,

I'm just lucky!

as he smirked unconvincingly at his accusers.

Robert hung around with other local guys who frequented Untermyer Park. The Portanova brothers, Joey and Tommy, were members of what he called the La Pier Park gang, a loose group of guys that partied and gambled their way to serious crimes. Joey was a big, intimidating guy with twenty-inch biceps. He carved his personal path, a path different from his father's. His father was a Yonkers PBA Chief who was highly respected by his fellow uniformed officers because he exemplified loyalty while he fought for better pay and benefits. Joey was respected despite following a different set of rules that supported his partying and gambling habits. He found loan sharking compatible to his thinking since it provided addicts fast cash for sports betting.[13] The going rate was one-hundred-fifty to two-hundred-fifty percent interest rates. It was an immense figure that financially raped addicted gamblers. Sports betting rings operated under the protection of Larry Centore, a senior member of the Genovese crime family in Westchester. Centore, in his seventies, acted like "The local Chairman of the board" who assigned territories and resolved disputes amongst organized crime members, but rarely, if ever, did he carry gambling or loansharking records.[14] That was Joey's job. He promoted gambling in the local area, acted as a loan shark to local businessmen in debt, and found means to collect delinquent payments. Joey paid good money to collect unpaid debts. He used intimidation and threats of physical violence to anyone who didn't pay. This was supplemental income for Robert, knowing many drug dealers who were short on cash, and so convinced Joey to loan them money. They were building their network of criminals indebted to them. It worked well until Robert's own gambling habits of twenty-thousand dollars' worth of debt to Joey put him behind the eight ball. Joey was now on his own, he had to do his own collecting. One evening after dinner, Margie heard some knocking on the front door and opened it to find Joey demanding to see Robert. Robert shooed her back into the kitchen and assured her everything was fine. Joey threatened, but Robert pulled out his Glock and waved it in Joey's face yelling:

What? What ya wanna do, fight me you fucking asshole? You want money and you come to my house! Fuck you, I work for you! Where am I going, you think I'm not going to pay you?

Joey relented, knowing he wasn't going to get any money that night, and he never collected it. Instead, he was involved in an investigation of illegal sports betting, and he was sentenced to six months in jail and a one-thousand-five-hundred dollars fine for felony, criminal usury, conspiracy, and gambling. Wiretaps were later ruled inadmissible, but he pleaded guilty to a misdemeanor charge of attempted criminal usury and sentenced to three years' probation. Joey never stopped his criminal activities and was eventually shot, getting shot in the ass in 1980 while collecting money from Ronald Pezzuti, a local plumber who had accrued a large debt later that year.[15] By 1982 Joey was caught up in a larger sting operation that lasted eighteen months, and that netted thirty other lawbreakers involved with gambling, loan sharking, and drug trafficking. That ended Robert's supplemental income through Joey, but he found other ways to make money.

Robert, Dave, Matty, and a pill-popping work-out buddy named Stan DeRuggiero robbed and stole whatever they could get their hands on.

I was a bad boy,

is how Robert explained it. They pulled a van to the back of a sporting goods store in Larchmont, squirted shaving cream into the alarm system, the type of alarm that was made of a red bell attached to the wall. A muffled sound couldn't be heard beyond ten feet and within twenty minutes they were gone with bicycles, guns, knives, and anything they could get their hands on. Stan wanted the guns, the others sold what they could at local high school parking lots, opening their trunks to the students after school. Within a few weeks, everything was sold. They would rob the arcades at the Cross County Shopping Center, or the games in the back rooms at Nathans. Quarters were often left in the machines overnight, and a crowbar would do the job quickly. They would get thousands of dollars in quarters per night. Robert would bring bags of quarters to the bank where his sister worked as a teller. Patty, embarrassed at her nineteen-year-old brother's behavior, would call her mother:

Ma, Robert and Dave are up to no good. They're coming here with thousands of dollars in quarter. This is crazy.

Vinnie, Patty's husband, pleaded with Robert to stop this craziness, saying he was going to get her in trouble. His response was:

This is a free country, I got quarters, I exchange them for bills, what's the problem?

Eventually he would spread out the visits to the bank on a weekly basis, so he would only cash in a few hundred every week. From these thefts he bought a new '72 Cadillac. He had a nicer car than his father, Jack's '62 Chevy Impala.

Where the hell are you getting all this money? Jack asked.

You hardly work, how much money are you making from painting?

Never mind, Pop, business is good, I get big jobs.

Jack wanted to believe, wanted to think his son was turning things around. What could he do?

Chapter 5

So fallen! so lost! the light withdrawn which once he wore!

—John Greenleaf Whittier

Jimmy, it's Robert, any chance you can get me a job at the union?

Jimmy Boy worked at the United Paper Workers International Union as a Pension Fund Administrator. The year was 1974. Robert Fabio decided to give Jimmy Boy, his half-brother, a call. Basil James Fabio, Jack's eldest son from his first marriage, was affectionately called Jimmy Boy. I met him in 1973, at Robert's sister Patty's wedding. I was twelve, the youngest at the table next to his. After dinner was served, I found myself seated alone. I watched the adults dance to music that I only heard from old black-and-white movies. I spotted Uncle Danny on the dance floor as he glided with a lady I did not recognize. My aunts marveled at his form as one of them commented:

Oh, nobody does the Peabody like Danny.

As I watched Uncle Danny glide and spin around the dance floor, now mindful of his gallantry with his dance partner, my attention was interrupted by the sound of a chair being moved as if someone was about to sit down. I glanced over to see who now occupied the chair next to me and was surprised to see a man extend his hand to formally introduce himself. He looked at me with a gleaming smile—a sincere smile—and introduced himself as James Fabio. Confused and curious at the same time, I marveled at the idea that another James Fabio even existed. He was handsome, elegant, an articulate thirty or so year-old man. He warmly introduced himself as the son of my Uncle Jack Fabio. I never knew Uncle Jack had a son other than Robert. As I was still trying to comprehend that the man speaking with me was a relative, the gentlemen noticed my confusion. To put me at ease, he asked what every adult asked me that evening:

How's school?

I hated that question because I hated school. James Fabio peppered me with more questions, but as a twelve-year-old kid, I gave a lot of one-word answers, mixed in with a sentence or two that elicited a head nod as if he was understanding my jumbled thoughts. After ten minutes he excused himself and said:

It was nice to meet you.

We shook hands and he got up and blended with the others at the table next me. I continued to watch the wedding guests dance, laugh, socialize, and drink. What a party, I thought.

Jimmy Boy lived in the Crestwood section of Yonkers. His uncle, Joseph Tonelli, Union President of the United Paper Workers International Union, had recently invited him to move in. The cunning regarding Joseph Tonelli's purported wealth was mystifying, and malicious tongues disseminated rumors that spread like wildfire. Questions about the provenance of his money caught the attention of many. Questions about his posh house were baffling to all sorts of people because they wondered about how a union man garnered all this mysterious wealth.

Jimmy Boy was just a preschooler when his parents divorced. PFC Jack Fabio completed his tour of duty in 1946 having served with the 11th Marines in Guadalcanal, Peleliu, and Okinawa. Unfortunately the excitement and expectation of being embraced by his loving family celebrating his sacrifice and safe return was met with sorrow. Jack returned to the Bronx and found an empty apartment. Stella had abandoned her husband and took his son. He was devastated yet resolved. A divorce was granted in 1947 but he secured his right as a parent. Jack and Stella both remarried several years later but the damage was done. Jimmy Boy was raised on the west coast with his mother and step-father. Jimmy Boy graduated Lowell High School in San Francisco[1], and then enrolled in the San Francisco School of Mortuary Sciences. He moved back east in the late nineteen-sixties. When Robert learned he had a brother and that he was moving close to home, he ran up and down the block in glee shouting to anyone is earshot,

I have a brother! I have a brother!

Jimmy Boy found employment as a pharmacist and then as a mortician in New York City with Frank E. Campbell —The Funeral Chapel. He trained hard for this line of work, but the emotional distress was overwhelming. The technical part of the job—handling and preparations of human remains, embalming, and the restorative arts—were skills he mastered. He could not master the emotional toll that this line of work was exacting on his psyche. He could not understand why family members of the deceased stood around the casket with a big smile. And he thought that the taking of pictures of a dead body in an open casket was uncouth. The most disconcerting aspect of the job was working on children. He lost sleep, had nightmares, and was unsettled. The burden of the actual work on these precious innocents, coupled with interacting with tormented families, was too much to bear. He had to get out. Seeing how unhappy Jimmy Boy was, Stella pleaded with her brother-in-law, Joseph Tonelli, to find him work in the union.

Jimmy Boy had limited contact with his father during his formative years. The young Jimmy barely knew his half-sisters and half-brother, Robert, but he enjoyed getting to know his father's new family. The bonds of *consanguineità*, familial blood, innately demanded loyalty and devotion. Robert tested the limits of this bond. Robert, now an eighteen-year-old high school dropout, was desperate to do something meaningful. He abhorred painting all day long, mixing colors, climbing on ladders, and reeking of paint and paint thinner. Jack urged Robert to reach out to Jimmy Boy and outright ask him to help him to find work with the union. Despondent, Jimmy Boy could only offer this response:

Robert, I can't help you right now, this U.S. District Attorney, Giuliani, is all over my back. When this settles down, I'll be in touch.

Disappointed he had no choice but to wait. Two weeks later Jimmy Boy was dead. He was thirty-one years old, the death certificate stated he died of a heart attack. It was hard to believe a man in perfect health died of a heart attack and Jack thought something was fishy: no toxicology report and no thorough investigation. I never heard my parents mention anything about it, it was all hush hush. He was gone. There was lots of speculation about foul play, but there was no tangible evidence. While he was Jack's son, the wake and funeral were arranged by his mother Stella and the plot at Gate of Heaven Cemetery in Hawthorne, NY was paid by Stella's sister, Mary Tonelli. He was interred on July 2, 1974. The Westchester County District Attorney, Carl Veragri, ordered the body to be exhumed on October 2 and it was reinterred on October 3, 1974. All this remains a mystery. The family had no knowledge of a post burial forensic examination or were privy to the results. Rumors abounded, and then the news. On Tuesday February 4, 1975, eight months after Jimmy Boy's untimely death, *The New York Daily News* printed an article on a UPWI pension fund scandal.[2] Jimmy Boy was the administrator for the pension fund. He died unexpectedly, and he was found in his bedroom with a prayer book on the side table. He was dressed in a suit, hands clasped over his waist. There was no suicide note, however there were three simple instructions: Jimmy Boy did not want to get embalmed, he did not want a wake or funeral service, and he did not want a headstone. He wanted to be completely forgotten. He is not forgotten.

His body was placed in a closed casket and was subsequently buried the next day at Gates of Heaven Cemetery in Hawthorne, NY amongst the towering tombstones of the rich and famous. But now this article provided a little more insight into Jimmy Boy's relationship with his Union boss uncle and what he was involved with. In death he was labeled an unindicted co-conspirator in a pension fund scandal. A federal grand jury in Newark, NJ charged two separate groups of bankers and business executives of swindling close to one million dollars from the United Paper Workers International Union.

Joseph Tonelli was married to Jimmy Boy's aunt Mary, sister of his mom, Stella. Even though he had no experience as a pension fund administrator, that didn't matter since nepotism, although odious and anti-meritocratic, was widespread and created opportunities for those who were able to game the system to their advantage. Joseph Tonelli was a highly respected Union President, who in 1972, was successful in his campaign to unite mill workers with papermakers under a new national organization called United Paper Workers International Union. He had reputable oratory skills, was a capable union organizer, a seasoned negotiator, and hobnobbed with influential people in high places. He was appointed as chairman of the New York State Racing Commission by New York Gov. Nelson Rockefeller and was impressively appointed to the Social Security Advisory Board by President Johnson. Additionally, he was named to the Air Quality Advisory Board of the Environmental Protection Agency by President Nixon and was also vice president of the AFL-CIO's International Executive Council and industrial union department. Joseph Tonelli was honored by His Eminence Terrance Cardinal Cooke as a Knight of the Order of St. Gregory the Great, and he was invested into the Ecclesiastical Order of the Knights of Malta during a ceremony held at St. Patrick's Cathedral in New York City.[3,4] He had a private audience with Pope Paul VI who honored him with a special medal, Pro "Ecclessia et Pontifice."[5] These honors were bestowed on men of influence and power. Now a man in his seventies, Tonelli had fallen from grace as he was embroiled in a complicated scheme involving the scandalous embezzlement of union funds.[6] As the investigation continued over the years, Tonelli; Henry Segal, treasurer of the union; George Carroll, deputy clerk; and Anthony Loiacono, vice president of Local 318 of the union, were charged with embezzling a total of $360,000 of union funds; $290,000 was earmarked as expenditures for organizing campaigns and strike benefits for union members; $20,000 in union money was collected by submitting false expense accounts to the union, and $50,000 of union money was set aside to pay two lawyers from an Atlanta based law firm, one who received an appointment from President Jimmy Carter when he was Governor of Georgia, to thwart a grand jury investigation.[7] An additional charge was that Tonelli conspired with Loiacono, Carroll, and his nephew, James Fabio, to get kickbacks from deposits of union pension funds. Several checks totaling $100,000 were used as collateral for loans to an unindicted co-conspirator of which a portion was turned back over to Tonelli and his associates.

It was alleged that Jimmy Boy wrote six checks from the union's pension fund and deposited them in non-union accounts. A pension fund manager overseeing millions of union workers pay and dues has a lot of responsibility. Depositing money without authorization was not one of these responsibilities. These checks were made payable to Bankers Trust Co. in Huntington Station, LI, and Totowa Savings and Loan Association of Totowa, NJ. Bankers from those branches were contacted several times by Jimmy Boy and James Tonelli, Joseph's son and Jimmy Boy's cousin. The charges were that the bankers siphoned money out of the pension fund in a check kiting scheme.

Check kiting is not a new fraud scheme. In fact, it dates back to 1920. The term "kiting" originated from a 19th-century practice of issuing IOUs and bonds without collateral. The name is traced to "flying a kite" which inferred that there was nothing but air to support the loans. The term check kiting refers to the same concept of an account holder creating credit where none exists by leveraging clearing or float times. Check kiting takes advantage of "the float," or the lag time between when an individual provides a check as payment and when the recipient cashes the check and the recipient's bank requests funds from the check writer's bank.[8] A deposit is made to bank "B" from a check originating from bank "A." Bank "A" has insufficient funds to cover the check deposited in bank "B," but before bank "B" discovers the scheme, money is already withdrawn through a check or loan.

Four of those checks were deposited then transferred to the president of a real estate company known as P & H Realty Corp. Two of those checks were allegedly routed to a produce broker from Corona, Queens also named as an unindicted co-conspirator. Teddy Potash, who had a record in narcotics trafficking, was an operator of a prosperous grocery store. As an associate of Loiacono, Potash agreed to deposit the checks and kickback money to union officials. His grocery store became a meeting place for Tonelli, and for Carlo Gambino, head of the Gambino crime family, and his associate Joseph Zingaro from Rye, NY, a leader in Gambino's garbage racketeering operations in New York and New Jersey. Years later, Zingaro was sentenced to five years in prison for racketeering, gambling, numbers, loan sharking, and extortion of garbage carters.[9]

Loretta Lustig also appeared in a separate indictment. Miss Lustig, a thoroughbred stable manager at Patricia Stables at Aqueduct Raceway was well acquainted with Joseph Tonelli as chairman of the NYS Racing Commission. She also happened to own thorough-bred horses and had horses in the winner's circle in 1972 and 1973 at Aqueduct and Belmont. Fillies with names like: Swift Sky, Squalus, Appear, Roman Spinn'r, and My Son The Lawyer brought her good earnings. But the winning streak ended, and a scheme was plotted to get needed income. State investigators show that in 1973 and 1974 Jimmy Boy shifted $583,000 into three accounts that were opened without proper authority from the union and then withdrew most of that money and signed it over to Loretta Lustig. Her involvement was to receive union funds through bank accounts opened in her name by Jimmy Boy. Jimmy Boy executed a total of $15 million in illegal loans from the pension fund to Loretta Lustig. These loans in the form of checks were then deposited to separate bank accounts one of which was Baker's Trust in Huntington LI, an account set up in her name by Jimmy Boy.[10,11]

James Tonelli, Joseph Tonelli's son, had no official affiliation with the Union or the Fund, but was also found to be involved with the Pension Fund's purchase of three certificates of deposit, valued each at $100,000, from a South Carolina bank. In subsequent years, four bank officers were charged with helping in the scheme and were fired by their respective Banks. James Tonelli was charged with stealing pension funds and perjury by none other than US Attorney Samuel Alito Jr., now a member of the Supreme Court of the United States.[12] Miss Lustig pled guilty to stealing funds for her own personal use and was sentenced to a year and a day in jail.[13,14] Her scheming continued after her conviction and jail sentence. In 1987 she was charged with paying a loan officer $40,000 at the First National Bank of Louisville with the intention to approve a $2.5 million dollar loan for her business Double Development Inc. The loan officer later confessed to the charge of fabricating references.[15] Later that year, she defaulted on a loan from the First National Bank of Columbus.[16] In 1991 she was involved with supplying false letters of credit of her business Double Development Inc. to the First Financial Savings and Loan Association in Lutcher, LA. She presented a false letter of credit and was loaned $500,000 from Trustmark National Bank in Jackson, MS and paid a senior vice president and loan officer for his complicity.

Joseph Tonelli ultimately pleaded guilty and made a deal with the government to serve a maximum five-years in prison and a $10,000 fine. U.S. District Judge Jack Weinstein said at his sentencing in 1979,

There is no question that you stole from the union, and you knew others were stealing. You had a wonderful contribution that you made to the union and in the last years you went bad.[17]

He served ten months in jail. The pension fund received 90% of the misallocated funds back.

While the others were fired or fined or imprisoned, Jimmy Boy paid the ultimate price. He was gone. No one ever saw the composite picture of Jimmy Boy's involvement with embezzling union funds or other details of his death besides it being ruled a suicide. Jack's efforts for transparency went nowhere.

Jack had once explored getting the results post burial toxicology report to determine if he had been poisoned as a result of a homicide, but he was advised not to open a can of worms. Robert thought about Jimmy Boy for years. He tried to make sense of something that didn't make any sense. He knew something wasn't right. People in high positions hold power. An uneducated house painter has no sway and his quest for truth was futile, especially when a union president with presidential appointments and religious titles wanted to bury any potential witnesses that could shed light into this sordid affair of embezzlement.

Chapter 6

The price of excellence is discipline. The cost of mediocrity is disappointment.

—William Arthur Ward

Death arrived early and often. It lingered in his mind, affected his sense of future, it was futile. Robert was adrift in a nebula of confusion. What will he do now that his chance for a union job came tumbling down? He needed to do something, but his prospects for legitimate work were shrinking. He needed to transition to something else, and that something else required trial and error.

He decided to start with what he knew, and he knew painting, but he also knew that he hated painting, and he took random jobs here and there. He found a job as a delivery man for a local butcher on Yonkers Avenue. A friend from Dunwoodie Pizza who knew the owner gave him a strong recommendation, and Robert was hired. He drove the truck for nine months and he learned all the back alleys of his delivery routes, but repetitive routines bored him to tears, and so he quit after a tedious nine months of misery. He was lucky that a neighbor, Nick Capone, who owned a dinette center that supplied kitchen tables and chairs to the area could use some help. Nick knew Robert as a kid and understood he had a tough go of it, so he wanted to do what he could to get him on his feet, make some money, and stay out of trouble. Robert was a likable teenager, and it worked out. He made deliveries, unpacked, and set up the dinette sets, removed all the packing material and returned to the Dinette Center and make another round of deliveries. His hourly wage was supplemented by tips, not much to speak about, but something, nevertheless.

One night Robert was hanging out with a few friends and while chatting and chugging down some Heinekens, a guy who knew him from the bar motioned him over and said,

Bobby, go to Mike at the gym and try out. It's good money.

Robert knew how to fight, and his reputation as a street brawler was known throughout the bars and dives all over Yonkers. But he needed to learn how to box, and that is a horse of a different color. There were several boxing clubs around; he would go and spar with other amateur boxers. He had a solid right punch, but still no match for a trained boxer. He got his ass kicked quite a few times.

Kid, you got a good punch, but you got to move, you got to pivot and throw faster. You need a quick punch.

The trainer at the club was willing to give him a few tips while watching him spar and told him that with some efforts he would be a good fighter, and that he could hold his own and even be competitive.

Robert began training at the Yonkers PAL gym and was good enough to be selected to compete in the Golden Gloves tournament. Of course, around the holidays we'd get the update on the family: so-and-so is doing this, someone is traveling, and oh, Robert is doing amateur boxing. My brothers and I responded incredulously,

What, Robert is boxing. Ok, whatever.

What did we know about boxing outside of the heavy-weight fights broadcast on TV? The Golden Gloves amateur boxing tournament had boxers start in preliminary rounds and if they won three fights, they advanced to compete in the Forum quarterfinals followed by Forum semifinals and then the Madison Square Garden Finals. His first fight was on February 11th, 1976, at the Felt Forum. He was listed as 160 lb. sub-novice, a designation for boxers with no prior amateur boxing experience. Robert's first bout was against Liberty Usera representing Midtown Gym. The result was RSC, referee stopped the contest at 1:39 of second round.[1] He was kicking this guy's ass, and the fight was stopped. Jack was ecstatic, bragging to everyone within earshot. As I was researching for this book, I mentioned that I found a newspaper clipping of his boxing matches.

I told you, I was a good boxer. No one believes me. I don't lie, you understand?

He said as he tapped my arms and nodded his head. Yes, yes, you were a good boxer, I responded, but added that I had seen another clip. His next fight was on February 18th against James Hardy representing the Times Out Club. Robert's brother-in-law Lenny was there watching the previous fourteen matches, and he came to the holding pen and said:

Robert don't fight, they're gonna kill you!

Lenny saw that these boxers were the real deal, much more prepared and disciplined. Robert looked at him in disbelief and told him to get lost. He was trying to focus and didn't need the mental distraction and doubt. He had trained at Gold's Gym in Yonkers for many weeks. He was one of the few white guys but got noticed for his for his constant movement: punch and move, punch and move. He was feeling tired after taking the train to the city with his father and walking ten or so blocks to get to Madison Square Garden. He partied the night before the fight and was certainly not in prime condition to fight. His match was up and as he entered the ring, he spotted Jack ringside yelling and carrying on. He was amused at his father's enthusiasm but failed to meet his expectations. He thought he could come in with a hangover and compete, but he was sorely mistaken. He put up a good effort but lost on points. He admitted he wasn't disciplined enough to compete and made an excuse that he was completing against a marine. Training took a lot of work, and he wasn't willing to do it properly. Jack was more excited about the prospects and bragging rights. Robert lost the fight and quickly lost interest.[2]

Robert continued working at the dinette center, and his evenings were even more productive, and he earned more money than before. He continued to engage in petty robberies with his friends, but now was taking it to another level. It was a Tuesday night around seven-thirty, he was low on cash. He walked into Homefield Bowl, the bowling alley on Saw Mill River Road and Odell Ave. As he descended downstairs to a meeting room, he approached a man, his father's age, and put a gun to his head and yelled for money. Another man walked in, stopped in shock as Robert again demanded money. They both gave the same answer:

We don't have any money.

Robert tensed up and fumed and cursed them, but he knew that it was pointless. He then demanded that they get down on the floor. He then sprinted away, but the getaway car was gone. I'm fucked, he thought. Joey P. set this up and now he was gone. He made his way over to St. Mary's Cemetery on Sprain Road and hid amongst the tombstones. After a couple of hours, he decided to make his way home. As soon as he reached the street, a cop car turned the corner and grabbed him. As they approached him, he dropped the gun, a starter pistol. He was charged with attempted robbery third degree and was sentenced to five years' probation.[3]

If there were easy money, Robert was eager. Dave found out about a massage parlor on 38th Street and Park Ave. that was easy for the taking, most of the girls were working illegally. They did tricks on the side and kept their money in bags or shoe boxes hidden in their rooms. Robert and Dave entered late one night with guns drawn. Robert had a gun pointed at the madam and told her to round up the money as Dave had his back to the wall. After the money was collected, a big Asian bouncer jumped out of nowhere and placed a gun to the back of Robert's head.

I was shitting in my pants, I thought he was going to cap me. Dave fired his sawed off shot gun, the guy went down immediately. I ran out like a motherfucka.

Total take was $40K. Robert saw no reason to save and invest. He gambled and partied and lost his take in two weeks.

Stan DeRuggiero, Dave Stephanik, and Robert hung out with Vinny C., another Yonkers friend whose basement was loaded with free weights and machines. Stan, ten years older than the rest of them, was a Vietnam vet with long brown hair who liked to get high and pop pills. Vinny had a Great Dane named Sheba who had twelve pups. Three of the pups, Cisco, Sybil, and Cory were given to Stan, Dave, and Robert. They had a pact with each other and with the dogs, namely, they would never rat on each other and always would watch each other's back. When Robert was telling me this story about these dogs, my memory was jarred about the time my father and I went to visit Jack and Margie one summer afternoon. I was fifteen and just finished my freshman year in high school and had yet to find a summer job so agreed to tag along. Robert took my father and me down to the basement to see the recent upgrades Jack did to the laundry room. As we descended, we were met with a dog that looked as big as a pony. I never had good experiences with dogs. Blood spilled many times as I had been bit in the ass, arm, and knee by aggressive German Shepherds. I kept my distance and a watchful eye on this Doberman. This dog was huge and intimidating and it kept a sharp eye on Robert and watched his every move. Robert had trained him well. I was impressed. There wasn't much interaction with Robert being he never said a whole lot outside of, *Hey, cuz, how you doing?* We stayed with Jack and Margie for a while, and I was no more the wise about my nineteen-year-old cousins' life. My father never got much detail about Robert's escapades. I just assumed he graduated high school and worked with his father as a painter. Little did I know. I didn't see him for another eight years.

Chapter 7

> Vengeance, retaliation, retribution, revenge are deceitful brothers—vile, beguiling demons promising justifiable compensation to a pained soul for his losses. Yet in truth they craftily fester away all else of worth remaining.
>
> —Richelle E. Goodrich

For centuries it was customary to anoint someone with a moniker, a sort of an alias, to describe a unique characteristic of a family or individual trait. Adding a *soprannome*, a nickname for someone's last name, was an excellent way to differentiate the distinct families of a clan. In Italy, a soprannome is added after an individual's surname, *cognome* that is, to describe a unique family trait. Julius was a common Roman family name. The Romans understood the word Caesar to mean mortally strike an enemy, and the name Caesar eventually was associated with dictatorial power. Caesar was the soprannome attached to Gaius Julius, forever known as Julius Caesar. Butchy, while not a soprannome, was such a moniker, considering the personality and the background of Butchy. The name Butch has English origins, and it has a dual definition that it is interestingly contrasting. Butch could mean illustrious, but it can also refer to a butcher. The name and the word conjure up someone who is tough, rugged, or aggressively masculine. And Butchy was all of those things.

Butchy employed Robert to perform many shady jobs. His full name was Ronald Rocco (Butch) Futia. He was thirty-four years old, born in White Plains, NY and was married with two children and currently living in New Rochelle, NY. His criminality involved a burglary ring that targeted homes in Westchester, Rockland, and Connecticut. He was recently arrested for trafficking stolen property and loading it on his boat on the Hudson River near Ashburton Ave.[1] Butchy was a rugged looking guy. He exuded a bad vibe with his burly body and his full set of dark hair. Butchy looked like the stereotypical criminal with his low forehead, his massive jaw, and his bushy eyebrows.

Butchy had a history of trouble since he was in his teens. He devised a scheme where would bring a female accomplice up to gas stations in Connecticut, and while she distracted the gas station attendant, he brazenly emptied the content of the cash register and returned to the car. He stole from local appliance stores and was involved in armed robbery at jewelry stores in Bridgeport and Stamford, CT and Bedford, NY. A judge once commented that

He started out as a seven-year-old shoplifter and was a source of trouble ever since.[2]

He was a small-time crook, and because of ties to the mob, he operated with impunity. He associated with Ken Masiello, another son of John Masiello Sr., and Nick Greco, all associates of the Genovese crime family.[3] John Masiello Sr. was indicted in 1969 for insurance fraud[4] and in 1977 for his strong-arm tactics to take control of a Bronx based business called Westchester Poultry. In his efforts to take over the chicken processing business, Masiello, under threats of violence, forced the owner to sign over executive control, and sign promissory notes payable to Masiello himself, and give him large sums of cash from the firm's assets.[5]

The Masiello's owned a house on Durst Place, a few blocks

north of where Robert grew up. Neighbors were cognizant that the Masiello family was somehow connected to the mob. Schoolmates of John Masiello Jr., Ken's brother, sensed something different, about their schoolmate. John Masiello Jr. was a senior at Lincoln High School in Yonkers in 1962. When the seniors posed for their yearbook pictures, it was customary for one's peers to write a sentence or phrase under the portrait of their fellow graduates to describe their schoolmates' best qualities or aspirations. How apropos it was, this double entendre was cynical, and it was observant. It was written without fear of repercussions or consequences. The quote read:

If clothes make the man, he's made.[6]

Ken had his run-ins with the law. He once tried to bribe cops to release Butchy Futia and a guy named Charles Guida from custody.[7] Guida was known to the cops for spending time in prison for six years for bank robbery and conspiracy to commit bank robbery in 1966.[8] In 1958 he pleaded guilty to first degree manslaughter for stabbing his estranged wife sixteen times.[9] In now 1972, two cops spotted Guida running from the bar and jumping into Butchy's car while ablaze.

The pair had just firebombed the business called the Executive Lounge on E 149th St in the South Bronx, probably for lack of payment to their extortion racket, were now in custody at the 40th Precinct in the Bronx. The cops quickly arrested Masiello for bribery, as he offered them two-thousand dollars to release Guida and Butchy while they were held at the local precinct.[10] Butchy was also an associate of Lawrence "Larry Black" Centore, a man who had a rap sheet going back to the 1930s and who was viewed by law enforcement as a senior member of the Genovese family, as well as; a man who could and did settle mob disputes.[11] Centore controlled the flow of illegal and untaxed cigarettes through his South Bronx warehouse. Butchy made sure that Centore's Jet Automatic Vending Machines distributed throughout local businesses in the Bronx and Westchester were stocked with their cigarettes. Centore and the Genovese made a killing. Truckloads of cigarettes arrived at the warehouse every week, each truck carrying up to eight-thousand cartons. These cartons were legally purchased from a North Carolina distributor at $2.42 a carton and through up-charges to middlemen and finally the consumer would sell for three dollars and fifty cents,[12] roughly six-thousand six-hundred dollars profit per truck. Millions of dollars were made annually. It was good business, except that selling untaxed cigarettes in New York was illegal.

Butchy found out that a new Subway franchise had opened, and he was not happy about the vending machines, or the cigarettes, which were not the same ones he had in the stores in Yonkers. This Subway shop became an object of his fury. Robert's two sisters, Jackie and Patty and their husbands, Lenny and Vinnie had just opened a Subway Franchise on Saw Mill River Road in Yonkers, some store fronts near the Yonkers Diner. They were excited about the possibilities. They scraped together fifty-thousand dollars between families and friends to open up. They were now competing with established Italian delicatessens spread-out all-over Saw Mill River Road and surrounding areas. If you wanted cold cuts, you went to the deli, if you wanted sandwich platters, you went to the deli, you wanted a meatball hero or pepper and egg sandwich on a roll, you went to the deli. Subway could give you submarine sandwiches with pre-sliced cold cuts on bread that were not of bakery quality and were delivered to the deli every morning. It didn't matter, Subway was part of the franchise craze and Jackie, Lenny, Patty, and Vinnie wanted to be part of the growing trend since they were optimistic about the possibilities to make a good profit. It didn't work out that way, and within a short span of time just before opening, they were surprised one day to find smashed, broken furniture, and a screaming maniac coming in later that day and demanding his vending machines to be used to stock his cigarettes:

My machines, my machines, you use my machines and my cigarettes, or something worse will happen.

Robert knew that the destruction was authored by Butchy. Who else would have wrecked the place? No one else in the area managed the cigarette machines and stock except for Butchy and his associates Dave and Matty. He told Jackie and Lenny it wouldn't happen again, and they should just absorb the cost of fixing up the place and allow cigarette machines in the store to operate and move on. They were beyond upset, they seethed to the point of inner rage, and thoughts of retribution streamed like floodwater down a sewer. They had just opened a few weeks earlier, but this setback of borrowing money from family and friends to fix broken tables and chairs and install new windows was an ominous sign. They were the newest kids on the block, so they needed to dangle the shiniest object of all and compete with the local delis. It didn't work out, for they were losing money month after month without getting ahead, it was like running in place in a financial treadmill, toiling and sweating with nothing new accomplished. Their investment was smashed, and they licked their wounds and anguished over shattered dreams.

Butchy didn't tolerate anyone who slighted him, no matter who it was. There was one score where Butchy thought Dave didn't pay up: he didn't give him his thirty percent cut of the money Dave acquired through targeted robbery. He was pissed and let Robert know it. At night he would take jobs from Butchy, bringing along Dave and Matty. They wanted easy money and Butchy seemed to know the easy targets,

Ok, this guy is around the corner from McLean Ave., he's a bookie and got lots of cash, lives alone. He's usually home on Wednesday evening after nine.

Robert, Dave, and Matty scoped it out, and drove around the block four or five times. Lights were on downstairs and by ten-thirty the lights were out. A lone light was on in the back upstairs. They parked down the street about half a block, and when they returned, they each wore a pull-over mask with cut-outs for the eyes and mouth. These masks were the knitted kind from a discount clothing store like Caldor's. They jimmied the back kitchen door open and made their way upstairs. The man in his late fifties was as surprised as hell. He reacted with ire in his eyes and stood up and angrily asked:

Who the hell are you? Get outta here!

He was about to grab the telephone nearby on the night table but before he completed his sentence Robert and Dave grabbed him and shoved him on the bed. Matty grasped and applied a choke hold while Robert got in his face before he screamed:

Where's the fucking money? We know you got money!

The big galoot posed a defiant resistance, trying to dislodge the wiry fingers from his neck. He desperately whistled and wheezed attempting to say:

I don't have any money, get out!

This torture lasted five minutes before Dave busted into a rage. Dave pulled out a Marlboro, lit it, and as Robert held those flailing legs, Dave hoarsely threatened him with cigarette burns. In a moment of pure rage, he extinguished the Marlboro cigarette tip on the exposed skin of the old man's worn feet and ankles. The man screamed, and tried to get free, but Matty punched the beleaguered man squarely in the face and jaw. Dave continued to torment him with yet another cigarette clinically pressuring the pale, white skin. The man howled and shook like a man convulsing uncontrollably. He reached a braking point and with a choking voice broke out:

Ok, ok. In the closet, I have money, take it, please don't kill me.

Robert calmly headed to the closest and found a cashier's bag behind some boxes on the top shelf. There was no money. Disbelieving, they threatened and punched the beleaguered victim. They took off empty handed, leaving behind a crazed man unable to seek assistance because criminals could not expose themselves to authority.

The next day the bookie spread the word on the street that he was robbed of $100,000. He showed anyone who would listen the burn marks and black and blue welts on his torso, arms, and legs. The trio partied at the Hide Out and lamented over their lack of success while the bookie lamented of his misfortune. Jack's motto swam through Robert's mind:

Free money.

But the robbery of the bookie came up short. They never did get any money. They couldn't find any. Butchy Futia believed otherwise.

Butchy didn't tolerate anyone who slighted him, no matter who it was. This was one score where Butchy thought Dave didn't pay up: he didn't give him his ten percent cut of the money that Dave acquired through petty larceny. He was pissed and let Robert know it. Dave was nineteen years-old and he spent good money from his earnings to rent an apartment on the third floor on Cook Avenue in Yonkers with his Great Dane, Sybil. It was a stifling hot and humid day on a July evening, the air reeked of stale cigarettes and body order, and without central air conditioning. Dave fell asleep with a window open and a floor fan droning an obsessive tune after a night of bar hopping. A neighbor and his wife, awoken after hearing the sound of breaking glass and screaming, pulled the fire alarm. It was around five-fifteen a.m. The heat from the fire was so intense that the fireman who arrived within minutes could not enter the apartment. Once the fire was under control thirty minutes later, they entered and found Dave dead, badly burned and lying in a fetal position.[13] Robert knew something was up, he had no proof, but a random fire was out of the question. He knew Butchy would exact his revenge. Robert told Dave's parents to get an autopsy because he suspected that his head was bashed-in, as was Sybil's. The Great Dane was very protective and would have gone berserk if a stranger entered the apartment, or some random fire blazed up. Someone would have heard the dog barking uncontrollably; no one did, not Mrs. Danka next door, nor the landlords living on the first floor. The Westchester County Medical Examiner ruled asphyxiation as the cause of death due to smoke inhalation and body burns. Robert thought otherwise, and so did others. Robert, Matty, and Dave played with the devil. Dave paid a price with his life, and this devil showed no honor among thieves. He wanted his money and would go after whoever slighted him. Robert was the next target.

Butchy blew in like a hurricane. Robert was working as a delivery man during the day for Nick Capone's Dinette Center. Suddenly, this stocky, burly, unkempt man headed for the first guy he eyed and tensely uttered:

Does Robert Fabio work here?

Yes, he does.

You better tell him to come see me or I'm going to chop him up, you understand?

Um, ok, yes, I'll tell him.

Robert came back to the store an hour later. He looked at Nick who turned ashen, as if a vampire had sucked his blood and all shaken said:

Listen, Robert, this guy came in here looking for you. He looked mean and nasty, and was threatening you, you better call the cops. He said you owed him money. You better call the cops.

No, no, I'm alright, don't worry about it.

Robert responded. Butchy was still looking for his cut. He thought Dave and the others made a score and that Dave didn't pay up. Dave was dead and Robert was next on the list. Everyone thought Butchy killed Dave, now the tables turned. As Robert, Matty, and Stan were pumping iron in Vinny C.'s basement, they shifted their despair to revenge. They all thought Butchy was an asshole and had no loyalty to any of them. They all thought Butchy had something to do with Dave's death. To add to the murmuring about Butchy, Stan complained that his nephew was roughed up by Futia a few days before and he and his family had enough of it. They started talking about working him up and knocking him around for good measure. Robert chimed in:

Let me tell you something, you beat this guy up, you are all going to be fucking dead, you gotta kill this motherfucka.

Stan replied,

You're right Robert, you gotta fucking kill this guy.

A few weeks after that ominous conversation, Butchy lay dead on Saw Mill River Road in Yonkers. Butchy was self-assured and fearless. He had intimidated, beaten, and killed to get what he wanted. And did that for most of his life. Not affected by the prediction of the proverb: live by the sword, die by the sword, he maintained his reign of terror. He had a routine; he would go around to the local businesses with his black El Dorado and collect money from everyone who wanted in on his private lotto racket. It was Monday around four p.m. on this mild November afternoon of 1976. The balmy breeze gently caressing his puffy cheeks. At one point, Butchy exited the Yonkers Diner. He wore a flannel shirt with an unbuttoned collar that accentuated his disheveled appearance of messy hair, untrimmed beard and hairy chest, giving him an uncaring and imposing stature. He collected some of his number rackets money from this diner, one of many stops on his collection racket.

On that fatal November afternoon, he cockily walked to his car, but he heard the hum of another car slowly approach. It was a dirty tan Chevy Nova. He froze before he could react to a leveled sawed-off shot gun blasting two ricocheting shots: Boom! Boom! The sound echoed down the street. Butchy's head dropped, and his lifeless body thumped as the Chevy Nova pulled ahead fifteen feet past the open front door of his Cadillac. Second guessing their aim, the assassins reared back to the lifeless body, pointed the barrel of the sawed-off gun, aimed for Butchy's bloody head and put a final bullet on it.[14] It was a gangland hit, a common practice, a signature method of mobsters.

Scattered witnesses identified two white males screeching off, driving a tannish Chevy Nova. The cops had a general idea of Butchy's identity and his associates. Butchy was a notorious prick, a mean motherfucker, a selfish, hellbent son of a bitch determined to the nth degree to succeed with his crime sprees. The cops didn't care about him personally, but they could not let this happen under their watch. They also knew from experience that this was not a random attack: it was theft or revenge for some scheme gone awry.

Butchy's murder rattled the Yonkers underworld as no one in the top ranks had ordered a hit. Weeks later, the cops found a torched tan Chevy in an East Yonkers apartment lot. The nondescript vehicle, perfect for the crime, was stolen specifically for the hit. Someone poured gasoline all over it and flung a match that set the volatile Chevy Nova to crackling sparks that seared the hair and eyebrows of the associate of the assassins. One of the trio's friends showed up at one of the local bars looking freakishly odd. His eyebrows looked like they were shaved by some cosmetologist. The thug appeared strange with his tough-looking facial features contrasted to an effeminate eyebrow make up. Their buddy was mercilessly teased for weeks on end.

Dave's death over the summer was ruled death by asphyxiation. They couldn't pin Butchy's death as revenge for Dave's death. But they knew Robert, Matty, Stan, and Brian were in cahoots with Butchy. These guys spelled trouble! They were locked up and released many times. Robert was paranoid, fearing the worst. He came home one evening and had a weird sensation that there was someone spying on him. He parked his car in front of his house, walked up the front pathway and just as the front door opened ajar, while the key was still in the lock, a rush came from nowhere. Suddenly, ten uniformed cops surrounded him with guns drawn. More police officers pulled up with their car lights flashing and their sirens blaring. The cops thrusted Robert to the ground while his Great Dane Cory came out on the front stoop and barked menacingly at the cops. *Calm this dog down or it's going to get shot*, one cop yelled. Robert shooed Cory back into the house and was soon handcuffed to the front railing. Margie came out of the front door in her housedress and immediately started crying,

Oh, my son, my son, what is happening?

Jack came out demanding to know what Robert did now. The cops calmed everyone down and matter of factly said they are bringing him to the local precinct with the charge of conspiracy to commit murder. Jack and Margie were shocked. How could this be? How bad was this kid?

Once at the station they questioned him profusely, but didn't have any evidence that he was at the murder scene or actually killed Futia. But because he was heard on Butchy's wiretaps talking about the murder with specific details of the hit and agreeing with the others that Butchy had to go, he was now compromised. The prosecutors had many false leads but narrowed their suspects to three: The DeRuggiero brothers and their nephew. Roger, Dominick and John DeRuggiero, and nephew Stanley DeRuggiero were the prime suspects. A waitress at the diner, and a neighbor from an apartment building overlooking Saw Mill River Road who witnessed the commotion near the diner, agreed to testify. A court order was issued to record conversations via a bugging device in Roger's living room and wiretaps on Roger's and Stanley's phones. The taps revealed that Robert and the others attended the wedding of Joey Portanova, a mutual friend. The DeRuggiero's were clearly involved in the crime. Any information implicating Robert was however not permissible because the court order only pertained to the DeRuggiero's. Robert sat in jail for months, but eventually walked out a free man. Case dismissed! As the DeRuggiero houses were searched, ten-thousand dollars' worth of rifles and shotguns were discovered. These weapons matched the guns that were reported stolen from the Big Indian Gun Shop in Ulster County in February 1976, the robbery that Dave participated in.[15] Robert is still in possession of a hunting knife from that robbery. It was a gift from Dave.

The DeRuggiero family was selling stolen guns, and Stan was eventually convicted of a misdemeanor weapons charge and possession of a .44 Magnum Ruger. They discovered a gruesome female skull with a hole in it. This horrific skull was sent to the medical examiner where it was thought to be a souvenir from Viet Nam. Stan took it home as a prized possession after his tour of duty.[16] His uncle, John, served time for possession of stolen property and criminal possession of a weapon. As Dominick was awaiting trial, he was arrested with several others including Ken Masiello's father, John Masiello Sr. on charges of distributing cocaine, phenobarbital and amphetamines in western Pennsylvania. By 1978 Roger and Dominick were given life sentences for the gangland execution of Butchy Futia.[17] Even though Robert was free, Jack was disgusted with him. He caused so much pain and anguish for Jack and Margie that they wanted him out. But Jack also hoped that something better would come along, hoped that he could be proud of him and find reasons to boast. Robert was free, but not from his vices. Gambling, partying, and free money was all he thought about.

Chapter 8

Learning never exhausts the mind.

—Leonardo Da Vinci

Robert was distraught; his friend was gone, a friend who was close to him, but just another dead friend, and now that Nick Capone simply let him go, money was tighter than ever. His world was rocked as life itself changed. Nick didn't need some guy arrested for conspiracy to commit murder on his payroll. Petty crimes and robberies he committed with Dave, Matty, and Brian were drying up, but from time to time, he collected money for Joey Portanova. Boxing was no longer part of his game plan. He hoped to earn money by scoring big when he gambled, or he helped Jack with painting. Going back to work for Jack wasn't working out well, so he started his own business, and Elite Painting was born. He worked at some jobs here and there, and whenever he bought something expensive it was easy to tell Jack that he was busy doing work through Elite.

Dealing cards now became his steady source of money. He explained it this way:

I was at the Hideaway, a local bar on Bailey Ave in the Bronx with Joey Portanova. We were drinking, having a good time, and this guy Tony Perez knew I had been in some boxing matches, comes over to me and says "Kid, that's not for you. You're gonna win some and you're gonna lose some and your face is gonna take a beating. You gotta a pretty face, not like those other ugly motherfuckers, you'll get all scarred up and for what?" Out of the corner of my eye a door opened to a room, it was all black except for some lights on a blackjack table. A game was breaking up. Nothing but Asians in the back room getting up to leave. I was fascinated, this was what I wanted to do! Tony said Look, learn how to deal, you make good money and have steady income, plenty of clubs need dealers. I thought I can do that, beats fucking painting, I hate painting, and I like my face.

Tony stared right in his eyes and said: *Come back Saturday around six p.m. We'll train you for two weeks. Two weeks later I finished. They told me that I was fast and that I was good. Next thing I knew was that I was heading down to a club on 61st Street between First and Second Avenues where I was working for a well-connected Irish guy that I had never met.*

Johnny Mac was a legitimate businessman. He drove a Canada Dry truck for years, but when his partner died, he opened his first neighborhood bar. After a decade of small Mom and Pop games for the locals, he decided to test the waters and ran a casino night venue at a local bar in the Bronx. Around 1976 New York State passed a new Las Vegas Night Law that allowed for the operation of bingo and casino nights as long as it was run for charity. Johnny Mac was onto something, the bingo/casino charity was a money-maker that grossed ten-thousand dollars a day. When the former Johnny Mac Bar was raided and shut down in the Kingsbridge section of the Bronx, it was known as: *The biggest money illegal gambling house in the city*. It comprised twenty-five blackjack tables, roulette wheels and numerous other games of chance for about three-hundred bettors.[1] After that shut down, Johnny Mac negotiated a deal with the mob on Belmont Ave., in the Bronx, to provide security, discretion, and muscle for casino operations in exchange for money payments. Eventually Johnny opened other bars, and soon found locations to operate illegal gambling in back rooms at other various legitimate businesses.

Blackjack, poker, and other games were often run from local bars in NYC. Although illegal, they were not sophisticated. These gambling jaunts attracted elder citizens who wiled their time away by gambling and socializing.

The Hideaway was one of those cozy places where locals gathered to have a good time. This old but well-maintained establishment had a regular customer base. Mary, a freckled, plump, fiftyish Irish woman dealt cards. She dealt mechanically, as if in slow motion. Each card was deliberately placed face-down, then just as slowly she would deal the cards facing up. After each card was fully down, she would unemotionally announce the card with an intentional hushed Irish accent. Old men playing cards with slow reflexes were happy to play cards with a deliberate rhythm. But the slow pace hindered the bottom line, and the house felt the financial pinch: this was not a recipe to make money, and nothing else mattered to the house but to make money, no matter what. The house favored a lot of games, not fewer.

Robert was asked to deal a few nights a week. Here was a young Italian guy, dealing fast, yelling out the cards, turning over hands, and winning for the house. The old men laughed and commented how his fingers blurred while shuffling the deck.

He's playing tricks. Look how fast he deals!

Commented the men through the slurs resulting from drinking all afternoon. Johnny Mac knew instinctively that this young Italian had the goods to make him some serious money. Johnny Mac kept Robert busy five nights, and sometimes six nights, a week.

George "Kelly" Ambrosini was nearly thirty years older than Robert, and in spite of the age gap between the two, he developed a fast sympathy for the younger man. George was divorced as many times as a Hollywood celebrity. Now free of female encumbrances, he made many rounds hopping from bar to bar until eventually he hit the upstairs of the Hideway to crash for the night.

George was also the bartender and the muscle at the 61st St. club. He was a big, fat, jovial guy with a mean streak and had his own side hustles. He secured illegal driver's licenses through a connection at an auto driving school based in Yonkers.[2] He also did some collecting of gambling debts and often took Robert to tag along. If George needed to bash a few heads and send a memorable message to a debt delinquent for not paying in a timely fashion, he would throw a brick through the storefront window. Big, fat George acted like a muscle-head superhero, he was tough, and he was proud of his exploits. Robert witnessed his brutality in action many times. On a cold winter evening, a cab driver who had borrowed money from George was sitting at a blackjack table. He was having a good time as his chips told everyone he was up a thousand dollars. George recognized him and demanded his money. The cab driver hesitated and offered to pay a partial amount next week. George was having none of it and retrieved a heavy snow shovel from the back office. As the cab driver focused on the cards Robert was calling out, George came up from behind and swung wildly. Bam! He whacked him on the back of his head. Blood gushed from the large gash as his head slumped on his red jack of hearts. He was out cold as his warm blood splattered everywhere. Robert, dressed in a white shirt now covered in red blood quickly took him outside with George's help and lay him on the side of the building. No more games the rest of the evening. He took Robert under his wing and showed him the ropes: nothing like learning on the job. He offered one hundred dollars on several occasions to throw bricks through store front windows, a good sum of money those days. George treated Robert like his young protégé. He became his self-appointed guru and would tell him anecdotes of his exploits while in the mob. He told his stories with a flair for the sensational, and Robert listened with intensity, for he was intrigued when hearing stories about retributions and vengeance. These stories raised spiral hair and excited the imagination to new levels. Robert loved the gory details that George graphically described, as if living those moments afresh. It was all about blood and money, violence and retribution, and ultimately power and submission.

One listless evening at the 61st St. club, George turned to Robert, looked him squarely in the eyes, and with his melodious baritone voice cryptically intoned:

Watch this fucking guy, he don't like you. This guy is jealous of you. Watch this prick, remember, you're a fighter, he's a fighter.

Ronnie was the manager of the club; he was poised and outwardly calm. He sat at the bar wearing a blue blazer with a drink in his hand, and he stared at Robert with knives darting out of his emerald eyes. Robert dealt blackjack at the table, and he was too busy to notice the glaring manager. But Ronnie had something festering in his head, something that was eating him up, but that he suppressed very deeply in his psyche. He suppressed his angst by concentrating on that scotch and water that he grasped in the cup of his hand; simultaneous ready to crush it, yet holding it gingerly. He watched the dealer, and he watched the spotter making sure no one was ripping off Johnny. He wasn't talkative to the staff, only talkative to the other Irishmen who came and went in the back office. There was always chatter behind the door, on the phone, or with a group of guys with thick Irish brogues talking about the clubs, money, and guns. Ronnie didn't gamble or do drugs. Robert did both with manifest authority. As a short Irish guy with not a lot of success in boxing, Ronnie made his way to the clubs through his Irish connections and friends at Johnny Mac's bars. He was a likable guy who earned the trust of those in the clan for his loyalty. He didn't steal. He made sure the money in the trap was counted and was given to Johnny Mac's number two man, Eddie.

Johnny Mac had a plan for Ronnie. He wanted to unionize the bouncers at all the discos and illegal casinos in Manhattan and in the Bronx. The idea was that most club owners paid the doorman/bouncer $125 a night to watch and protect clubs' interests. By paying a union fee of $25, the bouncer was guaranteed protection and back-up on demand. Big money was to be had. Johnny Mac and Eddie calculated that $500,000 could be earned over a weekend. Any doorman could be wired and be able to have ten guys at his disposal. Ronnie was all in on the gig. Ronnie was not big guy, but what he lacked in size he made up in mettle and in toughness. As a retired welterweight boxer, he was ever ready to throw a punch when needed and he could be persuasive without having to resort to violence as his first tactic to get what he wanted.

After dealing one night at 61st St., Robert headed over to the Iguana Club, one of the new hot clubs that attracted the type of cute party girls who were thrilled to dance after a few drinks and a snort of coke while flirting with guys who peeked up their short skirts if they started to dance by the bar. Robert, who could not keep his hands to himself, grabbed one of the girls under her short skirt; she shrieked:

My boyfriend is a bouncer, he's gonna kill you.

Ronnie dashed on the scene upon hearing the screeches and could not believe his eyes when of all people he sees none other than Robert. Ronnie's face turned to stone. His feral eyes expressed rage, he wanted to kick ass, but not just any ass, he wanted to kick Robert's ass. But common sense prevailed, and Ronnie took a deep breath, slowly ambled toward Robert, then stopped and gave him a look over, meekly advised him to calm down, and simply walked away. Robert continued to party and paid the bathroom attendant twenty dollars to guard the door and not let anyone in as he made his way to the bathroom every hour to snort some lines of coke with his dealer friend Zorro, a light skinned Dominican kid. As the night wore on, they stayed in the bathroom longer than usual. Several patrons were pissed off having to wait to take a leak. Soon ten bouncers bust in screaming:

What the fuck is going on in here?

Instantly, Zorro pulled out his gun and shouted:

Who wants to get shot?

Everyone backed off as Ronnie observed everything and screamed that no one could do blow in the bathroom. Robert yelled back:

Hey, fuck you, I know your boss.

Ronnie knew he was Johnny Mac's dealer who made him a lot of money, and so no one was going to touch him, not Ronnie, not the bouncers. A few days later Eddie came in laughing:

Johnny Mac loves you, says you really got a pair a balls; don't take crap from anyone.

Eddie then chewed out Ronnie, telling him that he had one incident at the Iguana Club and could barely handle it, then he continued his reprimand:

How are you gonna manage all these bouncers? We want to unionize these guys!

Ronnie stiffened up. He had no answer. Ronnie fumed in his silence.

Bengi, the daytime manager of the 61st St. club, was a big Black Irish guy with a handlebar mustache accenting his square jaw. His fellow clansmen were always going and coming in and out as blackjack games were in progress. While Robert dealt cards, he overheard bits and pieces of information about guns, ammo, hand grenades, and shipments that the IRA monitored. Robert registered the conversations, but he stored all that information in the recesses of his memory. One day after the club closed around four a.m., George offered Robert a ride home by saying:

Listen, I have to make a couple of stops.

Ok, George, sounds good.

They quietly walked to George's beat up blue Toyota, and without a word spoken George opened the trunk of his car. The open trunk revealed an arsenal of deadly weapons ranging from handguns, machine guns, rifles, and a lot of ammunition. George warned Robert to watch out for these guys from Ireland, they were killers. They flew them into the country and commissioned them for assignment: they chopped victims up and vanished in the mists of Ireland.

Don't argue with these guys!

Robert didn't say a word, he couldn't, but he did the math, kept his mouth shut and did what he was paid to do, deal, win for the house, and make Johnny Mac lots of money. He never had any other run-ins with Ronnie and kept his head down, focused on the game, and often relaxed with a Heineken and a cigarette during breaks.

Joseph "Ronnie" Gibbons hailed from an Irish family from Liverpool, England. He came to New York at the age of nineteen to enter the boxing circuit as a welterweight. His boxing career ended in the late 1970s. Because of his boxing schedules he forged various connections in bars throughout the tristate area. Boxing was an exhilarating experience that led to connect with and eventually manage many of Johnny Mac's clubs.[3] In the early 1990s, casinos were summarily raided, disrupted, and harassed, causing Ronnie to embark for greener pastures. He went for big-time money, and that entailed risky, illegal activities.

He planned a heist in concert with an unlikely trio, a Melkite Priest from upstate NY, a former Irish Republican Army guerrilla, and a retired cop who worked security at a Brink's Depot in Rochester, NY. A total of $7.4 million was stolen, and even though Ronnie was in on the planning, and was not part of the actual robbery, he wanted his cut. Ronnie drove from Manhattan to Rochester two years after the heist in 1995 and was never seen alive again. Years later George says:

Oh, you won't see Ronnie no more, they chopped him up.

A chopped-up torso and lone foot were found on the shore of Lake Ontario in 1999 and 2000, respectively. DNA samples later confirmed that the body parts belonged to the welterweight Irish boxer. These DNA samples matched those collected from his mother living in Liverpool.[4,5,6]

Stevie was yet another manager in Johnny Mac's club. Robert knew Stevie for a long time. Stevie was well liked. He was enterprising and made the club good money by means of wheeling and dealing. He earned a promotion, but he got greedy. Stevie was stealing from Johnny Mac and mistakenly believed that he could disappear after he whisked a large amount of cash from a safe. He also liked heroin and got his fix from a dealer in the Bronx. One evening, as Robert was giving him a ride back to Yonkers, Stevie persuaded him to drop by Pelham Parkway in the Bronx so he could make a score underneath the "L" by Boston Post Road. Robert was tired, but he agreed, being it wasn't that far out of his way, just off exit 7E on the Bronx River Parkway. As he pulled over under the "L" around four-thirty a.m., the area seemed deserted, when out of the shadows, a dark figure approached the car. It was the dealer. He jumped in the backseat on the passenger side. After some small talk back and forth, the trade was made, cash for heroin. The voice in the back sounded strangely familiar, and as Robert turned around, he couldn't believe who it was. Of all people it was Johnny Fabio whom he hadn't seen in years, and now he was dealing heroin. Just two years younger than Robert, Johnny was our first cousin. He was the son of Joe (and Rose) Fabio, and nephew to Jack and Paul. Johnny was the youngest of five children growing up on Westervelt Ave. near Allerton Ave., north of Pelham Parkway. Johnny, his parents, Joe and Rose, and the rest of the family, moved to Neill Ave. in the Morris Park section of the Bronx when this neighborhood was encroached with home break-ins. Johnny was street-wise and spoke with a thick Bronx accent. Like Robert, he never finished high school. Johnny became addicted to drugs in his late teens, and his addiction spiraled down from there. I didn't see much of my cousin Johnny after he turned sixteen years old, neither did Robert until now, now that the deal was consummated. After the exchange took place, Johnny got out of the car and staggered down the street not to be seen by his cousins and aunts and uncles until his father's, Joe Fabio, seventieth birthday party in 1987. He was as high as a kite even then. It was not too smart for Stevie to steal money from Johnny Mac, it was a real bad move. He attempted to hide fifty thousand dollars in a cabin in Woodstock, NY. He eventually was tracked down, and gruesomely, some psychopath chopped off his right arm.

Robert tried to keep his focus on dealing, and he made sure not to be high, drunk, or disrespectful while working. Off-nights was a different story, as he liked to party and play the ladies' man.

Hey, how's that pussy? Is that pussy worth dying for?

What? What are you talking about?

Robert responded with surprise, as he walked into the back office at the club on 61st Street and was about to shoot the breeze with Eddie. Eddie was hunched over in his swivel chair; glasses were down to the tip of his nose when he slowly looked up and decided to set Robert straight.

Look, I know you've been fucking around with K O. She's Dennis' girl. He will shoot you in the face, stuff you in the truck and I won't be seeing you anymore. Leave that shit alone.

Robert played dumb, denying he was physical with her. He knew who Dennis was, he was called The Fox because of his distinguished silver-grey mane that was combed back, neat, and trim. He had a club on City Island and everyone in the know considered

K O his girl. K O was a gorgeous, blue-eyed redheaded Irish girl from the Bronx. She was petite, with dark, auburn shoulder-length hair and an engaging smile. Her lilting Irish brogue sounded like an Irish lullaby. This Irish enchantress was of all things a blackjack dealer. Robert met her at Johnny Mac's clubs. She occasionally was on shifts with him as she dealt cards, and men placed bets as if under her spell, not caring about draining money out of their pockets. After a long night or on breaks, he was under her spell, especially after sharing a joint with her, and snorting coke. They relaxed together, drifting off in laughter and flirtatious conversation. They loved to be together as they shared a sexual attraction augmented by the bubbles of champagne, the smoke of weed, and the powder of cocaine. But Eddie was that pesky fly in the ointment. The Fox had a claim on K O. The Fox could never know that he and the Irish enchantress floated together in those bubbles of champaign. Valor is stability, and safety is more important than forbidden pleasures. Robert denied rumors and obeyed the laws of survival, came to his senses and gave up his dream woman. She was a magnetic force of nature, a stunning beauty, but she was not worth dying for. He concluded that no woman was ever worth dying for.

Eddie had another warning.

Did you hear anything about that robbery?

No, I had nothing to do with it.

Eddie looked at him suspiciously with a smirk.

OK, well, whoever got that ring better send it back because he is going to kill everybody.

Robert thought long and hard and spoke with Matty a few days later. The ring in question was a four-carat emerald cut diamond on a wide gold band. A week earlier Robert and Matty got a tip where to make a quick buck. A poker game was taking place in a tenth-floor apartment on 48th Street and Madison Ave. Everyone had lots of cash. They went in with guns drawn and masks over their faces. A wise guy from Brooklyn couldn't believe it:

Who the fuck are you guys? I will kill you!

Shut the fuck up!

was the answer as a gun was shoved in his face followed by a determined command to turn over the ring. The guy with the ring was a wise guy with an attitude. He was full of cash, thirty thousand dollars, a massive sum to bring to a game. In total, Robert and his buddies heisted one hundred and seventy-thousand dollars, plus the ring. Eddie gave Robert an address in case he heard anything. He heard loud and clear, and Matty mailed the ring to an address in Brooklyn.

Matty had his own side hustle. He found a job with Con Edison as a meter reader in Westchester and earned a steady income. But that wasn't enough to feed his drinking and partying expenses. He was also dealing Tuinal, a highly additive pain killer. Unfortunately for Matty and his older brother Donald, the police were tipped off that the pair was dealing drugs, and Donald's house in Yonkers was raided. Between the two, police confiscated Tuinal powder, syringes and needles, and $10,000 in diamonds and other jewelry. Matty burglarized several homes in Harrison, NY during his meter-reading route and made a big score. Now he was out of a job and out of commission and struggled to stay out of jail.[7] Donald succumbed to his vices and died of a drug overdose six months after his and Matty's arrest. He left behind a wife and young daughter. After jail, Matty continued with his side hustles and worked for Robert by keeping an eye on suspicious guys who loitered around the clubs. Matty hooked up with Maryann C., Vinny's younger sister. Matty wasn't husband material, let alone a model father. They divorced and her parents' gained custody of their granddaughter.

Robert was a valuable dealer for the clubs. Money flowed steadily from the blackjack tables into the club's money sacks. The Korean gamblers won just enough to keep them coming back and that kept the clubs busy, and kept a stream of revenue flowing in. As he worked his way up, he earned the respect of Johnny Mac and Eddie, and he became a dealer at other New York City clubs. He also knew he had to move and live in New York City. His reputation in Yonkers with the police was well established, and he was a target. Once when he was pulled over for speeding on Yonkers Avenue, Captain Jack McMahon searched his car. He didn't find anything illegal, no pot, no coke, no guns. However, the stop came with a warning. Times were changing and the cops had no appetite for a guy like Robert whose record and reputation spelled trouble. The message was clear:

If we see you around anymore, we'll lock you up.

Robert clearly understood: the authorities had no tolerance for him, and the next infraction he could expect trumped up charges. It was time to move on. Off he went to live in New York City.

Chapter 9

Man is not what he thinks he is, he is what he hides.

—André Malraux

Robert accumulated a troubling arrest record in New York City. Throughout the eighties, he was locked up and released nineteen times.[1] He was referred to a lawyer and hired him on retainer, and if he had any problems, he found disposable cash. His lawyer, a seasoned gentleman, always managed to pay for the fine, even if it meant receiving double pay from the club.

In February of 1982 a TV camera crew and a squad of armed New York Police officers methodically raided an illegal club that operated on the Upper East Side of Manhattan. The atmosphere was tense. But this nondescript storefront was a front for the real money maker, a gambling room in the basement, somewhat reminiscent of speakeasy settings in old gangster movies. The room was somewhat ample as smoke swirled and produced smells of cigars, cigarettes, and marijuana. Johnny Mac, responsible for this carnal business, kept a low profile in the back office while George "Kelly" methodically observed the joint to ensure smooth operations and to keep an eye on tables and possible intruders. Aggressive cops and snoopy reporters busted in with weapons drawn and cameras clicking and whirring.

A dozen or so fanatical gamblers froze like children about to be reprimanded by a disapproving father ready to lay down the law. In a moments time their stiffness was replaced with flailing arms, contorted mouths, flaring nostrils, and cards tossed recklessly as a matching number of officers stormed in, disrupting the quite smoky atmosphere juxtaposed with the din of the dealers calling of cards. This tableau incapsulated a moment in time that featured shock and awe in a gambler's haven. An irritated Johnny Mac looked like someone ready to slash some throats, but he also looked like somebody restraining his rage, and all he could do was to yell at a reporter:

I don't care if they close me down every day, I promise you, I will open up somewhere else the very next day, I promise you!

The police did not like that kind of bravado and Robert was arrested. He was arrested ten subsequent times in 1982. The charges were almost always identical: Penal law, PL 225.05, Promoting gambling or Possession of a gambling device 2nd degree. Status: Plead guilty. Sentenced to fine or imprisonment. $150/15 days, PAID IN FULL. All these infractions were misdemeanors. Arrests were predictable. Wednesday or Thursday nights cops would come storming in from the Midtown North or Midtown South Precincts. When Robert was brought to the local precinct the questions were always the same.

Who do you work for? ... We know you work for Johnny Mac, where is he? ... We know you are the manager. You are going away for a long time!

Robert cursed the cops out, but never said anything else. There was so much pressure on these illegal clubs that Johnny Mac installed gates in front of the door to make it look as if the place were closed.[2] If a gambler showed up at the door, someone would pop out of a nearby car or building and radio inside for someone to open the gate and let him in.

They had other pressures. One time the club was raided by a group of seven Black guys. These robbers were organized. They had automatic weapons. They busted in through the front door and pushed the doorman to the floor. As guns were waved around, they demanded money from everyone and demanded the manager open the safe. Several customers started to cry as they prayed to God that they would not be harmed. The robbers didn't get away with much because the few dealers only had a couple of thousand dollars among them, and there was no money in the safe. The gunfire attracted the attention of the police and within minutes detectives from the 19th Precinct swarmed the club and questioned the customers and staff. The detectives knew Robert from prior arrests and hoped he would be cooperative being he was now a witness to a crime.

Mr. Fabio, what did you see?

Not willing to divulge any information Robert responded:

The only thing I know is this rug needs a cleaning.

They were not amused.

Georgie, come over here. Georgie, what happened?

They put us in the back room and then they shot the machine guns, all the lights went out. I heard a woman crying, I put my arm around her, when the lights came on, it was JC, crying!

Everyone started laughing, the detectives, staff, and customers. The detectives knew they would probably not get a straight answer, but they tried anyway. The thieves were never found, and no arrests were made. But Johnny Mac learned a lesson.

Afterwards, Johnny Mac installed a double door system for every club he operated, a total of twelve clubs. He was not going to be robbed again.

Once, when Robert was arrested during another police raid,

the judge offered him community service. Robert whispered to his lawyer:

Listen, I don't do community service, I'm too busy, I don't do that shit.

The gentlemen lawyer rejoined:

Sorry your honor, we don't want community service.

The judge, unperturbed, clamored:

Ok, $5,000 fine.

Robert was free and didn't pay a dime. It was Johnny Mac who paid the lawyer and paid the fine. Robert was well liked by Johnny and Eddie. They rewarded his loyalty and gave him the responsibility to manage payroll. He was responsible for scheduling, paying the dealers at the end of their shifts, and keeping Johnny Mac informed through his conversations with Eddie. Robert earned extra cash by lying about how many dealers worked in a given week; he'd say he paid out money for ten dealers, when in fact only seven dealers worked, and he pocketed the rest. With no one to check on him, money rolled in. No one questioned him.

Robert knew all the dealers. He and Zorro worked different clubs together. When Robert worked on side jobs that needed dealers, Zorro was always the first he called. Zorro was a light-skinned Dominican from the Washington Heights neighborhood in Manhattan. Zorro came with his brother Cabo to meet Robert and work as a dealer as well. Cabo was dark-skinned and Robert hesitated to say we don't hire Black people; we don't even let them in to play. But he asked Johnny Mac and Eddie permission to bring him on board because Zorro vouched for him. Zorro was well liked so their prejudices were set aside for the sake of the business, the business of making money.

Johnny Mac operated a club on 26th Street between Second and Third Avenues. This club wasn't as profitable as he would have liked. These gamblers were mostly Chinese as opposed to

Koreans. They loved playing *pai gow* poker, a game which used the usual fifty-two card deck but had a rule which allowed the Joker to be used as a substitute card to complete straights, flushes, and straight flushes, or act like the fifth Ace card. The club was managed by a lackey named Danny. Danny's girlfriend was the dealer. She didn't like losing, and she had a loathsome disposition, a disposition that engendered rebuke. She was nasty to customers, and to dealers, and to the bouncers as well. She copped an attitude every time a customer won a hand. She reacted with a muted snarl, as if she lost her personal money. People stopped coming. Johnny Mac wasn't happy and told Eddie to give Robert the keys. Robert was cordial to the customers, and he made sure they were comped with plenty to drink and eat. Robert, who was charming, endeared himself with positive comments when guests won. Gamblers came because they enjoyed their gambling experience at the club. The club was profitable, earning fifty-thousand dollars a week. Eddie #2 picked up the cash to deliver to Johnny Mac, or Robert himself would deliver the cash himself, passing the money to Pops, Johnny Mac's father, at the Hideaway Bar in the Bronx. Some customers brought in more people, and the word spread. More people and more games favored the house. Danny's combative girlfriend, who turned her physical beauty into an ugly persona, was finally replaced with the more friendly duo of Lana and Rita, two Russian girls who dealt blackjack in the front room. Meanwhile, a Japanese youth named Kamata was dealing pai gow poker in the back room. Robert turned the club around, and everyone was happy. Everyone, except the new floor manager, an Irish girl named Doyle. Doyle was responsible for collecting the money at the end of each shift, and on average she collected ten-thousand dollars. Doyle was a pretty but temperamental woman in her thirties. She was a hardened bitch who scoffed at people who were carefree and happy. When Robert delivered less than a nine-thousand-dollar profit per night, Doyle accused him of cheating. Jimmy M., the new manager, who happened to be Johnny Mac's brother-in-law, was not going to go against her adamant claims. They told Robert that he couldn't deal at that location anymore. Doyle, with her caustic temperament, was responsible for Robert's termination. There is nothing more unsettling then when a pretty woman does ugly things. Eddy and Robert decided to focus on the 61st St. club, a joint which consistently made more money than all the other clubs. Eddie had his suspicions but told Robert:

I don't care what you are doing, keep on winning, baby, and keep the money flowing.

He did just that.

Johnny Mac's clubs were not in the habit of loaning money to gamblers, that's what loan sharks did. They simply didn't just hand out chips and give an IOU. This policy, however, had exceptions. There were three dealers floating around the 61st St. club. Jerry was acting manager that night, he was an iron worker and a big drinker. He sat most nights at the club and drank and drank, and constantly pushed his eyeglasses up his long, thin nose. Paul Castellano, the Gambino family boss, was in the club that night with his bodyguard. A hot Latina, whose low-cut shirt revealed a cleavage that tempted the most discreet observer. Paul Castellano knew the sensation that this *chica caliente* stirred as she jauntily paraded in the large gambling arena. Paul Castellano scanned the gambling zone for affirmation of his power as his ego was being massaged. With his paramour on his side, Paul gambled with striking zest, but after losing a hand with Kamata, he started to lob some wisecracks about gooks derisibly spouting:

We won the war, why do I got a jap dealing to me, I thought we killed all these motherfuckers!

After he went through a shoe, he demanded a new dealer as well as some additional credit. The club had a policy of no credit, and now Jerry was in an impossible situation, that involved Eddie #2. He explained that Big Paul wanted ten-thousand dollars in chips. Eddie told him that no credit would be awarded to anyone. He then sent word to George Kelly to come to the club to ensure that nothing got out of hand. Jerry gave him the bad news and Big Paul threatened:

I'll make this place a parking lot. Don't you know who I am? I will bury you!

At that point, George sauntered in and saw Big Paul. He stopped, looked Eddie in the eye and uttered to Eddie and Jerry:

I quit. Are you fucking kidding me? You want to get me killed? I no longer work here.

He proceeded to sit down next to Paul and pulled out an aspirin bottle full of coke and poured it on the table. Everyone settled down, and eventually, Jerry decided to extend a loan and handed Big Paul a thousand dollars-worth of chips. Carl, who replaced Kamata as the dealer, now stepped in and had no clue who Paul Castellano was or what just happened. As Big Paul started winning, Carl wise-cracked that:

If I didn't know any better, I would think that you were cheating.

Big Paul didn't take too kindly to the jab and yelled:

Hey, you, I wouldn't cheat you, I would kidnap your grandmother and you would pay that way.

Seeing that Big Paul was upset, Jerry told Robert to start dealing. After some more wins and a few losses, Big Paul was having a good time, and the club closed early in the morning with no further theatrics.

Johnny Mac and Eddie were always looking for new sources of revenue. Eddie got wind that a rabbi in Queens was looking to rent out the synagogue basement. With a shrinking congregation, the rabbi had to be more creative in generating revenue. A series of casino nights, if done correctly, could provide essential money for meeting the financial needs of the congregation. These were completely legal; tickets were purchased by congregants; those sold tickets covered food expenses and the games provided the profit. A vendor was secured to provide a cash bar and raffle prizes brought in even more money, sometimes as much as ten-thousand dollars. These events were advertised as fundraisers for building projects, or to honor valued local politicians, business leaders, or members of the synagogue. More often than not, it created an opportunity to socialize and have some fun. New York State allowed congregations to host up to twelve casino nights per year, with a limitation that chips could be bought for no more than twenty-five dollars.

At this synagogue, the casino night was illegal. The law was circumvented by virtue of Eddie's powerful connections.[3] The casino managed to set tables, deal cards, use chips, serve alcohol, and provide food. Chips could be purchased for any amount: twenty-five dollars, fifty dollars, one-hundred dollars, and lastly five-hundred dollars. Dealers received five-hundred dollars for five hours' worth of work. The Rabbi cleared five thousand dollars for his imprimatur. Eddie # 2 ran this synagogue casino for months. The house made money, the rabbi was paid, the dealers got their cut, and everyone had a good time, except for the occasional guy or group of friends who were losing big. Robert brought along Zorro, and they were happy making five-hundred dollars a night. Their rapacious greed was a powerful inducement to pilfer money by skillfully employing sleight of hand to appropriate about eight-hundred dollars per night. Two slick-looking gentlemen walked in scoping the area, looking for Robert. They were twin towers dressed in deep black suits and sporting bright, gold rope chains and slowly walking with purposeful intent. Their attires were as dark as their intentions, and with those sinister designs they approached Robert Fabio, and the gentleman with the scar on his left cheek coolly sneered:

You know what, JC, your arms are too long, you're ripping us off, someday you're gonna lose those arms.

Robert was baffled. He eyed these imposing men suspiciously. He had no idea who they were. Friends of Eddie, he guessed.

Robert was no mechanic, not in the automotive terms, but in the card dealing cheating mode. He never used that scam, but he did know he owed some bookie $17K and couldn't be sure if this threat was from that. The two men walked around the tables, then one of them vanished into the bathroom.

Zorro, give me your .38.

Zorro always carried his gun wedged on his lower lumbar under his blue pinstriped jacket. As the scar-faced slickster stood shaking his phallus in the urinal, Robert crept up and menacingly said:

You threatening me, you motherfucka? I'll drop you right here!

Robert pushed the gun on his skull just behind his left ear.

Whose arms are you gonna chop off cocksucka, I'm gonna blow you away right here!

Robert now remembered; these were the guys looking to collect the seventeen-thousand dollars. They called his house and freaked out his wife Sae Hee, threatened her and Robert. The two slicksters broke protocol; you never bother family members for debts. Now the other slickster, sporting black hair and blue eyes, approached Robert, and Robert looked him over intensely and said:

I know you just had a baby, I'll put that kid in a garbage bag and slam him against a tree, you hear motherfucka? Who you talking to?

The two goons had not expected a gun to be pushed in their faces and backed off, as if a light switch suddenly turned on:

Look, JC, no harm done. It was nothing but a misunderstanding. We were just leaving. We will never bother you again, Ok?

Robert snickered, put Zorro's gun under his jacket as the scarred tower zipped up and put his flaccid member away. He eyed the slicksters:

Get the fuck outta here.

They never looked back and left. Robert downed a Heineken and went back to dealing.

The casino nights at the Synagogue were over after three months. The NYPD was tipped off and started taking pictures of license plates in the parking lot. Most plates were registered to owners from Brooklyn, the Bronx, Manhattan, and Yonkers. Several of the names were well known to detectives who worked in the organized crime investigation division. Fifteen cops stormed the synagogue, many Asians were astir with lots of chips on hand. The dealers were all dressed in suits and looked professional. The operators who managed the money and chips scrambled at the sight of the cops. It was a big mess and Robert, Suzie, and Zorro, all repeat offenders, were taken in to be booked. The NYPD weren't after the dealers, they were after the organizers. Robert and the other dealers were booked for misdemeanors. A week later Robert was at Tango's raking in cash, partying, doing blow, and having a good time. A few weeks back, the pit boss walked over and said:

Hey, JC, these two guys are looking for you.

Robert says to bring them over to the table where he was dealing. While switching to a new shoe, two big guys, six-foot-two, and six-foot-four, whispered to him:

We own Tango's on 24th St. between 2nd and 3rd Avenue, we want you to work for us.

They talked terms, Robert asking for a thirty percent take. Tango's was a popular place, as it attracted professional sports-figures, actors, and other sectors of society willing and able to spend their money. Scotty the Jew, and another Jew named Al, who was nicknamed House, were running games at Tango's. Scotty, who loved the snap of newly minted bills, was the man who handled money. House was a big, fat man, with hands like claws that would clamp down on anyone getting out of line. This hulking boar hailed from Brooklyn. He spoke arrogantly of anyone not of his tribe. He often watched the perimeters of the gambling area casually to see what was going on. He appeared somewhat distant as if distracted by a thought, precisely the impression he wanted to give. He watched without being noticed, without rousing suspicion, but in fact he was a prowler ready pounce like a lion after a prey. These two kept the place in check and operations ran as smoothly as silk. Robert brought along other dealers to work shifts. Robert relished a good time and made sure to wallow in it. House kept a watchful eye on Robert. A stranger with a reputation, he didn't like his partying, always admonished him to stop smoking weed, and doing blow. Robert ignored him: He dealt for Johnny Mac and Eddie and this new partnership with these Jews from Brooklyn was not going be disrupted by a blustering fat man.

House and Robert's mutual animosity spilled over into their gambling as well. Robert explained it this way:

There was sit-down with me and House in Coney Island. One night we were playing craps together in a club and I was down ten-thousand dollars, House was down ten-thousand dollars and that lasted for a while. My losing continued, and now House started to win. He was now up ten thousand, then he was up another twenty-thousand dollars, and finally he was up forty-thousand dollars. I asked House to loan me five-thousand dollars or even ten-thousand dollars. Fuck you, JC, I'm not loaning you a thing, how are you going to pay me back? I already loaned you money and you lost, you can't pay me back, you're getting nothing else. I was pissed off and yelled: House, you're a Jew and you are going to play with me? House tensed up, his fists clenched, his teeth grinded, and he was ready to rumble, but he forced himself to calm down a bit, and with a bit of sardonic tone he uttered: We are going to have sit-down over this, this is bullshit. Oh yeah, I'll show you who has power, you're a Jew and I'm Italian, bring it on.

Scotty did not like this kind of infighting; it could lead to worse problems. It did not sit right with him. Scotty and House were protected by a mob family in Brooklyn. They paid a percentage of their earnings to stay in business and operate freely. There was a sit-down with several made men from Brooklyn. Robert made his case that they were partners, had always loaned each other money, and now he was a tightwad. He then tossed out the ethnic card by saying:

I'm Italian, my grandparents are from Sicily, that means something.

House lost and was made to pay a mob tax for wasting everyone's time.

One night late into the morning, Robert needed a break, it was four a.m. Making money was Scotty and House's focus, and they didn't like to party, so Robert decided to go to Scores by himself. Scores was a topless bar with a second location now on 28th Street. The doorman greeted him with an attitude:

Hey, you, pay up, forty to get in.

Robert was incensed:

Listen, buddy, I deal down the street, your owners are in my place all the time, cut me some slack, all I want is a Hamburger, a beer, and to watch the girls, what's the problem?

A screaming match ensued. The doorman wouldn't budge:

You know who I am motherfucka? I'm JC!

I'm Willie!

Well, fuck you, Willie! I'm not paying, try to stop me.

Robert prevailed. The doorman was pissed, but he didn't feel like fighting at four a.m. with no back-up readily available. Years later it was revealed that the doorman, Willie Marshall, was a retired corrections officer who became a government informant against Jr. Gotti. Willie kept a low profile, and once jokingly described himself to his girlfriend's parents as a two-bit leg breaker for a loan shark. Many a truth was said in jest as he was collecting for mob boss Greg DePalma from Yonkers. Willie eventually pled guilty to one count of racketeering and one count of money laundering and both he and his wife went into the witness protection program.[4]

Chapter 10

Rejoice with your family in the beautiful land of life.

—Albert Einstein

The nineteen-seventies ushered in changes that had been set into motion the previous decade. An upheaval in politics, values, cultural norms, the economy, and relationships continued to transform the collective consciousness. I watched the 1972 debates in amusement as my father and uncle called President Nixon, *mignolelle*, a Sicilian word they commandeered to mean little dick. Their negative impressions of President Nixon were validated with his resignation two years later. As the next election cycle was in full swing in 1976 I was vaguely aware of the campaign issues that were important to my parents. My brother Greg never expressed any political leanings, but I soon became aware of his interest when he returned from a campaign rally for President Ford at the Rockland County Courthouse. He gleefully quoted the protesters chants:

Ford, a liar, we'll set his ass on fire!

I was not convinced if he was just mocking authority or truly made a decision based on his understanding of policy positions. No matter what, we all were impacted by the failures of the Carter administration: inflation, an energy crisis, and Iranian Islamic fanaticism.

At the same time the country was mesmerized by the made for television spectacle, the battle of the sexes. Bobby Riggs, a retired tennis champion and self-proclaimed "male chauvinist pig," challenged Billie Jean King, the world's top ranked tennis player, to a $100,000 winner-take-all match. Despite his pronunciations of the inferiority of female tennis players, Billie Jean won the match in three straight sets. While the exhibition was campy and tongue-in-cheek, women were roused, becoming more outspoken in the workforce and demanding equal rights and equal pay.

The Beatles took the pop rock music world by storm. Their domination of pop charts, increased radio and television exposure, and music that was relatable across generations allowed them to become icons of youth culture and social change. Their musical transformation from pop to psychedelic was heavily influenced by drugs. This cultural shift mirrored the social transformation of the youth culture and portended to more change on the horizon. Psychedelic music gave way to acid rock and then heavy metal. Readily available drugs swept through youth culture and became almost equal in popularity as alcohol. I was shocked as I watched television with my parents and witnessed Alice Cooper hurl wads of dollar bills of all denominations out of second story window. He looked psychotic with crazy eye make-up, disheveled hair, and ripped shirt exposing his emaciated chest. Self-induced psychosis was dually being celebrated and ridiculed on a television news segment. This same era heralded the unprecedented force of OPEC. I became acutely aware of the influences of unfriendly countries half a world away. Arab OPEC members banned petroleum exports and created chaos throughout the industrialized world. I remember sitting in the car with my dad as we waited hours in line to buy gasoline. His freedom to choose when and where to buy gasoline was superseded by mandates of the local authorities. Fuel purchases were now limited to alternative days based on a vehicle's license plate ending in odd or even numbers. The banter around the dinner table exposed us to: homosexuals wanting recognition, women demanding a right to an abortion, Palestinians kidnapping Israelis at the Munich Olympics, and the buffoonery of Billy Carter, President Carter's brother, marketing Billy Beer.

The justification of my father escaping the growing chaos of the Bronx became evident as he read weekly newspaper articles about how his old neighborhood descended into crime and neglect. We rightfully kept our distance from New York City which was an affront to the senses and sensibilities of my father seeking a refined suburban experience for his family. When we took the occasional trip into NYC, we were often perplexed and amused when hordes of minority families commandeered the Palisades Parkway as their personal picnic area. Loud Spanish music could be heard blasting from car radios in the grass median between the north and south lanes as people sat around grilling chicken and drinking cervezas. We mockingly termed these impromptu parties as Puerto Rican picnics.

Our only excursions to New York City were the occasional trips to Yankee Stadium, Shea Stadium, or a school trip to some museum or the theater district, and the seasonal trips to the Bronx for holiday gatherings. City blight and intimidating squeegee men further reinforced my father quest for suburban bliss. Filthy Black men rushed to my father's baby-blue Plymouth station wagon and squirted dirty water from a plastic ketchup bottle. They hurriedly attempted to clean the windshield before the traffic light turned green. The result was an additional layer of dirt and water schmeered with a wrinkled newspaper. My father refused to hand over money for the beggar's unsolicited service. He drove away as the stranger banged on the roof demanding payment for his services. It was chaos. Barely a few inches, a car window, separated us from the instability of New York City street-life.

Mayhem and lawlessness crept into our backyard. My schoolmate's sister was murdered in Nanuet. Lisa Thomas was found bludgeoned to death behind the Nanuet Mall. A dance instructor was shot dead in his apartment in Spring Valley. The body of a known gambler from Yonkers was found riddled with bullets in the parking lot of the Clarkstown Plaza Shopping Center. A customer of the Carvel Ice Cream Store in Nyack was shot in the chest, dead on arrival at Nyack Hospital. None of these murders have been solved. As theories circulated, it further created a climate of uncertainty and the random nature of violence. Son of Sam played on our emotions like no other because this was a serial killer. He was a crazed lunatic who claimed the devil spoke to him through a dog. The claim seemed preposterous, but his crimes of targeting young couples for murder was all too real and unsettling. While the killings were in New York City, we all thought, who's next? As I was entering into my teens, I increasingly was more aware of random violence. My parents attempted to keep myself and brothers isolated from malevolent influences that could cause distress but what is life without rebellion.

Robert and I grew up in a similar social and familial environment. We believed in the creed of family values and the Calvinistic work ethic, a work ethic that was foundational in the making of America. But Robert and I diverged when it came to education and religion. We were certainly aware of the tragedy of the three deaths that my Aunt Josie and my cousin Linda experienced, Robert more so, but I had no idea of its effect on any one person. Everyone evolved over the years as Aunt Josie endeared herself to a new partner, a retired engineer named Joe DeGrazia. Linda married a police officer named Vincent Newman, and Garry focused on his grades at SUNY Albany pursuing a degree in Economics and eventually a PhD in Economics and Econometrics from Columbia University.[1] I remember going over to Aunt Josie's house one Sunday sometime in 1971 with my parents and two younger brothers, Tim and Paul. We went to the usual nine-thirty a.m. Mass, and after we dropped off Greg to some activity he was involved with, we went to Rockland Bakery to pick up some pastries and then headed over to Yonkers. Before dinner, we sat down in the living room and were formally introduced to Aunt Josie's new friend. My aunt and father were very cognizant of how we reacted to my aunt's new relationship, even though several years had already passed since Uncle Jack Schinasi's death. As the adults sat down in the living room, each one of us was formally introduced to Joe. Even though I was only ten years old, I quickly understood the formality of the situation and stood up and hugged him saying: nice to meet you Uncle Joe. He nodded, smiled, and giggled, as my parents and Aunt Josie smiled in approval. Soon thereafter, off we charged to watch television in the side room next to the bathroom adorned with the pink tiles. Aunt Josie fussed over her simmering tomato sauce while she prepared a family favorite: chicken with garlic and lemon. Always followed by the homemade *pignolata*; *deliziosa!* The was the sweetness of life captured around the dinner table.

My brothers and I never merited an allowance. My parents demanded a pound of flesh before awarding spending money. I was too young to appreciate the merit behind their moral teachings, perhaps a little resentful that my friends always seemed to have a few dollars in their pockets. I worked hard for my money as I was responsible for a paper route. I delivered the *Rockland Journal News* come rain or shine, whether well or ill, no matter what I was obligated to do it. I netted maybe twenty dollars a week which I indulged myself on albums purchased at EJ Korvettes in Nanuet. I purchased clothes, gas for the car, soda, and snacks, and sampled every local pizzeria. After several years of this afternoon drudgery, I grew tired of being a paperboy. I was as fed up dealing with inclement weather. Riding a bicycle loaded with newspapers in rain and snow was horrible. I was fed up being attacked by unleased dogs. I'll never forget the afternoon when the Manning's dalmatian, the size of a pony, knocked me off my bike as I rode past their house. Two baskets of newspapers flew in every direct on that blustery cold autumn afternoon. They unapologetically whisked their menacing dog back inside, demanding their paper as fifty newspapers were dispersed by the wind. I spent the next hour rounding up whatever I could, knowing that some homes would not be getting the lifestyle or sports sections that afternoon. Several customers were very unpleasant when I came to collect the weekly fees. I was challenged on the amount that was owed. Even when I displayed the payment ledger to the homeowner and that they were behind payment for a week, they sneered, and reluctantly handed over the cash. I once tried to get into lawn mowing business, and I developed a small clientele consisting of several houses in my neighborhood. I cut grass on a regular basis and thought at one point I could do more. All incentives ended when my father demanded a cut of the money. He cited wear and tear on the lawnmower and money spent on gas. My mom couldn't believe my father's demand and reprimanded him with,

Oh, Paul, I can't believe you.

I refused to put up with the nit picking about giving him money. Mom's words had no influence on his demands and so I stopped cutting grass and eventually gave up the paper route as well.

My grades stalled in mediocrity when I transitioned from middle school to high school. My brother Greg, conversely, was a book worm, kids in the neighborhood dubbed him as *Mr. Encyclopedia.* I wasn't much of a student as I was unmotivated and content with Bs and Cs. My father berated me non-stop. I surprised everyone when I earned respectable grades in math and science, but those results were an academic mirage when I switched my focus from academics and sports to getting high.

We used older kids to buy beer, weed. Another friend secured a fake driver's license. When I was sixteen years old, I frequented bars in Pearl River, Nanuet, and New City. We listened to bands, downed kamikazes, smoked weed, and cruised around the county in my friend Dominick's Gran Torino. I'd often borrowed my father's baby-blue Dodge to meet my buddies in Dom's basement. We played pool for an hour or so, then we headed out to local bars. Every now and then, we drove to Portchester to a bar called Detroit. This bar was much larger than the Rockland County bars because it hosted bands like the Good Rats and Twisted Sister that attracted much bigger crowds. My father was always suspicious of the mileage I put on the car. As a chemist, systematically collecting data, he required his sons to keep meticulous records of gas mileage. I was forced to record the price of gas, the mileage at time of purchase, and calculate the miles per gallon. There was an entry for every time I bought gas, and if I didn't record it, I lost driving privileges. He somehow divined the author of the journal entries as he deciphered the penmanship. But I was the creative sort, and the explanations of my travels seemed to satisfy him.

We learned to swim at the Pearl River Nauraushaun Swim Club, a private swim club opened only to residents in the Pearl River Fire District. I swam competitively for years and eventually became a licensed lifeguard. I should have pursued a lifeguard job over the summers, but I was as blind as a bat with my glasses off. All the Fabio boys played little league baseball, and I continued playing in high school, and while I was not a starter, I had my share of solid hits to keep me interested. I tore my ACL in the fall of 1977, when I fell off a small trailer that flipped when a kid we called Beta took a hard turn around the flagpole of the swim club. My right knee swelled like a balloon, and I couldn't put any pressure on it for weeks. An x-ray showed no broken bones, but this was before MRI machines were commercially available, so no one knew the extent of the damages. I certainly knew something was off because my knee kept popping out of the socket. It didn't help when I ran to catch a fly ball during a game and my knee popped out. This was not for me, and in my senior year, I decided I would rather goof off than sit on the bench during games. Asthma was also a problem. I suffered with asthma. When I was a kid, I never took any medication for it. I always felt winded with intense physical exertion, and it always took much longer for me to catch my breath. I was constantly exposed to secondhand cigarette smoke, as my mother's cigarette addiction increased to a pack a day. Her cigarette smoking became a health hazard for those around her—and for me in particular—as it affected my breathing, especially when I caught a cold, or when I ran an uphill incline during a competition and felt a sting and a burn in my lungs, and as a kid I was concerned not knowing why it was happening to me and not to others. I did not understand why it took so much longer to recover my breath after a competition. My mom took me to an allergist, a middle-aged German man with short red tightly curled hair with an intense gaze. Skin tests revealed that I was highly allergic to cats and dogs. That same intense gaze met my mother's eyes. The doctor sternly intoned:

Does anyone smoke in the house?

Mom looked puzzled, and meekly said that she did. Doctor Stein's expression now turned truculent as he cleared his throat and rasped:

You shouldn't smoke around your children, especially if they have allergies, smoking is detrimental.

Mom looked miffed and embarrassed, but she said nothing and simply eyed Doctor Stein and me. We walked out of the office with a better understanding. Or, so I thought. As we headed home on that frigid, windy afternoon, mom lit up a cigarette, as she always did. After Doctor Stein's reprimand, I was emboldened and said:

The doctor said not to smoke around me.

Mother tensed up, looked at me with a large pinch of indignance, and growled:

Well, then, just roll down the window!

I recoiled, thinking I was doomed at my own mother's indifference. I would like to believe it touched a nerve because soon thereafter she sought a hypnotist. It worked, and Mom kicked the habit, and we all expressed how proud we were of her.

Regular church attendance was a normal Sunday activity, as was it for Mom and her two sisters in Pearl River. My father's family refrained from regular church attendance, but I didn't realize that until much later. At my cousin Patricia's wedding in 1973 in Yonkers, when it was time for the congregation to approach the altar to receive the Holy Communion, only we: Mom, Dad, and the four boys, and a few old ladies from the groom's family, were the only ones who participated in the ritual of the priest offering the Eucharist. The priest's face looked revealing as he froze for a nano second. It was comical and pathetic as he attempted to coax others to step forward, but no one did. Mother whispered to father:

What is wrong with your family?

My three brothers and I received our first Holy Communion at St. Anthony's Church in Nanuet and received our Confirmation at St. Aedan's Church in Pearl River. We all attended St. Anthony's Parochial School for most of our elementary school years. Mass was performed in a lone gymnasium of an otherwise undeveloped property. Folding chairs were laid out in rows on a basketball court with the hoops and backboards folded up at each end of the court. It looked somewhat bare, with no candles, no stained-glass windows, or ornately decorated altar. We attended service punctually at nine-thirty, but often we partook the ceremony Saturday evening at five-thirty. Pops would say we are going on Saturday to,

Get it out of the way.

The five-thirty Mass only lasted thirty minutes, being the homily was scaled down due to the priest's recognition that the congregation was eager to get home and have dinner. We also attended religion classes one afternoon a week as part of the school-year program to learn about the seven sacraments. We never read the Bible verse by verse but gained a general gist of the sacraments by virtue of reading specific scripture verses that supported the lesson. Naturally, we were taught to memorize some passages, but never had the full context or understanding of what we were memorizing. My brother, Greg, once caused quite a stir with our next-door neighbor when he quoted a passage from the Bible. Frank Fornabio, my friend's father, was helping some neighborhood kids practice their hitting and fielding skills in preparation for an upcoming little league baseball game, when out the blue he asked Greg where I was. Greg responded dismissively:

Am I my brother's keeper?

Mr. Fornabio wasn't too pleased with the disrespectful and insolent response for a neighborhood kid in his early teens. He mentioned that exchange to my father. Greg got a mouthful from my parents at the dinner table as I sat wondering why anyone would say that to an adult. I never felt fully connected to what was taught in church, nor did I fully understand it. When I asked my parents about some religious questions and the answer was

Go talk to the Priest.

I thought:

I'm twelve years old, who the heck is going to talk to me and answer my question?

I never read the Bible on my own, and it was not encouraged in our house. As the years passed, I started to realize I did not really know much about the Bible. Not knowing where to start I thumbed through one small bible we had on the shelf and found myself opening to the Book of Job. I had heard the name Job before and decided to read this portion of the Old Testament. I could not make heads nor tails of what the message was and after one read through, my curiosity turned to disenchantment. I read parts of the New Testament, and I remember reading about the fruit of the Spirit in the book of Galatians:

> *But the fruit of the Spirit is love, joy, peace, patience, kindness, goodness, faithfulness, gentleness and self-control.*
>
> Galatians 5:22–23

I churned through the list in my mind, and I concluded that I didn't have any of these fruits, except maybe goodness, whatever that meant. Besides, what did fruit of the spirit mean anyway? There was nothing readily available for me to investigate and I wasn't going to ask my parents. I would have received the same phatic response about me having to consult a priest.

Most families in my immediate neighborhood were Roman Catholic except for two families who were Lutheran and Presbyterian. As kids, we didn't interact much with the Jewish families. With names like Cohen, Kadoff, Kaufman, Klein, Londoner, and Pessel they were clustered on the other end of the neighborhood. I asked my mom why all the families with Italian names like Vitale, Fornabio, Giuliano, Piraneo, Dorangrichia, and Mariconi were near us, while Jews were on the opposite side of the neighborhood separated by families of other ethnicities with names like Jacobson, Ryan, Maughan, Hook, Redman, White, and Olszewski.[2] She thought for a while, then remembered that when the realtor sponsored an open house, he divided couples who shared the same ethnicity. This was my first lesson in segregation. Most kids in the neighborhood gathered to play wiffleball in my backyard, softball in a nearby park, or stickball on Standish Drive or on Pilgrim Court. Softball was a weekend sport because it required more organization. Stickball was a pick-up game where all that was needed was a pink Spalding ball which we bought at the L.H. Martin Department store on North Middletown Road, and a broom stick cut down to four to five feet and wrapped with black electrical tape at one end for a good grip. We never had a problem rounding up six guys or more. Someone would knock on doors after dinner, or a few guys came out on the street and joined in. There wasn't any base running, we simply hit the ball and fielded our position. The game was a summertime ritual. We learned respect for your opponent and earned the right to brag when we hit well or fielded a scorching, screaming, pink ball bearing down on your head. Rituals had laws, or rules of engagement: balls hit between the curbs was fair territory, balls hit outside the curbs were foul; anything caught on a fly was an out; a ground ball hit to the first guy standing halfway down the street was considered an out; if it went past him and the guy standing further behind caught it, it was considered a single; a line drive over the first guy's head, but caught on a bounce by the second guy was a single; doubles and triples followed suit if there were enough guys. Joe V. was the only guy to hit homeruns in stick ball, but we all came close. I remember knocking on different doors throughout the neighborhood to see who wanted to shoot hoops, play softball, stickball, or just hang out, but there were a few kids who would never participate, and claim to be buried in schoolwork. The Jewish guys, three of them, never seemed interested in playing stickball, softball, or wiffleball. It wasn't for a lack of effort, they just simply had no interest in these neighborhood activities. Either they were not athletic or were anti-social. With plenty of other guys around, we didn't give it a second thought.

When my brother Greg befriended a Jewish schoolmate, it was a novelty to me. By the time I was in high school, his friend became a regular at my house and am sure he found our family dynamics just as much a novelty as we found his. Jonathan Cahn was a smart, articulate teen who was musically talented and generally artistic. He was just as sarcastic and quick-witted as my brother. They enjoyed mocking their teachers, classmates, parents, siblings, anybody and anything. During Jon's later years in high school, he would come over with his artwork and give presentations to whoever was sitting around the large round kitchen table. He took his time to explain the content behind each painting or drawing. He enjoyed the attention, the comments, and his role as commentator. As a musician he played lead guitar in pick-up bands in high school. They argued spiritedly about the virtuosity of Eric Clapton, Jeff Beck, and Jimmy Page. And rejoiced when Greg scored tickets to see Led Zeppelin on June seven of 1977 at Madison Square Garden.

The protective envelope my parents sought to secure around their sons was bursting. We were adventuresome and saw the opportunities, excitement, and new experiences that New York City had to offer. Rockland County was twenty-five minutes north of NYC. It represented an escape from crime, chaos, and uncouth characters my father sought to avoid. For teen-age boys, NYC represented an escape from the routine bucolic boredom of suburbia. Rock music stations like 102.7 WNEW and 92.3 WXRK routinely advertised concert venues at MSG, the Palladium, and the Nassau Coliseum, and kids from around the area flocked to these shows. I pleaded with Greg to sell me a ticket to the Led Zeppelin concert, but he refused until the last minute as he and his friends piled into the car. He yelled for me to come now, spurring me to jump into the open door as the car glided down our sloping driveway. This was my baptism into New York City. And it started by getting stoned on marijuana, on the trip south on Palisades Parkway. My brother introduced me to the marvels of Thai sticks, an ancient way to combine marijuana, hash, oil, and resin placed on a bamboo skewer. The six of us piled into my father's blue Plymouth station wagon and headed toward the excitement of the city. By the time we reached a parking lot, I was so disoriented and could not remember where the car was after walking a block away. Greg procured tickets through some PO Box address advertised in the back of a magazine and was lucky enough to get the maximum six tickets allotted. He paid $8.50 each for six seats in section four hundred twenty-two row F, in the mezzanine section. The blue seats were not ideal for concerts as you could hardly see the band members on stage. Greg knew it, and figured he could try to upgrade them, as scalpers were out in droves. When we approached the Garden, it became an ant trail of people whisking around smoking, drinking, buying, and selling. There were plenty of people selling seats by chanting:

Tickets! Tickets! Who needs tickets?

Black guys holding a hand full of tickets approached desperate concert-goers and showed their tickets. Greg was an opportunist, a fast talker, and knew how to turn any situation to his advantage. He persuaded a guy wasted out of his mind to trade his four yellow seats that were at eye level of the stage for four of the less desirable blue seats. Greg convinced him he was getting great seats. Chris Farrelly and I took the remaining tickets and were relegated to the worst seats in the house, the blue seats situated behind the stage.

The concert was amazing! But once over, Chris and I wandered around NYC for three hours looking for the parking lot. My brother, Greg, left with the others after a futile attempt of driving around the maze of one-way streets. Chris Farrelly and I roamed the streets for hours in a drunken pot fueled daze. Waiting for us to come home, my father quickly ascertained I was not with Greg.

Greg, where the hell is your brother?

He had been home for an hour and tried to rationalize why I wasn't with him. Pops displayed his usual expression when frustrated or disappointed and let out a slow high-pitched breath through his clenched teeth, the same sound you would hear when releasing steam pressure from a car radiator cap. Mom was equally upset and cried out:

Where is my son? You left him in the city? What is wrong with you!

Sobering up, Chris and I realized we didn't have a dime between us so I made a collect call to home hoping that someone would answer the phone. My father drove down to pick us up on 8th Ave and 42nd St in front of the Port Authority at three a.m. This area of the city was a cesspool of vulgarity and vice; opportunists exploiting the vulnerable. Pops said nothing during the ride home to suburbia twenty-five miles north as the spectacle of pimps, prostitutes, peep shows, perverts, and castaways faded away from the sideview mirror, and then out of memory; two worlds colliding for a brief moment, each left pondering the elements of the others universe.

Chapter 11

Un-winged and naked, sorrow surrenders its crown to a throne called Grace.

—Aberjhani

I was disillusioned with the choices I had to make regarding my future. My high school years were coming to an end, and I was in an emotional limbo. Asthma and a bum knee kept me from being competitive in baseball, and I decided not to play ball in my senior year. The asthma that afflicted me was not medically managed at all. I had very little stamina and I often struggled to catch my breath when physically exerting myself. The injury to my right knee limited my ability to run and pivot. The ligaments were so weakened that the knee often slipped out of joint even when doing the simplest of movements like descending a staircase. My lower back suffered as well as pain in that area flared with increased regularity. It took twenty-five years for me to discover that I had suffered a severed anterior cruciate ligament. The scope of my life changed as I socially shifted from competitive activities to partying with my buddies at the local bars and splitting to the city to catch a concert at Madison Square Garden, the Palladium, or other venues or larger bars in Westchester.

I did not plan to enroll in any college, as I was detached from the world of academia requiring discipline and focus. I made a feeble attempt to convince my parents that I wanted to get into a trade like carpentry or electricity, but they snickered: they actually demanded that I attend college. I did get a scholarship to the Rochester Institute of Technology for a degree in package design based on the art portfolio I submitted as part of the application process, but I had no interest to live in a suburban campus near Lake Ontario. I was accepted into SUNY Oneonta, not because of my grades, but more because my mom was an alumnus. Although my post high school future was determined, I still did not have a future to be excited about. I felt in my bones that there was something more to life than simply college. I wanted something different, something more, but what I had was nothing more than ambiguous desires. I had foggy visions of a future living on my own with a wife, a job, and a house. Yet I had no concrete plans of how any of that would happen through my own efforts.

My friendship with Jon Cahn reached a new dimension in my spiritual journey. The intersection of my lapsed Catholicism and his abandonment of reformed Judaism united us to experience a new reverence for the message of the Bible. This experience transcended simple relationships as we grew in character and depth. Here we were, me growing up Catholic, and he raised Jewish, and we found a bond that intensified our friendship. Jon often came over to the house and we discussed current events and delicate topics, topics that were difficult to thread through. Jon argued that the first Christians were Jews, and that Mary and Joseph, Peter and Paul, were also Jews. That Jesus was the Messiah, the fulfillment of every promise that God made to Abraham and the Jewish Patriarchs, Prophets, and Kings. I understood that we shared the tenets of the Abrahamic religions but started to comprehend that there was more to all this than intellectual knowledge. I was often dumbfounded that this Jewish kid had so much insight into the Bible and Christianity. My parents—mostly my father—were skeptical. Our discussions generated a seed of curiosity, and that curiosity elevated thought into action; a transformative action that would make me a new person. Any activity that resulted in me to depart the Catholic faith was not received well. But the seeds had been planted in my mind and in my heart. Jon Cahn was the catalyst. His influence over the years was consequential as I was to become a new person in Christ.

As Catholics, at every Mass, we heard the priest announce the acclamations of faith:

Christ has died, Christ has risen, Christ will come again.

This was a powerful trinitarian acclamation, one that remains seared in catholic souls, one that is always past, one that is always present, and one that is always future. Intellectually, we knew of Christ's promise to return, but had no idea about that meaning, about that intent. What did it mean for the here and now? The answers to these deep spiritual questions evaded me.

Jon's pursuit of these answers awakened my inquisitiveness, and I was increasingly eager to listen, to question and to challenge. Jon liked to share what he read about prophesy and offered me a book: *The Late Great Planet Earth* by Hal Lindsay.[1] It was the first time I heard about Bible prophecy. We spent many hours discussing Biblical passages that reflect communications from God through prophets. What makes someone a prophet? What prophecies that have been fulfilled? What predictions have yet to be fulfilled? My father listened to many of these conversations, and he asked questions, with a healthy dose of skepticism.

The Late Great Planet Earth was turned into a movie. Somehow, I convinced my father to join me and several friends to check it out. We went to see it on a cold, February evening in nineteen-seventy-nine at Cinema 45 in Spring Valley. The booming, deep voice of Orson Wells echoed throughout the theater. His narration seemed an endorsement of the topic's credibility. And contrary to what most mainstream Catholics would consider a fringe topic, roughly twenty five percent of the New Testament is devoted to discussing end time prophesies and events. The film warned about looming calamities of the twenty first century that included military clashes, polluted cities, and ravishing famine. We compared the movie's theatrics to what we read in the Bible and pondered how this applied to us. We did not have answers, but this was another goad to our sides that drove us closer to the Bible.

The Holy Name Society promoted fraternity among the men of St. Aedan's parish. At the time when the movie came out several members asked the parish priest, Father Edward J. Quirk, to discuss the essence of the apocalyptic film. Father Quirk, a large, balding man with knock knees and a hunched back, lumbered his battered body like he was dragging a massive crucifix across to cavalry. He looked weathered by time and pain. Much older than his fifty-eight years of life.

Parishioners described him as the gentle giant, for he stood a head taller than the common church-goer. My father invited me and Jon to attend. We politely sat in the gymnasium waiting for the meeting to start as the HNS members finished reciting prayers in the side chapel. As the meeting came to order my father introduced us to Father Quirk and the men of the church. Most had not seen the movie but were aware of the sensational advertisements on television. All the men were much older than us, being fathers and grandfathers. They clearly noticed Jon, whose physiognomy appeared different than the typical Italian, or Irish, or northern European congregant of this parish. They were eager to hear an interesting discussion. Father Quirk pensively looked around before joining the meeting to address the subject of Christ's return and end times. Jon broke the ice and broached the topic. He commented that as a Jew he found the subject of Bible prophecy, and the rebirth of Israel fascinating. Father Quirk looked transfixed, as this moment was both a challenge and an opportunity. But he looked deterred. He cleared his throat and then spoke slowly and carefully. He found the whole notion of Christ's return and end times interesting, but didn't fully endorse the idea that it would happen in the near future. He opted not to address the topic of prophecy in any detail and short-circuited further discussion. Congregants sat silently for an eternal second hoping to hear more on the subject. The subject of prophesy was quashed. To break the silence, the HNS Chapter President interjected and thanked Father Quirk as he gracefully returned to the parish rectory. The president then transitioned the discussion and had the organizing committee share the plans for the spring dance. Everyone clapped as the meeting concluded. It was a surreal experience. Jon and I left the meeting as my father remained to discuss other social activities and charity events. I had hoped to learn what the Catholic Church had to say about Christ's second coming, about the events described so vividly in the Book of Revelation and throughout the New Testament. I left know little more than when I entered. What I really learned is that I would need to seek the answers myself.

Jon was passionate is his pursuit of biblical truth. And discovered, of all things, a Christian radio format on a local AM station, WWDJ, 97.7. I was familiar with this number on the AM dial as it hosted a pop rock programing during the early seventies before they converted to a Christian teaching format later in the decade. Jon discovered a local preacher whom he liked, and his teachings and unique preaching style prompted Jon to attend church services. Jon encouraged me to go and listen to the preacher. He stimulated my curiosity by telling me that the preacher played the guitar like Eric Clapton. The idea of a preacher playing rock music certainly piqued my interest. I loved the hard rock of the seventies and was inquisitive to how the contiguity of scripture and guitar solos would be presented in a Protestant church.

One Saturday night in '98, I agreed to go to church with him. Early evenings over the summer were usually uneventful. There was a predictable lull between dinner and when I would go out to meet friends at a local bar. Jon was not available on this particular day, so I decided to go myself. It was a warm summer evening, and after this church service I planned either to go to my usual haunts, The Barn in Nanuet, or the Gran Saloon in Pearl River. I figured I would go to listen some Clapton music and then listen to a simple Bible teaching. I drove to this small church in New Milford, New Jersey uniquely called the Maranatha Church of the Nazarene.[2] It was situated on a quiet, tree-lined street and resembled a typical small Protestant church tucked in a small mid-west town. It was something you might see on a Christmas card. It was a small, white, wooden structure with a steeple, stained glass windows, and a sign with stick-on letters for announcements. As I got out of the car and walked down the street, I questioned what the hell was I getting myself into. Little did I know that I was getting on board a spiritual journey that would change the course of my life. As I drew nearer the building, I envisioned that I was going to sit next to older, slumped-over men dressed in buttoned-up light blue sweaters bracing themselves with canes, accompanied by their gray-haired wives dressed in blue pastel dresses and head coverings. As I walked up the steps, I was greeted by a burly individual in his late twenties flashing a big smile. His hair was parted to the side over his ears, and his beard and mustache covered his otherwise masculine features. He wore blue jeans and had a light blue denim shirt. He appeared to be an older version me. But upon my approach, he almost bounced to his feet, extended his right hand and waited for me to do likewise. I looked at him for a spit second, somewhat uncomfortable and proceeded to extend my right hand. He gripped my hand firmly, assuredly, and warmly welcomed me. I found an open aisle seat in the pews to the right of the main aisle. As I looked around, I spotted mostly teenagers sprinkled with people in their mid-twenties and thirties. They looked like me, long hair, dressed in dungarees, sneakers, and tee shirts. Certainly, they didn't look like people dressed for Sunday morning

Mass. My perceptions of a Protestant church were immediately dashed, even though I never sat through a Protestant church service before. There was a palpable energy, an excitement, and an expectation from the congregation. This wasn't a perfunctory service that people rushed through for mere appearance. People wanted to be there. I thought to myself:

What teenagers would go to church on a Friday night? Not anyone I knew.

The church was decorated simply with a small wooden pulpit off to the side to make room for the musicians. When I entered, there were pews on either side of the main aisle, and stained glass windows on the right wall. Beyond the left pews, there was an open area with additional pews occupied by people sitting on the floor by the stage. Downstairs there were classrooms and bathrooms. This church did not have the trappings of other churches that I was accustomed to, it lacked the holy water at the entrance, lacked the iconography of the more lavish Catholic Churches, and lacked the formality of Sunday Mass. As the music amped up, I became amused; this wasn't any church I've seen before. Absent were church organs, choral music, and familiar hymns. Instead, eight-foot speaker monitors blasted guitar riffs as the bass, rhythm guitar, keyboard, and drums played the rock music I liked and was familiar with. The singer performed a melody about sin, repentance, God's love, and forgiveness. I was fascinated!

After twenty minutes or so, the music stopped, the pulpit was moved into the center of the stage, and the lead guitarist started to teach. This guitarist with long hair around his ears, and a buttoned-down shirt with blue jeans was Charlie Rizzo, the church pastor. He was a Bronx transplant eleven years my senior who spoke with confidence and conviction. I don't remember the specifics about the sermon, but I certainly remember that, as I listened, I thought he was talking directly to me. I looked around a few times to my left and my right because I felt like this was a setup, like this message was being said just for me. He spoke about the need for repentance, not penance. He said that I could know Jesus personally and that He cares for me. Pastor Rizzo was animated, logical, and spoke passionately about scripture. At the end of the sermon, he asked the congregation if anyone wanted to know Jesus personally. This was an invitation. An invitation to bow at the altar and ask Jesus to come into your life. He instructed those who were interested to step up to the altar, while motioning to the side that someone was willing to pray with them. I wanted to jump out of the pew but hesitated, looking around to see if I was the only one who felt this way. Seeing others have the same reaction I was the third person to make it up front where I shook Pastor Charlie's hand and knelt on my knees. The individual who greeted me at the door came over to talk and eventually we prayed together. He shook my hand and asked me to repeat a prayer. It was commonly known as the sinner's prayer. I said that I repent of my sins, that I believed that Jesus died for my sins, and that he was crucified and had rose on the third day, and that I will be forgiven and given a new life through His Holy Spirit, and that I can know Him personally. He asked if I had any questions, and I did! I wasn't sure about a lot of things, and I began to question why the four gospels were different. Why did one gospel say Peter would deny Christ three times after the cock crows twice, while the other gospels only said he denied Christ once after the cock crows. He looked at me quizzically, as if that would even matter, and he had no answer. He said to keep reading the Bible, to pray, and that God would fill me and give me understanding. I walked out with a lot of questions about following Christ, and these were questions without answers. I knew I needed purpose and direction, but this was the beginning of years of soul searching, procrastination, bad decisions, failures, and eventual life-changing commitments.

When I stumbled into this church service, I knew nothing about this pastor or ministry. Charlie Rizzo, the guitar-playing pastor, was born to second generation immigrants from Italy who settled in the Bronx, but moved to New Milford, New Jersey in the mid 1960s. By his own admission, he was not a distinguished academic, or athlete. He was a man who had fallen prey to amphetamines, known as speed. He liked playing guitar, and like many kids of his day, he used his garage as a setting for rehearsals and creativity with his newly formed band as they played under the influence of drugs imagining they were like their idols on the record albums they purchased. They strummed guitars, banged the drums, plucked the bass, and hammered the electronic keyboard. They played the music they heard on the radio.

Reverend Paul Moore, a former gospel musician and son of a Nazarene pastor was recently asked to lead a struggling congregation of eight people in Northern New Jersey. He was keenly aware of the paucity of younger people attending church, he wanted to create an environment where they would feel welcome on their own terms yet be willing to hear a gospel message as well. He walked around town and spoke with kids at the local pizzeria and street corners informing them that he was starting a coffeehouse on Friday nights and that they could come and play whatever they liked. Charlie liked playing psychedelic music mixed in with Beatles songs. He brought his friends to play along with other bands. This went on for months but ended after a stereo and other equipment was stolen from the church. Charlie continued to interact with Pastor Moore even after the coffeehouse ended. After a conversation with another young acquaintance, he tossed his stash of speed down the toilet and committed his life to Christ.[3] He returned the stolen stereo, and Moore convinced him to use his musical abilities for Christ. Charlie and his buddies became the house band for the newly christened Maranatha Coffeehouse.[4] The coffeehouse and the gospel message thrived with renewed energy now that it was led by volunteers in their teens and twenties.[5,6]

The musicians called the band Maranatha and collaborated to record an album called "Soon" in 1971.[7] A slew of people, mostly in their teens and twenties, attended Friday and Saturday services. The coffeehouse played music but held rap sessions where small groups of people would sit around and talk about scripture. Music was always a big part of the draw, and attendance grew through word of mouth. Word about this youth revival spread to other churches. Disenfranchised teenagers from traditional church services and eastern religions flocked to this congregation. As part of their outreach to youth in NYC, Maranatha and the Nazarene church sponsored a series of concerts called Jesus Joy![8,9] They invited Andraé Crouch, a renowned gospel singer, and his band called The Disciples, and another band called Rock Garden to play at Carnegie Hall. They performed in the iconic theater in April of 1972. Charlie Rizzo and the Maranatha Band also played at Madison Square Garden's Felt Forum in April and September of 1972. The MSG event was called "Jesus Joy: A Solid Rock Gathering at the Garden" featured bands with names Love Song, Danny Lee and the Children of Truth, Katie Hanley, and Lillian Parker. Speakers included Tom Skinner, a former leader of the Harlem Lords gang, Scott Ross, a "Christian disc jockey," Moishe Rosen, a Jewish believer who became a Baptist Minister and founder of Jews for Jesus, Bob Mumford, Jerry Davis (editor of New York's Jesus paper, *Good News of Jesus*), Father Jack Sutton, a Roman Catholic priest and Rev. Paul Moore of Maranatha. Charlie Rizzo spoke as well. He was also asked by the Nazarene denomination leadership to perform at their regional Nazarene youth conventions Expo '72, an event at the Cotton Bowl in Dallas, Texas and dubbed the "Christian Woodstock" which ran from June 12th through June 17th. And attended the denomination's General Assembly in Miami Beach. With all this going on, Charlie, only twenty-one years-old, was engaged in home study in preparation to be an ordained minister. He did this while helping oversee a congregation of three thousand with close to twenty home Bible study groups and a dozen coffee houses in the area. He became assistant pastor in 1973, and his zeal was the catalyst for many people to hear the gospel message in a way they had not heard before.

In the summer of 1980, I heard the message loudly and clearly, but that was all I did. The transition from high school to college was a portal that pushed students from the familiar to this wonderous world of the mind. Gone were the mundane classrooms where you traveled from room to room tethered to a daily schedule of everyday sameness with imperious teachers barking information without examining the wherefores and the whys. My first year of college was a bewilderment, it was an intricate maze for the quest of knowledge. But not the knowledge my parents and student loans were paying for. Those winding paths promised an educated mind, a responsible citizen, a son worthy of praise, promising the golden fleece at the end of the maze. I chose a different path.

I attended SUNY Oneonta, a small college southwest of Albany, NY. Studying was not a priority, and I mostly skipped classes or just didn't take them seriously, as I still felt the vestiges of high school. I had no contact with my family from late August until Thanksgiving. I was either stoned, drunk or hungover. By the end of my freshman year, I was on probation having a combined GPA of 2.0, the highest standard of mediocrity. I really didn't have much ambition and wasn't concerned about a career. I was interested in getting high, hanging out with my friends, and bar hopping.

This behavior continued over the summer but in parallel to my spiritual awakening. A few days after attending the Maranatha Church of the Nazarene for the first time I remember one night tossing and turning in my bed struggling with the concept of committing my life to Christ. I thought, I can't do this, I am a young guy, I have so much stuff to do, I would be missing out on so much.

I wasn't cut out to be a missionary, a preacher, or whatever other misconception I had at the time about what it actually meant to be a Christian. I distinctly remember saying to myself:

I'll just wait a while.

That seemed plausible, I'll just get serious later, I mused.

A few weeks after going to the Friday night service, I was working on a temporary job through Kelly Services at a small perfume manufacturer in Rockleigh, NJ. The job required a few workers to go through pallets of boxes that contained square perfume bottles. Each perfume bottle had to be removed and measured individually to determine if they would fit through the gauge. We used a metal gauge and passed each bottle through it. If they passed through the gauge, they could safely travel on the conveyer belt. Those that didn't were discarded. This job went on for weeks and I became friendly with my co-worker, a fellow student on summer break. He hailed from Englewood, NJ, and was a fellow fan of Jorma Kaukonen. We smoked pot during breaks and met on weekends at local bars to share a few drinks. He was a great guitarist. I listened to him playing True Religion, one of my favorite Hot Tuna songs. I knew this by heart, having copied Jorma's 1978 solo concert at the Suffolk Forum in Commack, NY on a cassette tape. As I hummed the song to myself while I cut open a box, I noticed a small white pamphlet on top of the bottles. We opened boxes for weeks and never saw anything but square perfume bottles. I was curious. What could this piece of paper be? I picked it up, it was roughly 3 x 4 inches in size and had writing on the front. It had a line-drawing of an old man that read: The Gospel According to John. It was a religious pamphlet, and I flipped through it quickly, but stopped on the last page. The very last sentence jumped out at me, and I nearly jumped out of my skin. It read:

The Devil says Wait a while.

I stood there in shock, my exact words, the very words I used to convince myself that now was not the time to believe and follow.

As I stood there in stunned silence, my co-worker stopped, he noticed the look on my face. He made some comment, but I couldn't respond, I couldn't talk, I was breathless! I flung the pamphlet in his direction and walked away from the assembly line seeking fresh air. My inner thoughts were exposed, and challenged, but by who. I had no idea what it was or what was happening and was unsettled for weeks.

I returned to college that autumn and I travelled through the same road as I had in my freshman year. I partied, and I continued to live in my academic cemetery. By mid-October, my three quad mates and I sat in front of Dean Foti's desk, somewhat apprehensively as we looked at each other for moral support. We were summoned to his office to answer for some extracurricular activities on campus. Dean Foti eyed us gravely as he flipped through a stack of papers.

You guys are in serious trouble. Fabio! Donohue! There is no reason for me not to throw you out of school. You are both on academic probation and now you are on disciplinary probation. You other two. You should be thrown off campus because you are now on disciplinary probation.

We sat dumbfounded and blindsided. No one informed us, not the RA, not anyone, that we did anything wrong! He made a comment that our behavior was unacceptable, and if he let us stay in school, or on campus, we would continue our disruptive behavior. Silently I recalled the infractions: kicking off doorknobs, smoking pot in the quad, playing Pink Floyd's, *We Don't Need No Education* at full blast with the speakers out the window at four a.m. on a Thursday night. As the others sat in silence I spoke in our defense. I argued that, had we known about how serious these infractions where, we would have not continued to do them. Dean Foti looked in my direction unconvinced. He said would let us know his decision in two weeks.

I'll never forget the phone call to my parents, that there was a real possibility I would be expelled from college. My mother was calm, supportive, and assured me that things will work out, no matter what happened. My father was in a rage. He was disgusted with me and put the blame squarely on me. He berated me the whole time I was on the phone. I expected nothing less and endured his wrath.

As the four of us quad mates sat around, smoked pot, and pondered our futures, one of them was in full panic. He was anxious and complained that his life was ruined. That he could never get into grad school or get hired by a reputable firm in NYC if he was expelled. The other fellow, also in his junior year, planned to call his father, a Police Captain out in Suffolk County Long Island. Surely a police captain could reason with Dean Foti, he hoped. Donohue snickered at his fate as he pondered revenge on the dean and the school. I pondered the future. I reluctantly began to accept that I would now have to attend RCC, Rockland Community College.

RCC for you!

If I attended RCC it would be an affirmation of my father's prediction for me. He mocked me every time he reviewed my high school report cards and every time he reviewed my college transcripts at the end of each semester.

RCC for you!

I had always laughed back at his antagonistic commentary. Now it just may come true. I would never live it down. The look from my father would be ever-present and undoubtably my brothers would have gleefully joined in the derisive chorus of condescendence. Fortunately, that scenario never materialized. The two juniors were given warnings and put on probation. Donohue and I were allowed to stay in college but were expelled from campus. We were none the wiser.

Chapter 12

Now, God be praised, that to believing souls / Gives light in darkness, comfort in despair.

—William Shakespeare

Six weeks into my first semester of sophomore year the verdict came in and I was exiled from campus. The availability of housing was limited in the middle of a semester and so we settled. Steve and I and two other students, the Bill's, found a rundown house on Lincoln Street, just behind Golding Hall. This house looked like it should have been condemned. It met basic needs such as a small serviceable kitchen, small sized bedrooms, and a repurposed attic. The only bathroom was a configuration of mismatched fixtures with a rusted clawfoot cast iron tub that had with it a makeshift shower head. The first floor was dominated by a dark wooden staircase. Narrow and steep, these stairs had to be ascended and descended sideways. These were clearly unsafe, and it was a miracle no one was ever injured as we traversed them in all states of inebriation. The front porch overhang was supported by two twelve-foot tree limbs that the landlord cut and positioned to replace the rotted porch pillars. We shared the house with repellent, gnawing mice that scurried through the uninsulated walls. These mice generously donated excrement pellets that scattered throughout the cupboard. More than once the kitchen cabinets crawled with huge carpenter ants swarming a sugar bowl knocked over by said mice. The house was cold and drafty; we mostly cared less, because we had cheap lodging, lived independently from school authority, and had no one to account to.

We were as free as the beer on the Two-for-Tuesdays mid-week special. The Filling Station was a gasoline station converted into a bar, and I often decided to get my money's worth of free alcohol by ordering Rusty Nails. It got the job done quicker. When pot and alcohol weren't enough, we occasionally descended into the vortex of psychedelic drugs or cocaine. For many students the decision of whether to partake of LSD or mushrooms was not a matter availability, but what level of post drug side-effects they were willing to endure. We often plunged into an altered state of consciousness induced by undulating colors, collapsing depth perception, heightened auditory awareness, and fractured thoughts and nonsensical conversations never to be remembered. I'll never forget my first—and last—time I used LSD.

It was at a Grateful Dead concert in Buffalo NY at the Aud. Six of us took a hit of LSD. It was referred to as "Window pane", named so for the clear gel wafer that contained the drug that dissolved on your tongue. It took a while for the psychedelic effects to kick in, but I remember distinctly after the show that I was having paranoid anxiety attacks and minor hallucinations. We parked in some alley that was surrounded by eight story brick warehouses. We talked about the show, drank beer, smoked more pot, and decided what to do next. As I was leaning against the car, a piece of paper fell out of the sky. It was a flyer for the concert. The word *dead* jumped from page. My imagination immediately conjured up a scene from an obscure horror movie shown during Chiller Theatre, a TV program that broadcast classic horror movies on Saturday evenings. The movie, called *Dr. Terror's House of Horrors* featured Peter Cushing, Christopher Lee, and Donald Sutherland.[1] The premise featured a fortune teller, a ghostly old man, who divined the future of his fellow travelers. All five travelers, businessmen dressed in suits and ties, had their future demise revealed through the reading of Tarot cards. The last card each man was dealt was the death card. They looked at each other in shock and panic as they concluded what the cards had revealed. They concluded that they had no future. Wanting to know the fate of the old man, they inquired.

What about you?

The man obliged and dealt to himself. He lifted the last card and presented it to each rider. Death.

Who are you? They implored.

Have you not guessed?

In the black of night, the train made its last stop. The riders exited onto a deserted railway platform. Relieved that they had reached their final destination they gathered under a single black pendulum light fixture. A newspaper suddenly dropped out of the sky. As the gentlemen chuckled about the crazy old man, the headline read: "Train Crashes—Five Dead." Horrified, the gentlemen turned their attention to a man in a black cloak. Dr. Terror turned and revealed himself a skeleton. He was death. They were all dead.

My drug fueled, paranoid imagination when in full gear. As I read the concert flyer, my eyes hyper-focused on the word dead. My conscience screamed inside my head. I was embracing death. My partying and lifestyle led me on a journey that led to spiritual death. I did not want to be on that train. But how could I get off? The life I was following was contrary to the teachings of Jesus. I needed another way.

Later in the evening we whiled away hours near a park dimly lit by the ambient light of the city's streetlights. The effects of the "Window pane" morphed into a psychedelic screen that featured an open field with swaying trees beckoning me to frolic in the twilight pasture. I slowly drifted away from friends to the edge of the vacant parking area. I wanted to be in the midst of this new phenomenon of tree limbs that trailed each other, leaves that sparkled, and an open field that undulated, that invited me to explore.

The blend of reality and illusion created a metaphysical canvas full of fantastical fauna and flora where striking color palettes billowed in my mind's eye. My friends had no idea on my mental state and called me back, curious to what attracted my attention. I was unable to explain what I perceived, muttered something, and rejoined them around the car. I was slowly overcome with restlessness and fatigue, finding it increasingly difficult to stand, converse or focus. I found myself alone, staring blankly in the backseat of Donohue's old Mustang. The Mustang's interior was olive-green with ebony-black upholstery, ripped and worn, and a chrome dashboard that was dimly lit by the interior overhead light, yellowed from cigarette smoke. As the banter of my friends droned on outside, the visual display of ripped upholstery, dirty windows, and inoperable dashboard gauges soon became an abstraction. I slumped motionless as my perception was reduced to two-dimensions, length and height. Objects appeared as if they were on a flat surface without depth. Colors, by contrast, were vivid. The interior of the Mustang glistened with equal intensity and soon morphed into a whirlpool of swirling colors absent of a focal point. The effect of the drugs rushed to my head like a surging wave in a stormy sea. I became agitated, maniacal, and wanted it to stop. I felt like screaming but could not. Time did not exist in my mind. The reference points of passing time faded into the background, imperceptible. The hushed tones and laughter of my schoolmates drifted to a whisper; the music playing on the car radio slowly muted to background noise, no beginning and no end; the measure of time from a breath, an inhale, an exhale, was insensible. I retreated into my mind. Distorted and surrounded by color I became anxious and confused. How long would this suspension of reality last? How long have I been like this? I was captive and could not escape. Through this alternative reality a still small voice provided comfort. A coherent thought provided reason and hope. This suspension of normal perception was only temporary. It was the byproduct of a chemical interference with normal brain function. Reason alone did not alleviate my anxiety and confusion. Why was I so stupid to take drugs that could alter my brain chemistry and perhaps alter it permanently? I prayed. I asked for forgiveness for being so stupid, and so careless. A peace came over me and eventually my perception returned to normal. I had no idea how long I was in the back seat of Donohue's Green Mustang. Not aware of how much time had elapsed, the drug's hallucinogenic effects ended, and I regained enough control of my faculties to rejoin my buddies standing outside the open rear passenger side door. The next afternoon, frazzled by the sensory overload, I drank until inebriated at a Rolling Stones concert at Rich Stadium. Not until days later, did I take stock of my behavior. My choices were leading me down a path that was detrimental to my mind, my body, and my spirit. I learned a valuable lesson from this trip. Something had to change.

School was school and unfulfilling. I was taking compulsory courses as part of the core curriculum, but I bristled at the tedious slog involved in these useless courses, courses that were mandatory to complete the liberal arts curriculum. Registration for courses was hectic as a crush of students lined up to register, but underclassmen were mostly locked out of their preferred classes because upperclassmen had first choice. Useless courses like, "Civil Rights for Students and Teachers," and "Intro into Astronomy" filled my days. When I finally took classes in my declared major—psychology—I was stimulated by comparing the contrasting theories of human behavior by Freud, Jung, and Skinner to each other.

I floundered in a career vacuum, for I had no idea as to my future calling. I could not imagine a career in psychology or envision any possibility of graduate school. I was as carefree as a vagabond in a homeless camp. I was cavalier about my grades, about school, and about life in general. But the party life was equally as unfulfilling as it was taking its toll on my mind. I meandered through my first three years of college. It seemed as if I was just going through the motions and didn't find any true purpose for why I was doing it. While I yet applied the means to live a Christian life, there was an inner longing that the Bible had the answers. Over the summer between my sophomore and junior year I regularly attended bible studies that were led by Jon Cahn. I started a trend that summer that was compatible with my thirst for spiritual knowledge and my vices: Friday night bible studies, Saturday nights at the bar. The bible studies led by Jon were insightful and uplifting. Jon's bible studies were my lifeline as I meandered in the deepest black hole induced by narcotics, alcohol, and other carnal choices. Knowing about virtue and sin was not enough to follow the salvific path. I learned that carnal temptations were a potent obstacle to spiritual growth.

I knew what the truth was, but just didn't fully grasp what I needed to do. Smoking pot on a regular basis depressed my spirit and inhibited any ambition. Marijuana kept me in a state of stupor. Summer employment gave me the opportunity to earn money, and at my tender age, the real meaning of money was to have fun and to satiate my physical wants. I now developed a penchant for cocaine, an experience like none other. The euphoria from cocaine allowed the party to continue into the wee hours of the morning.

Before heading into yet another bar, my friends would spread lines of coke laid out in neat rows on a small square mirror. The parking lot behind the Grand Saloon in Pearl River was a favorite spot to get a quick high. It was dark and deserted and we could quickly escape into the bar if need be. We laughed at our good fortune as we snorted the white powder through crisp one-hundred-dollar bills. We often gathered behind the Orangeburg Pub, snorting in Dominick's Gran Torino and drinking beers before we entered to listen to music provided by the local talent.

The fortunes of five of us almost ended in disaster. We sat in the car with a plan to get a quick cocaine buzz before we went into the bar. The radio was cranked up, we downed beers, and snorted cocaine on a six-by-six mirror. As I sat in the front passenger seat with two parallel lines of coke on my lap, suddenly I perceived movement across my peripheral vision. It was no illusion; the reality was that a car was heading toward the back of the parking lot and about to turn the corner in our direction. My eyes were hazy, glass-like, and then became laser focused as it became evident this was a police car. I leaned forward, for I realized that I needed to remove any evidence, and like a magician, I slid the mirror under the car seat. Dominick quickly turned the radio off and hurried out of the car while the others were already turning the corner on the opposite side of the building. I screamed:

Get the fuck back here and turn up the radio and act like we are just hanging out.

I couldn't believe it; I had a mirror with lines of cocaine on my lap and the local Orangetown cops were feet away from me. Dominick came back, put the keys in the ignition, turned up the radio and slouched himself over the open driver's side door. As the cops approached the passenger side door, they looked in, I nodded and tipped back the beer. The officers simply glared, drove off slowly and turned the corner behind us. We collectively took a sigh of relief. I was inches away from getting busted and possibly going to jail. As the cops drove out of view, I quickly snorted the rest of the cocaine, headed to the pub, continued to party, and laughed as we collectively had dodged a bullet.

By the spring of 1982 I was a mess. While my peers poured over books and class notes to complete their requirements for senior year, I languished in academic limbo. I barely accrued enough credits in psychology, and I would not graduate if I came up short.

When I came home that spring for Easter break my parents were oblivious to my plight. They were just happy to have all their boys home for the holiday and we celebrated by having a casual meal at Pickles, a restaurant nearby in the Nanuet Mall. It was a Friday night and as I waited for the assistant waiter to serve water, I felt a pang of anxiety. My pulse beat a little faster, and somehow a sense of emptiness came over me; I felt a spiritual void, it was as if my mind was in turmoil for some arcane reason. I needed to hear a spiritual message. I needed to gain a sense purpose and be filled with spiritual truths. I knew the Friday night bible study was where I could find that.

I have to go!

Without another word, I got up, avoided my father's eyes, briefly glanced at my mother, and I rushed out of the restaurant like a bat out of hell. I then rushed to my car and sped away without fear of a traffic violation. My parents sat there, dumbfounded, but said nothing.

The sound of spiritual music soothed my mind; I bathed in a sea of tranquility. The bible study was a venue for me to forget about myself and to focus on Jesus. As I prayed, I asked for Jesus' spirit to enter my body and purge my soul from toxic waste and give me the will power to simply say no to pot, say no to drunkenness, and say no to a life of waste. And to fill me with His spirit. I yearned for a spiritual connection with a higher power!

When I returned to school, I planned to attend a Jorma concert scheduled for April 11, 1982. I determined that this was to be my last hurrah with marijuana. For the first time in my life, I took stock of my situation, my values, my ethics, and my moral rectitude. I evaluated my lifestyle, my wants, my beliefs, my ambitions. It was a true soul searching. I knew I was headed in the wrong direction with all the partying and wanton behavior. I now realized that if I didn't turn my life around, I would end up living at home with my parents and be endlessly berated for my failures. With no plans for anything else, this is where I was headed. I ended up alone at the concert, high as a kite and hoping to have a last hurrah with marijuana. However, I could not help but compare the internal peace I had the week before worshipping at a bible study vs. what I had felt now. It was actually a lack of feeling. My head was buzzed but I had no inner peace, no connection to a higher power, no mental clarity. Getting high and listening to Jorma was the same as it always had been, great musicianship, a party vibe, and carefree fun, but now I realized I wanted more. I had personally experienced a totally different feeling the week earlier as I desperately longed for direction and purpose from God. I had felt an inward tug by the Holy Spirit, and I wanted that. That was the last time I smoked pot. And the last time I had any desire to indulge. It was completely removed. I knew intellectually about God but had never put the lessons of the Bible into practice so that the word of God through the power of the Holy Spirit could transform me. Growing up Roman Catholic and attending Mass almost every Sunday I absorbed enough from the lessons that Jesus was my savior, and He was the only path to Heaven. I believed the scriptures and never bought the argument that there are alternative paths to heaven.

> *Enter by the narrow gate. For the gate is wide and the way is easy that leads to destruction, and those who enter by it are many. For the gate is narrow and the way is hard that leads to life, and those who find it are few.*
>
> MATTHEW 7:13–14

> *I am the way, and the truth, and the life. No one comes to the Father except through me.*
>
> JOHN 14:6

I had rudimentary understanding of how following Jesus was about change in attitude and behavior. This verse in Paul's letter to the Ephesians explains exactly what was happening as I started to devote myself to change.

> *To put off your old self, which belongs to your former manner of life and is corrupt through deceitful desires, and to be renewed in the spirit of your minds, and to put on the new self, created after the likeness of God in true righteousness and holiness.*
>
> EPHESIANS 4:22

The change occurred because I stopped what I was doing and replaced it with something better. The change occurred because I replaced those old behaviors with new behaviors. I was no longer adrift in the foggy haze of marijuana; it was a cleansing of the mind, and an embrace of the real. Over the summer I regularly attended Jon's bible study on Friday nights and church services on Sunday at Maranatha in New Milford. I remember talking to Jon about the challenges and temptations I was going to face when I returned to school. Before I headed back for the fall semester of my senior year, he made a list of activities I should do to keep on track with my spiritual journey. It included reading the Bible, praying, finding a church to attend, avoiding bad habits, etc. Jon's counsel was exactly what I needed. His passion for the gospel was evident and he had impacted my spiritual journey immensely.[2,3,4,5] When I returned to school my friends were in disbelief that I quit pot. I was offered many times to indulge but there was no desire to go back to the mental fog and prison that had entrapped me for years. I occasionally drank alcohol socially but never to the point of inebriation. I made a commitment to read some scripture almost every day, pray, and seek out different churches. I started reading the Gospel of John, one chapter per day, and then pray and ask for insight on what I just read. I continued with this daily routine as I made my way through the New Testament.

One afternoon I walked to the upper quad. I was headed toward the Fitzelle Hall campus coffee shop and thought about some passages in the Bible. I read the Bible many times but now found myself contemplating how scripture applied to my daily life. My head was in the clouds when I noticed a girl walking with a guitar. She seemed absorbed in thought as her big brown eyes gazed upward. Her face was draped with long, dark, wavy, chestnut-brown hair. She looked contemplative and peaceful. My pace slowed to a crawl and my eyes and head followed her gentle stroll. I thought:

Lord, is this the one?

The thought popped into my head out of nowhere. It was strange and disconcerting. I never saw her on campus in my previous three years. Who was she? Where has she been? I deeply pondered this brief encounter for the rest of the afternoon. I retreated into my apartment and as if in a dream. Lord Byron's poem, "She Walks in Beauty," perfectly captured my feelings.

I
She walks in beauty, like the night
Of cloudless climes and starry skies;
And all that's best of dark and bright
Meet in her aspect and her eyes:
Thus mellowed to her tender light'
Which heaven to gaudy day denies

II
One shade the more, one ray the less,
Had half impaired the nameless grace
Which waves in every raven tress,
Or softly lightens o'er her face;
Where thoughts serenely sweet express,
How pure, how dear their dwelling-place

III
And on that cheek, and o'er that brow,
So soft, so calm, yet eloquent,
The smiles that win, the tints that glow,
But tell of days in goodness spent,
A mind at peace with all below,
A love whose heart is innocent!

I usually fell in lust, but now I pulsed with something different. Only the iambics of love could quell the cries of the heart. I imagined the purity of her soul more than the curves of her figure; I remembered her delicate visage more than her attractive physique.

I dreamt about this brief encounter but soon put it out of my mind. Why should I delude myself about some chance encounter. I determined to focus my thoughts on hard reality: my daily routine of class attendance, completion of assignments, and time devoted to scripture reading and prayer. While I studied at the Milne Library, I noticed a flyer advertising an off-campus bible study. I had never been to a bible study at college and decided to check it out. The bible study was held in a private house two doors down from my new apartment. I had no excuse to not attend. Chris and Barbie Deemer, the local staff for Campus Ambassadors, a national ministry focused on Christian outreach to college students, had graciously opened their home to students attending SUNY Oneonta and Hartwick College. I marveled at what a coincidence it was to have an off-campus bible study so close to where I lived. As I walked in, I immediately noticed the girl I spotted on campus two weeks earlier. She was lively, pretty and seemed to know everyone. I chuckled to myself thinking, no wonder I never saw her; this was where she has been all this time. Not at the bars, but at a bible study. Over the next few weeks, I thought about her, but I made no attempts to date her. I was in no condition to be boyfriend material. My head needed cleansing, my soul needed revival, and my spirit needed awakening. I remember reading the verse from Psalm.

> *Delight yourself in the Lord, and he will give you the desires of your heart.*
>
> PSALM 37:4

I did not know what that verse meant at first but came to understand that growing closer to the Lord should be my focus. If I align my thoughts and behaviors with the messages of the Bible, He will take care of the rest. There was another verse in Jeremiah that gave me great comfort. God had a plan for me, and I didn't need to be anxious about the future.

> *"For I know the plans I have for you," declares the Lord, "plans for welfare and not for evil, to give you a future and a hope."*
>
> JEREMIAH 29:11

Senior year was the year of change. I was focused on growing closer to Jesus, practicing discipline, and doing all activities as if I was doing them for Him. My grades were the best ever, despite a more demanding schedule. I worked at a local pizzeria, attended Bible Studies and church services; first at a Baptist Church and later at a non-denominational Evangelical Church. My discipline had results. I turned around my academic failures and graduated college. Mom and Dad were pleasantly surprised, proud ,and relieved. The chance encounter with the girl with the big brown eyes morphed into a friendship. A friendship that would blossom into something more than I could have imagined.

Chapter 13

Trust is earned, respect is given, and loyalty is demonstrated.
Betrayal of any one of those is to lose all three.

—Ziad K. Abdelnour

In the 1980s, America rose from the despondency of the Carter presidency. During his administration, President Jimmy Carter instructed Americans to wear heavy sweaters, to respect the odds and even days for fueling automobiles, and to rely on his diplomacy to free American hostages from the medieval clutches of the Iranian revolution. Carter's feckless leadership created a pall that draped the country in malaise. Actor Ronald Reagan emerged as the Jimmy Carter antidote. Reagan was that indomitable Hollywood star who used his photogenic charm, his mordacious wit, and his common sense to spray sunshine in an otherwise bleak America. The world changed as Yuppies entered our nomenclature, reflective of the economic prosperity that Wall Street speculators, investors, and bankers created. American hostages were set free, and the Berlin Wall soon was dismantled after Reagan stood at the Brandenburg Gate and sententiously boomed,

Mr. Gorbachev, tear down this wall!

While Reagan facilitated the collapse of the Soviet Union the headlines focused on the idol worship of Princess Diana. Diana Spencer, a blue-eyed British beauty with a radiant smile captured the imagination of the entire world. In contrast, First Lady Nancy Reagan was mocked for her big head, adoring eyes, and ineffective directive about doing drugs.

Just say no.

Mount St. Helen's exploded, reminding us of the frivolity of our efforts to control the environment. The power and unpredictability of earthquakes with the resulting destruction and pollution humbled the nation. Something else exploded, even more loudly than the volcanic mountain, an explosion that reverberated in the collective psyches of our nation, an explosion that was also unexpected. The Challenger space shuttle disintegrated before our eyes. A teacher, Christa McAuliffe, was the first civilian aboard a manned mission in space and the program failed her and the rest of the crew. An investigation into the explosion revealed NASA's organizational failure to properly assess their own engineers' technical concerns about O-rings and temperature.

Moral failures were on full display across our television sets and newspapers. Jerry Falwell led the Moral Majority in a crusade of pro-life, pro-traditional family, and pro-American values, while televangelists Jim Bakker and Jimmy Swaggert were publicly castrated for their moral failures. In New York, U.S. Attorney General Rudoph Giuliani spearheaded efforts against corrupt elected officials, white-collar criminals, drug dealers and organized crime. The disinfecting light of law, order, and scrutiny scattered criminal elements to the shadows, alleys, and backrooms of legitimate businesses. Quality of live improvements were palpable; squeegee men disappeared, 42nd Street transformed from the porn capital of the US to a retail hub that welcomed the Disney Store. But crime and criminals morphed with the times and hid in plain sight. They blended in with legitimate occupations and transformed themselves from sleazy underworld characters to white collar businessmen fronting an appearance of wealth and virtue. The true nature of their illicit gains and vice was hidden and only revealed through creative law reform and enforcement. Reagan and Giuliani were the artificers of the renaissance that ushered in one of the most consequential decades of the 20th century.

Robert was summoned to a meeting.

Bobby, this is Johnny Mac, you need to get down to the 79th & 9th Ave club tomorrow at nine a.m.

What's up?

Never mind, just get down here!

The boss, Jimmy, didn't like flashy dressers, didn't like expensive suits, and didn't like the look of disco-clad guineas. He hated Italians but tolerated them when it was convenient. He cozied up to the them when he needed to bolster his troops during turf wars. He liked Bobby, but he had some misgivings about his appearance. It wasn't Robert's imposing physicality, especially now that he beefed up his physique to tip the scale to 225 lbs. He knew that Robert was an obsessed gym rat who lifted weights regularly, and used steroids to further enhance his massive presence. Robert took umbrage when someone hurled insults to his nationality, to his appearance, or especially when someone called him a pretzel. This particular slur motivated him to go full bore on weights and challenge those who hurled the insult. He determined to obviate that insult in the future. He was now a man of the '80s: he styled his long, flowing hair, he sported tight shirts with a cropped athletic style, he hung gold chains around his neck, he wore a gold watch and gold bracelets, and he wore white Air Jordan's. His attire showed the world that he was financially successful, and that he held everyone with a tinge of arrogance as if saying: "Don't mess with me, or else!" Few dared.

Give him a coffee

barked Jimmy, as Bobby took a chair from long table in the basement. There were boxes of untaxed liquor, beer, and cigarettes.

The basement was a windowless space with only a few lights on the wall and one major light overhead. Robert didn't know what to expect, but he was fearless. He didn't steal. He was blameless, in his mind. He went wherever he was needed; he collected gambling debts from people who borrowed, sometimes as much as $50-60,000. He forced people to pay, not all at once, but made sure they paid. Otherwise, he resorted to physical therapy in the form of a beating. Jimmy remarked:

Bobby, you look like a mobster, you look like those fucking guineas from Brooklyn, you are drawing too much attention to yourself, tone it down. I don't want to see anymore gold chains and cut that damn hair; you understand.

Ok, I will. Sorry, I'll tone it down. Robert demurred.

Robert continued to deal and collect for Jimmy the boss while working at Johnny Mac's clubs on the Eastside and the Bronx. His work with Jimmy the boss was considered supplemental income. Robert liked working with Johnny Mac. He was loyal to his boss, respected, and as long Robert kept the money flowing, he was protected. Johnny Mac's hired muscle were members of various motorcycle clubs, usually the Pagan's. They used to escort Robert from the club to his car. One member of the Pagan's MC drew Robert's ire to the point of rage. This Pagan had the audacity to flirt and hit on Mink, a Korean woman Robert knew from the club. This guy Paul and Robert had words. Robert had wanted to date Mink, and his jealousy escalated into an all-out brawl on 1st Ave. Fists flew between the two, and eventually Paul, battered heavily, retreated into a twenty-four-hour diner. Robert followed him in a rage and ran back into the kitchen area and grabbed a cleaver and pounded this head and face with the dull end. Paul was in bad shape and landed in the hospital with his faced bashed in. When Eddie #2 asked why he was beating up on his security detail Robert said,

Hey, he's hitting up on my girl and I'm not going to put up with that.

Johnny Mac and Eddie #2 respected him for that and there never was any retaliation by Johnny Mac or the Pagan's.

The Pagan MC became a problem that Robert had to solve. It was solved with a threat. Robert was asked to pay a visit to a club in the Bronx operating in a back room at the Wishing Well located on W. 238th Street under the "L." The bar was run by an old man called John O'Sullivan, who was past his prime when it came to enforcing respectable behavior of the gamblers.

Bobby, please go up there and find out what the fuck is going on, we're having a problem.

A dozen or so members of the Pagan's MC were drunk and pissed off because they lost big money and the owners and staff wanted to close up, but they would not leave. It was after one a.m. and Robert walked in and yelled,

You guys gotta go, you're all gonna get killed, Johnny Mac's gonna send a crew and kill all you motherfuckers.

Paul was now a lieutenant of the Pagan's. He knew Robert and he knew Johnny Mac would do exactly as Robert said. He left begrudgingly with some cursing and vailed threats but otherwise without incident. Robert's bravado and connections were consequential.

Mink was a cute, petite, Korean woman, several years older than Robert. He was intrigued with her. She always had money, exuded confidence, and he admired her ability to lead as she operated several hostess bars and massage parlors in Flushing and Manhattan. She now managed a massage parlor down the street from a club owned by Jimmy the boss at 38th and 9th. Business was profitable and demand was high as her earnings supported her gambling habits. Robert was jealous of this lady always coming in with lots of money; he didn't like some Korean woman acting like she was a big shot. He asked Jimmy the boss to close down her massage parlor. Robert wanted to demonstrate who really had power and influence. This was a dumb move for Robert who didn't take into account all the other people that would be affected by this closure. Out of work, the Korean girls stopped drinking, stopped gambling, and Robert stopped making money. Mink didn't bat an eye and opened another massage parlor on the upper east side. She was now coming into Johnny Mac's other club on 61st and 1st. Again, she would show up and lay down big money to play poker. Robert eventually took notice and started to pursue her. She was ten years older than he was, but he lusted over her tight leather pants. Mink was equally attracted to this big, musclebound blackjack dealer, not aware that he was the catalyst for the closure of her massage parlor. Ever the businessman, Johnny Mac handed Robert $10,000 and said, "Go the 55th Street club, go play and promote the game."

Ok, sure, no problem.

While poker was not his favorite game, Robert was all for playing with someone else's money. One hand ended up with fours Jacks and he figured the other player would throw his cards in, lose, while he would walk away with the $14,000 pot. Instead, a different gambler threw down four Queens. Robert was pissed. He had been bested, his strategy failed him, and stood up quickly slamming his Glock pistol loudly on the table.

This is bullshit, this is rigged.

Everyone's ears perked up, gamblers and masseuses alike. Calming down, he retreated to his chair and was suddenly distracted by the Korean seductress, Mink. She maneuvered through the crowd, pressed her hips into his shoulder and whispered is his hear.

I need $3,000 to play.

Robert, amused at the brazenness and titillated by the flirtation, bargained that he would only give her cash if she promised to go out with him. She playfully hesitated, then nodded yes with a sly grin.

Robert took every opportunity to make money. Easy money

was his business and dealing per se was easy. His reputation earned him a chance to deal and eventually manage a club on 57th Street. Korean men loitered around a blocked gate masking the club entrance near a subway entrance. The only way to gain access was to personally know the gate keepers; Robert later discovered that the people running this club were members of KP, the Korean Power gang.

These guys were sleaze bags, hung around the club all the time, ate there, slept there, watched every dealer like a hawk.

These unsavory thugs smelled like fish because there was a fish market nearby. These "Little Brothers," as they were known in Korean circles, did the bidding for the "Big Brothers." The Big Brothers were the organizers and brains of the operation. They ran prostitution rings, gambling clubs, and engaged in robbery, extortion, and smuggling of illegal immigrants.[1] Mink, Robert's new Korean girlfriend, warned him about doing business with KP.

These guys are not your people, they will steal from you and hurt you.

Robert ignored the warning and made arrangements with Mr. Sung, a well-dressed old man who agreed to let him manage and deal. Tiger, a Korean gangster, who was the muscle for this club, barged in. When not working he came into play and was displeased at Robert's presence. Tiger was an imposing figure, standing six-feet and three-inches and was marked by scars on his face and his hands. His physicality clearly indicated that he was a force to be reckoned with. He was riled and nasty whenever he lost and started to rant and curse in his native Korean language.

A few months earlier George Kelly and another bouncer forcibly removed Tiger from the club on 61st Street. Upon losing, Tiger hit the discard rack and cards flew everywhere. Despite his protestations, he was removed. Tiger associated this misfortune with Robert, the long-haired Italian guy surrounded by seductive

Korean girls. Robert's presence provoked a visceral reaction. Tiger grabbed him and yelled:

Get him out of here, he's no good, he's not one of us, ssi-bal-nom, fucking guy, gae-sae-ggi, fuck you!

Shocked at all the commotion, Mr. Sung came over and spoke to Tiger in a hushed voice:

Everything is alright, he is working for us, leave him alone.

Tiger starred at Mr. Sung, surprised at his defense of the foreigner. He loosened his grip on Robert's shirt, sulked as he drank a beer, and joined players at a different table. Making money brought respect, it brought protection, it brought power.

Money seeks for more money; power begets more power. Robert wanted more of both. The idea of independence and the idea of managing his own clubs started to percolate in his mind. He would make more money, he mused, and why not, he had a good reputation with his customers. Robert now felt a sense of independence, for he had enough of doing for others since now he could do for himself. He tired of doing side jobs requiring violence and threats of violence. Robert sought Johnny Mac's blessings. The man who gave him his start now nodded in approval with one stipulation, no stealing his customers.

Robert opened one club on 37th and 5th Ave, and another on 79th and 1st. He was buoyed by his investors who promoted him by trusting him with their personal investments. These two clubs were more upscale, as they featured a greater variety of gambling machines in a more exclusive setting. Robert's clubs now hummed with the rolling of dice, the shuffling of cards, the grating of roulette wheels, the chatter of gamblers, the clinking of cocktail glasses, and the roar of winnings in Blackjack and poker. Weed wafted through the smoky air, and the smell of liquor escaped the breaths of heavy drinkers. Scantily dressed women strutted around looking for free drinks and hook ups with the lucky winners. Everyone paraded with fashionable clothes and conspicuous jewelry that bespoke of wealth, or the appearance thereof. Even the dealers wore black slacks and white shirts, and often with matching vest. The decor of Robert's clubs was a departure of the spartan décor of Johnny Mac's clubs. No wood paneling reminiscent of a suburban finished basement, or exposed electric wiring. Contractors were paid to create an ambiance of a mini casino. Details mattered. Food was no exception. Runners picked up whatever the player wanted: lobster, steak, pasta, bulgogi (Korean beef bar-b-que), just ask and it was done.

Mob connections provided gambling instruments: cards, tables, roulette wheels, chips, chip trays, card-dispensing shoes, and drop boxes. The mob took a percentage of the take. Liquor was stolen from legitimate business and purchased at a discount. Word got out to prostitutes that these places were lucrative to their trade. Robert skillfully dipped into everything he supplied. The casino catered to anyone who gambled, for color of skin did not matter, green was the only color that truly mattered. Asians and Russians were liberal with the green, they loved to play and play until they were broke. But they always came back.

When word circulated that an afterhours locale was nearby, everyone who wanted to continue their nightly entertainment from the sports bar, strip club, or watering hole closing would make their way over. Bouncers, cabbies, and livery drivers enthusiastically disseminated information about the new club. While Johnny Mac had no problem with Robert spreading anew on his own, he had issues that Robert paid the dealers fifty dollars more per night.

You just increased the cost of me doing business. What the fuck are you doing?

Robert heard from Eddie, #2. Robert, cognizant of his faux pas, cajoled Eddie to relay to Johnny that he was sorry and gave him an envelope stuffed with two thousand dollars as compensation before a serious rift developed.

JC, I'm selling my club above Dangerfield's, you interested?

Vikki LaMotta, ex-wife of boxer Jake LaMotta, stated with the intention to arouse Robert's interest. Vikki knew Robert from her frequent gambling at various clubs. She was cognizant of his autonomy and successful launches of his new clubs. He listened as the bustle of the dealers, players, bartenders, and bouncers droned in the background as his thoughts coalesced and concluded:

This is an easy business, free money.

The business model was simple, entice partygoers of the popular comedy club Rodney Dangerfield to continue the fun by simply walking a flight of steps to the afterhours club upstairs. Food and drink were plentiful, customers could play Blackjack if they wanted or just hang out. Coke and weed were always available. The business model fit in with the upper East Side vibe, where handsome patrons with money to spare sought the thrill of games of chance while they could continue to party throughout the evening. Eddie #2 cautioned him:

Don't get involved with those guineas, it will be nothing but headaches.

Vikki had friends associated with the mob, but Robert didn't see that as a risk, but he saw this as a step-up from the usual basement or back-office club he'd been working for the last few years. This was the big stage, First Ave, Upper East Side, and this would be his for the taking. He ignored ominous warnings and came to an agreement to pay her thirty thousand dollars in cold cash up front. Another twenty thousand would be paid in cash installments for the next six to nine months. The money was given to a middle-aged man everyone called Wassel. Robert had no idea who he was, but Vikki used Wassel as a middleman and the deal was consummated.

Money rolled in at a $20-30,000 per night. Income that Robert used to fuel his own gambling habits. The club opened at four in the afternoon, and it closed by nine in the morning. Robert often closed up himself, and often left strung out from hours of cocaine, which made him paranoid as he slung an unassuming sack filled with cash over his shoulder. Matty and another bodyguard, both armed, shadowed Robert from behind as he made his way home. The club above Dangerfield's was located on 1st Avenue between 61st and 62nd Streets, while Johnny Mac and associates continued to operate his club around the corner. As promised, Robert did not steal customers. The Dangerfield clientele of yuppies and late-night partiers was different from Johnny Mac's customers, mainly working-class, hard-core gamblers. The club above Dangerfield's was attracting an educated white-collar crowd, whereas Johnny Mac's were blue collar. After several months, Robert found himself over his head trying to maintain a decorum of sophistication, exclusivity, and loyal customers. His resorted to borrowing money to cover his expenses. He usually had no intention of paying it back unless threatened.

The veneer of wealth, sophistication, and power are the false advertising of many of gamblers at after-hours clubs. The legitimate path to these positions is usually education and business acumen, culture, and influence. Most partakers of these clubs lack these attributes. Club owners, managers, bouncers, bodyguards, and bartenders were astute observers and needed to be that way in order to make money. Astute observers could quickly ascertain the sophistication of a gambler: professional, compulsive, social, or novice. They could ascertain their level of influence; did they have juice; a confidence that superseded their physical presence. Ascertain their wealth; did they acquire chips with c-notes, were they exorbitant tippers, or flash expensive clothes and jewelry. These were all tells, a conscious or sub-conscious way, one communicated. Someone's identity or moniker were equally as important as observed behaviors. Being that a gambler, dealer, or club worker rarely shared their legal name, a first name or nickname, picked or assigned were usually the only identity anyone could refer to. The anonymity of the people who work, support, and frequent these clubs inhibits any scrutiny into anyone's real background. A façade is created through rumor, whispers, and half-truths. Underestimating someone's façade in the world of big money can have deadly consequences. Robert's description of many of the characters frequenting his clubs were simple observations of physical characteristics and keen awareness of their reputation and habits.

Chinese Paul and Chinese Davy were two such characters. No one knew each other's real names, and Robert referred to certain associates by their ethnicity. Chinese Paul was a member of the White Tigers and was also a killer. Chinese Paul hung around the clubs, always seemed to have lots of cash, and was comfortable with Robert. Robert was friendly, often greeting the gamblers with a direct look in the eye, outstretched hand, and offering a,

How are ya, or *looking good; glad to see you; what can I do for you?*

Gamblers who won and felt welcome came back. Gamblers who lost but felt a bit of sympathy, came back. To the losers, Robert said,

Rough night? Don't worry about it. Come back tomorrow, you might get lucky.

These comments were a means to an end. Gamblers, no matter how much they won or lost, always meant profits for the club. Chinese Paul won and lost, but always had a good time and kept coming back. Familiarity breeds content, and when Robert shared his predicament, he skillfully convinced him to loan him $50K. A large amount of cash was needed to operate a club. If you wanted customers back, you have to pay their winnings. This required large amounts of cash on hand from a money guy who either took a cut of the profits or a loan shark to bail you out for 30% or more interest. Chinese Paul handed Robert the cash with terms of payback. Full payment with interest over six months. He wasn't someone who forgave some else's debts.

Chinese Davy was also a member of the White Tigers. He

made his money from dealing coke at various clubs. Robert let him deal coke at the Dangerfield's club. This arrangement allowed Chinese Davy another revenue stream and gave Robert access to a ready supply of coke for his personal use. But after a few months, Chinese Davy disappeared. He was delinquent on paying $35K for a kilo of coke and was found dead with hundreds of stab wounds. Chinese Paul got the contract. The White Tiger turned on the other White Tiger. Interrupt the money flow or fail to pay your debts was a deadly risk. Chinese Paul was arrested for his involvement and landed in jail. Word eventually got back to Robert that Chinese Paul wanted the remaining $25K he was owed and sent some young Chinese recruits to collect. Robert didn't know these thugs and told them to fuck off.

Tell Paul if he wants his money, come down and get it himself.

He never did. He was either dead or deported.

With the money put to good use, Robert focused on running the club, and Mink, now his partner and girlfriend, hired a few more waitresses, assuring plenty of food and drink for the customers, many of whom were Asian. Mink also hired an old lady she knew from her other massage parlors. She was no taller than five-foot-one and blinked when spoken to. She understood very little English and only nodded her head with an automatic reply, *OK*, whenever Robert tried to engage her. He ended up calling her OK Ajumma. OK Ajumma spoke Korean fluently and supplied cash to gamblers in exchange for whatever they were willing to sell. She, in essence, was a loan shark who catered to Asian customers. She amassed quite a collection of diamond rings, Rolex watches, chains, and bracelets over the years. She operated her own private exchange.

The Dangerfield club thrived. It was one thing if the club was making money but another altogether when a customer won consistently. One gambler stood out because every time he came, he walked away a winner. Sometimes he won a few hundred dollars, other times he won thousands of dollars. A spotter and a manager whispered to each other:

Wow, this guy is on a streak again, up $4000. What is he doing? He's been here the last few weeks and he's always leaving with a few thousand dollars. Something funny is going on.

One of the dealers on break pulled Robert aside,

Hey JC, you see that guy, that's the actor Jon Voight's brother, he's a professional card player.

Bullshit I don't believe it.

No, it's true, he's been here the last four weekends.

Jon Voight's brother was known as Chip Taylor. He was a native of Yonkers like Robert. Chip gained success as a musician with a trove of albums and hit singles such as *Wild Thing* and *Angel of the Morning*. He also loved to gamble and came up with a perfected a system of card counting. He won big over the years, and the legal casinos noticed; they suspected that he cheated. There were several systems of card counting that gamblers used over the years. One of the most popular was the hi-low system as described by a mathematics professor named Edward Thorp. The math professor lays out the swindling system in his book titled: *Beat the Dealer*, a book published in the early 1960s.[2] Thorp discovered that if a player were able to track the ratio of face cards left in a shoe, compared to low cards (2–6) the player had, the player had a greater probability of getting more blackjacks vs. the dealer. Chip was employing some method of card counting and his consistent winnings resulted in him being banned from every casino in Las Vegas and Atlantic City.[3,4] Chip was a calm player, didn't draw attention to himself. He was winning, having a good time, and after a few hours of playing, casually gets up from the blackjack table to cash in his chips. Robert says,

Hey, Chip, come over here, you cocksucka.

I'm sorry, don't kill me,

Chip responded in a hushed, apologetic tone.

Listen, you can't play Vegas, you can't play Atlantic City and now you come to my place and are taking money from me! What a shame. You're done. Don't ever come back here. I'll cut off your fucking arms. You'll be driving cars with your feet.

Ok, ok, I'm leaving, I'll never come back. Chip never did come back.

Months later, as Robert managed a late evening shift, a rough looking blonde with a raspy voice complained:

You're stealing from me, this club is rigged, what kind of dealers do you have here?

Vikki LaMotta came in earlier with some girlfriends and Robert had not noticed her until she spoke louder and louder. Vikki LaMotta was playing fifty dollars a game and lost big. The female dealer was high, and sloppy, and Vikki thought the whole game was rigged. After screaming at whomever was around, she went right up to Robert and accused him of running a fixed club. Robert pleaded with her, said the dealer was new, she didn't do anything. Vikki fumed; she lost ten thousand dollars. She walked out upset and accused Robert of ruining a good club. The next day, Nick Greco, a mob soldier and friend of Ken Masiello and Butchy Futia, walked in and told Robert:

Do not come in tomorrow!

Robert knew Greco through his association with a mob power broker who held power over the upper east side. Robert pleaded with him, but all Greco said was,

Too bad!

Robert knew that his club was going to get trashed, thus he made sure to remove the one arm bandits out of the club and to a safe location. He warned the grunt workers, the Korean Power *little brothers*. These grunts hung around all day and night making sure it was clean and that the Korean customers were kept in line. Unfortunately for them, they ignored Robert's warning. The following day the club was ransacked. Everything was wrecked:

tables were broken, the bar counter was shattered, glassware was smashed, rugs were torn, fixtures were cracked, and walls were crushed. Six men were seriously busted up and the ambulance rushed them to the hospital. Vikki's wrath played out and Robert paid the price. He incurred thousands of dollars' worth of damage, plus he lost many of his workers.

Within a week, the club was back in business. He borrowed money and bought new Blackjack tables, roulette wheels, and all the gambling instruments needed to operate properly. The same customers returned, happier than ever, and money streamed from purses and pockets to percussive slot machines; he was making money once again. However, he became leery of people with petty grievances, and paranoid with his own surroundings. Robert had some clout with Johnny Mac and Jimmy the boss, but this was his venture, and his alone. And that was not enough clout for an angry, vindictive woman with powerful friends.

Bang, Bang, shots rang out! Matty Dalton, Robert's childhood buddy from Yonkers, and bodyguard, ran out to the hallway and saw that Tony, the manager of the club, was pummeled by two Italian-looking men. Tony was a short tough guy, a Vietnam Vet, who managed the four to midnight shift, while Matty was the spotter eyeballing the dealer and the players making sure that no one was cheated. Tony was summoned by two guys to go out in the hallway. He saw these two goons coming around the club over the past few weeks to gamble and to drink, and Tony thought nothing of it. These two roughnecks were from Gotti's crew, and once Tony was in the hallway, they started beat the piss out of him by throwing him against the wall, pounding on his head, and kicking him all over his body. He was quickly overwhelmed, and as he tried to react to one blow to the head, two other blows came from behind in rapid succession, pounding away at him, hitting him as if he were a punching bag. Matty heard the commotion and immediately ran out to the hallway, pulled out his gun, and unleashed a couple of rounds over their heads. Just as the gun fired, Robert, who was trailing behind Matty, was struck with shrapnel below the eye. Robert's face became a mask of splattered blood that squirted directly over Tony's bashed-in face; blood spurted from his lips, nose, and scalp. The two goons, meanwhile, sprinted out as if their bodies had caught fire. After things settled down, Tony decided that he was done. He was not going to put his life in danger from some random goons determined to muscle in on someone else's gambling investment. Robert was pissed off and couldn't believe that someone had the nerve to muscle in on his enterprise. A few weeks later, as Robert managed the evening shift, a Dapper John Gotti came ambling in. Gotti sat at one of the Blackjack tables and was clearly agitated. He barked:

Whose club is this?

Robert coughed and retorted:

It's yours!

Somewhat amused, the Don slyly smirked:

I like you! You are a smart kid.

Gotti stood stern, unperturbed, as he held human life in the palm of his gentle hand. He looked around placidly as if nothing bothered him. Who would even dare challenge him? He was there to find out what the hell was going on and who had the balls to stand up to challenge his hired muscle, defy his power.

After several rounds of Blackjack, Robert looks Gotti in the eye and with a pinch of nerve said:

No disrespect, what can I do for you?

Gotti ignored the comment as he focused on his cards and his Cutty Scotch and water. He remembered Robert from the days when he played at a club on Prince Street. While playing with a few members of his crew, Gotti lost over sixty-thousand dollars. As Gotti went for a drink at the bar, Robert commented about the guy who managed the craps game:

You see that guy over there, we call him Frankie La Machine, he's a cheat, has something in his dice. No one ever wins.

Gotti angrily yelped, then stared menacingly, and with an outburst, he threatened to burn the place down. He was now shaking with ire and accused the craps dealer of cheating. The craps dealer froze still, unable to say anything at all. He simply looked down, waiting for this uncomfortable moment to vanish into his memory hole. Gotti remembered that, and just as he was about to leave, he motioned for Robert to come over. Robert was a dealer; he'd seen him around before. He looked into his eyes and in an intimidating hushed voice he uttered

You asked me what you can do, you can do this for me, my cumare *parents live in an apartment next door. Put in a security camera in the hallway—a buzzer—and a monitor in the apartment and get them a new hot water heater. Do this, I love you forever!*

He gave Robert his number, and a week later he came back to the club. The job was done. Gotti kissed him on the cheek and softly said:

I like you. Anybody gives you a problem, call me.

Gotti gave him his number on a scrap of paper. Gotti nonchalantly gave a thousand dollars for repairs and for money to pay protection for the club.

Chris was a regular who always hung around the club ready to run errands for the extra buck. He asked Robert if he could work as a doorman at Dangerfield's. Robert quickly agreed. He was untrustworthy, Robert soon discovered. When Robert attempted to open the club one evening, after a prolonged two-week break, he and Matty found that the locks on the doors had been changed. Robert fumed. He stashed one-hundred-thousand dollars in the safe, and now he saw red, and like a bull, he wished to gore the culprit. Within days they discovered who orchestrated the takeover. It was an old man named Wassel. This aging hustler was attempting to take over the club. Chris, who was paid by Wassel, was scoping out the club for months in his capacity as doorman. Chris informed Wassel about the large amount of cash rolled in day after day and reinforced that the club was a lucrative enterprise. As part of the terms with the previous owner, Vikki LaMotta, to take ownership of the club, Robert was supposed to make installment payments to Wassel. Robert did for a while but stopped. He now suspected that Wassel was the man behind the switched locks.

Wassel was a music producer. He was Bert Bern's partner who produced Van Morrison's first hit song Brown Eyed Girl in the late 1960s. Wassel was also prone to violence. There was a well-publicized story about Wassel smashing an acoustic guitar over Van Morrison's head and throwing Tiny Tim off a boat in the Hudson River.[5,6] Chris was pounded to submission, and under threat of death revealed where Wassel lived on Central Park West. Robert and Matty circled the block a few times before finding the building. When they casually entered the empty foyer, Matty spotted the balding doorman and impassively accosted him with the pretext of wanting to go to the bathroom. The balding doorman came near Matty to tell him that the bathroom was for tenants only. Matty quickly pulled out his handgun and pointed the barrel of the gun to the temple of the shaken doorman. Matty growled:

Listen, you piece of shit. Tell me before I blow your head, what floor is Wassel on? Take a deep breath and tell me.

The doorman hyperventilated and could not spit-out the words. Matty, still with the gun pointed at the temple growled again:

Listen, motherfucka, you tell me now or I'll blow your head off.

The quaking doorman took a hefty breath and blurted:

He's on the 72nd floor.

Matty and Robert flew on to the last floor and burst into Wassel's apartment. Matty looked stone-faced. He took a deep breath and kicked the door wide open. They grabbed Wassel and stuck his head in the oven. Robert turned the gas on, Wassel screamed and cursed and gagged, but refused to answer any questions. Matty grabbed Wassel, dragged the chocking man to the balcony and hung him over the balcony railing. Wassel screamed, and as Matty's hands tired, Robert grabbed him and lifted him back up. Convinced that these guys meant business, Wassel turned over the keys, and they never heard from him again.

Robert's debts piled up as he owed a guy two-hundred-and-fifty-thousand dollars. Bobby Glasses liked the Dangerfield Club. He gambled there several times and noticed that it was a lucrative business opportunity. The Dangerfield Club, as it started to be called on the street, had a good reputation as an afterhours club, although it had no financial relationship with the Dangerfield Comedy Club or Rodney Dangerfield himself. Bobby Glasses, who owned several coffee shops in Queens as fronts for his own illegal clubs, put the word out that he would like to meet JC. Robert met him months earlier when he was dealing at another club but had no idea who he was.

Bobby Glasses often sat at the table where Robert was dealing. Robert knew that Bobby had money, but nothing more, he just appeared to be a regular gambler, a high roller who played with gusto; no one ever connected him to the mob. Both men had the urge to relieve themselves and as Bobby stood at the urinal contemplating his mini empire of gambling dens, Robert pulls out next to him and attempts some small talk. Robert, every bit the chatterbox, but with an ulterior motive, floats out the idea about his need for some extra money. The club wasn't as profitable as he would like, and he needed money for some repairs for his apartment. Bobby Glasses acknowledged times were tough and said good luck.

The following day, the manager approached Robert, handed him a sealed envelope and matter of factly said:

This is from Bobby.

Robert smirked: great, free money to gamble with, and off he went to Atlantic City he fled. Several weeks lapsed and Robert had no intention of paying back Bobby. He gambled away the money, and nothing was left. He wasn't going to pay back a middle-aged man with glasses. If he asked for the money back, he would have told him to fuck himself. What the hell could he do. Bobby Glasses made his way over to the club, and while ambling around, finally spotted Robert coming out of the back office and motioned him to go outside. As they stepped out into the sidewalk, Bobby sucker punched him in the right cheek while he demanded his money. It was a shot across the brow. Robert recoiled! He was blindsided, never expecting to be challenged. Robert gathered himself as he clenched his fists, ready to throw a right and left to his face. He withheld. He froze both his fists and his tongue. He finally figured out that there was more to Bobby Glasses and that he was no push-over. He mustered a weak response; he apologized and said the money would be coming soon.

Several days later, Robert was informed that he needed to attend a meeting: *A sit down* at SPQR Restaurant on Mulberry Street. A Bronx cap named LoCascio will be there as well as a nephew of a capo. These men of honor barked at him:

What the fuck are you doing, not paying Bobby? You disrespected him. He could have you fucking wacked. What's the matter with you?

Robert was jittery. The four cups of espresso and snort of coke he did in the restroom compounded his anxiety. Despite his nervousness, Robert made light of it, saying with a little chuckle:

Look, everyone knows I'm a gambler, you don't lend me money.

They laughed, knowing he pissed away thousands of dollars by gambling on a weekly basis. Several men told Bobby Glasses that J.C. respected him by not retaliating. One of his henchmen said:

He's six-foot-two, 260lbs of muscle, and you are recovering from open heart surgery, he could have killed you, we think that punch is worth five-thousand dollars.

Bobby looked a little embarrassed and a little bothered, but in his own way, he respected the codes of the street that he lived by. Bobby bowed to ancient laws of honor and accepted the apology. Robert paid him back within two weeks, and there were no ill feelings.

Bobby Glasses was a shrewd operator, and he smelled opportunities like a bloodhound smelled his prey. He figured that Robert had potential with his various clubs, and he should strike while the iron was hot. He reasoned that if he supplied slot machines to Robert, he would make a bundle of money in the fertile Eastside territory. With these Eastside clubs, Robert could safely make money, and the slot machines would provide additional gaming revenue for his clubs. Robert didn't know Bobby Glasses well, but he asked around and found out that Bobby was an associate of the Gambino family. He looked like an ordinary businessman who sported large, rimmed glasses that gave him a muted aura. His thinning hair made him more distinct, but his thick Italian accent contradicted his physical appearance. After finally meeting, the deal was sealed over a cup of coffee and cigarettes at a restaurant on First Ave. Bobby Glasses gave Robert fifty-thousand dollars on five separate occasions to supply gambling machines for his clubs; Robert would pay him back over time plus twenty percent of the take; Robert would keep the rest. In his arrogance, Robert decided not to pay. His profits from the club were not as expected and he also gambled away much of his earnings. He had no allegiance to this mild-mannered looking businessman, so he thought to himself.

Fuck him, I'm not paying.

That was a bad move.

Bobby Glasses wasn't the type to walk away from his money, nor was he afraid of confrontations; he relished the opportunity to flex his muscles to teach his enemy a lesson. Bobby Glasses was not just some mild-mannered Gambino associate that left the rough stuff to someone else. He was a feared, powerful man not to be reckoned with. His real name was Bartolomeo Vernace, and he was a murderer. Bobby Glasses and fellow mob boss Frank Ricciardi were involved with two notorious murders back in 1981. Known as the Shamrock Murders, John D'Agnese and Richard Godkin, the owners of the Shamrock Bar in the Woodhaven, Queens, were shot dead following a dispute over a spilled drink. At two in the morning, on an April evening, Ricciardi was tossed out of the bar after reacting crazily to his girlfriend's displeasure over a drink that was accidently spilled on her. He returned twenty minutes later with the reinforcement of Bobby Glasses. D'Agnese was shot-point blank in the face, and Godkin was mortally wounded as he tried to intervene.[7] Bobby Glasses went into hiding for years but still expected payments through his associates. Months later, after not paying any money back to Bobby Glasses, Robert learned that a hit was put out on him. The pressure started to mount; he partied more than ever but didn't have a good time. He became more paranoid and anxious, as his debts mounted, and fear of retribution hung over his head like a pall. Illegal clubs were getting busted by the cops as Rudy Guiliani cleaned up organized crime. Robert paid off his lawyer to take care of the fines and keep him out of jail. But now he had no way to pay off Bobby Glasses. He needed to get out of town and regroup. He received word that a connected guy from Westchester wanted to buy his club. The word came from dealers he knew from 26th St. Linda and Stan were Westchester natives and knew the owners of several gambling and sport betting clubs in Yonkers and New Rochelle. A guy named Butch Cuzzo, a Lucchese associate from New Rochelle, was interested.[8] Butch's club manager Paulie made the exchange of one hundred-thousand dollars in cold cash. This Westchester guy Butch amassed a lot of money through his clubs in and around Westchester. This transaction was his first foray into Manhattan business. Butch was arrested in 1960 for "parking without lights" in Yonkers. A term the City Judge used to fine young people for parking cars to "neck" or to get intimate.[9] This arrest came a year after he was arrested for running a dice game when he was seventeen-years old.[10] The early arrests were innocuous if contrasted with the arrests in 2009 where he was locked up, along with eighteen others, for racketeering, illegal gambling, sports betting, loan sharking, and bribery as part of a RICO indictment.

With all these headaches, miscalculations and squandered opportunities, Robert thought about what Mink had said when he started to complain of his troubles:

You got the muscle, and I got the girls. Let's go to Michigan and open a massage parlor.

Now was the time to move on and cut his losses. He jumped at the chance. He knew he had a hit on him and couldn't take the pressure of constantly looking over his shoulder, so he bolted with the idea that if he could make some money and slowly pay off his debts, he could expunge the hit on him and eventually come back to NY.

Chapter 14

Physical maturity is bound to time. Spiritual maturity is bound to obedience.

—John Bevere

Robert's move to Michigan was a result of a culmination of decisions he had made over the previous twelve years. He was driven by his desire to make money, feed his gambling habits and support his licentiousness. His lifestyle was so completely different from those of his parents. He was an enigma, a black sheep who lost his way from his roots. He never adhered to his family values of hard work and an honest way of life. He was a law unto himself. He circumvented rules and regulations at will. His romantic affairs were fluid as he flowed from the arms of one woman to the arms of another, seeking satisfaction for his own needs. His defiance of the law bespoke of a frayed morality. His life in the mob world showed his indifference to his own wellbeing. Michigan was his chance to start over, free of anxiety, free of uncertainty, and free of threats. It did not quite work out that way.

My decisions over the last eight years also brought about a transformation. My reckless behavior in high school and college was interrupted by a spiritual awakening. I took life seriously and developed a personal work ethic that never existed before. I made a conscious effort to mirror what I read in scripture. A verse from Paul's letter to the Colossians perfectly describes the purposefulness of my intent and actions.

> *Whatever you do, work at it with all your heart, as working for the Lord and not for men.*
>
> COLOSSIANS 3:23

I was hopeful, feeling confident that God had my best interests at heart. I knew I needed to depart from my past behaviors and attitudes and knew that my spiritual growth would be a work in progress. My decision and commitment to grow in my faith became a priority. My values were changing. I was being transformed as stated so beautifully in a verse from Paul's letter to the Romans.

> *Do not be conformed to this world, but be transformed by the renewal of your mind ...*
>
> ROMANS 12:2

The effects of smoking marijuana, doing drugs and binge drinking had taken its toll. But the foggy haze and mental bewilderment dissipated and was replaced with lucidity and purpose.

The friendship with the girl I first glanced at on the upper quad and formally met at a bible study grew into love. Within four months of graduation, we were engaged. In December of 1983 I returned from the diamond district in New York City and presented my fiancée with an engagement ring. I had a mere four dollars left in my bank account. Without money, a car, or employment, we set forth without much of a plan. The only plan was that whatever we did, we would do together. A year and half later after that stroll on the upper quad we were beginning to build our careers, settled into an apartment, found a place to worship, and started our life's journey together. My degree in psychology did not lead to a well-charted career path unless I wanted to pursue graduate courses and that was out of the question. I worked several jobs through Kelly Services, an employment agency, to bankroll my basic needs. Adriane was an English major, and she was well qualified to pour coffee for lawyers at a law firm in NYC. We continued to meander professionally for several years until we seized on opportunities we had not envisioned.

For the short term we were slowly making adjustments to find work and save enough money. Growth in our spiritual lives was supported by bible studies under the stewardship of Jon Cahn, and being taught, and entertained, by Pastor Charlie Rizzo at Maranatha Church of the Nazarene, who brought the scriptures to life and had a great sense of humor. We searched for Christian radio programs that were contemporary, avoiding fire and brimstone preachers, overly emotional Pentecostal evangelists, and dry mid-western story tellers. A friend mentioned a program called: *A New Beginning with Greg Laurie.* We learned that Greg Laurie's ministry was forming a church in New York City called Harvest Christian Fellowship. It was located within easy reach of Brooklyn and Pearl River, where Adriane and I each lived, respectively, and we grew increasingly comfortable and involved.

My father had misgivings about Jon Cahn's bible studies, and he balked at the idea of me attending Born Again Churches. He viewed them to be nothing but brainwashing cults. When I showed him the scripture of Jesus' own words to the Pharisee, Nicodemus, and further examples of the need to be born of the Spirit, he discarded it all, asserting that Baptism had taken care all of that. He did not accept any teachings from scripture that was not sanctioned by the authority of the Catholic Church. My father argued that I should immerse myself with the doctrines of Catholicism instead of studying the Bible led by some Jewish kid. He rebuked me for encouraging my younger brothers to attend church services or bible studies not under the authority of the Catholic Church. I vehemently disagreed, arguing that I was learning more about scripture and Christian living and was better off than I ever had been. My father was agitated when I urged my brother Paul to attend a Good Friday service at Maranatha and bitterly told me to mind my own business. I challenged my father's reasoning, questioning why he would support Paul's barhopping on Good Friday instead of hearing a gospel message. My father was cavalierly dismissive, claiming Paul had his own religion. I was reconciling the emotional roller coaster that was swimming in my mind: for years I did drugs; I was expelled from college campus; I barely eked out a college degree, but now finally I was getting my act together, and the one important thing that reversed my life was somehow not worth sharing with my brother. How disappointing it all seemed. With just a little prodding Paul would have joined me and experienced a contemporary gospel teaching with people he could relate to. Instead, Paul was stepping onto a path I recently departed, the path of carefree partying. My Father, not a student of the Bible, felt alien to all religions other than Roman Catholicism; he could not be objective. I never understood his unwillingness to consider scripture teachings apart from the Catholic Church. From his perspective, I should never have switched to another religion, especially if I had been more serious and more attentive during Sunday Mass.

His attitude softened over the years as I liked to believe he saw the positive changes in my life. But he never acknowledged my explanation for my transformation. While he would directly acknowledge my success, he would imply it with an off-handed sarcastic remark,

What took you so long?

I always laughed when he made that comment and found it incredible that he could not make the connection that my good fortune went hand in hand with my spiritual transformation. One Thursday evening in 1984 my father called me over and pointed to a newspaper article.

Jim, Jim, take a look at this article, your cousin is doing what you are into, maybe you should call him.

My father showed me an article from the local newspaper, it was Section C of the *Journal News*, the people's section. Half the page was dedicated to my cousin. It read:

The Good News family returns to Rockland.[1]

As I read the article, I immediately recognized the last name of the person featured in the article. It was Berlingeri. I asked how we were related, and he mentioned that Richard was the son of his cousin Vincent, therefore he was my second cousin. I had no idea that I had a second cousin. My father explained that Richard's grandfather Benjamin was his mother Lina Berlingeri's brother. Vincent and his family moved from the Bronx and settled in Valley Cottage, NY. My father wasn't close with his cousins, so we never knew much about them and to what extent they communicated over the years. They exchanged Christmas cards and notified each other of milestone events in the extended family, births, marriages, and deaths. I did reach out to Richard and his wife Betty, and we agreed to meet at his parents' house. After some small talk, I asked what church he was affiliated with, and I discovered that they were itinerant preachers not affiliated with any church. They travelled around the world with their young son and soon to be new baby and shared the gospel. They depended on the generous support of others. I informed him how I became involved with Maranatha and how I regularly attended a bible study. I invited them both to the next meeting at a friend's house in Tallman, NY. Richard Berlingeri attended a few times, and the attendees were eager to learn about his ministry. There was a soft sell on his part as he asked for support, and while most of the people who attended were pleasant and asked questions, they didn't have much expendable cash to support ministries outside of their local church. Richard did eventually travel to Turkey, and I received some letters of his activities, but eventually we lost touch. My father never met Richard. But he was intrigued with his convictions and fascinated that he could pick up with his wife and young children and travel around the world with not much of a plan, depending on the generosity of others. It was the very opposite of his views on risk taking. He certainly didn't think this was a vocation that he wanted me involved with. I assured him that I had no intention of doing what my cousin did anyway. I envisioned marriage, family, a stable home life, and a solid means to support myself. Naturally, these ideas were somewhat abstract at the time, and I had no real short-term plan.

My mom, Nan, had returned to teaching full time in the early 1980's after her kids were almost out of high school. She loved the teaching profession, and viewed it as a calling, as a mission to impart social values such as punctuality, responsibility, respect, loyalty, and hard work. She didn't lecture about morality, she didn't believe in preaching a sermon, she led by example. She believed in hard work, accountability, discipline, independence and educating young minds. She eagerly returned and reconnected with other teachers and instantly embraced her students as members of her school family.

Her new income allowed her to spend her earnings the way she wanted. Within months, she refurnished the living room with new rugs, a large casement window, solid oak wall unit, abstract designer wallpaper in the kitchen, and new minimalist furniture known as Danish modern. Mom was pouring her earnings into the house and enjoying it, much to the chagrin of my father who thought the money should be used for household expenses. Mom was having none of that. She summarily rejected this spartan notion of essentials only. Why deny simple amenities? Why live in stark surroundings without things that turn a house into a home? She was tired of Pop's depression-era attitude toward money: Spend as little as possible. It was her own money, and she would spend it as she liked. While Dad was no longer going to have much of a say in financial matters, he had even less to say when Robert became the topic of discussion a few months later.

The school year was nearing an end in the late spring of 1984, the teachers retreated into the teachers' lounge one last time before the official end of the day. Everyone was in a convivial mood. As fellow teacher, Charlie, read the *Journal News*, he burst out in laughter and joked about Nan's mafia connections. Friends and colleagues with non-Italian ethnicity occasionally teased her because of her last name, and even more so when they learned that her mother-in-law hailed from Corleone, now an infamous city in Sicily popularized by the *Godfather* movies.

Hey, this is good, Nan seems to be in the money. Nan, hope you are going to share in the profits, better yet, drinks are on Nan tonight.

Everyone chuckled and perked up while waiting to hear what he was talking about. He read the article out loud:

A Bronx man charged with possessing more than five-thousand dollars in gambling records faces a hearing today in the Ramapo Justice Court. Robert Fabio was arrested Sunday in a Suffern motel room where police were investigating a disturbance involving a man and woman … Fabio … is charged with felonious possession of gambling records … Police say the records appeared to be from a policy (numbers) operation and the investigation is continuing …[2]

Charlie and the others had no idea that Robert was Nan's nephew, and she never imagined that she would be related to someone charged with gambling. To Charlie, this was playful teasing of a colleague, but to Mom this was surreal.

My mother knew this was no joke. Her nephew was arrested, and now she was grist for the mill. She absorbed the innuendos that came with this insidious banter. She maintained a dignified posture, as she had no other recourse. But her facial expressions revealed her true disgust. Her ears tweaked slightly back, similar to when a Doberman pincher's ears stand upright when excited. Her lips tightened and her gaze became intense. She was irritated, she abruptly left the lounge. Until now no one truly knew that she was related to this Robert Fabio mentioned in the daily newspaper, but now they knew. My father got an earful at dinner.

What is wrong with your family? I have never been so embarrassed in all my life.

She lamented, totally disgusted. My father shrugged his shoulders, but what could he do? They didn't talk about this article with their boys and hoped that time would remove this from everyone's consciousness. Mom's circle of friends were sympathetic to her embarrassment and no one broached the topic. I didn't read the newspapers, and none of my friends ever mentioned anything and knew nothing of this incident until I began to research and validate Robert's escapades.

The story behind the newspaper article is just as alarming and Robert recalled it in explicit detail. At the time, he had an apartment in the Bronx. His parents recently moved from Yonkers to Suffern in Rockland County and while visiting he had no interest in staying with them. He opted to pay $190 a night, cash, at the Holidome Hotel near exit 14a off the New York State Thruway. He was making money hand over fist, dealing, running sports betting rings, and earning big money from the clubs, so this was a convenient arrangement.

That summer evening Mink and Robert were drunk, tired, and arguing about money—or rather, poor money management—as his gambling habits often left them with little expendable cash. He screamed in her face and pushed her around. She was scared that Robert was out of control and managed to call 911. Mink knew how to fight. She trained in karate, and she used her prowess to swiftly kick Robert in the face. He stumbled, lost his balance, and crashed backward to a wall. Blood spurted from his nose and from his mouth. He thought his nose was broken; blood was everywhere. Instinctively, he reacted like he did with so many street fights and boxing matches, he threw a right jab that landed squarely on her left cheek and jaw. Pow! Mink keeled over, writhing in pain upon impact, and fell to the carpeted floor. Robert didn't think he hit her hard but down she was. Her facial tint turned from a reddish hue to blue as blood settled under her skin. Mink spoke incoherently in Korean, slipping in and out of consciousness. Worried that he had seriously injured her, he rushed to Good Samaritan hospital a few miles down the road on Route 59. Mink was released after an hour. As they exited the ER the police were waiting just outside. Robert was immediately arrested and was taken to the Ramapo jail. The 911 call Mink had placed from the hotel room spurred the police to coerce the hotel manager to let them in. Finding it empty except for mysterious blood stains, they searched the hotel room. Robert was charged with felony possession of 300 betting cards, gambling records, five-thousand dollars cash, and some marijuana. He called his lawyer and explained that he was at the police station but was unclear if he was officially arrested. His lawyer told him to hang up the phone and walk out. As he walked out, he was surrounded by eight police officers who were yelling with their guns pointed at his face:

Hey, where do you think you're going?

He was brought back in and interrogated.

What family do you work for? ... Whose money is this? ... Why are you here?

This went on for a few hours. He remained silent, didn't say a thing. Mink refused to press charges. Bail was set at ten-thousand dollars. He cajoled his father, Jack, to go drive from Suffern to the club above Dangerfield's and get some money from one of the managers. Upset but loyal to his son, Jack did as requested. Robert was out on bail but had to make court appearances for the next six months. His lawyer argued that there was an illegal search and seizure, even though the prosecutor said they were answering a 911 call. When they knocked on the door and there was no answer, they assumed the worst. Robert plead guilty to possession of gambling records and marijuana. He paid a seven-hundred and fifty dollars fine. He received his cards back and a check for fifteen-thousand dollars.[3]

I had not seen my cousin in eight years, so when he and an Asian woman randomly showed up at my house, I was quite surprised. It was mid-afternoon on this Saturday in early summer and I was the only one home at the time. Upon hearing the doorbell, I went down to open it up thinking it was someone soliciting for donations as I was not expecting any of my friends at that time. Standing there was Robert, who I heartly greeted with a handshake while he muttered his companion's name, Mink. We went up to the kitchen and I asked if they wanted something to eat or drink. I asked Robert a series of matter-of-fact questions:

How's it going? ... What are you up to? ... Where are you working?

Robert didn't respond to my weak inquiries and retorted:

You look good. Fabio's are good looking guys.

I'm good cuz, just painting. How are you? How's college? How's your brothers? How's Uncle Paul, Aunt Nan.

These rapid-fire questions were not uttered with the intent to learn anything, just perfunctory banter. No matter what answer I gave, he responded with,

That's good, or *Oh, God Bless.*

Robert arrived with Mink with the intention of meeting with my parents, Nan and Paul—his aunt and uncle. Robert stood at least a foot taller than Mink and he did all the talking. She did not utter a word and never gave me direct eye contact, which I thought strange, but then I assumed it was some Asian custom. I perceived that Mink was a little older than Robert. She looked more weathered than him. I felt the duty to ask if they wanted something to drink. I motioned to them to sit down around the large walnut-stained table that dominated the kitchen. They watched observantly as I put down some glasses, offered them beer and whatever crackers we had laying around in the pantry. Robert and Mink simply sat looking around, and finally offered,

Wow, you're a good host.

My parents were not home at the time, and I had no clue as to when they were coming home. They sat for a little bit but didn't touch a thing, decided they were not going to wait, and in fifteen minutes they were gone. Robert wanted to introduce Mink to my parents, but he never got the chance. I assumed he was living in Westchester County and was perplexed as to why they would make the trek to Rockland County without assurance that his aunt and uncle would be home. This was the height of impatience. But this rationale somehow didn't work for me. There was more to it than meets the eye. When my parents returned home closer to dinnertime, I shared with them their nephew's unannounced visit. My father was not surprised with his nephew's lack of planning and impetuous behavior. He knew more about Robert's history than he was willing to reveal. His reaction of tightening his lips and lowering his head while moving it left to right a few times said it all. The unspoken word spoke volumes. Robert was not living up to his potential. He was a disappointment. While my father knew his nephew was completely irresponsible, he had no clue of his involvement with organized crime. He would never find out. Robert not only left my house in haste, now he was leaving New York. With cash problems at his clubs, and nonsense with the Ramapo police, he and Mink were ready for a move and off they were to Battle Creek, Michigan.

Late in the summer of 1984, my career and Adriane's career were beginning to blossom. Marriage plans took a back seat to finding employment. I found work as a manufacturer's sales representative. I ordered products and serviced electric departments in home centers such as Channel, Rickel, and Pergament. For six months I travelled with a couple of colleagues throughout the Southeast setting up electrical departments in retail home centers, learning the products and department configuration. By the spring I was promoted to Sales/Service Representative managing a sales territory in New York City and Long Island. Adriane's prospects were more limited, as she was an English major and the pickings were slim. But she found a job as a Girl-Friday. She now worked for Otterboug & Steiner, but not as a lawyer or a paralegal, but mainly as a sort of barista who poured coffee for demanding lawyers. She hated it, but her options for work were limited; she needed the money, and this provided some income until she figured out her next move.

Our faith was paramount to us, and we sought to encourage one another in the faith while also being of service in the local church. Adriane still lived in Brooklyn with her parents, and it made sense for us to meet halfway on Sundays, hence we attended Harvest Christian Fellowship on W. 56th Street. It was a difficult choice because practicality overruled our love for Maranatha. Harvest, as we called it, was closely aligned with another California ministry called Calvary Chapel whose pastor was Chuck Smith. Pastor Chuck was nationally known for his outreach to hippies in the late 1960s and early 1970s. This unique religious awakening in California and throughout the US was documented in an article in *Time* magazine called "The Jesus Revolution."[4,5] Church plantings of Harvest Christian Fellowship were happening all over the country, and the New York based ministry started soon after an outreach in NYC that was advertised through Greg Laurie's radio program titled, *A New Beginning*. We listened to this program and loved its teachings. The pastor leading this new congregation was former Hoboken native, Mike Finizio. He was most welcoming, greeting everyone with a large smile, that matched his enthusiasm for the gospel and his flock. The people attending Harvest were friendly, hospitable, and down to earth. They were a cross-pollination of young and old, of mixed ethnicities and mixed income, to a certain degree different from Maranatha which mainly attracted a white suburban congregation. Congregants who attended Harvest, like Maranatha, did not attend out of obligation but were intent for deeper biblical knowledge and a deeper personal experience with Jesus. And while many attendees were just curious or wanted to be part of a movement advertised by a radio program, sincere and devote congregants filled the sanctuary on Sundays and at mid-week bible studies. This was a far cry from my personal experience with the Catholic Church and my family's attitude to church attendance. Church for us was an obligation, and the lessons learned on Sunday mornings or afternoon religion classes didn't seem to apply to our everyday lives. Going to church to *get it over with* certainly exemplified my attitude of church attendance.

It was 1985 and I finally marched to the altar to marry Adriane. I was the first to tie the knot out of all my brothers. The general feeling was that we were crazy young kids with no money, no set careers, and lots of college debt. It didn't matter to us that we had limited resources, we were in love and whatever adventures and challenges we were going to face we would be together. We belonged to a church without a building, but one with a deep foundation. The sanctuary was set up in a rented a studio from the Joffrey Ballet Company. The idea of exchanging vows in an unappealing rehearsal studio surrounded by mirrors, and balance bars, did not fit in with our vision of in a solemn venue. We had to find a church to rent, and one that would also allow our Pastor to officiate. We recruited Adriane's mother, Dottie, who found a Unitarian church in Staten Island, an alluring, traditional dark oak wood building with high cathedral ceiling, rich, wooden pews, formal altar, and stunning stain glass windows.

We planned for a June wedding, and Pastor Mike agreed to officiate. My parents were not very happy that we were not getting married in the Catholic Church, and I think they were quite insulted that we were not following the path that everyone else in the family did. We weren't attending Mass and did not feel connected in any way to the Catholic church. I had many heated discussions with my parents and their opinion that I was betraying my religious heritage. We tried to convey that Jesus would be at the center of our marriage and that the rituals of the Catholic Church did not appeal to us or motivate us. But we were consenting adults, and though we wished to propitiate our parents, we were free to follow our own choice to practice our faith.

Mike delivered a thoughtful and solemn sermon. Our wedding guests, our extended families, and our dear friends listened attentively. Not everyone could attend, and I wasn't too surprised that Robert wasn't there. I heard through the grapevine that he was in Michigan running his massage parlor, but I believed that it was a mere alibi that he concocted. A reception followed at the Mandalay Catering Hall which had all the amenities that were suitable for our needs: great food, beautiful venue, and easy parking. We were meticulous when it came to selecting the wedding band as there were many choices. We hired a wedding planner who alerted us to see this one band play at a ceremony in Freehold, NJ. We loved the energy and contemporary vibe they displayed. The band comprised a great lead singer backed by full band, which included a fantastic saxophone player. They easily transitioned from rock 'n' roll, to rhythm and blues, pure jazz, and romantic ballads. Our wedding guests frenzied over the music, although some eyebrows were raised when the lead vocalist started belting out

I've been born again, I've been born again.

There was a change in the air, a disquietude that was slightly visible, especially in the faces of my parents whose smiles now appeared to be forced, after all, social impressions were paramount, especially at something as monumental as a wedding. The moment lingered, as if forever. But, once the social tremor was over, smiles returned, dancing continued, and the sounds of laughter merged with the music. My aunt Jerry was a bundle of joy and her infectious energy roused others to dance with abandon, to improvise moves, to sway their hips, to create steps based on the beat of the drums, and to absorb the rhythms in the air. My father-in-law remained aloof, and the song selections grew louder. He stood right in front of the band, spread his legs apart, and stared down the band leader as if to a duel. He later exchanged words with the musician. He complained about the high voltage of the music, the deafening volume, the shrill brass, and the booming percussion. The band leader pushed right back saying:

You can't just lower the music!

Ricky Vella, my father-in-law, was a retired cop hailing from Brooklyn's 61st Precinct. He was a feisty man, one who tolerated no back-talk from anyone, especially a hired hand such as a band leader. I felt a little uncomfortable having to mediate between the sax player and my new father-in-law. Two grown men stared down each other like dogs ready to tear each other apart. I stepped in and told Ricky I would take care of it. Eventually everything calmed down when the band switched their repertoire to softer, melodic music.

We honeymooned in the archipelago of Bermuda. Adriane and I loved to sunbathe in those pink, sandy beaches overlooking the crystalline, cerulean waters of Church Bay. We rented scooters and traversed the shoreline along the serpentine, narrow roads. And drank in the breathtaking vista of pastel-colored houses as we meandered toward the lighthouse overlooking the tranquil seascape below. Restaurants had a definite English flavor, featuring fresh fish prepared to perfection, while offering classics like Beef Wellington. Our life together started in this paradisiacal setting. And then we returned to our basement apartment in North Flushing, Queens. My cousin, Joey Fabio, knew the neighborhood intimately, having many apartment listings through his real estate business in the area. The apartment we settled in was created from dividing up a one-family attached house converted into three separate living spaces. This was a far cry from my suburban existence of a big backyard, a quiet street, and plenty of living space. But my wife who grew up in an attached house in the Flatlands section of Brooklyn and no trouble adjusting to her new living conditions. After several months, Adriane decided that pouring coffee for lawyers was an insult to her intelligence. She learned about career opportunities as a librarian and enrolled at St. John's University to pursue a Master of Library Science. This degree opened doors like she could never fathom. When Adriane finally finished her studies and graduated with a 4.0 GPA, she became the object of my parents' praise. My parents valued education, and this earned respect as never before. They privately told me that she would be getting Grandma Lina's wedding ring, which had been passed down to my mother as recognition for being the most educated of all the females amongst the Fabio's.

My Uncle Jack had a different set of values. They valued hard work, respect, and money. They respected Mink, for she proved to be generous whenever she visited Jack and Margie. She charitably gave them one-hundred dollars every time she visited them, a much-appreciated gesture. She didn't speak English well, so Robert would interject and explain that is the way she showed respect. Mink valued the older generation which her parents instilled before they died years before back in Korea. Jack loved that kind of respect. He thought, good, they are making money and now they are going to Michigan to start a business.

My son the businessman!

Jack boasted. Robert's Uncle "D," his mother's brother, yelled at Jack:

He's not going to Michigan to run any business, he's running from the Gambino's, he owes them big money.

Uncle "D" was a union man, a delegate with the Teamsters, and word circulated that Robert's gambling and debts were causing problems in managing the Dangerfield club. Jack refused to believe that Robert was running from anyone. He was a card dealer, a low-level dealer at best, how could he know the Gambino's, or even be in trouble with them?

Robert's new adventure in Michigan began with a night in jail. He arrived in late July, and was pulled over by the cops the next day:

Officer why are you pulling me over?

The officer sternly retorted:

You made an illegal left turn from the middle lane. License and registration.

Robert, slightly perturbed:

Um, I just arrived from New York and must have misplaced them.

Officer, still temperamentally:

Son, are you telling me you have no license and no registration?

Robert, beginning to sound annoyed, intoned:

It's my girlfriend's car.

Now the officer spoke a little louder:

So, where is the registration?

Robert suppressed his annoyance:

I guess she has it.

The officer, now with a smidge of irritation:

Does your girlfriend have your driver's license?

Robert, feeling the heat:

I guess she does.

Now the officer, dripping with sarcasm:

Can you answer me this son? When you are in New York, do you drive with a driver's license and registration?

At this point, Robert suppressed a manifest anger:

Yes, of course.

Now, the laconic officer in a Clint Eastwood tone:

Well, son, it is no different here in Michigan. And if you don't have a driver's license and registration, you are not allowed to drive. Step out of the car, please.

Robert now burst into a rage:

Motherfucka now what?

Now the officer figured that he had him in a bind:

Excuse me, what did you say?

Robert needed to calm down before things got out of hand:

Um, sorry officer, I um, I need to call my girlfriend.

The tall officer broadened his smirk, totally self-satisfied:

Ok, son, step out of the vehicle, you cannot drive this car, it will be impounded, and you can make a call to the station.

Now Robert's temperature reached fever pitch:

Fuck me, fuck this.

Robert yelled out of control, raising and shaking his arms and hands in frustration. At the station he phoned several times with no answer. Mink was at a meeting with a girlfriend and didn't get home until the next morning. The red light on the answering machine was blinking. Mink didn't see Robert's car and once the red light caught her attention, she pushed the black play key button and listened to her partner's tremulous voice:

Mink, Mink, where the fuck are you? I'm at the police station and they will not let me leave, get the fuck over here!

Five messages with increased anger and agitation. Mink called over, got the address, and went to the bank for money to bail him out.

Mink was not kidding when she said to Robert:

I have the girls.

She had a long relationship with Mister Yu, a Chinese businessman who ran import/export businesses, massage parlors, and restaurants in New York's Chinatown and in Flushing Queens. Mister Yu provided female therapists for these ubiquitous massage parlors. Mink also had connections with desperate Korean girls who wanted to come to the United States. Many of these hopeless women came to marry American men who sought a bride for a fee but divorced soon after. The now divorced Korean woman ineligible to work legally found massage parlors easy money until they could establish themselves independently.

Robert and Mink's first massage parlor was called King's Garden. They bought the establishment for sixty thousand dollars from Mister Yu. They bought the massage parlor sight unseen, not knowing the structural shape of the place, and the necessary cosmetic overhauls. Robert hired contractors to put up a new sign, rip up rugs, put in new sheet rock, and install a sauna, massage tables, and showers. Robert applied new paint and made sure curtains were used for the womens room instead of doors. Mink secured the girls through her connections. Ten girls worked at a time. There was a total of thirty girls who worked throughout the week. Each girl had her own room with a single bed, a side table, and lamp. They performed massages, offered extra-curricular activities, and set their own rates. The lease was in Mink's name, and she managed the girls and made sure they were clean and cooperative. Robert worked up front and collected an entrance fee, did the laundry, and took care of the kitchen and lounge area. And when the girls were bored, they played a Korean card game called Go-Stop, or *Hwatu*. Mink implored him not to take the girl's money when he won, so he opted to gamble for their clothes. Once, Mink returned to find Robert surrounded by a group of massage girls in various states of nudity and undress as they giggled saying,

JC is winning!

His presence in the neighborhood caused a stir, not from normal businessmen, but from the "gentleman" who owned the adult bookstore, a massage parlor and bar down the street. Two men with shotguns walked in one afternoon while he opened up. One said:

Who the fuck are you? My family has been here two-hundred years, you can't just come in here, we'll blow you away.

Robert was clearly out of his element and said,

Listen, I'm from NY, they call me JC, I'm an associate of John Gotti. Call him!

After they cursed him out and threatened him, they left. Robert had John Gotti's number and call they did.

Don't touch a hair on his head

was Gotti's response. The local came back a few days later with a basket of fruit, some wine and cheese, and said:

I should have known, an Italian guy from NY, of course you can do business here, there is plenty of money for everyone.

There was peace and profits. Mink started to place ads for King's Garden massage parlor in the local paper. *The Battle Creek Enquirer* lifestyle section had a calendar of local events featuring advertisements for art exhibits, theater, concerts, movies, and massage parlors. The King's Garden ad was sandwiched between one touting entertainment from duo pianists playing at the Dalton Theatre, and a restaurant called Mr. Cribbins Sunday Brunch. The ad read:

Asian style, Reasonable price—be treated like a king in a palace ... experience the ultimate pleasure of a soothing massage ... Complimentary drink, body shampoo ... we're warm, we're friendly, we're not in a rush, and for added emphasis: *Also, we enjoy it.*

Mink's picture was included in some of the ads. She looked more like a businesswoman than a seductress. It seemed so legitimate.[6,7,8,9]

Massage parlors are often used as a front for prostitution. Most girls have little or no training as a licensed masseuse, and often they don't even have legal documents to be in the United Stated. King's Garden massage parlor was no different. Their business was raided many times and when they were questioned by the police investigating prostitution, Robert claimed that he never took money from anyone except an entrance fee of thirty-five dollars per customer. Mink had been involved with massage parlors for years and knew the law and knew that the flow of money determined if you were a pimp or not. When several girls were interviewed, they said they never gave any money to Robert or Mink. Robert and Mink managed the building and services, the girls determined their own advertised rates determined as half hour massages or full hour massages. The girls did legitimate massages, but also more for an extra fee. The business thrived because of tricks. At most a girl was slapped with a misdemeanor for prostitution, paid a fine, and was back at work in a day. Robert was arrested three times over a span of five years. The business was lucrative and opened three more parlors, all called King's Garden, in Grand Rapids, Kalamazoo, and Pontiac. The massage parlor in Pontiac was not far from the Silver Dome. Robert handed out fliers one weekend advertising thirty dollars a massage "today only" and cleared fifty thousand dollars during a Detroit Lions game. Ninety girls worked and split their time at all the locations. Money rolled in; Robert delighted, he had money to gamble, pay off his debts, and could travel easily back and forth to New York.

Robert was even on the local Toledo, OH evening news after bailing out thirty girls who were arrested and taken to the court wearing only night gowns and slippers. Mink thought it was a good business model to pay the girls' bail, get phone numbers, and expand her network of girls plying the trade. Reporters and local gentry screamed at him, as he left the courthouse. They shouted:

Pimp, pimp, you're a pimp, you're a massage parlor boss, you're a criminal.

The TV coverage was highlighting a growing problem of massage parlors fronting for prostitution. Upon his return home, the TV coverage flashed across the screen. Mink laughed, and said:

There's my guy, you are famous.

Robert brought Jack and Margie out to Battle Creek in 1985. He escorted his wide-eyed parents to his businesses. Jack was earnest to listen to his son describe the ins and outs of the business. And he was proud and bragged to everyone who would listen that Robert was running massage parlors and made lots of money. Uncle "D" would respond:

You are so stupid, open your eyes! He's a pimp! He's running whore houses.

Jack wouldn't listen, he wanted to believe that his son had turned a corner. However, no corner was ever turned. Robert income and lifestyle were based on doing things his way and not abiding by the law. While he was back East visiting Jack and Margie, he and Mink took them to Atlantic City. But there were ominous signs of bad luck. Robert was losing his shirt, Mink's terrier died, and two of his massage parlors were robbed: Battle Creek and Kalamazoo. He found out that a Korean troublemaker robbed the girls from two of his locations. The girls were largely immigrants who did not speak English well or at all. They had no idea about how to start a bank account and kept all their cash hidden away in boxes in their rooms at the parlor. There was a lot of cash on hand as some girls were earning fifteen-thousand dollars a month.

Robert and Mink met Chung when they opened the first King's Garden. Chung was a stocky character who was a Taekwondo champ in Korea. He was a hustler who supplied stolen televisions, tape recorders with headphones, blankets, rice, and other items the girls used. Chung's wife spoke with the girls and sold them what they needed; Chung told Robert war stories about his escapades and about his life in Korea. He spoke about gangs inflicting upon him agonizing torture, and he lifted his shirt, to show and tell about burn marks and scars he sustained over the years. Robert knew this man was trouble, and he had a feeling that he would have a problem with this shadowy figure. When they returned to Michigan, Robert and Mink went to a Korean disco to hang out. Robert was the only non-Korean in the place and a lot of dirty looks were launched in his way. His six-foot two inches stature, his long hair, and his tight clothes accentuating his muscles, built up from weight training and steroids, made him stand out even more. He ignored these playboy wannabees and motioned to Mink that he was going to the restroom. As he was zipping up, he spotted Chung, and without hesitation said:

Hey, you, you owe me ninety-thousand dollars. You want to die, you motherfucka!

Chung froze for a split second, took a step back, zipped up his pants, snapped back, arguing that this was none of his business and bellowed out:

You don't own these places, these are Mink's.

Robert was having none of it and started to pummel him in a quick succession of rights and lefts to his head, nose and jaw, while Chung registered some potent kicks and landed some solid strikes to the body. The fighting spilled out into the bar area, where Robert grabbed a Heineken bottle, breaking it over Chung's head. Chung didn't flinch so Robert slammed a chair on him which prompted a slew of Korean bar patrons to jump in. Just as the melee was about to reach its apex, Mister Sung, chimed in. He was also from New York and possessed a quiet presence of power and influence. The others backed off as Robert and Chung continued their fight, now exiting the disco. Robert told Mink to take his Rolex, chain, and bracelet and told her to open the trunk of his car and retrieve his .38 revolver. Mink pleaded with Robert to stop as she knew Chung would not relent as Robert demanded,

I told you go to the fucking car and get the gun!

Just as Chung made his way out of the club to come after Robert, Robert pointed the gun at him and fired over his head: *Bang!* Everyone froze. Chung didn't move a muscle as Robert approached and proceeded to smash his face with the butt of the gun. He hit him ten times and split his face wide open. Chung ended up in the hospital, and eventually paid Robert twenty-thousand dollar over the course of two months. Most of that money went back to the girls, but Mink pocketed some for herself.

His relationship with Mink scured after that. The massage parlors were not bringing as much money they wanted or needed to feed their spending and gambling habits. They were planning on going back to NYC permanently, and Mink wanted to arrange for Robert to meet with Mister Yu, an older Korean man they had done business with before. Mister Yu owned restaurants and a wedding hall around Manhattan. They gave him twenty-five-thousand dollars to invest on a massage parlor a year earlier. It was a down-payment for a future business that they would start when they decided to return to NY permanently. The love flame between Robert and Mink had faded. Robert lost a lot of money with his high stakes gambling habit. Mink stopped giving him money and stopped paying the lease for Pontiac Tempest they bought for Jack the previous year. Robert grew further suspicious of Mink's displeasure when they were at a house party in Michigan, and Mink disclosed that she knew where Chung was and how to reclaim the rest of the money. The owner of the house heard this and said yes, he's there right now, a few houses down the street. Robert drank his beer but stayed put, his radar was on high alert and thought this was too suspect. Mink schemed behind his back and saw Robert as vulnerable, with no power except for the connections she brought to the table. Robert was no fool and wouldn't just wander up to some house looking for a guy like Chung. He likely would have been ambushed and have no one to back him up. He knew then and there that Mink was no longer his partner in crime.

By 1986 Mink was gone. She won two million-six-hundred-thousand dollars playing the slot machine at Caesar's Palace in Las Vegas. She disappeared, and Robert never saw her again, no goodbye, no note. They were lovers and partners and now it was over. Robert was not going to manage this operation without Mink. Problems were compounding due to the emergence of the AIDS epidemic. The department of health was now mandating that all masseuses had to be licensed and get monthly blood tests. Robert knew the girls were not going to subject themselves to needles, and they would not pay for licenses.

He was done with his Michigan adventure. The positive thing for him was that he paid his debt to Bobby Glasses, and that he could safely return to New York and not worry about pending death upon having snubbed a Gambino associate. Every month he made sure that fifteen thousand was regularly pocketed by Bobby Glasses. He did this for two and half years, paying a total three-hundred-sixty thousand dollars on a two-hundred-fifty-thousand-dollar loan. Now he was back in New York for good.

Chapter 15

A good reputation is more valuable than money.

—Publilius Syrus

When Robert returned to New York and to his old life in the Big Apple. He tracked down Mister Yu and found him at his building on the West Side. Mister Yu was a successful businessman who had an uncanny resemblance to Oddjob, the menacing henchman protecting Goldfinger, one of the most evil and greedy characters in the James Bond canon. Mister Yu was a dapper dresser. He always wore a suit and tie that mirrored the fashion sensibilities of the Garment District neighborhood where his building was located. His snugly-fitting suit advertised his expanding girth and oversized confidence. Robert approached him and belched out:

Hey, Yu, I want my twenty-five thousand. I'm back and need my money now!

Mink and Robert had given Mr. Yu this money two years earlier as down payment in hopes Mister Yu could find space for a massage parlor. Mister Yu did find space in his building but was using the money to cover rent. Not comfortable with this demand from a menacing brute standing over him, Mister Yu gathered his thoughts, regained his composure and calmly assured Robert in a halting voice that he would have his money in a few weeks.

Robert was not pleased with Mister Yu's response but reluctantly waited. But as time moved on, he became increasingly frustrated with his financial situation. After waiting two weeks he convinced his father, Jack, to drive him to 8th Ave., not revealing the true nature of the trip downtown. Once they arrived Robert waited outside of Mister Yu's usual restaurant haunt. As Mr. Yu walked out, Robert ambushed him right on 8th Ave near 38th St.

Without saying a word Robert grabbed him by his tie and punched him in rapid succession:

Bang, Bang, Bang.

Then, once he finished a barrage of blows, he maniacally bellowed:

Hey, Yu, I want my money. I told you, I am not moving ahead with this massage parlor. Give me my money now!

Cowering, Mister Yu pleaded for patience, weakly offering that the money would be coming soon but he quickly changed his mind when Robert grabbed him again and raised his right fist to punch him again. Pleading with this menace, he slowly pulled out his check book from the breast pocket of his now disheveled suit. As Robert stood over him on 8th Ave, curious pedestrians slowed their pace to see the commotion. Mister Yu wrote a check made out to cash. Robert ripped the check out of his hand and threatened that if the check bounced, he'd die. Robert's reputation as a gambler, enforcer, with suspected mob connections, convinced Mister Yu to not seek retribution. Mister Yu had his own dealings with Asian gangs and was not willing to employ them for revenge. He tolerated the public humiliation and hoped to put the incident behind him. Robert's wrath was abated. He paid his debt, absorbed a beating, and gathered his composure while straightening his tie and reorienting his suit jacket. Robert disappeared into the shadows of 38th St. where Jack was waiting in his Cadillac and handed his father the check. Robert was invisible to the financial institutions and only did transactions in cash. Not having a bank account meant Jack would have to deposit the check and hand his son the cash, like he did many times before.

Now that he had a little cash in hand, Robert was intent on finding work and getting more money to support his gambling. His opportunity came knocking on the door when he came across an acquaintance at one of the clubs frequented by the Gambino's. He put the word out that he wanted a sit down to air his situation. A few weeks later, word came back that he was to meet with a few Gambino capos at a restaurant in Little Italy. Robert asserted that since he squared his debts, the hit on him should be lifted and he wanted to work and make money. Robert offered that he would do whatever was needed to earn some money. The message was relayed to Bobby Glasses. The capo honored Robert's request and all was forgiven and assigned him to be a debt collector once again. Collecting gambling debts, loans, or extortion money was usually resolved with threats of violence, destruction of property or a few well-placed punches. A portion of the debt would be handed over then and there and more was promised by the unlucky gambler. Robert would get a percentage of what he collected as his fee. But complications are complications as one collection job went awry. One owner of a fleet of limousines in his mid-thirties failed to pay a Gambino associate the sum of one-hundred-thousand dollars. That brazen business owner ignored the matter altogether. Robert was chosen to recover the debt with the usual ten percent commission. No one cared about the limo owners' reasons for not paying his debts, nothing mattered except the bottom line. He accepted the loan, agreed to the terms, and now had to pay. Organized crime was a banking system, as they substituted physical violence over incarceration, intimidation over legal entanglements, and enforcer over a judge.

A tip led Robert to a club in the Bronx. Once there, he sat

down, ordered a Heineken, and observed his target. The limo owner had made his routine stop into this club for a few hours before heading back home to Westchester. Bobby Glasses doubted the man's ability to pay but was determined that he would pay one way or another. Robert spotted him leaving and pounced on this unsuspecting customer as he approached his car. The man dropped to the ground quickly after he was met with a flurry of hard blows the face and chest. He then ordered the man to get up and pushed this wretched guy to his car while Matty held him at gunpoint. They then drove to a warehouse in the Hunt's Point section of the Bronx. They entered a dilapidated building and tied the limo owner to a chair. With eyes ablaze like a mad man and a vinyl pipe held above his head, Robert screamed:

You see this fuckin pipe? If you don't get me the money, I'm going to beat your ass. Where's the money!

Robert windmilled the pipe so that it swooshed. The thirty-year-old limo owner tensed, bracing himself from the blow. Robert raged but relented and tried to reason with the man, saying he really didn't want to hurt him. After forty-five minutes, the time for reasoning was over. Robert grasped the pipe, swung it with force and bashed it on his arms, back, legs, and shoulders. The prisoner gasped and pleaded for mercy, but none would come. Robert continued to pummel the helpless man who was now out like a limp body. Robert had delivered his brutal message. The beaten man remained tied as Robert left for the day. Robert was confident that the limo owner would contemplate his predicament and come to his senses when Robert returned. Robert came and left for nine straight days. He screamed, beat, and attempted to get the limo owner to hand over cash or tell him where to get it. As the limo owner slumped alone in this abandoned warehouse that was once a distribution hub for fruits and vegetables, Robert returned each day only to feed him one French fry. He continued to pummel the man who sat limp with his head hanging low.

Robert tried to extract any information he could but realized that his prisoner was determined to say nothing, no matter what torture he inflicted. Robert realized he would never collect a dime and had to figure out a plan to save face. Robert wasn't going to kill him but also could not display weakness to mob leadership by letting him go. While Robert would not earn any money from his efforts, he schemed to earn a reputation as an enforcer. So, instead of letting the limo owner walk free, he devised a plan that would be perceived as an escape. He loosened the rope around his prisoners' ankles and wrists as he slumped half unconscious from the beatings, sweltering summer heat, and lack of nourishment. Robert deserted his captive debtor as he left the rusted steel door unlocked. Robert returned two days later and did not find a single trace of the tortured man.

No one batted an eye when he explained that he was unsuccessful in collecting any money. But the ruse paid off because the mob valued his devotion to the task of collecting, and an escape by the limo owner could have been for a variety of reasons. The effect was immediate as Robert gained admirers within his sphere of mobsters. He was offered other jobs collecting debts and the money started rolling in. Cash was all that mattered. Making money was a means to an end. Gambling, womanizing, and partying was what he thought about and is what he did. Everything else supported these endeavors.

Robert's reputation was bolstered by his physical appearance. He bulked up from steroids and routine workouts. His ripped physique and menacing demeanor were an effective deterrence to most people considering a confrontation or resistance to his demands. His physicality became such a deterrent that his collections became somewhat routine. To law enforcement, they had seen his type before. He stood out as someone looking for trouble.

Robert's reputation for running a fast Blackjack game and making money for gambling clubs was highly desirable and he quickly found work on his return to New York. Nicky, a fellow dealer friend, put in a good word for him and he started to deal at a club on 64th Street, run by the Albanian mob. Just before he arrived at the club for his four-to- twelve shift, he stopped into a local deli and bought a pack of Marlboro's and a Coke. Exiting with his fix of nicotine and caffeine, he turned the corner and headed down to a side alley where the club had its entrance. Illegal gambling clubs do not advertise their locations and only people in the know knew where to go. He was twenty paces from the club entrance when he detected that the entry door was ajar. His pulse pounded and his eyes widened as an uneasy feeling sunk in his mind. He could not move farther, as he was gripped by paralysis. His inner voice urged him to move, and he quickly turned and headed back to the deli. Just as he entered the deli, out of nowhere, police stormed from behind and wrestled him to the ground.

You're under arrest! We have a warrant!

Robert looked up at the determined Irish cop who was reaching for handcuffs, and with a strangled voice Robert barked:

Fuck you! Show me the warrant.

The cop grimaced and waved a warrant in his face that read:

John Doe! You're John Doe! before he finally pronounced:

You're the manager.

Robert denied everything, denied even knowing a club existed. He was booked in the 19th Precinct but was soon released after a phone call to his lawyer.

Robert was acquainted with many of the steady customers frequenting the clubs. The 26th St. club attracted many Korean women, some masseuses looking to get lucky, some working girls looking to be entertained, some business owners, and the madams of the massage parlors, looking for a big win. Lisa, a Korean woman and a manager of a massage parlor, was attracted to Robert. He was known as the Italian Blackjack dealer with the attitude and connections. They had a casual, uncommitted relationship for a few months as he moved in with her out of convenience. Lisa didn't care but his philandering and knew he "dated" other girls. They never argued and Robert was agreeable to helping her out when she complained about some trouble she was having. Lisa explained that she and her masseuses had problems with Chinese gangs that demanded extortion money. The Korean and Chinese immigrant communities didn't trust each other, and this only exacerbated the tensions. Madam Lisa's parlor was smallish, but it had an ample living room with large, comfortable black leather couches, an L-shaped quartz countertop and a satisfying quantity of booze and portable a twenty-four-inch RCA television set. A row of masseuses were conspicuously scattered around the couch and upon request led the solicitor to a back room with a bed and only a curtain for privacy. Robert agreed to act as bodyguard and was handsomely paid a thousand dollars for a couple of weeks work. His presence provided security and no further disruption of income or profits. His good-will paid off because the girls returned the favor, took their earnings, and gambled in his club.

Robert was firmly back on his feet. He was dealing steadily at multiple clubs, some run by Albanians, others run by the mob, all run by organized crime. The gambling clubs in the mid 1980s mirrored the flashy discos of the era. Sparkling lights, attractive people with fashionable clothes and jewelry that falsely advertised wealth and sophistication. Robert played the part well. The tight-fitting Jordache blue jeans, white Reebok pump sneakers, and pull-over sweaters he had worn a few years earlier were replaced with French moccasins and Joseph Abboud suits. He wanted to exude wealth and demonstrate to the gamblers that they could have that too. He smiled, laughed, and sympathized with the customers, knowing if they had a good experience, even while losing a few hundred or a few thousand dollars a night, that they would be back. And return they did. And as fast as the money came in, Robert spent it just as fast.

My father heard his brother, Jack, brag about Robert many times. One Sunday afternoon Jack raved about how successful his son was, what nice girlfriends he had, and how generous he was. My father was an analytical man, frugal, and skeptical. He responded to Jack in a low voice,

Nigger Rich.

Pops called anyone who spent their money recklessly "Nigger Rich." He directed this crass comment at me once in the early 1980s. I was taken aback yet amused at his crass and impetuous use of this racial caricature; I could not believe what I heard. I confronted him as to what that term actually meant, and equally incredulous that he would employ such a derogatory expression. My father was not a racist man in any sense of the imagination, yet he now directed this ethnic slur at me. He laughed sarcastically while he mocked me for spending money I earned from a summer job. My father thought it was foolish to spend money beyond ones means and he thought my purchases of concert tickets were frivolous and unnecessary. I should be saving money for the future, was his common rejoinder. Robert surely did not save his money, and Pops didn't think there was any reason for Jack's praise of his son's spending habits. Robert had incurred my father's judgement. He thought, what a prodigal son Robert was with his reckless spending, his drug vices, his arrests, and his life of wanton living.

Robert's lifestyle was a world of gambling, partying, and womanizing. The underworld of the Midtown South neighborhood of Manhattan made all this readily available. As the business owners and workers returned home to the suburbs of New York and New Jersey after their arduous pursuit of the American Dream, a subculture of urban minions pursued their after-hour routines within the cavernous grid of the city. Nightlife was a necessary escape from the mundane workday and gambling provided the means to the hopes and dreams of achieving monetary success above one's current financial station. Robert was the master performer in this theater of dreams. He dealt cards while displaying wealth and vitality, which drew in customers who longed for what he was selling. Robert also yearned for what he did not have. And one evening a tall, attractive Korean woman became the object of his desire. A group of Asian women had been playing blackjack at his table while the others stood around, watched, and sipped their pink cosmopolitans. He noticed that the woman in the center of the table, a tall attractive girl, was losing money and getting frustrated with her losses. She had an innocent look about her and after she made several unforced errors it became obvious to Robert that she was a novice at blackjack. He dutifully obeyed when she adamantly commanded,

Hit me,

dealing her a card contrary to a move from more skilled player. She held a Jack of hearts and six of clubs when she demanded another card, which signaled to Robert that she was ignorant of the odds of being dealt a third card that would total the three cards to twenty-one. After several loosing hands, her upbeat demeanor faded into despair, and wanting to lift her spirits, he reached out from behind his perch of cards and patted her hand gently while muttering a few sentences in Korean that he picked up from his time with Mink. Robert was skilled in his assessment of odds and probability when gambling with cards, and gambling with relationships. He told her that she was a nice girl and shouldn't be in clubs like this. She smiled, keenly aware of his intents and responded bluntly that he should not get confused, she was not one of these massage parlor girls. The tall attractive Korean girl was very observant of her surroundings and sensed this flirtatious Italian blackjack dealer knew the madam, Lisa, more intimately beyond a casual friendship. To this tall attractive Korean girl, Lisa was a dirty whore. Robert sensed this novice's opinion of her own integrity and smirked but did not respond to the curt response to his overture. After another half hour of losing hands, the girls got up from the table and went for their coats. Nicky, the other dealer that evening, had also noticed and was attracted to the tall Korean novice, but failed to seize the opportunity to interact with her. Robert moved quickly from behind the blackjack table and as he was saying goodbye to some of the other girls playing, managed to get formally introduced to this tall attractive Korean novice, Sae Hee Hong. After a few phone calls, he convinced her to join him for cocktails at a bar of her choice. Sae Hee was apprehensive at first, unconvinced of his intentions and background. But his expensive suits, wads of cash, and displays of affluence overwhelmed her apprehension and they soon became a couple, intrigued with each other's attributes. Robert desired an attractive, submissive, traditional companion, who would not challenge his lifestyle and provide a comfortable home life as a refuge and sanctum. Sae Hee relished in having an attractive man possessing power, influence and wealth, her gateway to the American Dream.

Sae Hee arrived illegally to the United States as a child with her parents. With only a high school diploma and little ambition for a higher education she worked at the Dollar General on 14th Street. Just like Robert, she worked off the books. She yearned to work legitimately and was enticed by the promise of the American Dream but without a green card, those aspirations would never materialize. Robert and Sae Hee quickly realized each other's potential to fulfill each other's ulterior motives and soon moved in together. Sae Hee had worked at several Korean restaurants. A green card and restaurant ownership would be the next step in her ambitious plan. Through Robert's connections with influential lawyers and ten-thousand dollars she avoided the painful navigation through government bureaucracy. The Permanent Resident Card was now hers and she now sought her next goal, to manage a restaurant.

Sae Hee treated Robert like Korean nobility, acting as his humble servant. A hot bath waited for him every time he walked into their apartment, humbly washing him with a sponge before dinner or intimacy. Robert worked diligently to earn money. His regular shifts dealing cards provided a fraction of the income he made. His gambling habits kept him busy as a loyal patron of the local OTB, Atlantic City, or illegal after-hours casinos. Robert did not have a bank account, so all his earnings were kept in the refrigerator. When he lost playing the horses at the OTB, he would call Sae Hee and instruct her to bring down cash. Within fifteen-minutes he had cash in his hand and continued his torrid betting. The gambling income ebbed and flowed but provided enough net profits for them to have a comfortable apartment and lifestyle. Sae Hee wanted more than being a clerk at Dollar General and still dreamt of running a restaurant. She paid attention to the crowds at the dining establishments in the Garment District neighborhoods. She made note of which restaurants were busy in the evenings after the hordes of garment workers left for the day. Most restaurants were busy in the middle of the day, eleven a.m. through three p.m., but only those that sustained a stream of customers in the evening were truly successful. Restaurant failure rates were typically five years in the Garment District and Midtown South neighborhoods of the city which was low compared to other neighborhoods in Manhattan. A Chinese restaurant on the corner of 36th St. and 7th Ave. had attracted her attention. She had walked past this restaurant a dozen times during the day and evening and paid attention to the dwindling crowds. Sae Hee consulted with her friends who commented that it was poorly run, and the food was inferior to other Chinese restaurants in the area, and people just stopped coming.

Sae Hee asked Robert to investigate who was the landlord and find out who owned the business and if they were willing to sell it. Robert had his lawyer track down the landlord and discovered the space was owned by a Hasidic Jew. Robert made an appointment to introduce himself along with Sae Hee and they explained their interest in taking over the restaurant. Sae Hee's observations were correct as the landlord confirmed that the restaurant was losing money and that he had not received any rent payments in six months. The Hasidic landlord was so upset, saying he wanted the owners out. He disclosed that if Robert could get them out, he would give him the lease. Weeks later Robert and his crew of Matty, Chris, and others devised a plan and paid a visit to the restaurant. As the last of the lunch patrons left, Robert and his buddies walked in and demanded to see the owner. A middle-aged Asian man peeked out from the kitchen, and Matty, without hesitation, grabbed him by his neck as the other pushed, yelled, and manhandled the other three employees. With a few tables turned over, and glassware broken on the floor, the message was loud and clear. Before exiting, Robert threatened the older man and told him he's out, don't come back or you are going to get worse. This Asian had no legal recourse, he was an illegal immigrant, had no working papers, and was behind in rent. He left without a fight and never came back. Robert went back to the Hasidic landlord and explained that the restaurant had not opened in a week, let's make a deal. Robert put down a cash deposit and the lease was set up in Sae Hee's name. It was official. Sae Hee was a restaurant owner.

I could hear the roar of the World Series from my basement apartment window on 28th Avenue near Parsons Blvd. It was the fall of 1986 and in between the roar of jets departing LaGuardia Airport we could hear crazed Met fans scream as their heroes battled the hated Boston Red Sox. I was a New York Yankees fan and hated the Mets as much as I hated the Red Sox. This World Series had no meaning for me. I couldn't care less about the Mets which were so beloved by my mother and two brothers. I was more interested as to when the traffic would ease up on parkways around the stadium. I had never lived in an apartment and this basement apartment, like many others in this Flushing neighborhood north of Northern Blvd., was created by partitioning a one family, attached brick house, into three apartments. It was affordable for us newlyweds, struggling to launch a career and pursue graduate school. While not interested in attending Mets games, we did enjoy the diversity of restaurant options within a fifteen-minute drive. It was a new experience dining in a restaurant as a minority. Many of the restaurants in Flushing had menus with pictures but no English. And quite a few restaurants didn't even employ staff fluent in English. But we grew to love the food and took advantage of the affordability and convenience of the local eateries.

That spring Robert helped Sae Hee set up their Korean restaurant and by autumn it was fully operational. He bypassed the usual inspection processes and learned through other associates the easy way to have an official look the other way. After being fined, heavily and frequently for the first few months, Robert had enough. Fines for not cleaning the sidewalks, fines for inferior lighting, fines for kitchen infractions. He was now frustrated that these extra costs were eating into his gambling earnings. All that ceased when he was instructed to meet with the inspector and pay whatever fines were outstanding. But with a little payola.

When you are finished paying the fines, get up from the chair, place an envelope full of cash, two thousand dollars, in the inspectors' breast jacket pocket. The jacket will be on the chair next to you. Do not look at him, do not say anything and do not write anything on the envelope.

Robert did as advised, and that was the end of his dealings with the health department. His cash flow increased and so did the expendable cash for gambling.

I heard through family chatter that Robert was back in New York and was now running a Korean restaurant. I assumed he was running it with Mink, his girlfriend I met briefly a few years earlier. In the back of my mind, I was questioning how he had all these connections and business sense to run a restaurant. My father encouraged me to see what Robert was up to and go check it out. Pops was just as curious as to Robert's latest adventure as

I was. I found out that he managed the restaurant most evenings. Uncle Jack shared the address with my father. I didn't know the restaurant's name or even have a phone number, but I figured we'd just show up and surprise him. He had never met my wife, and we both liked Asian food so even if he wasn't there, we would still get a good meal out of our efforts.

It was a Thursday night around seven p.m., and we made our way to the restaurant. It wasn't a big place, maybe fifteen tables, and when we walked in there was only one couple eating. Behind the bar stood a tall, attractive Korean woman, and a smaller, heavy-set, older Korean man scurrying around with plates. I approached the woman without introducing myself and said:

Is Robert around?

Surprised, she and the older man stopped what they were doing and looked at each other and didn't acknowledge my question. I assumed they didn't speak English too well, so I said it again more loudly and a bit slower. They looked at each other somewhat concerned, but they didn't say anything. I turned around and looked at my wife, then I smirked, shrugged my shoulders, and said:

Maybe they don't know him.

I turned back and said:

I'm his cousin, our fathers are brothers.

That seemed to resonate with her and off she went to the side wall and got on the telephone. Progress, I thought, we are making headway. She came back and motioned that he was upstairs, and he would come right down. She sat us down as Robert walked in a few minutes later. He looked tired and disheveled. His uncombed long brown hair was as unkempt as his wrinkled, untucked long-sleeve shirt. He slouched and squinted at the bright lights while shaking my hand and introduced us to the pretty Korean woman, finally adding that she was his wife. We were just as surprised at this revelation, as he was with meeting Adriane for the first time.

After a little more banter, we ordered food and ate. Sae Hee served the food, while they both mumbled to each other in Korean. He usually wasn't very conversational, but even less so now because he obviously had been sleeping. He spoke with short obligatory responses, but I didn't expect much to begin with. After about an hour we asked for the check, but he refused our money. I was happy to see him and impressed with his new venture. My mission was accomplished, he met my wife and I could provide a firsthand update to my father on the travails of his wayward nephew.

Robert and Sae Hee lived together for several years before getting married in 1988, but troubles followed. She caught him cheating on her when they were first dated, but he talked her out of leaving him, saying he was a single man and had urges and they were not even married. She was mad as hell but after a month she got over it. That didn't stop Robert and his urges. Robert had an affair with a Swedish girl he met at one of the clubs. A cute, Swedish blonde dressed in short pants, a bikini, a halter top, and a cowboy hat pursued Robert. This blonde Swede spotted Robert as he dealt through his usual shift and asked the bartender to introduce her to him after a night of partying. Even though he was tired after his shift, he agreed to take her out for a few drinks. One thing led to another, and he started paying for her studio apartment in Alphabet City. It was a sleazy apartment in a sleazy neighborhood. He hated the place and reacted in disgust as cockroaches scurried about the floors and corners. This forced him to concoct a plan to have his way with this Swede in his apartment while Sae Hee worked at the restaurant. Sae Hee knew that something was going on. Incensed when she found a Michelob in the fridge, she confronted him, saying:

You only drink Heineken!

He came up with a slew of excuses, but the die was now cast.

His gambling was out of control, losing tens of thousands of dollars. He would spend most of his time in the OTB located at

38th and 7th, two blocks from the restaurant. Every day he went down and bet. She complained that he was hanging around with what she called "the dirty people," but he pushed back, saying he was making money and why should she even care. He would bring back thousands of dollars at a time. He gambled by placing large bets and knew if he bet large the winnings would be larger. On weekends he traveled to Atlantic City to bet big. If he was low on cash, he would have her take a limousine to his loan shark and get $20,000 in cash and head right back down to Atlantic City. Back in the early 1990s Robert was approached by an Albanian dealer offering a job dealing at some club in the Bronx. It was at a small club at 187th St. and Arthur Ave., a few blocks from 188th St. and Bathgate Ave where our grandfather, Basilio Fabio, settled with his young family seventy years earlier. The rumor was that Frank LoCascio, a Gambino underboss, ran this hot club. Robert made $150 a night to deal blackjack, but sat for hours instead, bored out of his mind as he watched customers drink demitasse or cocktails. One evening, two well-tailored men walked in and asked the manager for a cup of coffee. Martin, the club manager, walked over to Robert and spewed:

Hey, those two want coffee, make them some.

Robert nearly blew a gasket.

Hey, I'm not here to make coffee, I deal!

Martin, as cool as a cucumber, advised Robert to pipe down. He then paused for a second, went up to his ear and whispered:

Listen, JC, the guy over there is asking for coffee, just make it for him.

Begrudgingly, Robert relented, made a regular cup of coffee and brought it over to the table. One of the guys handed him a $200 tip. With a generous tip like that, Robert thought to himself he would serve him whatever he wanted all day. By the end of his shift, he learned that the well-tailored gentleman was called Zef, the Albanian, and supposedly he was the foster son of Frank

LoCascio. Zef clearly had powerful connections. Word spread that Robert was dealing in the Bronx in one of the oldest Italian American enclaves in the city, and he earned great respect. But that didn't matter to him, he was bored because no one actually wanted to play Blackjack. However, he did make connections and learned that a guy named Rudy splashed his cash round. Rudy, a loan shark, supplied Robert with cash through an intermediary named Louie. Louie liked to gamble and party, and he and Robert became friendly when Louie lost a few thousand during one of the rare games Robert dealt at this Bronx club. Robert, always the talker, said to Louie:

Hey, I'm sorry you lost, I prefer you win a few thousand and throw me a $500 tip.

Appreciating Robert's sympathy, Louie and Robert became gambling buddies. They traveled to Atlantic City many times as Louie observed Robert's propensity to bet large sums of money. Robert's risk-free style of betting large amounts of cash signaled to Louie that Robert could benefit from easy cash from Rudy, the loan shark. Through Louie, Rudy supplied the cash. When Robert was in need, he instructed Sae Hee to take a cab to the Bronx to pick it up. She was driven so many times back and forth from Atlantic City to the Bronx that finally she was fed up. She pleaded to one of the casino floor managers, asking that Robert be given a marker.

She made the case that he was always gambling and had access to cash, and he was good for the money. When one casino gave him a marker, others followed suit, including Golden Nugget, Resorts, Sands, and Tropicana. He signed a marker, and they gave him $20,000 worth of chips. When he was up in winnings, he spent.

I would spend, I never saved a dollar in my life!

Robert boasted. Robert bought jewelry, cars, clothes, expensive meals, and whatever he needed. He could pay off the loan shark $1000 a week until he needed more and pay back the marker when he was up. When he was down, he was down by a lot. Robert was down one hundred thousand dollars and Steve Wynn, owner of the Golden Nugget said,

Take a break, I hate people losing big money. Everything is on me; you are always welcome here. Take a break, go home.

Robert took his advice and left. He abstained from Atlantic City for two weeks, but the allure was too great. He would bring Jack and Margie, stay at the Dean Martin suite, order surf and turf, cigars, champagne, whatever Jack and Margie wanted. He lived high on the hog. He was comped front row tickets for Frank Sinatra. Jack and Margie no longer questioned his gambling. Robert was a high roller and everyone around him benefitted from the casino propensity to comp their best customers with whatever amenities they wanted. Eventually he stopped paying everyone. At Sands he went through $20,000. When a high roller was penniless, a casino often granted the gambler $2000 for car service for a ride home.

No taxi money for you!

An argument ensued after he was denied taxi money, to which Robert responded:

Oh yeah, go fuck yourself, I'm not paying cock!

After that he never paid back his markers despite the casino's attempts to track him down. Sae Hee couldn't believe the amount of money that was flowing through his hands. She finally had enough when $300,000 disappeared and he asked her to get more from Rudy. She refused and a verbal barrage ensued. She was so upset that she said she was not going over to Jack and Margie's for Christmas. That was an insult that Robert would not, could not, put up with. He made an ultimatum that if:

You don't come with me to Suffern for Christmas, our marriage is over, and I'm gone.

She didn't think he was serious, but after he left, he never returned to the apartment or stepped foot into the restaurant again. Sae Hee had put up with Robert's philandering and gambling throughout their relationship. But the relationship was on his terms, and now it was over.

Chapter 16

To believe in God is to yearn for His existence, and furthermore, it is to act as if He did exist.

—Miguel de Unamuno

After our honeymoon, my wife and I settled into our routine of work and church and we both were involved with the different ministries at Harvest Christian Fellowship.[1] The church didn't own a building since it was a relatively new ministry in NYC. Several large rooms on different floors were rented from the Joffrey Ballet School on West 56th St. between 6th and 7th Avenues. These ballet studios were housed in a pre-war building that featured high ceilings and no windows. A single door was the only ingress and egress to the sanctuary, except for the door that led to the fire escape providing some semblance of ventilation. Church services were held on the 6th floor while metal folding chairs were stored on the 4th floor. Every Sunday for nine years, the ushers and set-up crew loaded hundreds of folding chairs onto an old, lever-controlled elevator operated by the building maintenance supervisor, a Black man named George. The ballet studio was our Sunday morning sanctuary. After service we folded the chairs up, loaded them onto the elevator, and stored them back on the fourth floor. My wife was on the worship team and went to church for early practice with the other musicians while I grabbed some coffee and bagels down the street and then I headed upstairs for what we called chair duty. It was tedious work that was made easy by a group of guys who wanted to serve and make sure the growing congregation had a place to sit. I expressed interest in becoming more involved, and I was asked to act as an altar counselor. At the end of Sunday morning sermons, Pastor Mike invited people to commit their lives to Christ and accept Jesus as their savior. As he led them in prayer, he invited people to stand up from the chairs and stand before the podium. Although we had no church pews or altars, the act of moving forward was known as an altar call. I would be doing what someone did for me when I first went up for an altar call years earlier. Greet them and pray. This role was a little more detailed in that I spoke with everyone who walked forward and gave them a gift called the growth packet. I shared the contents of the large envelope which included a welcome letter from Pastor Mike, a NIV study Bible, a daily devotion guide, a pamphlet on "How to Read the Bible," information on what prayer is, and information about the church. I asked them to fill out a small form printed in triplicate and requested that they provided their contact information. I always motioned people to follow me to the fire escape door just to the right of the stage. Every Sunday there was always someone who came forward for prayer and requested more information. I met so many people who earnestly searched for God and felt honored to be part of their spiritual journey. The majority were sincere seekers. Many attended some type of church in the past but sought a deeper faith and understanding of Christ. Others had no religious background at all. We met many wonderful people through the years, and we have remained friends to this day.

Over the years I had come to appreciate the difficulties and challenges pastors, clergy, and church leadership had to endure. Some incidents were comical, but others were disturbing and negatively affected the congregation. One event that stood out vividly was when I and a few ushers observed one lady's unique style of breast feeding. She was doing double duty, simultaneously breast feeding her five-year-old and infant at the same time. No one had a problem with her breast feeding except that the five-year-old kid just stood there like he was drinking from a fountain. Both of her breasts were exposed as she made no attempt to modestly conceal her bosom with some sort of covering. We watched in disbelief. A few of the ushers chuckled, another shook his head in disgust, and finally the lead usher approached her discreetly. She quickly put her breasts back in her bra while the embarrassed usher informed her that we had a room in the back where she could breastfeed in privacy in the future.

The congregation was encouraged to attend bible studies and to read and discuss the scriptures amongst themselves. Occasionally there were congregants who followed a particular belief other than what Harvest taught. One such doctrine spread like wildfire as a few people went around to others in the congregation and asked if they believed in eternal security. I was asked this very question and began to realize that there was quite a division amongst the church attendees as whether they believed in this or not. The Pastor and church leadership needed to address this, but Mike first made sure the leadership was fully informed and in agreement to what the scriptures taught. He also chose to speak on the subject individually, not wanting this controversy to hijack his regular Sunday messages. We all hoped that the congregation would accept Pastor Mike's teaching on the matter but were not naïve enough to know that not everyone would be in agreement and either continue to cause controversy or leave the congregation altogether.

Eternal security is a doctrine that implies once a person is saved, they are always saved. Meaning that once you have salvation from Christ, then you cannot lose it. You are eternally secure, no matter what, there is no possibility of apostasy. I never felt that this was a correct interpretation of scripture and was in full agreement with our church's teaching on the matter. It was simply explained that a believer is eternally secure as you abide in Christ. This is a conditional statement which implies free will, the possibility that one can abandon their previous commitment and be separated from God. The scriptures below provide a basis for this position.

> *My sheep hear my voice, and I know them, and they follow me. I give them eternal life, and they will never perish, and no one will snatch them out of my hand.*
>
> John 10:27–28

> *Abide in me, and I in you. As the branch cannot bear fruit by itself, unless it abides in the vine, neither can you, unless you abide in me. I am the vine; you are the branches. Whoever abides in me and I in him, he it is that bears much fruit, for apart from me you can do nothing. If anyone does not abide in me he is thrown away like a branch and withers; and the branches are gathered, thrown into the fire, and burned.*
>
> John 15:4–6

Less than a dozen people disagreed with our church's position and soon left for other congregations. It was upsetting to the congregation that this issue had caused such a stir, but I admired Pastor Mike handling of this situation with forbearance.

People from across NYC and other parts of the country and even foreign nationals made their way into our church services either from hearing Greg Laurie on radio or attending one of the outreaches held in NYC every fall.

The Fall outreaches, called HARVEST, featured special messages by prominent pastors associated with Calvary Chapel Ministries on the West Coast including Greg Laurie, Raul Ries, and Chuck Smith.[2] These outreaches were held over consecutive nights, or spread out over weeks at the Days Inn on West 57th St where we rented a ballroom with a capacity for a thousand people. The ballrooms were usually full in large part due to the popularity of Greg Laurie's radio program: "A New Beginning." Christian musicians such as Roby Duke, Marty Goetz, and Richie Furay played their genre of Christian music. Eventually the featured speakers shared an evangelistic message. Adriane and I participated as well with Adriane singing with the worship team at the beginning of the event, and myself assisting as an usher. It was a privilege to be part of a large outreach and assist seekers in their spiritual journey.

I expressed an interest to Pastor Mike as I wished for greater involvement with Ministry. Except for the pastor, we were all volunteers and wore many hats. I led the counseling ministry, led home bible study group in Queens, and served on the leadership board. Occasionally I taught the Thursday evening bible study when Pastor Mike asked. It was a special treat and honor to teach bible study in NYC as my wife led worship beforehand. Thursday evenings attracted a smaller crowd than Sunday morning and usually had no more that forty people. Many of those who did come traveled directly from work. We had a certain order to the midweek bible study, and it didn"t include an uninvited random person walking up to the pulpit declaring they had a word from God. Services usually began with a prayer, several worship songs, followed with a teaching, then an invitation to accept Christ into your life or to pray with someone, while soft music played. Then the service ended. On one particular evening, I was asked to teach. After Adriane finished her last song, I walked up to the music stand facing the congregants. I was a little nervous as this was my first time teaching on a Thursday night. As I scanned my notes and readied to deliver my message, I spotted a disheveled fellow who looked homeless or on drugs. He stood as if hugging his acoustic guitar and he sauntered in front of the ballet studio as I was about to lead the faithful in prayer. He was a familiar figure in our church community, a street preacher who preferred to roam the city like a vagabond in search of an audience. We often noticed him as he sat on a bench surrounded with garbage bags full of his belongings, a pull cart, homemade signs of scripture, and homemade recordings of his songs and sermons for sale. He was a diminutive fellow of short stature but with an out-sized eccentric personality. He referred to himself as born-again Spiros. He never divulged his last name, but we ascertained he was Greek. His whole demeanor revealed someone who was passionate yet unconventional, approachable yet distant, determined yet ineffectual.

He made his way forward as he swayed his shoulders and guitar as if he were following a choreographed introduction to the stage. The whole congregation eyed him equally as they eyed me to see what was about to go down. I said a quick silent prayer as he was approaching me. I was very conscious that I should not raise my voice, or loudly confront him, or physically stop him if he started talking over me or just started playing his guitar and singing. I was ready for the worst and made eye contact with one of the ushers ready to motion them over to gently ask him to step outside as a last resort. As he stood next to me, he said that he had a word from God and wanted to share a song. I looked at him incredulously and said that God is a God of order, and since God didn't inform me of him having a word to share, and that this is not how we do things here, he should just go back to his seat and share after the service was over. I wasn't sure what would happen next because he seemed like someone who did whatever he wanted to do. To my surprise he did exactly as I asked. He sat down, remained quiet, and we continued the service as planned. I took a deep breath and a sigh of relief after the service was over.

I had frequent conversations with Pastor Mike about my interests in counseling. He paired me up with another congregant with a similar passion and we started reviewing books by Dr. Jay

Adams. I would go over to his house in White Plains, and we studied the book: *Competent to Counsel*.[3] This book provided a stark contrast to the current trend in churches that relied on secular psychological methods for counseling their flock. The text stressed the sufficiency of the scriptures to enable pastors and laymen to counsel their congregants in biblical-based counseling. I related with this principle because of my dissatisfaction for psychological theories that I studied while pursuing a psychology degree. The book *Competent to Counsel* offered insight into the power of the Holy Spirit through scripture. A divine authority that provides strength and direction while challenging men and women to grow more Christ-like. I read many of Dr. Adams' books and put the lessons into practice when Pastor Mike asked me to counsel members of the congregation. The teachings and counseling methods came in handy as I was asked to speak with a single woman who was suffering from bouts of depression. She had two daughters and struggled with the idea of giving her infant daughter up for adoption. My wife was fully supportive of me as I traveled weeknights to meet with this lady for an hour. We met for months as I shared many of the practical biblical principles outlined in Dr. Adams' and Wayne Mack's books. The long winding spiral of depression was slowly uncoiled as she took gradual, achievable steps to reverse her attitudes and behaviors. The lady slowly came out of her depression and decided she would keep her baby. I was amazed that I could be used in such a powerful way to help someone struggling with overwhelming issues.

To augment his weekly sermons, Pastor Mike had decided to buy time on a radio station devoted to Christian programing. It was a thirty-minute segment on an AM radio station, 770, WWDJ. He asked if I wanted to do an eight-minute segment about biblical solutions to depression, anger, and greed, among others. I was excited and I immediately accepted the challenge. I pre-recorded tapes every week and handed them to him every Sunday morning. These were inserted into the half hour segments. I researched the topic, wrote down and practiced my presentation, and finally recorded it on a portable cassette player. For one segment, I interviewed Wayne Mack, author of several books on counseling. His books were compatible with the publishing's of Dr. Jay Adams.[4] Mike and I drove out to Wayne Mack's home in Pennsylvania, and it was a real treat to meet him. I did these radio spots for several months, but this media endeavor was short lived. It was a lot of work that I was ill prepared to handle, and Mike also decided he was not going to pursue it further for the time being. I decided to focus on my role in the church and I was eventually asked to join the leadership team.

While our spiritual cup was overflowing in the later part of the 1980s, my financial situation was precarious. My income suffered greatly after the stock market crash of 1987. My commission checks dried up because do-it-yourself homeowners also felt the fallout from Wall Street's decline and became reluctant to undertake home improvement projects. Inventory sat on the shelves in the stock room of home centers like Rickles, Channel, and Pergament, and smaller home building and lumber supply outlets throughout Long Island and Queens. Even though Adriane now had completed her Master of Library Science degree, her income as a Cataloger at The Pierpont Morgan Library was helping us just get by. My father was aware of our financial situation, namely living from paycheck to paycheck, covering rent, student loans, and debt from Adriane's graduate courses. My mom was also clearly aware of our money situation exemplified by her comments on the homemade Christmas gifts we decided to hand out that year. My family always made it a habit to buy each other Christmas presents and whether we were struggling financially or not we made the effort to buy within our means. I had recently received several compliments on photographs I took so I figured a framed picture would be an appreciated gift for the holidays. A local photographer on Northern Boulevard had a unique technique of mounting pictures by adhering them directly onto particle board. Adriane approved of this idea so I thought my pictures of flowers, of the Statue of Liberty and other NYC landmarks would be a fun gift idea. I thought everyone would appreciate these iconic photographs, especially because we really did not have expendable cash to pay department store prices. Everyone was polite and seemed to appreciate them. My mom flippantly commented that I needed to get a real job and stop giving out cheap gifts. I did a double take as I glared at her in disbelief. I sarcastically responded saying maybe you would prefer another thoughtless gift basket of toiletries or perfume. Sticking to her sentiments she responded that she would have preferred those. I rolled my eyes and took a deep breath, anticipating that I would have to calm down Adriane's reaction to her mother-in-law's callous comments. My father said nothing.

After the holidays he pulled me aside and suggested I should investigate pharmaceuticals sales. Outside of knowing that he worked at Lederle Laboratories as a chemist, I had no intimate knowledge of the healthcare industry. I had no clue that once the FDA approved prescription medicines that they were then marketed directly to a provider, to a hospital buyer, and to pharmacies. He took the time to educate me. He then pulled out the PDR, a large book with red binding, from the bookshelf he installed on both sides of our fireplace. Those bookshelves served as the family library. He saved every *National Geographic* magazine, and when younger, my brother and I tore through the articles and pull-out graphics. No comic books for his children! He had books with titles like *The Rise and Fall of The Third Reich* by William L. Shirer, or *The History of Rome* by Valerie M. Warrior, and multiple books on rhododendrons, gardening, music, and tropical fish. And his graduate textbook, *A Textbook of Organic Chemistry* by A. Bernthsen. The PDR, short for Physician's Desk Reference listed every pharmaceutical manufacturer and the drugs they made. It was filled with descriptions and pictures of the unique identification and product label of every tablet, ampule, syringe, and injectable a company manufactured and sold. We first turned to American Cyanamid, the parent company of Lederle and looked at their product portfolio. I was dumbfounded trying to pronounce the generic and brand names of these products. It was going to be an uphill battle to learn about a new industry, but I was willing to try. The Health Care sector seemed inherently more stable than the Consumer Discretionary sector, so I was motivated to explore a new career path.

Through my father's connections I was granted an interview for a sales position in Astoria, Queens. The interview was in Nashua, NH and I was tense and excited as I zipped on the Delta shuttle from LaGuardia to Logan Airport. A taxi took me to a hotel in Nashua where I would meet the New York / New England Regional Sales Director. I prepped the best I could. I finally interviewed with a tall, middle-aged gentlemen who was buttoned up in a suit and tie with large glasses. He was professional and friendly. I communicated the details of my current position, the market, my sales successes, the challenges, and other topics of interest. After the formal interview questions, he directed me to take an aptitude test. The test results were reviewed with me over lunch, and he didn't seem too impressed. A full day's interview with an actual aptitude test was not what I was expecting, and the drive back to Boston in the snow followed by a flight back to LaGuardia was worse than any roller coaster ride I had ever experienced. My nerves were frayed!

I didn't get the position but was determined to use this as a learning opportunity. I scoured the *NY Times* daily for pharmaceutical sales position, and I was eventually interviewed by Adria Laboratories. After a phone interview I was invited for a live interview at Newark Airport. When the hiring manager mentioned that the eight a.m. slot was already taken, I said I could be there at seven. He was impressed and he agreed to seven-thirty. When I was done an hour and half later, I departed and came face to face with the next candidate who was visibly displeased with me making him wait. I was offered the sales representative position a week later. Compensation included salary, company car, benefits, pension, and vacation. This was a whole new world. Adriane was ecstatic.

I was assigned a sales territory covering South Queens and Brooklyn, an easy drive from our apartment in Flushing. The two weeks I spent in Dublin, OH at sales training was designed to prepare me to sell three products, one which was a new product for the company. My customers were internists, cardiologists, hospitals, and pharmacies. I was excited to get out in the territory and meet with my new customers. I would be selling a product called Nitrol Patch. Nitroglycerin was well known as a vasodilator and was used to relieve the symptoms of angina for decades. Adria Labs had a marketing advantage in that they owned the brand name Nitrol and received FDA approval to market nitroglycerin ointment. The product was received well by the providers for its convenience of including a flesh-colored adhesive bandage. I quickly experienced my first set back. The patch was a great idea but when a female patient with angina complained about the quality of the bandage it was unceremoniously pulled off the market. The hot weather in Arizona had compromised the adhesive bandage and it slid down the patient's chest, soiling her blouse. The sales force was now responsible to promote the remaining well-established products, a prescription potassium supplement and an anti-nausea over-the-counter elixir. These products did not provoke any meaningful scientific discourse but required salesmanship to increase market share.

A million glides down the GI tract. That was the message from the front cover of the sales aid created by our marketing department. This marketing piece was designed to provide confidence and assurance that the potassium supplement was delivered to the gut and would be absorbed as intended. Generic potassium supplementation was an important component of managing adverse events caused by the use of diuretics for patients with congestive heart failure. While diuretics would help lower blood pressure, patients often experienced swollen feet and ankles caused by excessive fluid and salt in the body, and an unhealthy loss of potassium. Potassium supplements helped restore the electrolyte imbalance caused by diuretics. There were at least eight other companies selling potassium supplements in the late 1980s. The doctors were well versed in the importance of these pills as companies were well versed in the profitability of these pills.

To separate ourselves from the pack, our marketing department came up with a program labeled Physician of the Week. The program exploited the doctors own view of their self-importance and rewarded them and their staff with meals and a candy dish. My colleagues and I were tasked with selecting the highest prescribers of potassium supplements and tell them that they were the physician of the week. Several doctors who would never meet with me were so happy to learn that I would be bringing them and their staff a meal every day for a week and receive a cut glass candy jar for the waiting room. My sales jumped dramatically as I was hustling to promote this new marketing initiative. For one Internal Medicine practice on Nostrand Ave. in Brooklyn, the doctor gladly accepted the decorative glass candy dish but politely declined the meals saying he worked late afternoons and evenings and unfortunately could not take advantage of the lunchtime meals. Without hesitation I responded that I would bring him and his staff dinner for the evening office hours. The doctor was Jewish so I assumed a kosher deli platter from Grabstein's Deli in Canarsie would make him happy. I planned with the office manager to bring dinner to the office at five-thirty p.m. When I showed up with the deli platter he came out from the back and thanked me, but said he could not eat any of it because it was not kosher. I was befuddled and confused and said I thought that Grabstein's was a kosher deli. I was about to be educated on the nuances of conversative Jewish eating requirements. He informed me that the deli platter was not kosher, only kosher style, and not Glatt Kosher. I had no idea what he was talking about, I never heard of a Glatt Kosher meal. But resolved to meet my end of the bargain, I agreed to bring him a Glatt kosher meal. He was so thankful of my offer instructed me to order Chinese food from a place called Glatt Chow located a few blocks away on Avenue J and Coney Island Avenue. I rolled my eyes but thought, I'll do whatever I needed to increase my potassium business. Feeling adventuresome I brought some home for dinner. Adriane and I gagged trying to swallow the food. I swore I would never eat from Glatt Chow ever again. While my stomach was upset, my boss was very happy being that sales from that practice doubled for the quarter. And while this kind marketing initiative could be lucrative for business, it was not intellectually stimulating.

As the 1980s ended I had to navigate salesmanship and integrity. Corporate guidelines were designed to keep the company and employee constrained within the boundaries of the government policies and regulations. Harvest and Pastor Mike allowed me the opportunity to remain grounded in my faith. And with my father's help, career opportunities expanded dramatically. This launched a pharmaceutical career that impacted me professionally and personally for decades. I was grateful for the blessings I had received and focused on growing the spiritual gifts described in Galatians Chapter 5. And due to the dramatic change in my finances I made sure I was not going to be accused of buying cheap gifts again.

Chapter 17

The undisciplined man doesn't wrong himself alone—He sets fire to the whole world.

—Rumi

Crazy Ronnie was a mad man known for his hair-trigger temper. He ran the club located on 15th Street and 9th Avenue in lower Manhattan. This club needed a dealer to cover for the regulars, and Robert was drafted to oversee the club when other dealers took their breaks. Robert Celestino, a student raised and bred in Yonkers, was among the dealers needing someone to fill in.

This was a vibrant club perched on the top floor of a building and featured a sleek, white interior that made the area look spacious and inviting. The club's modern looking bar was backlit by lights that gave it a vibrant atmosphere as opposed to bars with the bare minimum of chairs, tables, and unfocused, dim lights. Games were scattered in several rooms. The most prominent space was a large, oval room with three Blackjack tables; then another room featured darts and a couch; yet another room displayed baccarat; and there was an office where a guard watched monitors for security cameras posted in the lobby of the building. The climate was edgy as employees made no effort to hide that they carried guns which made gamblers feel a fair amount of nervousness.

A golf equipment store operated at street level of the building which contributed to the upscale vibe of the neighborhood. Across the street, a warehouse was garrisoned to approximate a police precinct for a TV show about cops was filmed. Robert was suspicious when he first started dealing as he observed scattered cop cars across the street each time he came to work. Crazy Ronnie mockingly told him:

Why so nervous? It's for the show?

The club attracted other attention, this time from celebrities. Pamela Anderson and Tommy Lee once came to the club. They created a buzz with Pamela exuding sexuality from every pore of her smooth skin and Tommy Lee's male magnetism enveloped the whole environment. It was short lived. Tommy Lee had somehow managed to break the glass doors at the club entrance. They were large double doors with a flamingo design, and they shattered when he drunkenly slammed into them, reducing the works of art to shards of glass sprayed everywhere. It was a mess and Crazy Ronnie was pissed off claiming the doors were worth fifteen-thousand dollars. Tommy apologized and laid a couple thousand on the bar to cover the damage before ordering a few more drinks. They left shortly after, leaving Crazy Ronnie even more upset.

Robert knew most people who worked in the club but took special notice of a gorgeous brunette bartender he had not seen before. She looked like a model and wasn't accustomed to getting ordered around by anyone except the boss. When Robert ambled over to the bar, demanding a Heineken, she became indignant and sneered:

I don't know you; I've been working here for months. Who the hell are you?

He laughed.

Listen sweetie, I'm the dealer here, get me that beer and think about moving in with me.

She grimaced as she tossed the bottle cap in the garbage while slamming the beer on the bar, refusing to make eye contact with him as he smirked in her direction. Robert's method to capture his prey was to assert his bravado, make her defensive, and flirtatiously interact with her over the course of hours, days, or weeks to get his prize. His charm would soon weaken her resistance. The brunette was defensive at first as she watched Robert deal blackjack with authority; fast and intense. She had her own method of conquest and subtle flirtation was the means for good tips. Her looks gave her authority as she poured drinks for gamblers who entertained delusions of taking her to bed, all the while she raked in generous tips for a good pour, flirtatious smile, and an extra hundred at the end of a shift. Robert smiled and made small talk with her during his breaks. She laughed nervously, flirted cautiously and eventually accepted his offer of weed and coke as they disappeared into the storage room under the rouse of getting a couple extra cases of beer. In the early hours of the morning, she joined him at his apartment near the Dunwoodie Golf Course in Yonkers.

This gorgeous brunette claimed to be a Penthouse Pet, but he soon discovered that she was just an exotic dancer, a stripper, billed as the Amazon Girl. She boasted that she was the main event at the nightclub where she worked. She gloated how she was the only dancer to have her own poster, a poster that showcased her considerable skills as a dancer, not just any dancer, but a stunning beauty, an exotic brunette with all the curves in the right places, and her dark, brown shoulder length hair that perfectly matched those big brown eyes; and those full lips with the bright red lipstick that craved kissing. She was the object of many men's, and women's, fantasies. This temptress of the night, conqueror of jungle beasts, sported long wavy dark brown hair, flowing out from under her cowgirl hat, two shiny silver Saturday night specials perched in her holster draped around her undulating hips, firmly planted in cowgirl boots that oozed with dollars bills. The poster captured her as the victor of the masses, the savior of mankind from the wicked beasts of the wild. She was no savior, but she was wild. Her mid-western ethos of generosity and wholesomeness worked very well for Robert. He benefitted from the thousands of dollars in cash she brought back home every Thursday, Friday, Saturday, and Sunday night. Her earnings fed Robert's gambling habits but when his loses were greater than her profits, he grew tired, especially when she complained. He realized he could never introduce her to his family like his previous Korean girlfriends. She was not family material as she was either too coked up or too drunk in her free time. He unceremoniously kicked her out after he noticed blood stains from the frequent nosebleeds on the bedroom pillow. The coke had its downside, and he had enough. The relationship lasted six months before he loaded her and her stuff in his car and dropped her off to one of her girlfriends in Manhattan.

He thought to himself that he should stick with New York Asian women that had respect for family and tradition and stay away from girls who were non-stop partiers. Susan, a half breed of Korean and Japanese parents fit the bill. Robert met Susan at a club called Tango's. Susan was the waitress there and sported a sincere smile that exuded confidence and independence. She had a friendly face, manicured hands and spoke like a Long Islander, direct and brash. Like all his other women, she liked to party, and her only aspiration was to make money. Robert made headway and before long he was involved in yet another relationship.

Jimmy V was the enforcer and doorman at Crazy Ronnie's Club. Jimmy V had a reputation as a tough guy, one who extinguished troubles in a flash. He was a valuable man who was well paid because he was efficient. Crazy Ronnie rewarded Jimmy V handsomely with a stipend of four-hundred dollar per night. He rotated from the Forum to the Palladium and to Webster Hall. Jimmy V was a brash character, as he was both emotional and fierce. And he also knew Robert's new girlfriend, Susan. When

Susan visited Robert at work, Jimmy V thought nothing of greeting her with a passionate tongue kiss which she readily reciprocated. Not escaping Robert's gaze, he fumed as he approached the stalworth bouncer:

Hey look, Jimmy, you don't kiss her anywhere except the cheek or I will beat your ass.

An intense exchange of stares lingered on like two fighting dogs preparing for the kill. Robert was intense, but not eager to face a man ready to explode on him and rip him like a rabid dog. Robert felt Jimmy V's ire coming out of his nostrils. Robert decided to be temperate and let the incident simmer down, after all, he knew that Jimmy V had no real interest in Susan.

One night six Irish looking guys walked in around three-fifteen a.m. They were rowdy and clamored to continue gambling and partying. Robert slowly walked over to inform them to come in when the gambling area reopened at four in the morning. The rowdy bunch hissed and readied to start trouble.

Fuck you!

shouted one of the more imposing guys.

We're coming in.

Hey Jimmy, these guys aren't listening to me.

to which he responded

Fuck you, JC, kick their asses.

Robert was tough, but facing six towering men full of drunken stupor was not valor, but foolhardiness. Jimmy V's blood bubbled with rage. He lived for these scenarios, and he jumped at any opportunity to challenge anyone who did not fear to tread on his turf. He knew martial arts and grabbed the largest guy and applied a choke-hold and dropped him unconscious. The five hoodlums riled up to fight. Jimmy V proceeded to punch, kick, and choke every one of them. Robert looked on dumbfounded by Jimmy V's exploits. Jimmy V glared at Robert and smugly and jokingly commented:

What are you going to do if I kiss your girlfriend? I'll choke you out too!

Robert suppressed his emotions and kept his distance and was now concerned with other matters at hand.

On slow nights or after the last of the gamblers left, party girls would continue to hang out at the clubs for the last rounds of free drinks from gullible men. Robert was well acquainted with several of these ladies, and they had a general idea where each other lived. Robert had an apartment in Airmont, NY at the time that two of the ladies asked if they could get a ride home from him, not wanting to pay car service, livery, or a taxi, which would easily cost eighty dollars or more. Robert apologized and said he was staying in Manhattan for the night and could not be of service. Another regular of the club overheard the conversation and offered his services. Vinny was heading up to Rockland County and welcomed the late-night company. Vinny, the volunteer, had been drinking for hours and he and the two ladies laughed and swayed as they attempted to walk a straight line as they descended the narrow pathway leading to the parking garage. They weren't very successful as the clouding power of alcohol was in full effect, disorienting their judgement and impairing their motor skills. The ladies opted to sit in the spacious backseat and soon closed their eyes as the hum of the car lulled them to sleep. As Vinny made a right turn onto the Westside Highway from West 41st St., he felt a slight bump as the rear, passenger side, jolted a little. Not noticing anything unusual, he reasoned that he must have hit the curb as he was making the turn. It was dark, he was tired, and his judgement was impaired. He sideswiped a cop on a police scooter. The cop fell to the ground and radioed for backup. Vinny was pulled over before he could make it past 57th St. Vinny was in shock as the bright lights screamed. Vinny pulled over and quickly lit a cigarette and opened the windows to mask the smell of beer. While he was questioned about where he was coming from at that time of night he responded with slurs and the smell of alcohol. The officers quickly surmised his condition and arrested him for DUI. As he sat in the patrol car, he said he was coming from an after-hours club and was giving the ladies in the back a ride home. The cops, skilled in interrogation made him feel comfortable while asking for the location of this club. Vinny sang like a bird. The car was impounded, and he was given a ticket and a court appearance.

The next day the cops raided the club and noticed that this was no ordinary after-hours club. After they called headquarters, they were instructed to destroy everything in sight. All the gaming tables were busted up, glassware was scattered in pieces, holes punched in the walls, and the light fixtures smashed; it was total devastation. When Crazy Ronnie arrived at his usual time in the afternoon, he was beside himself as he couldn't believe his place was destroyed. He had no citations, no warnings, no nothing. And now this. He was pissed off. He wasn't called crazy for nothing. Ronnie had a temper and would take it out on anyone who crossed him.

His first order of business was to clean up and restore his cash flow. He borrowed large sums of cash, paid a crew of contractors, and had the club up and running in a few weeks. The Rockland girls got wind that the club was back in business and decided to retreat into their usual routine of after-hours cocktails after a night of dancing. Gabbing away about their escapades the last time they partied there, the bartender's ears were alerted to what he overheard. And Crazy Ronnie was not going to like it. The bartender relayed the story to Crazy Ronnie who became incensed. He could not wait to get retribution.

Vinny was an electrician who found work in Manhattan, a world away from his home in Monroe, NY. He was just a regular working stiff who liked to gamble, hang out in after-hours clubs and be in the company of seductive party girls, fine liquor, and if lucky, hook up with a girl who drank too much. After his arrest he was able to convince a judge for a conditional license, one that would allow him to drive to and from work. He also heard that the club was busted up and felt bad. He had no idea how pissed off everyone was and how much lost income was incurred. He innocently decided he wanted to apologize for what happened. It did not cross his mind that he would be blamed for the club's destruction. As he entered the building Robert spotted him on the security camera. The bouncer buzzed him in. As Vinny walked out of the elevator, Robert warned him,

What the fuck are you doing here? You can't apologize, it's too late, they are going to kill you.

Friends of Crazy Ronnie were also watching the security camera and rushed from behind Robert and grabbed Vinny and beat the shit out of him. Vinny didn't know what hit him. He had no time to react and could barely defend himself against the barrage of blows and insults. Robert stayed put as Vinny was escorted outside. Robert never saw him again. Robert decided he was out and was done dealing for Crazy Ronnie. Crazy Ronnie's volatility and unpredictability didn't sit right with him, and it was only a matter of time before he would be in his crosshairs.

No matter how disappointing a wayward son or nephew drifted from the fold, Robert always found family as his last refuge. He reached out to his mother's brother, Uncle D. Uncle D knew Robert's history and wanted to help in any way he could. Uncle D was a union delegate with the Teamsters and had many connections with the Department of Transportation. Needing a job and a place to stay, Robert moved in with him, in his small cape cod style house in Mineola, NY.

Uncle D used his influence to benefit Robert. For a year and half Robert worked in a diversity of jobs: he dug holes, he placed road barriers, he hauled dirt, and he did whatever odds and ends came his way. Robert was not accustomed to manual labor, and he hated the bureaucracy that accompanied union work. Many times, after working a day or two with a crew assigned to a particular job for a few weeks, he would be pulled aside and be given a check and asked to never come back. Uncle D puzzled over his nephew's lack of work ethic. Robert once argued with the foreman on an important job by the Brooklyn Bridge. He was instructed to put on waders and jump in a flooded trench. Robert was instructed to set up a sump pump and to drain the water in order to resume the excavation. He recoiled at the sight of slithering rats with long, segmented tails flailing in the murky water. Robert's disgust showed in his face as he walked up to the supervisor, refusing his assignment:

Fuck you! I'm not going in there.

The supervisor wasn't going to argue. He shrugged his shoulders and told him not to come back.

Another job required three workers to dig a twenty-by twenty-by-eight-foot-deep trench. The job was supposed to take a month. Robert, not quite understanding union rules, decided it would be faster to call in a backhoe to do the work. The trench was dug in a day, but he got a tongue lashing from Uncle D who screamed:

You idiot. Who the hell are you calling for a backhoe, you were going to get paid for a month, now you won't work. It's a game stupid, play the game.

Uncle D kept getting him jobs and he continued to skirt the rules. He was paid union wages, but he never deposited his checks in a bank because he didn't have a bank account. He cashed the check at the Union Hall Bank on 57th Street and First Avenue and gambled with whatever money he had.

Fed-up with the union he moved out of Mineola and was onto his next venture. He now worked with a Greek in Astoria, Queens. He was well acquainted with Paul G. who would gamble at several of the clubs on the East Side. He was opening his own club and asked Robert to manage it, secure the tables, machines, dealers, and staff. Paul G. had his own connections for the muscle.

He also supplied the money to handle needed cash-flow. Robert asked Zorro, and Jughead—a young Albanian—to take shifts dealing. Jughead stood six-feet-five inches tall, perfect size for a doorman. Because of his stature he became a target for drunks and crazy people looking to fight without cause. Robert was fond of the kid and convinced him he would be dead by the age of twenty-five if he continued to work as security personnel. The young Albanian paid heed to the warning and learned how to deal blackjack, poker, and craps under Robert's tutelage.

OK Ajumma, the faithful Korean loan shark, secured the hostesses and spread the word that JC would be opening a new club in Queens. Business thrived as gamblers flocked in from all over the borough. The club was packed every night. OK Ajumma knew what Korean gamblers liked and contacted a nearby Korean restaurant and made sure they were able to deliver whatever the customers wanted, on demand. The casino was full, tables were humming, and Paul G was impressed.

Robert soon realized he was too trusting, and that Paul G could not live up to his promises. Paul G. didn't actually have access to the cash to run the games. A successful club needed twenty thousand a night to operate a well-oiled machine. This large amount of cash was needed to pay expenses and the winnings to the customers. When Paul G could not come up with the cash to pay customers who wanted to cash out, he suggested that they could return in a few days or accept more chips to play with. This nonsense went on for a few weeks and Robert voiced his concern, predicting that the customers would not continue to gamble here if they could not walk away with cash.

Robert soon found out about a reliability issue with his doorman. Tiger, another Greek, sported long hair, long fingernails, and had a reputation as a killer. Robert told him:

I don't want any Italian guys in here, you understand?

OK, boss, no Italian guys.

The only connected guy Robert really knew in Queens was some half-Italian, half-Irish local everyone called Hollywood. Hollywood ran his own clubs in Queens and his juice, enforcers, came from the mob itself. Robert knew he would find out about the new venture and want a piece of the pie, and this would spell trouble. No sooner after Robert told Tiger no Italians, Hollywood is standing in front of Robert as he is watching Jughead's dealing skills. With shit eating smile, Hollywood spots the man in charge and greets him with a big smile,

Hey, JC!

Dumbfounded, Robert got up and walked right over to Tiger. Without warning he threw a right jab to his face and knocked him down.

I told you motherfucker, you don't listen.

Tiger didn't know what hit him and didn't understand why he was even being hit. Hollywood laughed:

You're crazy, you're the only guy I know who punches out their own bouncer.

He's a fucking asshole, I told him don't let anyone in and he lets you in.

Robert's premonition was correct, Hollywood was not here to gamble. He had an ax to grind.

JC, we need to talk, you're stealing all my customers.

Robert was having none of it.

Listen to me, no fucking disrespect, I'm running a business here. I don't know who your customers are. I have Korean connections; this is how I run my business. I'm just letting you know these people are all my customers.

Just as the words left his mouth, several cute Korean girls at the bar spotted the two in conversation and waved,

Hi, Hollywood! Hi, Hollywood!

Robert couldn't believe it. A trifecta of problems. He was going to have to deal with Hollywood while worrying about cash flow and muscle issues. He sought greener pastures and left the club after several months.

Robert's family life was no better. As a single guy he had more expendable cash than either of his sisters or their hard-working husbands trying to earn a middle class living in Yonkers and Suffern. Vinny Mastrullo was an auto mechanic and Lenny Cirino was a painter. For many years they were good providers for their families, but their personal demons hindered their earnings and their family stability. Robert liked to play the hero, as he provided them with cash, gifts, dinners, and vacations. While Robert was an enigma, and they often questioned the legitimacy of his earnings, that never stopped them from accepting his generosity. He always had a pocketful of cash and dressed in expensive designer clothes. Robert would take Jack and Margie to Atlantic City or Las Vegas and generously lavished them with gambling money. Margie and Jack never went on vacation, so this was a dream for them. Patricia and Jackie did not delve into Robert's activities as he was always involved in schemes that he kept close to the vest. He was secretive for obvious reasons, and they did not wish to pry in his affairs, for all they knew he was generous beyond imagination, and they were happy keeping their nose out of his business. Robert was generous with his wealth and helped with car payments, mortgage payments, new clothes, gifts, and dinners when asked. Jack loved Robert's largess, and he extolled his son's success. On the other hand, Vinny and Lenny were sickened with Jack's boasting, and eventually it became a bone of contention that blew up over time.

In the mid-eighties Patricia and Vinny bought a high ranch-style house in Suffern. They relocated across the Hudson River in Rockland County to raise their two boys while Jack and Margie sold their house in Yonkers to live downstairs. Vinny, at some point, lost his job and relied on Jack's social security benefits and Robert's good will to get him through a rough stretch. Tension rose as Patty complained to Robert:

Vinny's not nice to my father, he put in a locked door separating the downstairs from the upstairs.

Vinny did this to create privacy and create a physical barrier to prevent Jack from wandering upstairs unannounced and keep the ever-present cigar smoke wafting into his living room. Jack complained to Robert:

Your-brother-in-law is miserable, he yells at me, tells me to shut up, he won't let me rake leaves or do anything around the house, and won't let me plant those tomato plants Uncle Paul just gave me.

Vinny barked:

Don't do nothing to my house. It's my house, not yours.

For months and months Robert heard these complaints. Margie called him a few times crying and saying how nasty he was to them. Robert finally got fed up. He didn't care who this guy was, something was going to happen. One Sunday he came accompanied by some friends in a limo. These friends from the clubs were bouncers, doormen, and enforcers. For them, a ride to the country meant partying, drinking beer, snorting coke, and going on a joy ride. And maybe a fight, if called upon. Robert exited the limo, leaving his friends, and walked into his parents' downstairs apartment to give a kiss to his mother and father. Pleasantly surprised, Jack asked what he was doing here coming from the city.

You don't call?

Robert angrily responded:

That motherfucker's gone, fuck him.

As he went upstairs, he spotted Vinny and yelled:

You see that limousine downstairs, there's ten guys down there ready to bury you in the woods you cocksucka.

Vinny defiantly yelled back:

I don't care!

Robert retorted:

I don't care? We'll see, tough guy. You want to die today? Today's your day!

Robert left and returned with two big, hulking, gorillas. As Vinny turned white as a ghost, Jack came upstairs and pled to Robert:

Don't do anything to him, you'll make your sister a widow, besides she's pregnant with her second son.

What's a matter with this guy, don't he fucking learn? I'm gonna kill this motherfucka!

Robert fumed as Patty sat nervously smoking a cigarette knowing that when Robert was mad there was no controlling him. Vinny realized that things could go downhill fast. He quickly apologized to his in-laws and Robert. Robert paced the kitchen and living room as he stewed in his own juices ready to pounce if he detected any sense of insincerity from his penitent brother-in-law. Cigarette after cigarette had its numbing effects and after an hour he retreated to the limo. Vinnie was left frozen, realizing that he dodged a bloodbath and that it would be best to avoid future confrontations and interactions with his wife's crazy brother. Vinny would remind his children as they grew older to stay away from their uncle, he is a gangster and up to no good. There was no love lost between the two.

Chapter 18

I am no bird; and no net ensnares me: I am a free human being with an independent will.

-Charlotte Brontë

The 1990s ushered in many changes to my relationships, finances, and career. We mourned and paid respect to our loved ones who passed into eternity. We rejoiced and celebrated new life. We built upon the spiritual foundations that grounded us. And we forged ahead with our careers, however uncertain of the specific path.

It was February of 1993 when a loud explosion rocked Lower Manhattan. A massive eruption carved out a large crater in the World Trade Center. Our eyes were affixed to the television set behind the bar watching as sirens sounded and firemen swarmed the building assisting women, distressed, coughing, gasping for breath, and covered in soot. We were grieving, but not for them. Our Aunt Agnes had recently died and after the wake at Ribustello Funeral Home on Morris Park Avenue in the Bronx, several of her brothers, sister, and spouses, and nieces and nephews gathered for a meal at a pub on Williamsbridge Road. Uncle Jack sat in the middle of the long table, holding court, telling stories to whoever would listen. My wife, seven months pregnant, respectfully listened, but coerced me to switch seats with her after thirty minutes because Uncle Jack tended to spit as he talked. She already had a shower and didn't want another. Aunt Agnes was the first to die of my father's brothers and sisters. She was now free of the burden of mental illness that had robbed her of joy for so many years.

More changes were in store as my father, Paul, decided to retire. Dad's career spanned over thirty-five years at Lederle Laboratories and now was the time to enjoy the fruits of his labor.[1] My mom hosted a large retirement party in the backyard of their quarter acre property. Pops was very pleased to be surrounded by family, friends, and colleagues commemorating this milestone. My parents beamed when showing off their new grandson, James. And were proud that their late bloomer son had now transitioned from adulthood to fatherhood.

I hadn't seen Robert for seven years, but he surprised everyone by showing up for the retirement party. He was sporting a mullet haircut and closely cropped facial hair. He looked worn but I couldn't tell if that was from exhaustion from painting, being hung over, or strung out on coke. After the typical exchange of,

Hey cuz, looking good, How's everything,

I was introduced to his newest girlfriend, Susan, a well-spoken Korean-American lady. She spoke English without any accent, which was different from the previous two girlfriends I met. I always wondered how Robert met these Korean girls: Did he know the language? Did he like Korean cuisine? Did he have an affinity for Korean culture? How does a painter who works all day meet these attractive Korean women?

Susan was much more talkative than his other girlfriends. I quickly ascertained that she was not an immigrant. She made a comment about having an argument with Uncle Jack. While I know he could be exhausting and opinionated, I viewed her willingness to challenge him as a lack of respect and temperance. Especially so, being she wasn't family. When I met her, I wrongly assumed she was like everyone else I knew, pursuing a career and working toward the American dream. She proudly stated that she was a pharmacist, but I immediately had my doubts when she quickly changed the topic as I attempted to engage her in professional banter. The bonds holding Robert and Susan's relationship together was not my concern but was also unknowable, for the time being.

The responsibilities of a husband and father are the very reflection of the love of God, a never-ending devotion. I strived to be the spiritual example and material provider. It is a lifelong journey. Through the grace of God, the indwelling of the Holy Spirit has allowed me to overcome obstacles and navigate unknown paths.

For the past few years, I was on the board of Harvest Ministries, yet I had to make the painful decision to find a church closer to home. It was not an easy decision, but because of a back ailment I was incapacitated for a week; a week of affliction that prompted reflection. I wrote a letter of resignation and called Pastor Mike and everyone on the board explaining my decision. While they were saddened, they understood our dilemma and they appreciated our sincerity. Pastor Mike informed Pastor Charlie Rizzo of our move and Maranatha Church of the Nazarene became our new home church. It was tough leaving, but we did not miss the trek into the city every Sunday with toddler in tow. Our Sunday routines became exhausting. We usually left our house at nine a.m. and didn't return until four-thirty. With all the activities and responsibilities with Harvest on Sundays, coupled with caring for a baby, it felt like another day at work. I was not looking to get involved with ministry at Maranatha right away but was concerned that Adriane would no longer sing. It was her passion. Many of the congregants shared how blessed they were to her soulful voice leading worship over the years. I assured her there would be opportunities to worship in some capacity in our new church. Adriane was a songbird that needed to sing. Soon, she would find a new home from where to perch.

By this time, Maranatha was a very large congregation. They had moved ten years earlier from the small wooden structure in New Milford to a new building, a repurposed Jewish Community Center, in Paramus, NJ. The sanctuary was specifically designed for sound and film recording as Pastor Charlie's messages and music were captured on DVDs. Sunday morning services easily had three hundred people in attendance, while Sunday evenings had half that amount. There were children's ministries for all age groups, a full kitchen in the basement, and multiple classrooms and office space for the various other ministries and bible studies. We hoped to get involved with ministry when the time was right. I reached out to our friend and Adriane's worship partner, Dr. Tony Panzica, who lived in New Jersey and had a flourishing chiropractic practice near his residence. Tony was a passionate musician, songwriter, guitarist, and vocalist. He had an extensive network of friends and gave us the phone number of Denny Vivolo, a gifted guitarist. Adriane procrastinated in making a telephone call uncomfortable in the art of persuasion, self-promotion, or with expounding her vocal abilities. I was the salesman and understood the dynamics of a successful cold call. I managed to convince a very skeptical Denny to meet with Adriane. Knowing that he was a proficient blues guitarist and liked soulful voices I made sure he understood Adriane's singing style. He latched onto my comment about her having a bluesy, raspy voice like Bonnie Raitt and agreed to come over to our house and explore this talent.

He showed up a week later with his guitar and a box of fig newtons. Denny looked like the majority of the friends I palled around with in college. He sported long brown hair over his ears, an open flannel shirt exposing a colored t-shirt underneath, blue jeans supported by a black leather belt, and tan fry boots. Several years older than us, he was confident, yet not brash. They exchanged pleasantries and compared their mutual acquaintances. Getting that out of the way, Denny became curious as to what this beautiful brunette, and mother of a one-year-old baby, could bring to the table, and with no further delay suggested they sing a few songs together. They jammed harmoniously as if they were an established duo. Denny and Adriane arranged a few more sessions to remove some kinks and establish a repertoire. They sang a few songs they knew, and it became clear they had musical chemistry.

Denny was well acquainted with Pastor Charlie Rizzo and with several members of the worship team including Harvey Auger and Chuck Corradino. Pastor Charlie was extremely accommodating to congregants who wanted to perform a few songs on special occasions, and recognized music as a universal bond and bridge between the divine and human. Adriane accompanied Denny playing special music for the pre-Thanksgiving evening service at the church. Denny wrote a song called "Thank You", which was appropriately selected for the occasion.[2] They were well received with their inspiring song selection and seamless execution of contemporary worship music. Six months later, Harvey, the leader of the music ministry called Adriane and invited her to join the worship ministry. She was back singing regularly on Sunday mornings and blessed the congregation with her beautiful voice. Years later we recruited Chuck to give my son drum lessons while Harvey was extremely gracious to include him as a drummer in the worship team during his high school years. Chuck would go on to be ordained and is Lead Pastor for the Church of the Nazarene in Butler, NJ.[3]

Besides the change in our home church, I made a series of career moves that greatly impacted our quality of life. For the last few years, I worked for the oncology sales division of my company. I sold chemotherapy products to medical oncologists in New York City. Between appointments I spent time at the Memorial Sloan Kettering Cancer Center faculty library. I researched relevant articles about the products I was selling and sought to learn more about the different types of cancers they were indicated for. I was naturally curious about my father's academic achievements, so I decided to scour various publications that my father authored. I enjoyed exchanging professional banter with my father. Even though I was a sales representative, and he was a research chemist, we had enough knowledge and interest in the life sciences that we could intelligently engage in informed, granular conversations regarding diseases and medications.

I found nine publications in the Journal of Medicinal Chemistry that had credited his contributions. To my great surprise, I saw one publication dated nineteen-seventy-nine about a drug class he worked on, called anthracenediones. That class of drug showed pre-clinical efficacy in leukemias.[4] That paper was one of many that enabled Lederle Labs to develop and eventually receive FDA approval for a product called Mitoxantrone. Its distinctive color motivated many employees to affectionately refer to it as Big Blue. Mitoxantrone was a direct competitor to Idarubicin, a product I launched in the mid-1990s, as both were indicated for acute myelogenous leukemia. We teased each other over the coincidence of being involved in the different phases of a drug's lifecycle. His role was in the beginning of drug development and my role toward its apogee as a medicine. My father never discussed his research at home. His work could not be easily translated into layman terms so his usual response to questions from his children was

Why bother explaining what I do, you wouldn't understand.

It was true but also displayed his lack of desire and inability to communicate in simple terms. I was one of a few blood relatives that could have some level of professional discourse.

Successful sales results and efforts are often rewarded with monetary incentives above and beyond a standard salary and pharmaceutical sales were no different. A quarterly bonus allowed the employer to recognize and reward the behaviors they valued.

Unfortunately for me, the bonus money I earned was not proportional to the financial needs of my growing family. I wanted more income and needed more income, especially since we lived from paycheck to paycheck. Mortgage, taxes, and student loans depleted our earnings. We had borrowed thirty-thousand dollars from my parents for a down payment on a house we purchased from my maternal grandfather, James Crosbie, back in 1990. My grandmother Isabel died, and I was the only grandchild, out of twenty-seven grandchildren that had any interest in purchasing it. This Dutch Colonial house was built in 1928. The house encompassed a modest thirteen hundred square feet in living space. With no upgrades since the nineteen-fifties, we were forced to spend a large amount of money for capital improvements. For years we poured money toward insulation for the attic. We then we upgraded electricity and plumbing, we built a new kitchen, we finished the basement, and we built a second bathroom. Through it all, my parents decided to modify the interest rate on the loan they originally gave us and increased it to ten percent. They justified the increase because the original rate no longer matched the current rate of return of their portfolio. Financially ignorant, I thought to myself, portfolio, who has a portfolio? While I had funds to make necessary improvements to the house, we precariously dipped into our savings. The birth of our daughter brought added stress to make ends meet.

With financial struggles and increasing job insecurity, I sought a change. We had changed where we worshipped a few years earlier, and we settled comfortably into our new spiritual home. I felt confident that a career change would also work out well. I was tired of working for a cash strapped company that consummated its second merger in just three short years. The mergers caused a change of identity as the name transitioned from Adria Laboratories to Pharmacia Adria to Pharmacia Upjohn. I sold the oncology portfolio for six years with Adria. Their most well-known product was named Adriamycin, a type of chemotherapy with a distinctive red color.[5] Oncology nurses called it red death. While extremely efficacious, it could cause serious side effects. It also had a Ph of 3.0, meaning it was highly acidic. If not injected properly into a vein, destructive necrosis would kill surrounding healthy, skin, muscle and fat. Doxorubicin, the generic name of the product, was part of a class of drugs called anthracyclines which was derived from bacteria taken from soil samples from the Adriatic coast of Italy. This clay soil was the same soil type used to by the Romans to dye their cloaks red. Two thousand years later it was discovered that the same soil harbored bacteria with anti-cancer properties. The FDA granted Adriamycin fourteen indications for use in a variety of cancers.

To sell such a product required intense training. The sales force was thoroughly educated on normal cellular functions and mitosis; cancer and its intrinsic and extrinsic risk factors; the different types of cancer; the efficacy, safety, mechanism of actions of the product; clinical studies that supported product approval, and our marketing messages. The final exam for the training class was ten blank sheets of paper. We were expected to write the Adriamycin package insert word for word. It was a pass or fail exam. After an intensive two-week training class, I was now certified to promote Adriamycin to our customers. Selling an oncology product to Medical Oncologists was drastically different from selling generic potassium supplements to internists and cardiologists, which is what I did my first two years with the company.

Oncology sales suited me because I could impact physicians prescribing behavior through discussions of scientific articles. I quickly found out that clinical data wasn't the only reasons these cancer doctors prescribed a company's drug. I pushed back my manager's request when I first started in my new territory. I was told that a three-man oncology practice in Englewood, NJ was not meeting their purchasing obligations. This practice had signed a volume contract which stipulated they had to order a certain amount of Adriamycin every quarter. The terms of the contract allowed the practices to receive a chemo chair and chemo hood. This special reclining chair had hardware attached to hold the medications. The chemo hood was a two-foot by fifteen-inch tabletop, ventilated workstation where pharmacists and nurses could prepare the medications for administration. The company wanted me to remove these and pack them up in the Ford Taurus provided to me by the fleet department. I laughed sarcastically at my boss and said there is no way I am removing these from this office or any office. The practice negotiated new terms and was allowed to keep these items.

After nine months covering a suburban territory, I assumed control over a Manhattan based territory. I was now interacting with doctors from Memorial Sloan-Kettering Cancer Center, NYU, and Cornell Medical Center. These doctors wanted to discuss the clinical data I presented. It was a whole new world when I moved over to oncology sales, and I proverbially pinched myself thinking a kid who nearly flunked out of school was now having scientific exchanges with nationally respected oncologists. I was allowed to sit in on Dr. Larry Norton's weekly meeting with oncology fellows and attended various tumor boards at NYU and the Manhattan VA. Dr. Norton, Chief of the Breast Service at MSK-CC, held court with the first-, second-, and third-years fellows discussing patient cases.[6] It was a privilege to learn and be exposed to brilliant minds and experience how they thought about tackling the challenges of treating patients with breast cancer. The NYU solid tumor boards focused on cases that the fellows saw during their hospital rounds. While patient names were never mentioned, their cancers and treatment plans were. Occasionally the doctors would ask a sales representative for updates on any new data about the product you represented that was being discussed at major medical meetings such as ASCO, American Society of Clinical

Oncology. If you weren't on your game when responding to a question, you lost credibility. Credibility and respect from the doctors earned you an appointment, or in the rarest of occasions, a seat at the conference table. It took me years to earn a seat at the table. I loved learning from the experts and was proud that I had earned their respect.

What a contrast my profession was to my cousin's. One cold winter morning, as I was leaving an early morning appointment with a private practice oncologist on 61st Street and Lexington Avenue, I noticed three men walking briskly toward me. I was wearing a long winter coat, juggling a black leather folio brief in one hand while slurping coffee from a disposable coffee cup with the distinctive Greek inspired design called Anthora. My head was tilted down as a tall, disheveled guy holding a dark duffle bag approached. He was flanked by two shorter men on either side. As they neared closer, I noticed that the man in the middle was Robert. He looked intent in his task. I spoke loudly to get his attention as my breath fogged up in the cold air. He was hunched over and looked surprised to see me. He slowed down and said:

Hey, Cuz, looking good.

I was raring to go as I felt hyper with two cups of coffee in my system. He seemed strung out after a long night of partying. I laughed and said something along the same vein to him. One of the guys mumbled something or other:

Do you want me to take care of this?

I eyeballed the guy as he eyeballed me, and Robert turned halfway around to his buddy and waved him off saying:

Nah, nah. Then he added a definitive *NO!*

I thought: what the hell is this guy's problem? I'm talking to my cousin and this guy seems like he wants to interrupt us. The brief exchange was over. I later realized that Robert was walking back to his apartment with thousands of dollars in cash from one of the clubs, and his buddies were there to protect him. What different paths we travelled. While Robert had his challenges with looking over his back and worrying about who or what was going to interrupt his money flow, I was hustling to get in front of medical oncologists hoping for some robust discussions about the products I was promoting.

A few months later I was pale, listless, and at death's door.

Mr. Fabio, you can't leave here without a doctor signing your release.

Ok, get a doctor here to sign the release.

Well, no one is here to do that.

Ok, then I want a patient advocate.

Sorry, but no one is here.

It was the evening of January 7, 1997, and I was in Pascack Valley Hospital in Westwood, NJ and stood in front of the nursing station in a loose hospital robe, a pair of socks, and my underwear. An IV hanged on my arm as I held the chrome pole where the bag of saline was hooked. I was frustrated and argued with the nurse and demanded that someone mercifully pull this needle out of my arm. I was determined to leave at once. The nurse, visibly annoyed that I was challenging her authority said that I couldn't do that without a doctor's approval and that was that. After two protracted days of waiting for my doctor to arrive, after making call after call to no avail, after howling at three different nurses, and even speaking with the doctor's wife, I reached my wits end. I needed to see Doctor Johnson. I had it with this place and was determined to leave.

Five days earlier I was diagnosed with infiltrating lingular pneumonia. This was a lingering condition that nagged me for many months. I coughed and felt sapped of energy. My wife pleaded with me to go see a doctor. My constant cough and lack of energy to even walk across a room was not normal. For months I took it one day at a time and figured I could power through it. But after our trip to North Carolina for the Christmas Holiday it became obvious I needed to see a doctor. I couldn't even walk across my parents living room without stopping to sit down and catch my breath. I knew I wouldn't be able to see my primary doctor without an appointment, so I found a same day clinic in Spring Valley, NY. After reviewing the x-ray, Doctor Johnson prescribed an antibiotic, a cough suppressant with codeine, potassium iodide drops for the persistent cough, NyQuil, Ricola drops, and Chloraseptic mouth wash. I was skeptical that any of these medications would work. Four days later I left a message with his office complaining of dizziness, a nasty cough, and numbness in the left fingers and toes. He called me back and advised me to go to Pascack Valley Hospital which was less than six miles from my house. He said he would arrange for me to be admitted. I figured if I was going to be admitted I had better pack a bag for a few days, and at the last minute I grabbed The Merck Manual, a medical textbook given to me as a sales award.[7] I arrived a little after two p.m. on January 6th, 1997. I was sent to the emergency room where the staff said they had no orders from any Dr. Johnson to admit me, but they put me behind a curtain and told me to lie down and wait for him to come. I waited, and waited, and waited some more. He never showed up, so the nurse sent for x-rays and CBC and confirmed that I had pneumonia. The staff was dumbfounded as to why the doctor was not responding so they finally admitted me around eight-thirty p.m. I called my wife and gave her a status update and said I'll be fine and should be home in a few days and not to bother visiting since the weather was very cold and it would be too much of a hassle for her to pack up an eleven-month-old baby and three-year-old toddler just for a quick visit. The next morning, I managed to speak with Dr. Johnson's wife who said the doctor should be over late afternoon. I settled in and waited. A couple of volunteers came to the room and offered prayers to anyone who wanted it. I said sure, I would love to pray. We prayed. They looked at me and wondered

Why you are even in here? You look so healthy.

I shrugged my shoulders and laughed and said:

Compared to this guy next to me, (a sixty-nine-year-old man hacking up his lungs), *of course I do.*

They chuckled and wished me well. After dinner I noticed the veins in my hands were dark and easily visible, and my hands were a blueish, purple color. My feet were freezing at this point, and I took off the white athletic socks I was wearing, and noticed they were purple as well. Something was clearly not right, and I called for a nurse. She was just as curious and put my finger in an oxygen finger monitor. I asked why my hands and toes were turning purple, and she looked at the reading and said nonchalantly that it looked like I had cyanosis and walked off. I was shocked, thinking,

Aren't you going to do anything about, like get a doctor in here?

I was pissed off and could not believe what was happening. I pulled out the Merck Manual and started flipping through the pages until I read the four stages of an acute asthma attack with cyanosis as sign of stage III (severe), followed by stage IV (respiratory failure). I freaked out, thinking if I stayed any longer, I would be dead by the morning. I was on edge and demanded a nurse come to my room at once. A different nurse came into my room, and I asked,

What are going to do about my condition? I want a new doctor being that Dr. Johnson never showed up.

The annoyed nurse came back and handed me a phone book and advised me to look one up. She said she was not allowed to make referrals. I looked at her in disbelief. It was after dinner, and I thought I was not going to waste my time calling random phone numbers at eight p.m. I called information looking to reconnect with my primary doctor. I eventually spoke with his answering service and explained the situation, and said I was leaving this hospital and would be driving to Good Samaritan Hospital in Suffern, NY. The answering service said she would relay that information.

That's when I got up and headed over to the nursing station and asked her to remove the needle. She would not budge, and after a tense exchange, my voice getting louder which each request, I ripped the IV out of my arm. She stood there with her mouth open.

You can't do that!

I threw the needle and tubing on the counter. I dressed, packed up, and headed out wondering why the hell this was happening, but I was determined to take action, and no one could deter me. I could not believe what I was going through. I have been in all kinds of hospitals in the New York area and interacted with so many respected MDs and staff. Never did I expect the lack of care from the doctor and floor staff.

It was a bitterly cold night, the dashboard thermometer read 27°. I made my way north on the Garden State Parkway toward the NYS Thruway. As I approached the toll booth just west of Spring Valley, my hands froze. They were completely numb, and I couldn't feel anything and was unable to grab the loose change in my pants pocket to toss in the toll booth basket. Instead, I drove straight through as fast as I could to Suffern. I pulled into the visitors' lot around ten p.m. and walked to the emergency room. I was haggard and tired since I had not showered for days. I was weak and could barely carry my bag of clothes. I explained my story at the admission desk. The young nurse behind the desk looked at me curiously, focusing on my disheveled, greasy hair, stubbled facial growth, and unkempt appearance. A male doctor joined her as they questioned me where I was coming from. I had my bag of clothes and some medication but had pulled off the identification wrist band given to me at Pascack Valley Hospital. The two grew increasingly suspicious of my story as their line of questioning led me to believe that they thought I was homeless. After adamantly saying that I had pneumonia and I had not been treated properly, they finally agreed to do another x-ray. As I miserably returned to the waiting room coughing, weak, cold, and tired, the physician on call said,

While your story is quite usual, you not only have pneumonia, but you also now have double pneumonia.

I responded sheepishly,

So, I guess I'm admitted.

To which he responded:

Oh, you are not going anywhere.

I was so wiped out I can't even remember the number of doctors and nurses that rotated through my room on an hourly basis. After several days it was determined that the antibiotics were not working, and that I needed a bronchodilator to open my airways. I was there for seven days before I was finally sent home. The care at the two hospitals was like night and day and thank God I found refuge in a facility that was doing what it was supposed to do. I was introduced to Dr. Osei, the pulmonologist who made the correct diagnosis and modified my treatment plan to counteract the effects that asthma was having on my response to the antibiotics. I counted my blessings and returned home to the comfort of my devoted wife and adoring children. I focused on my health and planned a career change.

I took stock of my career at that point, and I was satisfied with my professional interactions. However, after several unimpressive product launches, after generic competition and because of lack of innovative products, my opportunity for advancement stagnated. The European parent company of Adria Labs, Farmitalia Carlo Erba Spa, decided to partner with Upjohn based out of Kalamazoo MI. Now the company culture suffered as well. It no longer had a small company feel. It was Big Pharma, characterized as a bloated, impersonal bureaucracy with little innovation. Although I was offered a position in the sales training department in Kalamazoo, I did not consider this a promotion. I would have to pay for my own move and no longer have a company car. I was not ready to move to another state with two young children, no family support and a loss of income. I pursued other opportunities. A conversation with a colleague from North Carolina encouraged me to take a risk and explore more nimble and more innovative biotech companies. I explained that I had interviews scheduled with Lilly, but I was hesitant to jump to another Big Pharma company. She connected me with a former colleague of hers who joined a San Diego based company called IDEC Pharmaceuticals. She said just be open minded. After I spoke with the VP of Sales for about forty minutes, we agreed to keep in touch, even though he mentioned that IDEC would not be hiring until the end of the summer. He sent me an investor prospectus which I read but brought to work with the intent to share with some customers to get their opinion on the company and the molecule under development. As I waited to pay for my lunch at a diner on First Ave. and 30th Street, I spotted one of my customers, Dr. Bruce Raphael who specialized in hematology and oncology at NYU.[8] I called on him for years to talk about Adriamycin as part of chemotherapy regimens for non-Hodgkin's Lymphoma. As we were standing in line to pay our bills, I showed him the prospectus and asked for his opinion. After he read it, he commented that while it was not a panacea, an anti-CD20 monoclonal antibody will have some utility for patients with NHL. That didn't sound like a blockbuster to me, but when he proceeded to fold it up and put it in the breast pocket of his suit, I understood the real value. We smirked at each other as I snatched it back from him and thanked him for his opinion. Still not certain about the opportunity and with no definite timeline of when IDEC would be hiring, I pursued the position at Lilly. The final interview was a meeting with the regional manager at his office in Stamford CT. After reviewing my resume for about thirty minutes, he handed me a copy of The Journal of Clinical Oncology sitting on his desk. He opened it up to an article about a clinical study done with gemcitabine, one of Lilly's products, and told me to read it, and sell him on the product when he returned in fifteen minutes. I read clinical studies for years. My first exposure to reading clinical studies was in college. I had a course in clinical psychology and had an assignment to replicate a study. After reading a clinical study by Hermann Ebbinghaus on memory recall of nonsense syllables, I proposed to my professor to conduct a mini study with fifteen students as the study group. The first lesson I discovered from this assignment was that I easily comprehended the outline of a clinical study. The second was that conducting a study in a controlled environment was not an easy task. I had to approach random students as they drank their coffee or tea at the Fitzelle coffee shop during a break between classes and convince them to participate in my research project. Eventually I had to write up my research findings in the format of a published research paper which included the title, abstract, introduction, methods, results, supporting graphs, discussion, and reference. Professor Michael Siegel gave me an A on this project and commented:

Wow, students really do learn.

Little did I know that years later my career would focus on how to construct a sales call using the data presented in a journal article. I closed the Lilly regional manager on the merits of the data and shared the products efficacy, the adverse events, and the benefits for an appropriate patient.

I had a job offer by April seventh. I still was not excited about joining a company like Lilly with its reputation as bureaucratic and not innovative. I called the VP at IDEC and shared with him that I had a job offer, but that IDEC was still where I liked it to be. We met face to face at the ASCO meeting in Denver, CO that May and by mid- June I was working with IDEC Pharmaceuticals. After a slight delay Rituxan was FDA approved on the Monday after Thanksgiving 1997.[9] Four months later I understood the excitement this product brought to the medical community. While I attempted to have a sales call with a medical oncologist a few blocks from Montefiore Medical Center in the Bronx, I was yet again told by the office staff that the doctor had no time to see me. The bane of every salesman's existence is to be told to come back some other time. I left my business card with the receptionist and not so subtly said that the doctor will want to see me. I then wrote the product's name: Rituxan, rituximab. As I approached my car halfway down the block, I heard a faint voice. Thinking it was kids running around the neighborhood I ignored it. The voice got louder:

Mr. Fabio, Mr. Fabio!

I turned, and the office manager was running down the block after me.

The doctor wants to see you now! Please, come back.

I followed her back into the office, then waited a few minutes. After I reviewed the data for ten minutes, he clamored for more and asked about any local speaking programs he could attend. He heard about Rituxan from one of the medical symposiums he attended and wanted a new alternative for his patients.

Dr. Cieplinski had heard about Rituxan as well. He had prescribed it many times for his patients with lymphoma. I had had several clinical discussions with him over an eighteen-month period, but this appointment was different. As I was standing in his office, I asked him if he had any patients, he thought could benefit from Rituxan. He said yes and wanted to offer it to a patient with mantle cell lymphoma. This type of lymphoma was named for its location of origin, the mantle zone, an outer ring of lymphocytes that surrounded the center of a lymphatic nodule. It was an aggressive and rare form of non-Hodgkin's lymphoma and Rituxan did not have an approved indication for that cancer. I reminded him of Rituxan's approved indications, and that insurance would not likely provide coverage for a product used off-label. He was adamant about offering to his patient because he felt he was out of options. He also asked me if I could speak with the patient and explain a little about the product and how it worked. I said that if that patient wanted to learn more about the product that I could leave patient education material and that if wanted to use Rituxan off-label, the office manager should enroll the patient in our patient assistance program which would determine insurance eligibility or provide the drug for free. As he said,

Yes, yes, I know all that.

He surprised me as he motioned to the closed door of an exam room and said he had a patient in there and she is very upset. He pressed me,

Please, speak with her. Explain to her how your product works.

In an instant, I was overwhelmed with apprehension and reticent to proceed with his request. A flurry of thoughts swarmed around my brain as I tried to reconcile his desire to comfort his patient versus me adhering to my employers' product promotion guidelines. Direct product promotion to a patient was not allowed and not what I was trained to do or prepared to do. However, the Dr. was asking me to assist him in managing a patient in crisis, he was asking me to offer his patient compassionate empathy.

I agreed to meet the patient and listen to her questions, not fully comprehending what awaited me in the next room. I was being trusted to participate in the most privileged communication, the physician-patient interaction. As I walked into the room, a young lady sat on the exam table, tense, her legs were pressed together, hands clasped tightly, as her rounded shoulders broadcast her torment. I introduced myself and shared that I would be happy to answer any questions she had. Almost immediately, she teared up, as she shared her story. I offered my hand as she attempted to blot away the wet streams oozing down her cheek. This beautiful young mother had just given birth to her fourth child, a daughter. Sniveling, she explained that six months after daughter's arrival, she returned to her pediatrician complaining of abdominal cramps. It was determined that she had an enlarged lymph node, most likely an infection, and was prescribed antibiotics. As she now sat in her oncologist's office, the pathology report revealed that she an aggressive form of cancer. She cried out,

Will your product work for me? Am I going to live? I have a family that needs me.

I tried to maintain my composure as best I could. I had no answers, I made no promises. I could only explain the product's mechanism of action but could not assure her of the drug's efficacy. The only assurance I could provide was that her doctor would do the best he could to find an effective treatment. Dr. Cieplinski was very grateful and thanked me for assisting him in his quest to comfort his patient. I thought and prayed about the patient and her family for months, hoping for a miracle. None would come. When I spoke with the doctor six months later, he informed me that she died. The cancer was resistant to everything he administered. The battle against cancer, against pain and suffering, is difficult and frequently unsuccessful. I had a small part in the dynamic of patient care. Everyone tried to help as the challenge of finding a cure for cancer is ever before us.

Robert and his friends had a different approach to relieve pain and suffering, and it wasn't exactly what the medical community advocated.

Hey, Rob, have you heard about Billy? He's in bad shape!

Matty said as they spoke on the phone. Billy Sloan, a childhood friend who lived on Cook Avenue in Yonkers, was now dying at Memorial Sloan Kettering Cancer Center. Billy and his younger brother Alexander always liked to party, always enjoyed pot, and were mainstays at the CPW Bar on Central Avenue in Yonkers. In the 1970s drinking and weed were accessible, while coke and pills required a little more money and effort. They all made the effort to get what they needed; they needed to get high!

Alexander died in 1981 of a suspicious heart attack. He was twenty-one and he lived at home. His death was sudden. Robert dropped by the house on a June afternoon hoping to hang out with him. Alexander's mother muttered and scowled and denounced his presence. Her son was dead. Mrs. Sloan then took a deep breath and spoke:

You and your friends are no good. Alex died last night. He was doing things he shouldn't have been doing.

The door slammed in his face as he attempted to apologized and said:

Sorry for your loss.

What else could he do? Alexander and Billy liked to party with Robert, Matty, and other local deadbeats. Billy was always a party guy and when not drinking, he did *tuies.* The actual product name was Tuinal. It was a combination barbiturate for pain, and it was popular for recreational use for those with the right connections. Tuinal was highly addictive, especially when combined with drinking as it transported the mind into a liminal zone. Billy used his creativity to pinprick a hole in the pill so as to release the contents into his bloodstream faster. One night at the CPW bar, the owner, an Irishman named Kevin, told the bartender to stop serving this drunkard. Billy slurred vehemently and argued with other patrons, cursing the bartender for cutting him off. Billy was normally a mellow person, but now he was out of control and completely wasted. Robert quickly intervened when he saw the bartender grab Billy by the shirt:

I beat the cock out of him!

Robert boasted:

I stand up for my friends, and no one is going to shove Billy around.

After the commotion, the bartender's nose pumped blood like a broken faucet and his shirt stained red. Billy could barely walk as Robert and Matty carried his now limp body out like a sack of potatoes. Billy lost job after job, and his dignity faded like light at sunset. Billy scrapped by earning enough cash through cocaine dealing to meet his minimal needs. He and a few others made trips to Washington Heights and secured cocaine that they would later package in tinfoil to sell at various bars around Yonkers.[10] Four years later Billy was on his death bed. Matty and Robert kept in touch with most of the people that stayed in Yonkers. They learned that Billy contracted some sort of bone cancer, so they thought. All they knew was that Billy was in a lot of pain, that he looked emaciated, that his legs were swollen, and that he moaned at intervals. His condition was terminal. To provide some relief they offered him street drugs—heroin and valium—cut up and grounded into a powder to snort. Confident in their remedy they encouraged Billy to take a hit. Billy had his reservations, he hadn't partied for years since his sickness, and he didn't have the urge to get high. But Robert barked,

Too late, look at you, you're in agony, we are doing you a favor, bro.

With the angels of death at his bedside and too weak to argue, Billy took a hit. Over the next few hours, he slowly drifted into painlessness. His body never would recover from the drug combo he just snorted and died soon thereafter.

At the funeral, Matty was reproached by an angry aunt who blamed these misfits for the premature death of her nephew Billy.

You killed him. I know you guys.

Billy was entertained by his friends on Robert's birthday, September 11, 1998.[11] His death was announced the next day.

Chapter 19

> Beauty is mysterious as well as terrible. God and the devil are fighting out there, and the battlefield is the heart of man.
>
> —Fyodor Dostoevsky

Robert found a new opportunity with Nico the Greek and an Albanian nicknamed Turk. The club operated from 67th Street and Lexington Ave. Within time it was raided by the New York Police Department. Robert was handcuffed and arrested for possession of gambling instruments: chips, gaming tables, dice, cards, shoes, etc., and for operating an unlicensed bottle club. Robert was a recidivist, and since he had a number of prior arrests, he was sent to the Manhattan House of Detention. Known as the Tombs, it was a stark, gloomy complex. Nico instructed Turk to give to one of the waitresses a couple hundred dollars and post Robert's bail. Maggie, one of the bartenders, was a quiet Irish girl and green when it came to warrants and to bail procedures. She walked in apprehensively, stepped up to the cashier, submitted her name, said that she came to bail out Robert Fabio, handed over the required cash and was handed the bail receipt. Turk instructed Margie to wait after she handed in the cash for bail, but the place gave her the creeps, she was edgy and wanted out of that dingy office and walked out without the main man. An officer escorted Robert to the bail office, but there was no one there to show the bail receipt. Robert, fuming at the screw up, demanding to be released.

Robert was pacing in the holding cell for hours and wondered what the hell was going on.

Why am I still in here? Something's wrong.

He was miserable: no cigarettes, lousy food, and no phone calls. He paid a fellow inmate ten crispy dollars for a Snickers bar. After three days he started to bang on the cell bars and madly screamed at the guards:

What do I gotta do, kill a nigga to get a phone call in here?

Robert was only one out of two white guys in a pen with fourteen Black guys. He continued to bellow,

You all going to jail, motherfuckers, my boss has got my bail receipt, and I've been here three fuckin days. You're getting fuckin sued!

Finally, he was allowed to make a phone call. Completely agitated, he called Nico and screeched:

Where the hell are you? I've been in here four fucking days, get me outta here! No, I'm not in Atlantic City, I'm here you cocksucka. Get that bail receipt and get me the fuck outta here, you understand?

The bemused guards looked at him mockingly. Robert's voice rose a pitch as he ordered Nico:

Come down here and bring the bail receipt and get me out of here!

At once, the guards understood his frustration, and their oversight. Realizing the legal ramifications of holding a detainee after bail had been posted, they quickly thought to diffuse Robert's anger and brought him a McDonalds quarter pounder with cheese and fries. Nico finally arrived and presented the paid receipt. Robert was out that same afternoon.

If it weren't for his extensive arrest record, his attorney could have sued for millions. Robert was now a free man, and continued to deal at the club, as if nothing ever happened. Unfortunately, Nico had serious consequences: He lost fifty-thousand dollars gambling and now found himself owing ninety-thousand dollars to a loan shark associated with the Gambino's. Nico feared for his life. His imagined the vengeance he would receive. He had no means of paying the loan off. Even a monthly payment plan was out of the question. He was distressed and irrational and ran. He abandoned his wife and baby, retreating into the shadows, until there was no trace of him.

Nico's disappearance was a mere afterthought for Robert, for people walked in and out of his life like gloomy apparitions in the thick of night. Robert didn't linger into deep thoughts. He was a pragmatic thinker, for what truly mattered to him was the here and now since he lived in a constant moment where memories vanished in the mists of time, and the future was nothing more than a monstrous chimera, the illusory thing that is nothing more than an evanescent beast. So, Robert moved on, that's the only thing he normally did. He had no regrets and people from the past had no bearing in the moment.

This time he found another club to his liking, a club located above Giovanni's Restaurant on 38th Street between 9th and 10th Ave. He was back with his old partners working with Scotty the Jew who was the money man and with House, who supplied the muscle. Robert and eight other dealers rotated shifts dealing blackjack and poker. Trouble was brewing as the owner of the restaurant below the club came in and complained that their gambling club wasn't living up to its potential. Luigi, the owner, brought some enforcers upstairs and rewarded Scotty and House with a brutal beating, and for good measure he appropriated the club. Scotty and House were no pushovers, but they were outmuscled, and resistance would have been futile. The restaurant was owned by a connected man, someone within a heartbeat of the hierarchy of the mob, someone with power beyond peripheral players who were on the edge of the power structure.

As Scotty, bruised by the beating and hurt by his degraded ego was leaving the club with his tail between his legs, Luigi mocked:

Aw, these Jews, Hitler didn't do a good job.

Robert brashly replied:

Hey, Scotty's alright, leave him alone.

Fuck that. He's a Jew. Besides, what's he to you, who do you work for?

Luigi had no idea who Robert was, and he assumed he was connected with a family, but Robert voiced his independence:

I don't work for anyone, you want me to deal, you pay, you got it!

Luigi was impressed with Robert's resilience. He showed bravado, but at the same time he kept his level of respect, highly valued by made men.

Robert and Luigi came to terms and settled for two-hundred-fifty dollar a night, plus blow, and plus weed. Scotty was officially out of the club, a simple reason that when a mob connected thug wanted control, there was no one to stop him. Robert did not react before Luigi; it would have been futile and maybe even detrimental to their new understanding. Robert felt badly about Scotty. But loyalty was capricious and was used with discretion. Besides, his misgivings evaporated when he considered his lucrative outcome. Robert described him as such:

Luigi was a fat fuck who looked like Lou Costello from the Abbott and Costello comedy duo. He was a short, fat guy who liked to dress in suits, with a turtleneck in the winter, a button-down shirt in warmer weather, and always wore a diamond pinky ring. He was an arrogant prick who had a nasty attitude and tried to come across like a tough guy.

They were once jailed together. With a pen full of inmates and only one phone, tempers would flair over access. Luigi grew increasingly impatient with a Black inmate, demanding him to get off the phone, yelling,

Hurry up!

The enraged inmate turned and started to smack Luigi around. Luigi was both angered and humiliated, then yelled to Robert:

JC, give me a hand here. Get rid of this fucking mulignane.

Robert didn't budge, he wasn't going to step in to help this arrogant, fat, prick. Robert never understood where Luigi got his juice from, who provided financial support and protection. Eventually he learned about it when a cop shouted out:

Hey, Luigi, how's your Uncle Joe?

That's when the lights clicked! Robert finally knew who he was dealing with, what kind of power Luigi wielded, what kind of pedigree he was embroiled with. Luigi was the nephew of Joseph Massino, head of the Bonanno crime family in New Jersey.

Hey JC, see that guy on the machine, he's been here all night, he's not gonna leave, Luigi says. *I'm going home, you stay here and watch him.*

There was this Italian looking thug, thick black hair combed back, dressed in a sports jacket that fit tightly around his broad shoulders and massive arms. He was flanked by a couple of husky and imposing bodyguards, alert and protective of their master. This Italian was playing one of the electronic blackjack games and he was losing twelve-thousand dollars. He kept pouring money into the blackjack game all night long, and cursing:

I'm gonna burn this mother-fucking place down, it's got all my money.

Robert was dealing Blackjack, and during breaks, he'd go over and tell him:

Play at the table, you'll have a better chance.

The thug ignored Robert and continued the ritual as he pumped more and more coins into the mouth of the electronic bandit. There were hundreds of people in the club that night, and things turned sour. The thug decided he had enough with this fucking machine, and stood up, pulled out his gun, and started shooting it. Screaming and venting his frustration:

Bang! Bang! Bang!

Glass flew everywhere! Girls scattered and convulsed and screamed. Chaos followed. Girls frantically ran on high heeled shoes. Men tried to get the hysterical women out as fast as they could. Mayhem permeated everywhere as women ran out like bats out of hell and men chased them to grab them, hold them, and stop the stampede that could have resulted in mass injuries. The thug fully unloaded a seven magazine and regained his composure and calmly walked, out leaving a mess behind. All Robert could do was to get the crew to clean the debris.

Luigi was impressed with the recounting of Robert's cool handling of the volatile situation. He approached his now trusted man and asked him if he wanted to make an additional five-thousand dollars. Robert was gambling at the blackjack table while managing the club, and without hesitation nodded yes. He then said,

Now! I want it now!

Luigi reached for his deep jacket pocket and sank his money into Robert's jacket pocket. Luigi then proceeded to instruct Robert to go out front and move a car. He dispassionately said,

By the way, there is a dead body in the front seat.

Robert didn't bat an eye. The Cadillac was across the street with the keys in the ignition. He got in, a man in front passenger seat was slumped over liked he was sleeping, and Robert drove off. Three blocks away at 9th Ave. he got out and walked back to the club like any normal five a.m. stroll in NYC, quiet, no one around, and light from the horizon piercing the dark night. Harry, a well-known customer, was gone. Bullet to back of the head. He lived the high life. Loved to gamble, was always high on something, always had blow, and was accompanied with pretty, younger women. As I was interviewing Robert for this book I asked if this bothered him and what happened to cause his death. He really didn't know and said indifferently,

His luck ran out, I guess.

Robert graduated to the lofty position of enforcer as he had the physical prerequisites with his height and strength, with his temperament and his experience. Luigi always had a need for an enforcer and a debt collector. These side jobs required precise detail and smooth operations. Robert did his job without much ado as he was efficient, a much-appreciated trait. He beat up debt delinquents with a degree of indifference. Whatever the reason was not his concern, he was getting paid, that was all that mattered.

JC, go to Trump Tower and track down that Arab prick. He owes me $80,000.

Robert knew this polished Wall Street yuppie well. The Arab loved to flash his wealth. He brandished Brioni suits, Ferragamo shoes, a Patek Philippe watch, the symbol of haute horlogerie. Robert knew this oily guy well. He was in his early thirties, and he was always escorted with dazzling women who fretted over him like attentive muses. He was sufficiently arrogant to borrow risky money, overly confident that his insider trading prowess would rescue him from ruin. A piece of good fortune came to the Arab's rescue on this sunny day. Robert staked him out on the corner of the lobby where he could spy without being noticed. As he lurked in the hidden corner, he was surprised to see the Arab casually walking towards him. The Arab gleamed with a broad smile as he was happy to see a familiar face. The extravagant young Arab never imagined why Robert was truly in the atrium of Trump's Tower. The debt collection was the last thing on his mind, why it was sheer coincidence that the muscular Italian-American dealer happened to be there. But when Robert accosted him with a scowling face, the confused Arab started to retract. Robert cleared his throat intentionally like a hidden threat and said:

I'm here to get some cash, twenty-thousand dollars will do for now, the rest will be collected over the next six weeks.

But abruptly the Arab's face was drained of color, and he warned,

JC, stay away from me, I'm being watched. I'm under investigation for inside trading. You'll get caught up in all this.

Robert was shocked and his furrowed brows and menacing stare came with a final warning:

Pay up, or you're dead!

A week later the Arab was arrested. Luigi never recovered his money, and Robert never received his cut.

The connection to Luigi was a fruitful one for Robert. There always seemed to be new opportunities to make money and he rarely turned down an offer. Robert met fellow dealer Robert Celestino at Crazy Ronnie's club. Celestino hailed from Yonkers but kept his background close to his chest, as did Robert. Celestino was the godson of Dominick DeRuggiero, who was convicted of the 1976 murder of Butchy Futia. Dominick and his extended family played cards as a family activity and introduced Celestino to blackjack and poker. Comfortable around cards and casinos, Celestino found Blackjack dealing, a good, temporary side job as he attended The New School, a performing arts college, studying film. Celestino sought seed money for a new film project and knew exactly where to go. He approached Luigi for some funding. Film production was always predicated on a fistful of dollars because the dream factory can never be realized without substantial investments.

Celestino thought Robert was perfect for the role of Ernie in his upcoming movie. Filming would start in a few days, and he would need to travel to Yonkers for the backyard film shoot. The movie was titled *Mr. Vincent* and starred Frank John Hughes. The role of Ernie involved a jealous man who gets upset with some people at a party who ogled his girlfriend. Robert was told that he didn't need to act at all, all he needed was to play himself, nothing more. Robert would earn three hundred dollars for a day's work and two-thousand five hundred dollars for voice-overs. He was on board; why not, he thought? But things went awry and the unexpected happened.

His girlfriend, Susan, was working at a topless club jointly owned by Luigi and some associates of a Gambino soldier. Susan was a little concerned about working in a club affiliated with the mob, but Robert was assured she would be safe and didn't have to wear anything provocative. Besides, she would be among friends, and there was nothing that Zef the bouncer could not handle. Robert returned to his apartment around six a.m. and casually called Susan to check and chat for a few moments around eight a.m. He picked up the phone with a romantic:

Hey, honey, where are you? Let's meet for breakfast.

She fumed:

Leave me alone, I'm sleeping. Call back later.

I tried calling you and you weren't home. Where were you?

Why are you bothering me? I'm trying to sleep. I was with Zef, we were partying, drinking, getting high, no big deal. You know Zef! Besides, everyone knows I'm with you.

Robert recoiled and anger filled his heart.

What the fuck is this? he thought.

He wasn't just going to accept the rant of his crazy girlfriend. He needed to know more. He raged and impulsively picked up the phone receiver and with a growled voice said:

Hey buddy, how are you? Have you seen Susan?

No, JC, I haven't seen her all night.

Outraged, Robert screamed,

Why are you lying to me? I will beat your ass, you motherfucka!

Robert showed up at the topless bar that night with eyes aflame and fists clenched, and a ready stance to fight. The sultry voice of Barry White entertained the crowd. With brass knuckles on his right-hand Robert pummeled the towering six-foot-five, two hundred fifty-pound Russian bouncer. Those brass knuckles landed flush between the nose and the upper part of the mouth. The nose crunched like the sound of a palmetto bug stomped by the sole of a boot. The clubs' bouncers jumped in, followed by Barry White's security team. Robert's left-hand knuckles bled profusely. Blood streamed from his inner arm just above the wrist to the ball joint on his thumb. He was stabbed with a six-inch hunting knife and didn't feel a thing, adrenalin and rage became his pain killers. Blood gushed everywhere, on the designer suits, on the leather shoes, on the marble floors, and even on faces of bystanders. Luigi stood outside the bar, glaring with immeasurable enmity, waiting to unleash his ire and finally looked at Robert, and hollered:

What the fuck are you doing fighting in my club?

Robert still in a frenzy, pulled out his .38 Glock and everyone ducked. He then unleashed his fury and hollered even louder than Luigi:

Fuck youse all, this guy was fucking my girlfriend. You gonna fuck with me?

Robert stormed out of sight and ran to the ER at Bellevue Hospital. He continued to bleed, a small prize to uphold his honor, not so much for Susan, but for his damaged pride.

The subsequent week a filming crew was stationed for action in the back of a porch on a corner lot in Yonkers. Robert's left wrist was taped from the base of the thumb to the middle of his left forearm. He didn't want to draw attention to his bandage, but one loudmouth kept accusing him of being in the mob, giving voice to the whispers of the others. Celestino didn't mind injuries, bandages, broken noses, and other idiosyncrasies, what truly mattered was the cast had to appear authentic as if from real life; no need for Hollywood's glossy looks, the more elemental the greater the grit, as this film was to be a modern film noir.

Quiet on the set!

intoned the director.

Action,

he repeated with directorial authority.

Quiet on the set ... Action!

he sententiously repeated. Actors with bit roles moved around the scene looking busy, while the camera rolled and focused on Johnny Vincent, a gracile, moody singer/song writer. Johnny sang along, played the guitar to serenade, sort of, his girlfriend Lisa, who stood along her mother, her sister, her friend Julie, who in turn, looked lovingly at her boyfriend Ernie. Johnny Vincent was the silky, smooth singer who performed romantic songs with an extra dose of sentiment, and with a natural prolonged sigh reflecting his sadness. The atmosphere in the setting was festive as characters discussed the art of making melon balls while smoking cigarettes. The back porch was framed with miniature string lights, balloons, and streamers imprecisely spaced. Party guests milled around looking active, jovial, like they were having a good time, but Ernie looked somber, barely cracking a smile. He stood in pain, with the left wrist bandaged, and standing over Julie, his girlfriend.

The scene shifted from festive to suggestive as Lisa's mother started to grind her matronly hips around Ernie's backside. She gyrated like a drunken belly dancer, bereft of any shame, as Ernie pays no mind, solely focused on his flirtatious girlfriend adoringly facing him. The chorus of women started bickering at the middle-aged woman's wanton display of sexuality, upset at her indiscretion and lack of control. Frank, Johnny's glabrous friend, started flirting with Julie, but Ernie shoved in and cried out:

Hey, buddy, are you looking for a fucking problem?

Still tense, Ernie pushed Frank aside, but Julie pushed right back as Ernie yells:

I didn't want to come to this fucking party, I told you!

This fictional scenario was a shadow of the reality Robert experienced a week earlier. In the film scenario Frank sulked after he was pushed away and threatened by Ernie. In reality, Zef didn't fare too well after partying all night with Susan. Reality continued with more surprises as a Gambino soldier appeared at the Giovanni's Club to confront Robert about the outburst the week before. Robert wasn't going to back down to a challenge and retorted,

I don't back down to anyone fucking my girlfriend. Fuck Zef, fuck you. You need to pay a visit to that Russian motherfucker, not me.

The Gambino soldier did just that. After rifling through Zef's apartment, he found a credit card slider machine with copies of receipts from the dancers and customers. Zef was stealing. His fate was sealed. All his possessions and furniture were thrown out into the street, and Zef was never heard from again. *Mr. Vincent* wasn't a commercial success although it was featured in several Film Festivals.[1,2,3,4] Robert's film career came and went with a stab wound and two-thousand-eight-hundred dollars.

Luigi was a misguided clown, a caricature of a respected adult. His false swagger and impotence were masked by the fear his uncle and mob connections induced in those who thought to question his demands. He was dangerous and pitiful. He pissed off too many people over the years. He also lacked any self-awareness or empathy for his customers. After some of the gamblers were licking their wounds and losing a collective thirty-thousand dollars, Luigi went behind the blackjack table and performed magic tricks: he pulled out scarves from his clenched fist and fake thumb, and abracadabra there was nothing but a fist full of air. He was last seen shopping at a vegetable stand in New York City. Police found his battered body in an alley, slit from his groin to his chest. His performance was over.

Robert's relationship with Susan was contentious. Her combativeness oozed from every pore, poisoning any resemblance of a relationship. She was a bartender with an attitude. She once told a customer to twist her tit when he asked for a twist of lime and lemon with his vodka and tonic. She screamed at the patron and told him

Look around, motherfucker. This is an afterhours club!

This mob-connected guy was having none of her attitude and disrespect. He went off on her throwing the drink in her face and ran behind the bar to grab her. Several bouncers intercepted him, but Susan was left trembling.

Robert was dealing the four to twelve a.m. shift at one of the clubs and didn't feel like going out to a nightclub now that he was back in his apartment relaxing with his friends. He was physically and mentally exhausted. Susan didn't care. All she wanted was to go out and party. She badgered him relentlessly, calling him an old man. Robert pleaded with Matty and Zorro to take her out. They headed to the CPW Bar in Yonkers and after a few hours of cocktails and coke she started getting belligerent with the bartender, complaining her drinks weren't strong enough. The bartender couldn't believe what he was hearing. The audacity of his petite, obnoxious, Asian chick to demand stronger drinks. He told her to go fuck herself and called her a gook. Matty and Zorro, disbelieving, stepped in and pulled out their guns. Then the fireworks began. A shot was fired, fists were thrown, but all three were surrounded and kicked out. Another bartender recognized Matty as a friend of Robert. The next day Robert received a a call from an irate Irishman demanding compensation for the damage caused. Robert headed over to the CWP the following night and apologized to the Irish pub owners. The five hundred in cash remedied the situation.

It was spring of 1994. Margie had recently died of stomach cancer and Jack was not handling it well. Patricia and Vinny could no longer deal with Jack's temperament, and with his uncontrolled crying. Jack could not move in with Lenny because of Lenny's weakness for drinking. Robert lived in the Woodlawn section of the Bronx and welcomed Jack to move in with him.

One morning, while nursing his usual morning coffee and browsing the sports section of the *Daily News*, Jack heard a loud knock on the front door. Robert jumped up as he did not expect company. He whispered to Jack:

Don't let them in!

Robert rushed toward the bathroom to hide in the tub. Jack was confounded as to how did Robert figured out in a flash that the inquisitors were none other than the cops? There was a double knock. Jack jumped to his feet, rushed to the door to open it, and in a composed manner he let the police officer in. The police officer, as if he were a dog with heightened smell, walked to the bathroom and casually said:

Mr. Fabio, can you please come out of the bathroom?

Either the cops saw him through the crack in the bathroom door, or Jack motioned with his hand. Either way he was handcuffed and put in jail.

Robert had been dealing for a guy named Turk at the time on 62nd Street. The club was raided a month earlier. Robert was once again arrested, and bail was set. Giuliani was subduing all organized crime, and Robert was in his crosshairs. Robert was again nabbed, restrained, and led away. On his way out, Robert instructed Jack to call his lawyer. He never did. After a few days in prison Robert was being transferred to another floor and spotted his lawyer. It was serendipity; his lawyer was there to see another client but did double-duty that afternoon. Robert was out within an hour. When he arrived home, Robert thanked Jack for contacting the lawyer and to Robert's surprise, Jack removed the cigar from his mouth and leaned back from the kitchen table and guiltily blurted:

Oh shit, I forgot to call him!

It was a cold Sunday afternoon, the swirling wind howled outside the kitchen window. Jack was now living with Robert in Westchester. His beloved wife Margie died years earlier, and Robert was doing his best to comfort his struggling, incapacitated father who was grief ridden. Susan decided to do her part and make

Sunday dinner. Sunday dinner had been a mid-afternoon ritual for Jack and his family. Margie, like most Italian housewives, stood over the stove for hours and made sauce, which was served with pasta, and either meat, chicken, or seafood. It was the main meal of the day and centered the extended family as they gathered for their weekly ritual. Jack was in a belligerent mood, never quite getting over his loving wife's untimely death. He took his foul mood out on Robert, longing for the family life he once commanded.

Korean, Korean, don't you ever bring home an Italian girl.

Pop, it ain't going to happen.

Susan faced the frigid air that smelt like a coming snowstorm and returned to the apartment with a bag of groceries. Lasagna seemed easy enough to make. But ignorant of Jack's standards she bought cheap jar tomato sauce, and store brand ingredients of lasagna, ricotta, and mozzarella. Prechopped salad, salad dressing, and soft Italian bread complemented the meal. She anticipated words of satisfaction and praise. Jack and Robert ate the food like an obligatory task. Robert was not even subtle, he stood up, looked at Susan, and simply said that he was going for a shower. He had taken one bite of his lasagna, then eyed his girlfriend and angrily walked to the bathroom for his shower. Meanwhile, Jack took a few bites, and before the second forkful of lasagna reached his stomach, he bellowed in disgust,

This tastes like shit.

As Robert was drying off, he heard a commotion coming from the kitchen. China was rattling, pots were banging, voices were screeching, it sounded like a mad house. Jack and Susan screamed at each other. The arguments bordered on the physical as tempers were now on high voltage. Susan, disgusted by Jack's contempt for her efforts, attempted to hit him. A marine never forgets how to fight. Jack blocked and counter-punched from his wheelchair. Susan became increasingly irrational. Jack screamed:

You know how many Japs I killed? Hundreds!

He started to mouth the rapid shooting of a machine gun, an incessant sound, especially with Jack in a frenzy, repeating the percussive cacophony of a machine gun. Jack's screechy, irritating machine gun sounds freaked out an angry Susan who lost her composure and screamed:

He killed my ancestors! He killed my ancestors!

Robert's wrath boiled over, he grabbed Susan by her silky hair, and he flung her like a heap of garbage out of the house into frigid air. Robert's loyalty lay with his father, and no one was going to dishonor him, no matter what. Frozen, she shivered her way to a neighbor's house and managed to convince them to call 911. The Elmsford police arrived with siren blaring in a few minutes. Robert cautioned Jack to say nothing.

Just tell them we had a fight, just arguing, nothing more.

They questioned Jack who immediately admitted that Robert threw her out by the hair. The police were incensed, and they quickly applied handcuffs and escorted Robert into the patrol car. The officers sat quietly during the ride and Robert continued seething, more upset with Jack ratting on him then the mayhem that just happened. Robert was arrested and spent that night in jail. His lawyer took care of his release. Robert was out of jail the next day and Susan was out of his life for good.

Chapter 20

I have been one acquainted with the night.

—Robert Frost

OK, line up. You are all under arrest. Sgt. McFadden, collect all the guns and put them on that table. You, over here!

Robert was restrained by manacles. His documents were between his cuffed hands and back.

Oh, you're going to jail ... What's your name?

Robert Fabio.

Fabio, Fabio, where do I know that name from? That name rings a bell, are you related to Basil James Fabio?

There was stillness and stuffiness in the prison air. Robert stood as stiff as a statue. No answer.

Well, are you related?

Yes, my stepbrother.

You're going to jail, buddy. Yes, yes, now I remember. He was ensnared with another deceit, something that involved union's money. It didn't end too well with him now, did it? You are not in a good spot; this won't end well for you. Listen, we have now collected fifteen guns, if any of the guns we recovered are discovered to be part of any murder, you'll be charged with up to twenty-five years for murder. You understand me?

Robert continued with his silence as it was his best ploy under this interrogation.

My advice to you is to get out of this, but that's up to you.

The police officers led the detainees and Robert away to the local precinct. He sat for hours until he finally was taken into the District Attorney's office. A few officers from Internal Affairs arrived and opened a book that looked like a police roster with pictures. They began the interrogation:

Do you know this guy?

It was a picture of a cop.

What about this guy? ... What can you tell us about him? You must know this guy, what can you tell us about him?

This continued for twenty minutes. At last, finally Robert shouted:

Let me tell you something. I hate fucking cops, They're fucking scumbags!

Who pays the club's rent? ... Who pays you? ... What family are you working for?

Robert shouted even louder:

I hate cops, fuck youse all.

Oh yeah, we are going to garnish your pay for the rest of your life. We know you managed this club and that you know who owns the place.

Robert knew who owned the place, it was Jimmy V. Jimmy V who also happened to be a member of Hell's Angels. Who also owned tanning salons, gambling clubs, and massage parlors. But Robert wasn't talking. Rudolph Giuliani made his bones by relentlessly prosecuting the mob. He systematically decapitated mafia influence by coordinating raids of gambling clubs, by busting illegal massage parlors, by swooping in on illegal sports betting rings, and by pestering the mob and other gangs. He forcefully locked up people with bench warrants and unpaid fines. He was notorious for exploiting Racketeer influenced and Corrupt Organizations Act, better known as Rico. Robert was a freelancer, a mob associate, and didn't work for any New York family, but paid tribute to stay in business.

The Giuliani prosecutorial power was full bore directed at organized crime, rounding up big mob figures, decapitating crime families, threatening them with major prison time, and trying them for major felonies. Robert felt the full brunt of the law with police raids, incarcerations, and grave threats of life sentences. At best, he was looking to have his wages garnished for life or be in prison for twenty-five years. His lawyer paid his bail, and he was free once more. He came to the realization that his life as he lived it was over.

Robert was despondent: his spirits were low, he was discouraged, dejected, and disoriented; he needed to pull himself out of his nightmare; he needed to shift gears and change the direction of his life. He wondered how to reestablish himself yet support his gambling and partying lifestyle. He now needed to work and to sweat and to worry about earning a living wage. Eventually he came to the realization that he needed steady work and decided to bite the bullet and start painting again. His brother-in-law Lenny saw an ad in the local Westchester paper that a contractor was looking for a painter.

Robert met Frank Gennaro over a cup of coffee on Midland Avenue in Yonkers. Frank remembered seeing him deal at a club on First Avenue and said:

Hey, you're that Blackjack dealer. I know you, but can you paint?

Robert hated when anyone referred to him as "that Blackjack dealer." In his mind, he was JC, a man of respect, power, and influence. He now groveled with this painting contractor to do what he hated, painting. Robert explained he'd been painting with his dad and uncle since he was a child and could handle a brush. Frank put him on a job the following week and paid him one-hundred dollars a day. After one day Frank increased his pay to one-hundred and forty dollars a day, observing that Robert was good with the brush. It was steady work and while he hated the tediousness of painting, he kept at it. Robert was ready to quit after several years, but an agreement was reached that he would be foreman of the crew, a responsibility that utilized his experience and allowed him to escape the monotony of sanding, cleaning, and painting for hours on end. Robert now dealt directly with clients, answered questions, made sure the crew was prompt, and made sure that operations ran like a well-oiled machine. Robert kept in close contact with Frank. His boss ultimately made the final decisions, and he was usually a phone call away. One client on the Upper East Side had a question about dismantling a wall and if the new paint on the drywall would match the old paint on the plaster. Robert attempted to call Frank and discuss the particulars, but Frank was out of reach for the moment. When he finally did get through, he discovered that Frank was over his house making pancakes for Jack. Robert's boss was becoming a faithful family friend.

The skills and discipline Robert demonstrated over those past few years earned him more money and more responsibilities. He gained respect from his family, boss and work crew. But he could never fully separate himself from his past or his temper. Lenny Cirino, his brother-in-law, was a big, husky guy with dense curly, light brown hair. When I saw him, he always smoked cigarettes and had alcohol on his breath. One afternoon, I was working in Westchester and I stopped in a deli off Bronx River Road for my routine caffeine fix. As I was paying for my coffee, I heard a voice summoning me:

Hi, Jimmy, how are you?

Taken aback that someone would have known who I was, I looked up and realized that I was handing money to my cousin Jackie. I laughed at the serendipitous encounter not believing she was working behind a deli counter. We caught up a little, exchanged pleasantries, chuckled a few times, and promised to meet again. She ended our chance meeting by inviting me to her apartment around the corner from the deli when I was in neighborhood again. A few months later I did just that. I called Jackie and said I would come upstairs to say hello.

Sure, come on up.

As I walked in and greeted her with a kiss and said hello to her son, her husband Lenny stepped out of another room completely inebriated. He yelled incoherently, started to question who I was, and reddened with anger. Jackie jumped in front of me, and shoved her drunk husband back into their room, and in a reprimanding tone she said:

It's Cousin Jimmy!

I just stood like a lifeless lamppost. I had never seen Lenny in this condition and was embarrassed for Jackie that she had to treat her drunk husband like a child. I gathered my thoughts, and knowing it was bad time for a social visit, said:

It's nice to see you, you obviously have a lot on your hands. Say hi to everyone. I'll come by another time. Ok, see you, bye.

He hit me!

Jackie cried out on the phone. That's all she had to say, Robert was on his way over. Lenny was in a drunken rage. He was not working due to his drinking and multiple DWIs. Robert had bailed him out many times in the past, but Jackie was getting fed up with Lenny's pattern of behavior. Lenny had been put in jail for a parole violation and was recently released. He worked as a painter, but he continued his drinking. As Robert approached the door, he heard the commotion and as he entered the apartment, Lenny was confrontational, he yelled and walked toward him. Jackie was crying, screaming, saying that Lenny took a knife and stabbed the wall, and now turned his rage against her. Robert looked at Jackie's face and saw a bright red palm impression on her left cheek. He didn't wait for an explanation, he threw a right jab at Lenny, hitting him hard. In an instant, Lenny fell down face first. Blood spilled everywhere, seeping into the grout between the floor tiles. Robert grabbed him by his feet and dragged him down three flights of stairs, his head banging on the steps as they descended. Robert then dragged him across the street and punched him one more time and threw him on the sidewalk. Jackie was crying and yelled:

Stop, you're hurting him!

and then called the police. They arrived in a few minutes and Robert made his case that Lenny was out of control, hit his sister, wrecked the kitchen with a knife, and threatened his nephew. The officer listened, but after one look at Lenny he said:

You really did a number on him, and we will have to lock you up.

Robert was out in a day after a call to his lawyer.

Lenny's drinking problem was fatal. Late summer 1997, Jackie found him limp on the couch of her apartment. He was blue from his chest up. Jackie called Robert and the police. They confirmed his death and then took names of witnesses. Robert was arrested and handcuffed after a record search determined he had beaten him up years earlier. It was determined that Lenny died of heart attack the day after his birthday. He had just turned forty-five years old.

Chapter 21

You must not use wood to put out the fire.

—Bette Lord

Frank's painting business was running like a well-oiled machine, and it did not take much effort for Robert to convince Frank to be promoted to be project manager. Robert's bravado and reputation as a connected man earned him respect by the crew, and respect was a virtue achieved through leadership and not by brute force. Robert wanted to run Frank's business, he wanted to be paid off the books and he wanted an upgrade in his car. Gone was the Dodge Equinox, he was now driving a Cadillac Escalade. He managed with a firm hand and an exact idea as to how do things. He managed payroll, assigned the crews to specific job locations, created project estimates, ferried supplies to individual job sites, and assessed the workers performance. Robert knew what quality work entailed and didn't put up with sloppy work. If he didn't like it, he would make workers do it over. Robert was on location making his presence felt and making himself available for high-end clients. He met people like Bette Midler, Kelly Ripa, and Mark Consuelos. These clients didn't bat an eyelash at the expense required to get their houses painted, plastered, and wall-papered.

Price was not the ultimate denominator, quality and prestige was. Robert was handsome and personable, and those two things usually went a long way in keeping customers happy.

It was a sun-drenched day on 73rd and 5th Ave. Fifth Avenue was filled with a flurry of tourists, locals, and commuters. As rush hour descended, most people had thoughts of being somewhere else, anticipating the next few hours of human chaos.

Robert worked amid New York's combustion of volatile personalities and fluid timelines in this one particular project involving Merryl, an affluent woman. A screaming lady refused to let the crew finish the work. The plan was to paint the whole house, where the marble pillars framing the two entrances into the dining room were wrapped in plastic. The hysterical lady demanded that the plastic be taken down. She saw Robert and spewed her venom by cursing him out:

I want this down. I want this down, now! You don't take orders? You son of a bitch?

Please, Mrs. Merryl, Robert will take everything down after he finishes inspecting the painting, chimed a crew member attempting to deescalate her outbursts.

I want it down, now!

she shrieked and violently grabbed the plastic wrap. Merryl was the daughter-in-law of a billionaire real estate tycoon but an accomplished individual in her own right. She clearly had other priorities other than waiting for paint to dry. Dressed for a charity event, her dignified frame was draped with a handmade embroidered suit and a large pearl necklace, complemented by a diamond-framed million-dollar watch that had been delivered to her residence earlier in the day. But now that it was late afternoon, she was in no mood to deal with contractors. She continued to curse Robert and anyone within earshot:

You motherfucker, you don't take orders?

Robert had tried to remain stoic but deferred to Frank. Frank sensed Robert's urgency when he received five texts in a row, prompting him to call Robert back. He got an earful from Robert:

This bitch is screaming at me, if she continues with this, I will kick her down the stairs. I promise you, Frank, I will do it!

Frank did his best to calm him down and promised an extra five thousand dollars if he just dealt with her. Still ranting and raving, she left for the evening. Robert and crew worked a double shift just to get the job done and get out of there.

Robert spread himself too thin, his dual occupations overlapped and caused stress. Robert never did fully retreat from the casino business as he continued to supplement his income from his day-job with Frank by taking the twelve-to-four a.m. shifts at several gambling clubs. But Frank didn't like this double duty, observing Robert's hot temper flair more frequently as his stress level rose to a fever pitch. Frank gave Robert an ultimatum, either quit dealing into the wee hours of the morning or quit working for him. Robert balked at the edict, reasoning nine hundred dollars a week was not commensurate to his more lucrative nightly earnings which amounted to at least four times as much.

Frank tried to convince him that he didn't need the aggravation, and that he should just focus on his work as a site manager, but to no avail. Money in the gambling arena was steady, even if under the table, but he was not going to walk away from something that was in his blood. Robert entertained the thought of going legit after several of his dealer friends sought greener pastures securing employment and health benefits from well-established casinos like Mohegan Sun in Connecticut, Atlantic City, and the newly popular floating casinos that circled New York City's evening skyline. These party boats docked on the West Side and when they left port, they circled Manhattan for five hours. Guests laid down their money, and danced and dined, becoming another thread in the fabric of gambling revenue. Robert was intrigued about the opportunity and scheduled an interview with one of the managers of the floating casino. The interview required him to manage a craps table, oversee a poker game, and deal several rounds of blackjack.

After a few hands of Blackjack, the floor manager yelled:

Where the fuck did you know how to deal like this? Come over here!

Robert glared at him, anticipating a problem, but as he walked over to the bar, a Hasidic Jew called AV who loved to gamble shouted:

Do you know who this is? This is JC, the best dealer in the world!

The manager looked up at the Hasid. He was perplexed and he mused: how the hell could these two know each other? As Robert neared, the manager shrugged his shoulders, hitched his elbows into his waist while he lifted his trousers, with his hands stretched out palms down as if impersonating James Cagney playing Rocky in *Angels with Dirty Faces.* Robert smirked and explained that he knew the man in the yarmulke and side curls from a club. AV was a regular at Robert's Blackjack tables for years and was treated like any other paying customer willing to lay down their money for luck's sake, with attentiveness and cordiality. Robert knew he needed an edge, an advantage in getting the job, and casually dropped names of several well-known wise guys. The manager nodded, and within a few minutes' compensation, entered the discussion. Robert asked for hard cash off the books but was met with a reply disappointing to both the bearer and the receiver:

Listen, I can't pay you off the books, but we'll give you thirty shifts, benefits, and sick days.

Robert thought for a moment, but he declined. He wasn't thinking about the money and wasn't thinking about the health coverage. His mind was on the law. He never filed a tax return in his life, and if he filed real tax forms, he ran a huge with risk of being investigated by the IRS. He walked off the yacht, no closer to a legitimate job.

Robert thought that once Giuliani was out of office, his phone would ring. It was 2002, the year that Joe Schaefer and Abe V came into the picture. Joe Schaefer was a tough Irishman; they called White Tyson. He was the type of guy that would go out of his way to pick a fight. He pissed off a lot of people. Joe operated his own security service and charged eight-hundred dollars a night. He supplied high-end armed security to afterhours clubs with security personnel on rooftops, in cars, and on radios.

In early 2002, a week after Rudy Giuliani was out of the mayoral office, Robert received a call.

Hey, is this JC?

Yeah, who's this?

It's Joe Schaefer, I got your number from Scotty the Jew.

OK, what's up?

I hear you're the best.

I hear you're the best too.

Listen, I want to open a club. You handle the club, I'll do security, my take 30%.

Fine, Joe, but I got no money.

Don't worry I got a money man. Abe V, he'll sign the lease, put out money for the club. He's got great credit.

Joe, Robert, and Abe V met over a beer, and Robert asked:

OK. What about juice, who's protecting you?

Abe V laughed:

What are you talking about? You watch too many movies.

Listen to me, you'll be on someone's radar, and they will come here and bang, you'll be out, game over, don't give me that shit, wake up.

Robert described Abe V as a little greaseball spic who had money. Abe V put up the money for Scotty the Jew's clubs in the past and received a percentage. Robert had no respect for Abe V, he wasn't a tough guy, avoided confrontation with unruly customers, and relied on everyone else to do the dirty work. On the other hand, Robert loved Joe and had a good relationship with him.

For the first time in my life, I wasn't worried about someone shooting me, stabbing me, robbing me; Joe watched everything.

Robert had an earpiece and listened to the chatter:

Ok, come down off the roof, walk around the alley. Ok, now go to the cab in front, and let those people in. If another comes, don't let anyone in until I tell you.

Joe made sure that the club was full, but not overcrowded and unmanageable. Robert dealt and managed the other dealers and money flow. He felt that he was back in action, and that his earning potential just increased tenfold.

They opened a new club on 37th St. between 5th and 6th, but that wasn't their first choice. They originally wanted to open one in Soho around Carmine Street, but several of his friends said he needed the approval from The Chin, Vincent Gigante. Robert arrived by himself at Maria's restaurant on Bleeker Street and the negotiation began. Robert counted on a thirty percent take on the earnings. The Chin sternly countered with an offer of five percent. Robert was miffed with such an insulting counter, and he puffed:

What about my bank? If I lose, I need money to cover the losses.

The Chin smirked and with his Gigante eyes gave Robert a menacing stare, and with a darkened voice said:

If you lose, one of my boys here will kill you!

Robert froze for a second, but silently assessed the terms: Sure, I do all the work, hire everyone, manage the game, take the risk of getting busted and if I lose, your Sicilian zips are gonna kill me. After a long pause he uttered a decisive,

No, thanks.

Robert opted to return to the familiarity of Midtown South. Korean girls flocked to the 37th St. club. Fifty girls poured in from the massage joints in the area. They were exotically attractive and offered their bodies for exploitation. They also knew how to play blackjack and did not want to lose. These alluring women advised each other on when to hit, and how to hold and double down. The house wasn't profitable. They were happy to see the club bursting with alluring Korean women, but it was even more exciting to make barrels of money. Robert decided he needed to promote the club. He paid a skateboarder two-hundred dollars one weekend and told him to hand out cards with info about the club. Success. One weekend, the club was full of twenty-year-old hipsters high on ecstasy. They danced around and around as if the floor was moving under their feet. They gambled, they drank, played the machines, listened to the jukebox, and guzzled gallons of water. Joe was agitated!

Are we running Blackjack games or kiddy land?

Robert didn't care who was a paying customer, just as long as that customer departed from their money.

Joe, what are you worrying about, we just went through one-hundred cases of water at six dollars per bottle. We just made seven-thousand dollars.

Robert knew Nicky the Albanian and his brother Jughead for years. Nicky was contacted to supply machines for another venture this new trio was opening near 64th Street and Lexington Ave. Joe Shaefer provided the security while Abe V handled the credit and cash flow. Robert, Joe, and Abe V would each take a third of the profits. Robert asked Nicky if Jughead, who Robert encouraged to switch from being a doorman to a dealer years earlier, was available to take some regular shifts at the new club. Nicky responded quickly to Robert's inquiry. Not only would Jughead be able to deal, but he will also keep a close watch on the machines. He added that his extended Albanian family greatly appreciated Robert's mentoring of the towering Jughead.

Bad blood brewed when Abe V complained that Jughead was coming in late: games started at four in the morning and he was showing up a half hour late, drunk and high as a kite. Jughead came to work slurring, unfocused, and agitated. Abe V, usually docile, felt it was his place to confront and hassle Jughead for his tardiness and inattention. Tension was now in the air. Jughead, not amenable to Abe Vs obtrusion wanted to pounce on him, give him a beating, but instead—and without notice or explanation—quit, and never showed up for another shift. Robert was pissed off. The club was making money, everyone was earning a good cut of the profits, and now this had to happen. If it was any other dealer, Robert would not have cared. But Jughead was an important cog in the networking gear. He and Nicky were fully supported and encouraged by their *familje e zgjeruar*, that had their own organized crime network.

Other trouble was brewing as Joe Schaefer received a tip that the club was going to raided by the cops. The raid was only the beginning as more bad blood stirred with Robert's Albanian accomplices. The machines that Nicky had provided were worth $5000 each and were difficult to replace. With knowledge of the impending raid, they found a new location in a vacant apartment near 28th St. to operate. Robert had the machines removed and then placed at a new location. The raid took place as expected and everything that they could not remove was destroyed. They incurred heavy losses, but that was part of the business. The cops were efficient in disrupting a casino's operations, but always failed to completely shut them down. The demand for gambling at after-hours clubs was high and opportunists were always waiting for the next inauguration.

Nicky was shocked to discover that the three machines he thought were destroyed in the raid were now being used at the 28th St. club. When he paid a visit to the new venture, Robert matter-of-factly approached him and said:

You owe me fifteen-thousand dollars for the three machines I saved, everyone has to kick in.

Nicky protested but Robert, unperturbed, continued:

Hey, look, I saved your machines, they were going to be busted up.

If you want part of the take, which was the original arrangement, you have to pay.

Abe V had to pony up the cash from scratch, a new deposit, more rent money. Everything new. Nicky was not happy and said nothing. He left and calculated his next move. A few weeks later, Robert was at Aqueduct Raceway with his head in the racing forms when his nephew alerted him to the crowd forming around him.

Hey Unc, there are like twenty Albanian guys behind you.

Jughead towered over Robert and began to poke his finger in Robert's chest. He threatened him that he and his friends were either going to bust it up to 28th St. club or take control. Robert fumed at the upstart.

Hey, buddy, you know who the hell you poking? I love you like a son but keep this up and you're gonna lose an arm!

Jughead continued with his threats demanding that Robert not return to the club that night. The standoff continued with the Albanian entourage leaving as silently as the entered. Robert paid no attention to this rookie's demand and the club remained in operation. Nicky never did fork over the fifteen thousand that was requested, and Robert refused to give him a percentage of the weekly earnings.

Time marched on, and a few weeks later as Robert was stopped at a red light, he was approached by a group of intimidating men with baseball bats. He was in the Bronx heading south into Manhattan. A group of thugs froze then scattered after Robert pulled out his Glock and waved the weapon around. Faced with random threats from ruthless Albanians, Robert decided that it was better for him to pay off a ten-thousand-dollar loan he borrowed from a different group of Albanians. Short on cash, he called his former boss, Frank Gennaro, and pestered him to loan him the money. Against his better judgement Frank gave Robert the money he requested. With cash in hand Robert arranged for a meeting at Yonkers Raceway to settle up. The Albanians never showed up for the money. Robert called again, wanting to eliminate all chances of a surprise hit on his life. Finally, they agreed to meet at a bar on Arthur Avenue in the Bronx. As Robert sat down in the midst of his lenders, he pulled out his Glock and slammed it on the bar and shouted:

Who wants to fuck with me? You bring bats to a gun fight, you motherfucka?

The bar staff, startled, froze in place. The Albanians, backs stiffened, said nothing and awaited Robert's next move. An awkward silence permeated the bar but soon the atmosphere settled down as Robert displayed the cash that was to be handed over. The Albanians had a reputation for their ruthless dealings with people who owed them money or resisted their demands. They were provincial and uncultivated in the unwritten code of conduct of New York's organized crime. His debt was paid but this group of Albanians had pissed off other people and they paid a price. One of the clubs they operated on Jerome Avenue in the Bronx was busted up, but not by the cops. Enforcers from one of the five families executed the hit and left several men with broken bones and concussions. Jughead got in over his head and failed to heed Robert's advice to lay low and just deal cards. Jughead disappeared.

The 28th Street club did well, but neighbors were complaining about the noise late at night. Joe Shaefer anticipated that these complaints would escalate and create more problems. He hired carpenters to fix the club and create an appearance of a recording studio complete with control room, a workstation with mixers, monitors, microphones, headphones, guitar stands, and walls covered with acoustic panels to mute the noise. Total cost was around twelve-thousand dollars.

The club's landlord had no idea what he was looking at, he had no clue that most of the equipment didn't even work, except for the sound system. They never had another problem with the landlord again, but trouble was not far. Some wise guys started to come in every week, drop a few hundred, chat with Robert, and eventually leave. They knew this place was a gold mine, and they wanted in:

Fuck Joe Schaefer, fuck Abe V; me and you JC! I'm gonna make this place a nice place. We go mezzo, mezzo. Tell me yes, tell me yes!

Robert didn't want any partnerships with the mob. He didn't trust them, didn't trust the unseen power behind the front man. Didn't like the unpredictability of some wise guy having a bad day, shooting up the place and everyone in it.

Hey, I'm an honest guy and these are my partners. If you want to talk, here's my number, tell your bosses I'm JC.

Robert had his contacts, and if these guys asked around, Robert was sure he would have no problems. Linda, a short-haired Blackjack dealer who worked regular shifts, knew the wise guys that frequented the club regularly. She dealt at a club on Ave. B years back, which was owned by the mob, and they respected her. She liked Robert, was always paid on time, given any shift she wanted, and filled in when needed. She ran into a wise guy from Brooklyn when she was dealing at another club.

Linda, how well do you know JC? I want that club.

She knew when the mob had its sights on something, inevitably it would be theirs, either by agreement or removal.

Look I've been working with JC for two years, he's a good guy, always sends a cut to the Gambino's. Leave him alone, he's a good guy.

Robert nodded in appreciation and patted her hand when she told him that she put in a good work for him.

Thank you, God bless.

They never came back, never bothered him again about a partnership.

Upstairs from the 28th Street club on the seventh floor there was a special locale that appealed to licentious men and women.

They nicknamed it 7th Heaven. The decor was garish and gawdy, indiscreetly advertising that this was an establishment that catered to one's carnal lusts. With little effort except a lot of cash you could get what you desired.

It was run by some childhood personality who was popular on television in the early nineteen-seventies. Not blessed with good looks, this television child celebrity was more of a curiosity. His hook nose, bangs, and long, red hair was juxtaposed and contrasted to his witty and well-spoken persona. This childhood pitchman, now whoremonger, suspected that Robert was connected and gave him deference and space to run his affairs without meddling. Besides, the club was not only a good spot for selling sex, but he could also retreat downstairs and gamble at will.

They made an arrangement that if any customer wanted a girl, he would send them upstairs, and Robert would get an envelope full of cash at the end of the week. Robert thought the girls upstairs were pigs, crack whores, not worthy of anyone's attention. He reasoned if someone was drunk and wanted to drown out his depression from losing at his club, what did he care about the poor slob did? It was free money.

Robert had a penchant for submissive Asian girls. Yet, despite his urges, never had any desire to indulge in sexual escapades on the upper floor. One night, a bombshell blonde with blue eyes and a wide smile, was sitting with a rough looking man who looked like an uncultured construction worker. While the *cafone* hunched himself over the cards on the blackjack table, the blonde vixen eyed Robert as if she were measuring an item on sale. She was animated, friendly, and spoke with everyone within earshot. Robert's steady glaze at her masked his mesmerized thoughts about feeding his sexual appetites. An opportunity knocked when her date got up, told her that he needed to go to the men's room, and he'd be right back. Robert flashed a broad smile, an invitation for a conversation. Nothing was said, but when the blonde beauty casually stood, walked up to Robert, and handed him a scrap of paper with her name and number, he got the message.

He had no need to call her. She frequented the club regularly, and she drank like a fish, and snorted as much coke anyone was willing to offer. She was a thermometer that recorded the changes in temperature. Her disposition, intonation, and flirtatiousness increased in direct proportion to the amount of alcohol and coke she consumed. She didn't gamble, she partied, and she always had a good time. Coke was a catalyst to keep the party going uninterrupted into the wee hours of the morning.

To further supplement the club's income, Robert made an arrangement with a young kid in his twenties. He was called Julio. The kid came in several times to gamble and offered Robert some blow. He thought the blow was of good quality, and ascertained that Julio had his head on straight and not someone who just liked to party and get high all the time. Julio spoke Robert's language of making money. The means were different but in the end it was income. Robert and Julio came to terms and for free blow and rent money, Robert would allow Julio to be the exclusive coke dealer at the club. This was a new breed of drug dealer, a homeboy from the streets. He was Hispanic with baggy clothes, and a pullover sweatshirt with a Steelers logo. For the privilege of selling coke, he also had to pay the monthly rent of ten-thousand dollars. Julio didn't bat an eyelash. If anyone else was caught selling drugs, out they went, and Robert would keep the goods. All was well, customers had their fix, never had to leave the premises to get high, and only departed when their wallet was empty. One month Julio handed Robert an envelope and as he flipped through the one-hundred-dollar bills, he noticed he was short by a one-thousand dollars.

Where's the money? You're short?

Robert asked. Julio responded that he took the money out for the coke this Irish blonde was snorting.

She was asking for coke, so that's the difference.

Robert yelled at him:

Fuck that, I didn't say she could snort off of my dime, you owe me, and don't give it to her anymore.

The blonde who had willingly given her phone number was crazy, wild, loud, and without restraint. She did blow at the bar, danced on the tabletops, flirted with pretty girls, and cutely cuddled with indulgent men. Robert was captivated by her, and his friends secretly whispered that Robert was smitten by the seductive temptress. They were well matched as they loved to party, lived day to day, and when money was low, they hoped to rebound.

Enraptured by the allure of each other, the party blonde accepted Robert's invitation to move in with him. Within six months he kicked her out like a donation rejected from the Salvation Army. Robert had a menagerie of women with whom he could be intimate with. He didn't want to deal with her drunken tirades, hangovers, or crying after coming down from the highs from a night of cocaine induced euphoria. Joe and Abe V were also fed up with her antics and pulled her aside one evening. They tried to reason with her when she was sober. They stressed that her uncontrolled behavior was not acceptable; snorting coke out in the open, taking chips to play without paying for them, and hitting on other girls at the bar. They tried to explain that they did not want any undue attention. Clubs like theirs were always being watched by the cops and none of them could afford the having it shut down because of her antics. Robert told her she was banned from the club. She would not be allowed to step foot in there again. The crazy wench was furious. She went ballistic. Screaming at Joe and Abe V she threatened to call the police. Threatened to expose their illegal sources of income; gambling, drug dealing, prostitution. She was a greater liability then any of them realized. There was no way to reason with someone so out of control of their emotions and completely controlled by their vices.

The club went down for other reasons: the cops soon found out that Julio was dealing other things besides coke. He also sold guns, and illegal guns attracted police attention. Cops staked out the club by posing as ConEd workers. They parked a truck across the street and clicked pictures of everyone and anyone entering and exiting. Joe Shaefer's astute observations as head of security made him very suspicious of a ConEd utility truck parked outside the club. He knew instinctively that something was amiss when it remained parked overnight, highly unusual when there was no digging on the street. Robert, Joe, and Abe V were savvy and experienced to not wait around for something to happen. They simply locked up one evening and walked away. They operated the club for roughly for two years, made their money, and vanished in the dark of night. After gambling his money away, Robert asked Frank Gennaro for his job back but also if he could borrow sixty-thousand dollars. Robert got his job back, but the money never came. He would need to secure it by another source, an old friend, Eddie #2.

Chapter 22

When you go through deep waters, I will be with you.

—Isaiah 43:2

It was Robert's birthday and his first day in his new position as a crew foreman for Frank, the painting contractor. He planned to meet his boss at a new job site on the upper east side of Manhattan. A Wall Street Executive who lived in a high-rise apartment on 81st St. and First Ave. was ready to shell out seven-hundred thousand dollars. Robert arrived ready for his new responsibilities and excited to celebrate his birthday later that evening. The crew was abuzz with chatter and disturbed with news of the towers being hit and then collapsing. This was Frank's first big job in Manhattan and Robert, upset that the crew was distracted, demanded they focus and speed it up. He was concerned about getting the job done, and getting it done early. After the towers collapsed, he called Frank and asked if they were still going to celebrate his birthday later that night. Frank couldn't believe what he was hearing.

You're crazy, no we are not going to celebrate your birthday. New York just got attacked by terrorists. Are you that stupid!

I was in Chicago on September 11, 2001. It was early morning and the sales leadership team from IDEC huddled around a laptop in a hotel room. We gathered from across the country to listen to the oncologic drug advisory committee deliberate the merits of a biologics license application that had been submitted nine months earlier. The product under review was called Zevalin (ibritumomab tiuxetan) and was being reviewed for treatment of patients with relapsed or refractory low-grade, follicular, or transformed B-cell non-Hodgkin's lymphoma. There was hope and promise for patients, hope and promise for our growing company.

Committee members, I have just been informed that there has been attack on a government building. We are hoping to learn more as there also have been reports of a plane crashing into the World Trade Center in New York. We will continue with this review as we will not let the terrorists impede us in our mission.

We looked at each other, stunned as to what we were hearing from the committee secretary. A television set was wheeled in from another room. It was all so surreal. The laptop continued to broadcast the committee review of the clinical data while we all stood up and watched the first tower collapse. Our thoughts and prayers shifted to our country, the poor passengers and occupants of the Twin Towers. One colleague had the wherewithal to call every rental car agency and managed to secure the last four vehicles. I drove through the night with three other colleagues heading to the Northeast while everyone else scattered in different parts of the country in the three other rental cars. The next morning, I bawled my eyes out in relief when I learned my brother Tim had escaped from one of the towers as it had just been hit. His morning ritual of a restroom pit stop was interrupted by a bang and shattering glass. As he headed out of the men's room of the North Tower, he was startled by the rush of people running for the exits. Broken glass and smoke billowed down from above as he ran with the horde of fellow commuters to whatever safe harbor could be found. Later that morning I learned that the oncology drug advisory committee had completed their review and voted 13-2 for Zevalin to be approved. Tragedy, relief and hope, and a cascade of emotions enveloped my colleagues, friends, and family.

Life moved on through those difficult days, weeks, and months. I was promoted a few weeks later and like Robert forged ahead in my new role. Unlike Robert, I had no interest in the attraction, temptation, and fictitious presumption of beating the odds that keep gamblers captivated and willing to depart from their hard-earned money. I assessed the odds and likelihood of success in all aspects of my life. My spiritual birth had set me on a trajectory and adventure I never dreamed was possible. My mind, clouded by years of smoking pot, excessive drinking, and experimenting with psychedelics and cocaine, was no longer polluted. It was renewed, no longer conformed to my previous way of thinking. I no longer was controlled by my vices and impulses. Through reason, discernment, and prayer my paths forged ahead allowing me to overcome the obstacles that lay ahead.

> *Now this I say and testify in the Lord, that you must no longer walk as the Gentiles do, in the futility of their minds. They are darkened in their understanding, alienated from the life of God because of the ignorance that is in them, due to their hardness of heart. They have become callous and have given themselves up to sensuality, greedy to practice every kind of impurity. But that is not the way you learned Christ!— assuming that you have heard about him and were taught in him, as the truth is in Jesus, to put off your old self, which belongs to your former manner of life and is corrupt through deceitful desires, and to be renewed in the spirit of your minds, and to put on the new self, created after the likeness of God in true righteousness and holiness.*
>
> Ephesians 4:17–24

Promoting Zevalin was one such obstacle, but nothing would prepare me for the hand I was dealt with years later, professionally and personally. Zevalin was an extremely complicated product and therapeutic regimen. It was the first monoclonal antibody bound with a radioisotope that was approved for therapeutic treatment of cancer. This wasn't just an off-the-shelf product that a doctor could order, prepare and infuse in an office setting. After it was prescribed by a medical oncologist, it had to be prepared by a radio-pharmacist and administered in a nuclear medicine facility by nuclear medicine physicians. Many of my direct reports quit out of frustration. I attempted to remain positive and even volunteered to join a new sales team exclusively dedicated to the product. Unfortunately, management lost interest in the product and the sales team was dissolved. This was devastating for so many of my colleagues. I will never forget the uneasy expressions on the faces of my coworkers waiting to learn the fate of their employment. The sales and marketing team was summoned to San Diego in the fall of 2005 to learn what had already been pre-determined. As my peers mulled around a hotel courtyard, I heard a voice yell out,

Fabio, Fabio, what's up?

I had just left a meeting and was sworn to secrecy. I was silent as I greeted everyone with a hug. Many cried, knowing my silence said all they needed to know. Weeks later we all received pink slips that announced our dismissals. A sad end to such a promising product, and unfortunate dismantling of a biotech start-up.

I negotiated to stay with the company and joined a new division, rheumatology. My years of service in oncology meant nothing as the hiring manager rescinded an offer to supervise the Mid-Atlantic Region. This area director, a former marine with a Napoleonic complex, did not listen to reason. Instead, he offered the Southeast Region as my only option. The travel from New York to Florida, Georgia, Alabama, and South Carolina on a weekly basis was what I had negotiated but I reluctantly accepted because I did not want to part with the equity I had accumulated over the last several years. I was away from my family four days a week for three weeks every month. The plane travel took its toll hence by spring my health took a turn for the worst, and I was advised to go for sinus surgery after taking failing antibiotics for months. The surgery was akin to roto-rooter in my nasal cavity. The surgeon informed me that he cleared and widened three nasal cavities that had been completely obstructed. It was such a great relief, and my health rebounded quickly only to realize my father and brother's health would take a turn for the worse.

My brother Paul Fabio had a bold and adventuresome spirit. He was beloved by his friends and adored by his family. He could win you over with his smile and ask for forgiveness again and again. It was never denied. Mom would call him a lovable imp, a *scooch*, someone who would slide away from blame. Paul waked tall at an attractive six-foot frame. He possessed a pronounced smile with his frontal gapped incisors, a trait he inherited from Nan, our loving mother. He boasted dense, dark hair and his friendly deep-set eyes hinted at something from the dramatic landscape, that captured the attention of those who met his glaze. Paul had a swagger about him, an infectious laugh, he was a lover of life. He was a dreamer with big ideas and did not get bogged down in process and details. He believed and trusted in others without demanding much in return. That would be his albatross. His BA degree in communications from CW Post did little to help him find his career path. He dreamt of something more but did not know what. All he knew is that out west was the land of opportunity where he could reinvent himself. He was "California dreaming." With little more planned except to stay with a friend and look for work, he drove to Los Angeles with the clothes on his back and a few thousand dollars his brothers offered.

Paul, the prodigal son, returned home with a heavy heart and broken dreams. He returned to the soothing arms of his loving mother, to the skepticism of his pragmatic father, to the disappointment of his brothers, and to the elation of his loyal friends. He returned to Rockland County penniless after a ten-year journey in La La land. His indefatigable quest to find the American dream fizzled out like an illusion. His name changed as much as his jobs. He went from being Paul John to John Paul to JP. We didn't know what to call him, so we mockingly called him Paulie Mulignana. When he returned to NY permanently, he proclaimed,

I am Paul.

His first job out of college was selling office equipment in NYC for Monroe Systems for Business, Inc. He was an impassioned music lover who dreamt of a career as an artistic manager deeply involved in the mare nostrum of musical melodies. The world of selling office equipment was much too restrictive for Paul and soon quit to start a music artist promotion and management company called She Sang Productions. He did not have much success and decided to head out to California. He first settled in Torrance and his first night was greeted with an earthquake. Shaken to the bone, he called home for reassurance. As always, Mom provided soothing comfort. Paul would first find employment as a charter captain's mate, which did not last long. We all had a good laugh when he told us he was preparing fishing rods and hauling tackle. He was probably on three boats his whole life up to that point. When the weather turned cold, he landed a job at Irvin Arthur Associates in Beverly Hills. This was a talent and literary agency, and this was a good entry point for his career aspirations. That did not last long. As he sorted through mail and cleaned out discarded papers, he discovered a handwritten letter by Louis Armstrong to Irvin Arthur himself. Instead of seeking advice of what to do with such valuable memorabilia, he tried to hawk the valuable memento at a local pawn shop. Realizing the letter's value, the pawn shop owner called Irvin Arthur directly and Paul was immediately fired.

This was not the start of a career that he envisioned. Paul decided to go it alone and over the next ten years bounced around the music industry hoping to manage artists. He had better luck managing models. Young impressionable girls gravitated to his sales pitch much more readily than musicians. He was the model and talent director for Soundstage Studios, L.A. Models, IT Models, Zoo Models, and lastly, Eleven Model Management. He bounced around apartments as frequently as he bounced around jobs and every year was a new surprise, new hope and new disappointment. We became acutely aware of his financial distress when he revealed that the IRS had started to garnish his wages for defaulting on payments of student loans. My mother came to the rescue and bailed him out, just as she had so many times before.

Paul returned to Rockland penniless after a ten-year struggle and regret over not achieving his American dream in Los Angeles. Those aspirations of managing musical artists never materialized and when money-flow ran dry, he had no choice but to come back east. My mother helped him with expenses for years, bailing him out without question. My brothers and I acquiesced to his repeated appeals for financial assistance many times over the years, hoping that he would turn a corner and secure steady employment.

Jim, how are you, bro? I miss you!

Zio, Zio Paolo, what's up? What's going on?

How is Adriane? How are the kids?

Everybody's great, all good, what's going on?

Sorry to bother you but I need fifteen-hundred bucks. I'm short on cash for the car insurance and ....

I listened as I drove north on the Palisades Parkway and envisioned myself with him in his shiny, new, Atlantic Blue, Mustang convertible. I had visited him in LA two weeks earlier when I was on a business trip. We cruised around LA with the top down as we made our way visit his friends, pick up sundries, and sit down for a meal. Paul drove around like he owned the city. His right hand on the steering wheel confidently meandering through traffic. Paul was all about *joie de vivre, la dolce vita*. He had the unique ability to make everyone around him feel important, and often special. He was a loyal friend, a good brother, and a fun uncle. But naivety in the belief that people were as warm and sincere as he, was misguided. For years he got by with a big smile and a handshake and was oblivious to the hard realities of business. He believed that his affable comportment and his infectious charm would garner good business opportunities. Why would it be otherwise, but it was otherwise. Contracts, negotiations, and accountability were foreign concepts to him, and he readily accepted the happy talk and empty promises that most people peddled. His circle of friends were dreamers with lofty visions.

Los Angeles is crisscrossed with boulevards of broken dreams and Paul was another casualty. I knew Paul was struggling and I had no problem with helping my kid brother. But this time was different. After I sent him money, he called me a week later saying he needed more money, and when I pressed him, he sheepishly confessed that the money I gave him to cover car insurance, but now he needed more money because his car was now repossessed. I exploded on the phone. Did he take me for a fool? My generosity will only go so far. I screamed and told him no more money.

You are not getting another dime! The well is dry!

Within weeks he was back east for good. My parents paid for his ticket, and he landed with only the clothes on his back, new business cards, and a dream of managing models. I had no idea he was back east until I received a call from my father pleading with me to take him in. I protested to my father,

I have a wife and kids and major expenses, and now I have to be the responsible one and take him in. What about Greg? what about Tim?

Jim, you are his last hope.

I pondered his comments for a moment and thought, wow,

what a major responsibility and a heavy burden my dad is laying before me. What the hell? Why me? Only after getting my wife's approval, did we agreed to let him stay. Even though Paul was irresponsible with money, he was fun to have around, and the kids were especially happy to have Zio Paolo to horse around with. My kids loved Paul as he always indulged them when they wanted to play, and to read, or just talk. They loved their big, lovable uncle throwing them on the bed, and nightly rounds of pillows fights. I'll never forget when my kids were younger, and Paul got them so wound up and exhilarated before bedtime. My son just lay in his bed in his pajamas with his arms behind his head, leaning back on his pillow and with a big smile and a sigh said,

I love Zio Paolo!

as my daughter chimed in and sang out,

A little bit of Zio in my life,

to the tune of "Mambo No. 5 (A little Bit of …) by Lou Bega.

It was the fall of 2005, and we were resolved to provide Paul comfort and support while he attempted to get himself back on his feet. My wife was especially annoyed when he ate a half tray of leftover manicotti after a night of drinking with his friends. Unfortunately, his money management skills, or actually lack of them, was the catalyst for him getting kicked out of my house. It was late November Saturday morning, and I was in my office paying my bills. I couldn't believe what I was seeing. The Verizon telephone bill was over five-hundred dollars. As I looked further, I discovered it was for long distance calls to Italy from a month ago. I ran from my office to the couch in the den where Paul was lounging and drinking coffee and confronted him.

What the hell is this? I didn't make these calls …. What the hell are you doing?

His response was:

I thought you had the plan.

Well, I didn't have the plan, the imaginary long-distance plan he assumed would cover his new, long distance modeling management idea. He had the grand idea of managing a beautiful blonde from Northern Italy and get her modeling jobs in New York City. He never did get her any jobs, and all those calls got him kicked out of my house. He had an even shorter stay at my brother Tim's house but luckily found a downstairs apartment available to rent from an old childhood friend. As Paul settled down, he found employment at Verizon hanging cable lines. He was well liked and began thinking about pursuing an MBA through their tuition reimbursement program. We were back in good graces, and all was forgiven. I didn't hold grudges and never hassled him for the money he borrowed. I just wanted him to get back on his feet and be independent.

My brothers, Mom, and I were in the beginning stages of planning my dad's eightieth birthday party when the unspeakable was about to unfold. We had planned for a party in the fall when the weather was a little cooler in the evenings and started to think about locations. The usual arguing and battle for control ensued between myself and my brothers. Paul being the youngest, chimed in, but usually went along with whoever was the least irrational at the time. Nothing had been decided by late July and my brother Tim decided to drive down to our parents' house in Lake Norman on Dad's actual birthday not wanting to wait for a formal party to celebrate. I thought I could easily drop in for the night as well. I was in Florida doing mid-year business reviews and can just make a pit stop in Charlotte on my way back to New York. As I was in the middle of presenting a mid-year review to one of my direct reports, I received a call from my sister-in-law, Dorie. She asked me if I heard the news. I had no idea what she was talking about, but my chest thumped when she mentioned something about a complication from a surgery my father had six weeks ago. I tried to hide my concern in front of my colleague but clearly could not. My sales rep asked if everything was alright, clearly noticing that my countenance changed dramatically. I regrouped my thoughts and demeanor as best I could just so I could finish up and get to the airport.

Dad had health issues almost immediately after his retirement. Several years back during the Christmas holidays, we noticed that his abdominal cavity appeared distended, he experienced a loss of appetite, and he had a sickly yellowish pallor. He barely had enough energy to stand straight without the support of a wall. We quizzed my mother on what she thought about this condition, and she commented that he was just getting old. I did a double-take in disbelief of her explanation. When we questioned them further, we discovered that since they had moved down to North Carolina in 1994, they had not seen a doctor in seven years. Dumbfounded, we asked how two college educated people can ignore their health for that long. Why would they forgo annual health checkups at their age? It made no sense! We pleaded with her to take him to a doctor when they returned to Lake Norman. She did. After a routine blood examination, the doctor sent him immediately to the ER commenting,

How the hell were you even standing? Your hemoglobin is 5, when it normally should be between 14 to 18 grams per deciliter.

After a series of tests, he was put on Procrit, a red blood supplement, and soon his usual pale olive complexion returned to normal. We were all relieved and implored them to be more diligent about their own health.

Years went by and he was put on a newer medication called Aranesp which was more convenient due to a weekly dosing schedule instead of the trice weekly dosing he had had with Procrit. I managed to convince him to get a bone marrow biopsy to get a formal diagnosis. A doctor in North Carolina did the procedure, and I arranged the slides and labs be sent to a hematologist from NYU. Pops had a low tolerance for pain and found it to be a painful and uncomfortable procedure. He lay on his side so the doctor could get access to the upper iliac crest of the pelvis, the part of his hip bone close to the spine. After antiseptic was applied to the skin, local anesthesia was injected into the perioste-um, the membrane surrounding the bone. From there an incision was made in the skin so the large needle could pass easily to the bone. He was notably uncomfortable when the thirteen-gauge needle was turned and pushed repeatedly into his bone. It was a dull, deep pain that worsened before finally resolving after a week. But that was enough to convince him he was never going to do that again. He should have had another biopsy done because the sample was so poor that the doctor couldn't interpret it. The most we learned from their reports was that his red blood cells appeared to be immature and bizarre looking elliptical blasts, but no definitive diagnosis was offered. We poured through the internet to see if could find anything published that described Pop's condition. The only disease we found that seemed to match his laboratory findings, bone marrow report and symptoms was a disorder called hereditary elliptocytosis. His red blood cells were malformed, elliptical instead of circular.

This ordeal was frustrating. It was different from Mom's diagnosis of breast cancer in the early 2000s. Mom never had a mammography, and when she finally saw a doctor, he implored her to go for one. She was home when the radiologist called and nonchalantly told her that she tested positive for breast cancer. The radiologist was cold and indifferent as he shared the results of his findings. Mom was furious. Dad and my brothers did everything we could to comfort her and calm her down. Her emotions vacillated between a mixture of anger, sadness, and uncertainty. It was difficult to see her in that state and we surrounded her with the support she needed. Since I was in the industry and sold many of the chemotherapy drugs used to treat breast cancer and was keenly aware of the different treatment modalities, I was able to give her a greater understanding of what to expect. I related to her that it would be a long, difficult road, but that she had every reason to hope for a good result. When she told us about her consultation with her medical oncologist and shared that she didn't believe him to be very forthcoming, I stepped into action. I asked a breast cancer specialist associated with Lenox Hill Hospital in NYC about my mom's situation. Dr. Arthur Goldberg agreed to review her chart and treatment plan.

It was early November, and I was attending the Chemotherapy Foundation Symposium, an annual meeting of oncologists who presented, discussed, and debated the latest cancer research results. I had attended this meeting every November for the last ten years and when not managing the exhibit table for the company where I was working, I would listen to lectures on the topics pertinent to the cancer type my product was indicated for. During one on the breaks, I was chatting with industry friends and noticed a doctor walk over to my exhibit booth. My intent was to engage him in a conversation about the product I was selling as I did hundreds of times before. As I approached him and introduced myself, I noticed his name badge and city and state listed under his name.

Oh, hi, Dr. Krumdieck, I believe you are treating my mom, Nan Fabio.

Like most Drs. walking past a booth, they rarely want to engage with sales representatives unless they have specific questions, but my comment clearly got his attention.

I'm Nan Fabio's son, she lives down in Lake Norman. She mentioned she had just had an appointment with you.

He looked at me quite surprised and acknowledged that he had recently seen her. I thanked him and said I would be speaking with her about the proposed treatment plan. It was a quick exchange but sent a clear message to the doctor that her family would be involved in her care. Mom was diagnosed with stage II invasive ductal carcinoma. She had to endure surgery, radiotherapy, chemotherapy, and hormonal therapy. She never complained to her boys and always kept an upbeat attitude. Her support system of faith, family, and friends consoled, comforted, and cheered her through her treatment journey. Through it all, she was a role model. She endured the uncertainty of her own mortality, bore the pain of treatment side effects, and became a role model of determination, perseverance, and resoluteness. She would summon those attributes again to survive the most horrific events my family experienced the summer of 2007.

In the spring of that year doctors decided to remove Pop's spleen, believing that he would get relief from the symptoms of hemolytic anemia, mainly fatigue. A laparoscopic procedure was scheduled with the belief that the spleen could easily be removed without complications. During the procedure it was discovered that the size of spleen was significantly larger than expected but the doctor opted to continue as planned. Post-surgery, Dad was weak, lethargic, and lost his appetite. He would nibble on small amounts of food and then nap for hours. When awake, he was zapped of energy, not motivated to do the most minimal of tasks. The doctors were uncertain of why he was experiencing these symptoms and decided to do exploratory surgery. My brothers and I had no idea how serious this was and figured he would be home by his birthday. Pops had an aversion to pain and was apprehensive about the procedure. Mom kissed him and assured him that everything would be fine. Everything was not fine. The surgeons reported back to my mom that his small intestine was shriveled, essentially dried up and dead. They speculated that he had intestinal ischemia; a blood clot that blocked the artery that supplied blood to his small intestines. He no longer had functioning intestines and there was nothing that could be done. He never awoke from surgery. His last gesture was to kiss his loving wife of forty-nine years.

Nan Crosbie met Paul Fabio in nineteen-fifty-seven. As she was about to enter St. Margaret's Church in Pearl River to attend

Sunday morning Mass, she spotted him walking up West Central Ave toward the church. She thought to herself,

Now, that is a good man.

Pops lived in an apartment on Central Ave with fellow research chemists from Lederle Laboratories, Hal Ferrari and Herbie Brabander, while Mom lived with her parents while she taught fifth grade at George W. Miller School in Nanuet. They formally met at a church function called Catholic Action. It was a social gathering of singles with the intent to foster and advocate for Catholic values in the local community. When my brothers and Ibecame curious about how my parents met, they referenced this club they belonged to. When we inquired about the purpose of the club, Pops described Catholic Action as a place where Catholics went to get action. We all understood what he meant and laughed at his irreverence. A social club to meet girls.

Nan and Paul married in 1958 and had four boys over a span of eight years, with Paul John being the youngest. We were all especially fond of Paul with his big smile, friendly demeanor, and distinctive gap between his two front teeth: just like Mom. He was a big lovable guy that people gravitated toward. He resembled my mother with his infectious smile that lit up an entire room. I was the one who gave him a call to inform him of Dad's passing. He was on a ladder installing cable on a telephone pole. I called and told him to make travel arrangements to get to North Carolina. We were together, my brothers and their families, on Saturday, July 21st planning Dad's funeral arrangements. It would have been Pop's eightieth birthday, and now we were planning his funeral. As we visited the funeral home, Mom made funeral arrangements with the staff at St. Therese Catholic Church in Mooresville. She was involved with the church helping with various ministries and singing with the church choir. Dad was a member of the Knights of Columbus and helped with community work, including driving a bus bringing Nascar fans back and forth from the parking lot and racetrack. Years earlier my parents donated a large sum of money for St. Therese's building campaign. A large twenty-foot-high stained-glass window dominated a stairwell. Mom made sure that the artist commissioned to design the piece included the words:

DEDICATED BY THE FABIO AND CROSBIE FAMILIES.

No doubt Mom was inspired by the stained-glass windows in St. Juliana's Church in Mount Pleasant, PA, a church her Scottish great-grandfather, James Crosbie, and his sons, Daniel and Cornelius, labored to build in the mid-nineteenth century.

When making arrangements with the funeral home, we discovered that one of the funeral directors was originally from Long Island and a friend of Jimmy Carol, the husband of my cousin Ellen. He explained that, as a Catholic, he had to educate the locals on how Catholics from the Northeast conducted wakes. The local North Carolina custom was for a wake to last one hour on only one day. Family and friends of the deceased would stand in line and walk past the closed casket to pay their respects and leave. A few chairs were scattered about room. The funeral director educated them about the Northeast Catholic tradition where the wake consisted of two viewings per day over a two-day period. The body of the deceased usually lay in an open casket while mourners would stay and comfort the family and sit for two hours. The funeral director was great to work with and provided great comfort to our family. My brother Paul looked particularly distressed as he mourned the loss of Dad, sweating profusely and unable to stand up straight. Later that evening, when the family gathered back at the house, we planned on ordering take-out food, but the acute pain and symptoms Paul had experienced earlier came back with a vengeance. Concerned over his acute symptoms I took him to Lake Norman Regional Hospital. He received a barium enema in which they concluded he most likely had diverticulitis. He was discharged with antibiotics and pain killers. It was now Sunday morning, and we were all preparing for the Sunday morning funeral Mass for Dad. Paul was still in pain and couldn't even put on his suit. I decided to take him back to the hospital where they promised more tests. I phoned him after Mass, and he said he still hadn't seen anyone. I told him to start banging on the gurney until someone came back in. He banged on the gurney for over five minutes before a nurse came back in. I demanded to know what was happening and why was he so uncomfortable. The nurse had no answer and said they would like to admit him. When I arrived at the hospital, a nurse commented that my brother was probably reacting to pain killers. I was pissed off at their assumption and alerted them that he only took antibiotics the night before and didn't touch the painkillers. The staff wasn't particularly helpful when I suggested he be transferred to UNC in Charlotte. They just sent someone who was in a boat accident to UNC and the staff was thin. I suggested he get on a plane and fly back with me to New York. The nurse advised against that as he was too sick to move. So, there he stayed right there in Lake Norman Regional Hospital.

The final resting place for my dad was to be St. Anthony's Cemetery in Nanuet, NY. His second wake, and burial, would take place on July 25th. We were in a conundrum. My brother lay gravely ill in some small regional hospital while we were making plans to travel to NY to bury my father. My sister-in-law Dorie and cousin Carol Carpentier, daughter of Uncle Joe Fabio, graciously volunteered to stay with Paul, while the rest of the family returned to New York. While I sat in the plane, I was distraught, as I tried to wrap my head around what was happening to Paul while mourning the loss of my father; and trying to be strong for Mom. I stared straight ahead for the whole plane ride and made no eye contact with anyone. A Black woman sat next to me and observed my discomfort. As we deplaned, she commented that she didn't know what was troubling me but wished I would find peace and finally said she would pray for me. I thanked her as I struggled to vocalize my words while I averted my tear-swelled eyes from hers. Dorie kept us abreast of Paul's condition over the next few days. Doctors speculated that he had a parasitic infection caused by a tick bite, and ran some tests, which came out negative. No one really knew what was going on as Dorie pressed the doctors for more information. Wednesday, July twenty-fifth, was the day of my dad's funeral and burial. Early that morning Dorie called and said Paul took a turn for the worse and that we need to get Mom back there as soon as we can. I shook in despair not comprehending how a guy in the prime of his life was seemingly crashing before our eyes. I was emotionless during my father's wake. I had no answers for my brother Paul's friends who were equally shocked at his absence at his own father's burial. I agreed to accompany Mom back to NC. I drove with Mom from the burial at St. Anthony's Cemetery to Newark Airport and assured her that the doctors were doing the best they could to help Paul. No one knew anything, and we were in great distress. As I was about to exit the terminal in Charlotte Douglas Airport, Greg called me and informed me that Paul had passed. I was a few steps ahead of Mom and I let out a groan from deep within. I went into the men's room and some traveler saw me and asked if I was alright. I was speechless and waved him off as I splashed water on my face trying to gain my composure. I couldn't tell Mom that her son just died while at the airport. I put on a brave face, walked out of the restroom and told her Greg called just to check in and that we arrived. We headed straight to the hospital and as we walked in, Mom knew something was off when she spotted Dorie and Carol downstairs waiting by the elevator. Dorie tried to speak with her, but she was pushed out of the way. Mom and I made our way right up to the room where Paul lay. She was in the room no more than fifteen seconds when she blurted out:

That is not my son, he is no longer here.

She knew Paul was gone; his life was elsewhere, no longer trapped in his body that failed him over that last five days. She immediately signed papers for an autopsy. We left to mourn in confusion: how could this happen! How could Dad pass from complications of seemingly a simple laparoscopic procedure to remove an enlarged spleen. How could our baby brother be cut down before our eyes? How would any of us handle this grief, this all-encompassing grief? We made arrangements with the funeral director for the second time in seven days. As we attempted to make sense of what happened, all the man could say was:

Only God knows and He's not telling.

Dad died on July twentieth, and Paul died five days later on July twenty-fifth of 2007.[1,2]

As our loved ones gathered by the burial plot at St. Anthony's Cemetery for the second time in a week, they were in disbelief of the tragedy that struck our family. Robert walked up to me and whispered in my ear:

Fabio's don't cry.

I thought to myself:

What, is this guy kidding me? This is what you have to say to me?

as was about to bury my brother and make some attempt to comfort my mother. Was he oblivious that I just bawled my eyes out outside St. Aedan's Church as the casket where my brother lay was loaded into the hearse? Who was he kidding? Did he not remember his father Jack, crying over the loss of Margie? I ignored him, but I never forgot that whisper in my ear. Robert admitted to me that he never shed a tear when his mom died in 1994 or for his father in 1999. For solace, I went to the Lord for comfort and direction. In tragedy, Robert went to Yonkers Raceway. The morning he found out his father had passed, he went over to his sister Jackie's house. She was very distraught and sobbed uncontrollably while she made him breakfast. Robert and Jackie soon became aware that Jack did not make any final funeral arrangements, and whatever money he did have hardly covered the costs of a wake, burial plot, and headstone. After Robert finished his meal, he got up to leave. Jackie commented about whether he was going to the Bronx VA on Kingsbridge Road to speak with the morgue or going to Flower Funeral Home to make arrangements.

No, Jackie, I'm going to the track. Daddy had no policy, no nothing. How do you think we are going to bury him?

Robert bet a few hundred dollars on the horses and within two hours walked away with ten-thousand dollars. He called Jackie to come down to the track and cash the ticket, took the cash and then drove to Flower Funeral Home and gave it to the funeral director. Another six-thousand dollars went for the plot at Gate of Heaven Cemetery. Robert did what he trusted most: he gambled.

As the days and weeks went by after Paul and Paul John's passing, the immediate family acknowledged that God was sovereign and had His reasons and timing for everything. We resolved to comfort Mom and support each other as best we could. The weeks and months afterward were torturous, but we managed slowly. The autopsy report for Paul John came back, he had stage IV colorectal cancer. A mass on his colon dislodged, and ultimately, he died of sepsis. Paul Frank Fabio and Paul John Fabio have passed into eternity. We still shed tears over our loss, but the laughter and smiles prevail as they live in our thoughts and memories and are forever part of who we are. They were a gift from God.

> *… and the dust returns to the earth as it was, and the spirit returns to God who gave it.*
>
> Ecclesiastes 12:7–8

Chapter 23

Plus ça change, plus c'est la même chose. The more things change, the more they stay the same.

—Jean-Baptiste Alphonse Karr

Joe Shaefer knew the night doorman who gave him good intel on a new location. It was close to Henry Hudson Parkway and provided an easy escape route if trouble wandered in unexpectedly. Joe informed Robert that a large part of the basement was unused. A twenty-five-hundred-foot area lay behind locked doors. Personal storage areas were not available for the tenants, and this area was unused except for storing cleaning supplies, snow shovels, salt, and left-over paint. One-thousand dollars was pocketed by the doorman who faked blindness and gave Joe a duplicate key.

They referred to their new casino as the White Tower. This residential apartment complex was distinct with its glass exterior framed by white concrete columns. The White Tower stood imperiously over the red brick apartment complexes, residences, and municipal buildings made from local clay dug from the Hudson River. The Riverdale section of the Bronx was no different from the multitude of buildings throughout the Bronx, Brooklyn, Queens, and Manhattan. It was a maze of red brick only interrupted by the older structures made of wood or stone. Newer cement and glass buildings signaled a developers turn toward modernity and sophistication. All Robert and Joe saw was the green color of money.

The casino opened at two in the morning, and it closed by six a.m. From a van outside, Joe controlled the flow of people arriving. No more than one person ever entered or left at the same time. There were standard tables for craps, roulette, and blackjack. Bets ranged from ten dollars to two-hundred-fifty dollars. All types of players gravitated toward the machines: working guys who loved to play, hard-up guys who dreamt of the big payoff, and girls who loved to party.

There was the casual player who came with his buddies and didn't mind dropping a few hundred knowing it was the cost of an evening's entertainment. Customers were not the Korean/ Asian customers that the clubs in Manhattan attracted. These customers were mostly working-class white guys from the Bronx and Westchester. When Robert saw these guys he saw currency, many dollars. He looked at them with a broad smile and a glint in his eyes, he even looked welcoming and friendly. Robert greeted them with a:

Hi, how are ya?

or

Good to see you. Looking good!

He even sounded humble, and these gamblers felt at ease with Robert's affable demeanor, an attitude that paid off.

He wanted people to play and feel a high from winning; he wanted players to forget their life and feel the frenzy of the moment and forget the troubles of life because nothing mattered now. When he took a breather, he grabbed a beer, slipped into the bathroom, snorted a few lines, and the blow triggered a surge of dopamine, the neurotransmitter associated with pleasure and reward for the brain. His brain swam in the euphoria of his increased alertness. He knew that for the next thirty minutes he lived in his personal pleasure palace, and life itself took a backseat to the narcotic.

Robert kept a keen eye on the customers, their betting habits, knowledge of the games and if they were skilled in the nuances of blackjack. He paid attention to their conversations, to their gestures and to their body language. He felt secure, and knew that Joe was vigilant, and made sure that no one entered the club with knives or guns. He closely observed everyone and was as ready as a predatory eagle. Most gamblers did not turn their pieces over, they simply opted to go elsewhere.

As Robert was about to return to a blackjack table, his suspicious nature skillfully noticed a lean fellow who had lingered at the entrance doorway now slowly walking around the tables. Instead of buying a drink or buying chips, he seemed to be scanning the crowd, looking for something. He nonchalantly zoomed at the pockets and waists of targeted customers. He walked around keenly observing the outlay of different tables. His actions were a tell, all poker players had a tell, a sign that is barely perceptible, but will send a signal to a skilled observer. If a poker player twitched, rubbed his forehead, or stretched his neck, and repeated the pattern every time, he was a bluffer. Other astute players now knew and adjusted their bets.

This non gambler was giving off cues. Robert thought this individual didn't look like a policeman who could be looking to shut the place down, but maybe he was wired, and possibly in contact with someone outside. Robert watched and didn't like what he saw. He was in radio contact with Joe via a headset. He looked around a few times, and then walked in the back room and spoke loudly:

Joe, you're supposed to be the best fucking doorman. I smell pork mothafucka, why do I gotta a cop in here?

Joe laughed.

You're good. Don't worry, he's a nice guy, a friend of a friend. Don't worry about it, he's not gonna do anything. He's harmless, he just wants a few drinks and mingle with the club girls.

Ultimately the lawman was harmless. He played blackjack for a few hours at the twenty-five-dollar table, and he knew what he was doing. He spent his time guzzling beers, won intermittently, and chatted up the party girls. It was the end of an uneventful and profitable evening, just like most times when night turned to mornings.

Months later the White Tower was ransacked: tables were removed, alcohol bottles were shattered, the place was left like a war zone. The building manager had to clean up and deal with a slew of court appearances for operating an illegal casino, and for the unlawful sale of alcohol. Robert, Abe V, and Joe washed their hands of yet another pop-up casino, and they were on to their next location and began the process again.

Weeks slowly vanished; Joe Schaefer disappeared; he was beaten up badly. The details were sketchy, but apparently his tough-guy persona came back to bite him in the ass. Distressed that his partner and friend was incapacitated, Robert visited Joe while he recuperated at his mother's home. Several whacks with axe handles by unknown assailants did its job. Joe was forever out of commission, never again to be the unseen seeing eye. Robert resolved himself to Joe's fate, as he watched his friend sadly play with his toy Yoda while he proudly introduced his new pet, a picture of a chihuahua.

Opportunity came knocking again, when, out of nowhere, House contacted him.

Hey, JC, I got this spot, I want you to be on site but not to run the game.

Ok, but why not run the game?

Don't worry about it, you just hang out, your name is what is bringing in customers, you'll get free pot, free coke, free pussy. I also have a mechanic coming in so we'll be making good money.

House contacted Robert out of the blue needing his reputation and draw of customers. The mechanic he referred to was not a mechanic in the usual sense of the word, but rather a dealer skilled in cheating. The mechanic inserted ten cards with tiny brail imprints into a shoe of six decks of cards. When the dealer detected the cards, he pushed up the shoe to hold the card so it wouldn't be dealt. Robert knew the scam: he was cheated himself years ago at a small club in L.I. He lost sixteen-thousand dollars one night and had no idea that the dealer at the time was a thief. House and Robert were at a club named Tango when House alerted Robert to a man drinking at the bar. Robert recognized him immediately and said:

This is the same fucking guy who was dealing that night in L.I. when I lost big. No way, he's not coming in here! Fuck this, this is bullshit. Do you know who comes in here? If they ever find out you are cheating, you're dead! I'm dead! No way, this is not happening. Besides, I want my sixteen-thousand dollars back. This guy better pay up.

Unconvinced with House's assurances, Scotty appeared and calmed Robert down; they promised good money and said he could deal and pad his earnings on top of a thirty-percent take. Robert relented, as House and Scotty compromised. Instead of the L.I. mechanic, they hired a female mechanic. Robert described her as:

Italian girl, blonde hair, big tits, nice!

Scotty and House additionally brought in Jimmy V as their muscle. Scotty and House were old pros, finding a location on the upper east side located at 77th and York. The owner agreed that if Scotty paid the eight months back rent, the current rent, and buy the alcohol, they had a deal. The owner struggled for years to turn a profit, and he was taken to court several times, and now was desperate. Scotty and House seized on the opportunity, and as a result of Robert's reputation for attracting steady customers, money rolled in. They had a few blackjack tables and a few machines. Robert was paid for his presence and for endorsing the club. He didn't even have to deal if he chose not to. Just be there!

This female mechanic had no discretion when she cheated the customers. She was stoic and all business and felt no regrets. Men looked at her with voracious eyes as if they could swallow her. Her severe beauty was a challenge, but all she did was deal with total attention to the game. Her pleasant smile, sympathetic tone, and attractive figure created an atmosphere of trust; A look that was a cover for her dishonest sleight of hand. Her severe beauty cast a gambling spell. She dressed well but not provocatively, and precisely because of her sexual lure the gamblers had not suspected that the game was rigged. Nothing but the game mattered to her, she only saw cash in the eyes of longing men.

Robert never deceived customers, he didn't play that game, he dealt honestly. Robert confronted her aggressively:

You're killing everyone, let them play.

She felt his ferocity, his no nonsense, no pretense look. Intimidated by Robert, she threatened him, saying she was going to call her boyfriend, Karate Mike, another freelance dealer who ran a club down on 28th Street.

Oh yeah, call my fucking cock up you dumb bitch. You're on York Ave. baby, this is big time, Be careful!

Robert confronted Karate Mike in the past when he accused Robert of badmouthing his club on 28th Street. Robert denied it. She didn't call, and nothing came of her threats.

Black Charlie was a sorrowful soul who lived in the depths of desperation. He was stripped of any vestige of dignity as he wandered from club to club, looking for odd jobs to make money to support his own drinking and gambling habits. Scotty and House saw him as a useful idiot to run errands. Robert found an opportunity to use him a guise. One evening the game was slow and Robert found himself alone for a few hours. He went out for a break, smoked a cigarette, downed a beer, and made his way back in. Three people were now sitting at his blackjack table, drinking, smoking, and engaging in banter about losing $1000 over the last few blackjack games.

A thick-set man with short, dark, kinky hair and a prominent nose sat next to a well-endowed woman paying careful attention to his every word, while a big muscular man with larger shoulders sat indifferently listening to the two complain about their misfortune. Ill tempered, Robert returned from his break and interrupts the trio's powwow:

Hey, buddy, you need to move, I'm starting a game here!

Screeching voices and smoke-filled air blended into a nauseous cocktail. Obscenities echoed through the air and scattered words bounced all around:

Fuck you! Who the fuck you think you are? Fuck off!

Robert finally howled at Black Charlie:

Take the raincoats, lock the door, I'm gonna chop up this motherfucka!

Robert turned red. He was no longer tired, he no longer cared about dealing cards, he was now a rabid dog with saliva dripping from his mouth and ready to maul anyone in his path. Black Charlie played his part and did exactly what he was told: he took their coats, locked the doors and blocked the exit. The man with the prominent nose mouthed off while turning ashen; his girlfriend screamed:

Get me out of here!

to which Robert replied,

You're going too, bitch!

The crass looking couple ran to the exit door, and just as Robert was ready to pounce, he stopped on a dime and nodded to Black Charlie to let them go.

His life became a little more routine as he continued to work with Joe during the day and dealt cards at various clubs at night. He was paid off the books, naturally, and just as routinely he pilfered some money as additional income.

Stealing was easy, and in Robert's mind, possession equaled ownership. He developed a working scheme that ran like a well-oiled machine. His slippery hands took the cash that gamblers gave him for chips, and instead of putting the money in the money box, he would quickly slip a hundred-dollar bill in his shirt pocket, tucked neatly between two cards. His fast hands sometimes yielded an extra thousand bucks over the course of a week. All tax free. The work he did as painting foreman with Frank was off the books, and the work he did as a dealer and partner in the club was an all-cash enterprise. Even though he slipped under the radar of the IRS, he would not escape the raptness of loan sharks.

Hey, this guy Jose is looking for you. He's saying you don't call, and you don't respond to his messages. Rob, he is going to kill you, he says you owe one-hundred-thousand dollars.

Frank was very concerned for Robert and Robert was equally concerned that his loan shark was in contact with his boss. Robert was always in need of extra cash for his gambling habits. He wagered large sums of money to bet on horses, blackjack, and sports betting, and his weekly income could not support the level of losses he incurred. The marble contractor became his new source of money. Unfortunately for Robert, the marble contractor was not from the same mold of his previous loan shark from Arthur Avenue in the Bronx. The marble contractor was not Italian and held no allegiance to the mafia's code of criminal justice. He was associated with the blood-thirsty members of the MS-13 gang. Jose was not interested in negotiating terms of payment, he wanted his money now and his code, the gang's code, was to kill you off if you did not pay.

Arthur Avenue is main commercial hub and the center of

Bronx's Little Italy. It is the heart of the Belmont section of the Bronx and situated just south of Fordham University, and west of the Bronx Zoo. The Italian language church, Chiesa di Nostra Signora del Carmelo, Our Lady of Mount Carmel, served immigrants from all over Sicily and Calabria just like it did for our parents, grandparents, and their extended families. But every neighborhood changes and with the passing of time, Italian immigration died down, and the community aged. A new presence of Puerto Ricans and Dominicans would alter the demographic makeup of the area. That change would also apply to how Robert secured money for his gambling habits.

When Robert was short on cash and needed gambling money, he went to an Italian loan shark named Rudy, a regular guy who hung around Arthur Avenue establishments. Robert never met Rudy but was always told by his dealer friend who secured the loan that Rudy supplied the cash and set the terms of repayment. Robert understood the terms and understood the ramifications of not paying off his debts to a mob associate. He respected the code and was fearful of the hidden hand of mob justice. He had seen and heard what befell gamblers and others who crossed the line. They disappeared, no longer to be seen or heard from again. But Rudy died and in need of a new source of cash Robert was referred to a marble contractor, Jose. He had borrowed fifty-thousand dollars from his new money source. If Robert won at the blackjack table or OTB or with sports betting he would pay the loan back. He did that when he first borrowed fifty thousand from Jose and paid him back over the course of a few months. But now this was different. Robert pissed away the hundred thousand he borrowed and lacked the respect and understanding of Jose' criminal network.

Robert told his boss Joe:

Fuck him, he's not going to do anything, screw him.

Robert didn't respect this Latin American marble contractor, and doubted Jose had a large network of enforcers to ensure repayment. But Robert's lifestyle was catching up with him. The years of coke, lack of sleep, warning from his and nagging girlfriend grinded down his resolve. He slowly grew tired of the threats, the calls, and uncertainty hanging over his head. Jose pursued Robert, pursued his money for nine months and finally Robert agreed to meet with him. Jose was parked on Southern Boulevard next to a sidewalk bordering the Bronx Zoo. It was a quiet location and Robert approached the car from behind, making sure no pedestrians were in sight. While Robert sat on the passenger's side on the car, he pulled out his .38 Glock from his left breast coat pocket and pointed it directly at Jose's face:

You are threatening me? Don't ever threaten me, and don't call my boss! Who the fuck are you? I'll shoot you in your left eye. You understand?

Jose shuddered,

I'm sorry, I'm sorry.

as he was handed a couple thousand dollars to hold him over for the time being.

Turbulence was never far from Robert, and even though the threat of retribution from Jose faded, the unabated harassment from his boss, girlfriend, and casino partners was wearing him down. Frank was fed up with Robert showing up at work as if in a trance. Being a foreman required energy, focus, and attention to detail and Robert had none of that outside of the artificial situation with coke that he used to get him through the day. Frank was yet again frustrated that his star foreman was self-destructing.

Compounding the negativity from his boss was his girlfriend's accusation of his philandering. Robert had always been a ladies' man and an opportunist with a willing partner. But the Irish Blonde was his live-in girlfriend once again and in no time became suspicious of Robert during his long absences from her day and night. They both kept crazy hours and communicated by phone and text just to keep track of each other's whereabouts. One night she called him and asked where he was. He told her that he was in the city. He was actually in City Lights, a strip club on Yonkers Ave. just below the apartment balcony on Cowles Ave. that he shared with her. The strip club was the least of her worries as she began to suspect Robert double timing her with the blonde dealer from the York Ave. club. Robert was cheating on his Irish blonde live-in girlfriend with the Italian blonde cheat dealer. Robert was loyal to no one accept his urges. But his urges could not relieve his stress and compromised health. He was running on fumes, supplemented with weed, and coke. All this pressure made him agitated and short tempered with everyone. His moods fluctuated like the rolling tides of a storm, unrelenting and destructive to himself and anyone who would challenge him.

Robert's frustration came to head. Robert always thought House was a fat, sanctimonious prick and pissed off Robert when he preached about the harm of marijuana on brain cells, and the dangers of doing blow all hours of the night. House was now a partier himself as he smoked pot and snorted coke regularly like everyone else. The pot can't call the kettle black, Robert thought, and that idea turned Robert's stomach.

That fat fuck. I'm done!

Equally frustrated with his take home pay he concluded all this aggravation was not worth it. He figured he should be making two-thousand dollars a week; he was only bringing home nine-hundred dollars. He told Scotty and House that he was done, he was walking away from the partnership. Scotty and House did their best to try to convince him to stay, and they even asked Jimmy V to intimidate him, and Jimmy V tried.

JC, you can't leave!

Go fuck yourself, you're not going to pay me money, fuck those two Jews, I'm not making any money here, get the fuck outta here! Don't piss me off!

Robert erupted into a tirade of expletives.

His girlfriend was the next to go but not before they got married. Like all of his relationships, this was transactional. He did not have the capacity to love unconditionally. And neither did she. They met each other's needs, but it was temporary. The gambling, drugs, and dishonesty dissolved whatever glue they thought kept them together.

The day before their marriage, Robert was informed by his fiancée that she had two children from two previous marriages. She sheepishly asked if he was agreeable with the two boys moving in with them. His new bride was just like Robert: impulsive, impetuous, and explosive; she loved to party, gamble, and live fast. Robert agreed, not thinking it would be any trouble. He had no frame of reference of what responsible parenting entailed. And neither did she.

Her foundational years prepped her for partying, risk taking, and bad decisions. A product of divorce at a young age, she and her sisters were exposed to a life of high stakes gambling, nightclubs, and partying. Her mother remarried a man who was accomplished in a world of cards and gaming. Alvin Roth was a champion bridge player, had won twenty-six national titles, and wrote several books on Bridge which introduced new strategies and concepts to competing and winning at bridge.[1,2] He was so successful that he bought the Mayfair Club, a gaming club run out of the Gramercy Park Hotel in Manhattan and stewarded it from low stakes backgammon games to high stakes bridge and poker games.[3] This club was considered a high end establishment with well-dressed clientele, polite staff, expensive food, and attractive and attentive women. This club made lots of money and garnered national attention from the national press when reporting on tournaments held there.

Having young kids through his second marriage was not in the cards for Alvin, yet that was the hand he was dealt. Gaming clubs did not attract the most virtuous of men. While upright in appearance, many were lecherous fiends who preyed upon weak and willing women. Alvin's associates were not father figures to these young ladies, and each of the girls had their own unsettling experiences with associates of the club. Who would believe that outwardly respectable men would ever do such things to these vulnerable girls?

Robert's fiancée and now bride was an independent woman who was gregarious, generous, and determined. She was accustomed to money and grew up traveling in style. She wore pricy dresses, expensive suits, and had designer purses, shoes, and jewelry. She liked to look rich, which she did, but it was a charade. Robert's earnings as foreman, and whatever clubs he was involved with at the time, allowed him to have cash most times. And when he had that cash, his bride got her weekly stipend of eight-hundred dollars for her needs. They both lived beyond their means. When the money was steady, they ate well, partied heavily, and took nice trips to Las Vegas, or Mexico, or the Caribbean. When money was scarce, they wouldn't eat. She quickly learned that Robert lived on the edge. When she wanted to open a joint bank account he laughed at her, saying:

Are you crazy? I never had a bank account in my life, I never paid taxes. You want me to go to jail?

Not quite believing what she was hearing, she decided to put the rental lease and car payments in her name. She had no idea who she actually married. Robert seemed liked the respectable painting contractor foreman earning a good salary and benefits. But that was far from the truth. Robert was a gambler, first and foremost. Everything he did supported his quest to make money to support his lifestyle of gambling and partying. His female relationships served his needs.

When his wife was working, she exposed him to another world. A world of high-end restaurants and hotels. She gravitated toward fashionable and trendy people who were far removed of the seedy world of late-night casinos filled with massage parlor masseuses and immigrant gamblers. She floated around many trendy upscale establishments catering to a younger crowd who liked to party with disposable cash. Gay themed nights and other themed events happened multiple times a week, and Robert would often come down, get dressed and get with whatever was available: coke, weed, or alcohol.

Lady Gaga was in the house! Stefani Joanne Angelina Germanotta was going to be performing at a private event at the hotel where his wife was employed. Robert decided to go. It was a night out with pretty people, and he would spend his night doing what he liked to do best: partying and getting high. When Robert was warned that this private event was an all-male party, he retreated and found refuge in the backstage area to hang out before the show started.

As Robert inhaled a joint, he froze to the magic spell of a female voice. Lady Gaga was backstage getting prepped for her show when she sniffed a familiar scent.

I like your cologne,

she said, as she stroked his toned biceps. He looked up after his deep puff of marijuana and was stunned by Lady Gaga's arresting smile. He eyed her with a degree of wonder, and out of embarrassment he extended his hand and offered Lady Gaga his joint. She displayed a gleaming smile but declined his offer. Robert, unfazed by the presence of this famous performer, brazenly asked the diva if he could be her bodyguard. Lady Gaga simply chuckled and walked away with a bemused smirk.

He had another brush with fame, or rather, the infamous. His bride was particularly fond of a hair salon in the Bronx because of the quality of their hair dye. It was a blonde color that was unmatched by any other salon. The coloring cost her one-hundred-fifty dollars. Unfazed by the cost Robert drove her down and planned to walk around the Morris Park section not far from Neill

Ave where our Uncle Joe and Aunt Rose lived and Rhinelander Ave. where Uncle Danny and Aunt Agnes had lived. As he entered the salon, Robert introduced himself to the owner.

Hey, I'm Robert, but everyone calls me JC.

Without hesitation the owner retorts:

Hey, I heard about you, you're that blackjack dealer.

Robert winced and muttered to himself:

I hate that shit.

Robert hated that his persona was minimized to a lowly blackjack dealer. In his mind, he was so much more. His stature and his physicality and the reputation he built through intimidation and affiliations with disdainful members of the underworld had earned him respect. His inflated ego placed him as a club owner, as a man with power and connections, as a man with wealth and taste. But here he was, "that blackjack dealer," shaking hands with a bona fide man of honor. The salon owner, colorist, was called Vinny Gorgeous. A moniker he earned through the play on his good looks and the name of his salon, Hello Gorgeous.[4]

He told Robert:

Don't bother waiting at the salon, instead go out and kill some time at a local bar where you can bet on horses, have a few drinks, and relax. You don't want to sit here; your wife will be here for a little over an hour.

Robert heeded the advice and did what was offered. An hour later, Robert received a call and was told to return to the salon. He stumbled in drunk, high, and a few hundred dollars richer. Robert occupied his free time by getting high and gambling his money. He pocketed close to four-hundred dollars and paid the hair colorist two-hundred dollars.

His wife loved Vinny's masterful hair-coloring work, and she kept going back to him for years. Robert never saw him again after that brief interaction and had no idea who he really was. Years later he learned that the hair colorist had been immersed in a different line of work. Vinny was the acting boss of the Bonanno crime family, promoted after the arrest of Joe Massino. And like many men in that line of business, was convicted of racketeering, two murders, and for attempted murder of a federal prosecutor. It didn't work out too well, as he was eventually sentenced to life in prison.[5]

Robert's blonde Irish wife was a mystery to me and my brothers. We met only her after my father and brother died in 2007. Robert reached out to us during the holidays that year and invited us over. This was Robert's first ever overture to his younger cousins and we were all pleasantly surprised to be invited to a party at his house. All we really knew about Robert was that he was employed as a painting contractor, had been a dealer for illegal casinos on First Ave. twenty years ago, dated several Korean women and owned a restaurant for a short period of time. We all heard mutterings around the family dinner table. Robert was involved with this, and Robert was involved with that. Who really knew? None of us did. And we really didn't dwell on it. We had our own lives, families, careers, and interests. So, when Robert did reach out to us, we thought it was a great gesture for a member of extended family to offer solace and esprit de corps. He was inviting us over to meet his new wife; an intelligent, attractive, well spoken, Irish blonde who worked in hotel management. We were quite curious about what type of person is attracted to a guy like my cousin who always seemed to walk a fine line between respectable and dubious behavior.

Mr. and Mrs. Robert Fabio lived in an apartment in New Rochelle. It was the tallest building in the area, and they rented a top floor with panoramic views of Manhattan. In preparation for the evening holiday gathering, his bride instructed Robert to pick up some antipasto, some liquor for the party, and a couple of eight balls, eighth of an ounce of cocaine. Robert disappeared for five hours. He and his coke supplier, a Dominican he called Chihuahua, met in an apartment a few blocks from Yankee Stadium. Robert bought an ounce of pot, some coke, and in the interim proceeded to get high. He got so intoxicated, jittery, and overstimulated that he could hardly walk straight. He stopped at a liquor store to pick up a fifth of scotch to simply calm down. The alcohol calmed his nervous energy. It worked every time. When he arrived home, his bride screamed as if she had seen a ghost, and with a loud shrill she asked:

Where the hell were you?

He responded, bemused at her over reaction to his absence and laughed:

We're having a party tonight, I started early.

You're an asshole!

Well do you want some coke or not? ... Who's the asshole?

Adriane and I arrived at the apartment around eight-thirty in the evening. We quickly caught up with Robert, met his wife, and gathered around with my brothers and assorted other company. When we walked in, the apartment it was abuzz with activity, and after some obligatory niceties, we dug into some antipasto and some red wine. Robert pulled me aside and asked me if I wanted to do any blow. I did a double-take. I haven't snorted cocaine or was even offered it for twenty-five years. I associated coke and partying with my days in college, and those days were long behind me. I bleakly responded:

Um, no thanks, I'm good!

It became obvious that many others at the party readily accepted his offer, and they disappeared with him in the back bedroom. His circle of friends and acquaintances and type of partying they engaged in was not anything I wanted to hang around with. As it became more and more apparent that the drug high was more important than any conversation we attempted to engage in, we grew increasingly uncomfortable and made a quick exit. Robert played the jovial host as he offered his guests the high of their choice, coke, weed, and alcohol. The incongruity of the Christmas tree and it's symbolic meaning of Christ's birth juxtaposed with the those seeking a high through drugs and alcohol didn't escape my attention. That was me many years ago. I was no longer that person.

Robert's wife initially didn't understand the extent of his connections with powerful people, his gambling addiction, and constant quest for gambling money. But like all of Robert's female companions, his lifestyle was not sustainable for a stable relationship. A letter arrived from a collection agency. It listed nine casinos he owed money to. The line of credit that his previous wife Sae Hee helped him secure fifteen years earlier had come back to haunt him. He owed a hefty sum of one-hundred-thousand dollars that was lent to him over the years via markers. Robert's paranoia and anxiety skyrocketed as his debts and threats of retribution mounted. He had slowly been paying off the money he owed Jose and now the law was coming after him from unpaid markers from the Atlantic City casinos. If law enforcement could find out where he lived, he reasoned that they could certainly make his life very uncomfortable as court cases and lawyer's fees for his defense would eat away at any extra income he had and may likely garnish his wife's wages. Robert turned to his lawyer once again but found solace in the knowledge that a court of law would probably not hold him liable. His lawyer explained that the statute of limitations would not allow prosecution after nine years. Relieved and defiant, Robert decided to ignore his obligation to Jose and refused to pay back any more of the money that he owed his loan shark. He instead used money he siphoned from his wife to incur addition gambling losses. Robert prided himself on his gambling prowess, but it was an illusion. It was a vicious cycle that he refused to learn from. The enticement of a big reward, a big win, and the thrill of winning free money deluded him. His time and effort expended in gambling and losing his wives' and girlfriends' money taught him nothing. The winnings he did take home were quickly spent. But he could never claim that the money he won in gambling exceeded what he lost. He lost yet again.

Robert was joyless with his explosive temper, his gambling debts, and his constant mood swings. His relationship with his wife was built on a slippery foundation of partying, travel, and excess. He was oblivious to her growing frustration with the marriage and with his gambling debts. By 2012 the marriage fizzled. His wife packed up and left him. He returned home from work and found his apartment in New Rochelle empty. His sole possessions were his closet full of clothes, a granite dining room table and chairs, and a blow-up mattress. They never saw each other again.

Chapter 24

Let providence, not chance, have the honor of thy acknowledgements.

—Sir Thomas Browne

Despite numerous opportunities and setbacks in my professional career I always tried to maintain a level head. At times I struggled to remain positive and hopeful. It was difficult to be forward thinking. It was easier to doubt myself, to be distraught by my circumstances, be dejected by my fruitless efforts to gain employment, and cheerless with my loss of meaningful work. But these were momentary feelings. They passed. When I was faced with difficult choices, I consulted the Lord in prayer. When I lost a job and was left with no source of income, I prayed. I didn't just pray, I sought comfort and gained confidence through God's word. I never expected a job to fall in my lap. But I was hopeful that job opportunities would come my way. But hope is not a plan. I needed to put great effort into finding a new job. My confidence awakened when I realized I am not alone. The scriptures have always been my source of assurance.

> *What then shall we say to these things? If God is for us, who can be against us?*
>
> Romans 8:31

As the new year rang in, I was informed that if I wanted to remain employed with Biogen Idec, I would need to relocate and reside in the region I was managing. It was January of 2009, and my boss seemingly created this new rule out of nowhere. He mandated that I move somewhere, anywhere, in the Southeast region. I had resided in New York for two years while I managed a sales region based in Florida, Georgia, South Carolina, or Alabama. Now I was told I needed to move south.

Three times in my professional career I was offered to move closer to company headquarters and assume various roles. Adria Laboratories, Pharmacia Upjohn, and IDEC Pharmaceuticals all had offered me an internal position and to move me to their corporate offices. While I was flattered at the recognition that my skills were highly valued, I ultimately turned down the offers. Adria was based out of Dublin, Ohio, a suburb of Columbus. The John Deere tractor in front of the factory in the adjacent field demonstrated the area was more rural than suburb. The Mid-West was a foreign country to me, and I turned them down. Pharmacia Upjohn was based out of Kalamazoo, Michigan. I lead oncology sales training classes at the home offices several times and was asked if I wanted to relocate and take a position as sales trainer. I loved teaching science but questioned the judgement of the person making me the offer. The new VP of the Commercial team made a weak attempt of a sales pitch. She tried to convince me that Kalamazoo is just like New Jersey. I laughed to myself thinking that, while there is a lot to like about New Jersey, mainly its beaches, how could she possibly think Kalamazoo is an attractive place to live. I thought that comment was a joke, this lady doesn't know what she is talking about. Besides, my wife and I just welcomed our new baby daughter. I declined the offer. A few years later IDEC Pharmaceutical offered me a tempting position in San Diego. I was told if I moved out west that a position would be created for me. It sounded enticing as my wife imagined strolling the streets overlooking the La Jolla coastlines, as she pictured the waves crashing into the tumbling cliffs stretched along Pacific Ocean. My wife fantasized about being in complete harmony with the scenic world of southern California, the warm sun, gentle breezes, and endless summers. But in wasn't to be. Reality delivered a knockout punch. Her dreams came crashing down. I faced the truth about our finances. There would be no way we could afford living in La Jolla or anywhere near the water. And having two young children without the support of family and friends would be too great of an adjustment. I thought about it, but I ultimately passed on the opportunity.

And now, almost ten years later, I was not given the option to move: I was told to move. I became very suspicious of my boss' motives when he would not provide me a straight answer or support his reasoning in writing. I was even less confident with the company. I consulted human resources, and they could not produce any rule that required a director to reside within the region that they managed. Human resources told me I needed to negotiate with my manager. This mandate was too disruptive for my family, and I refused to move. Why would I want to work for a manager or company that arbitrarily created and enforced a mandate like that? Instead, I negotiated a buy-out, confident in my chances of finding work before the severance ran out.

As I was interviewing for a new job, an opportunity allowed me to serve on the board of trustees at Maranatha Church of the Nazarene. It was an honor to serve the faithful. I was now home during the week and had the time to attend the various board meetings. I was grateful to spend more time with my family and be able to serve the church in a leadership role. I had previously served as the junior youth teacher for the past seven years teaching sixth through eighth graders lessons from the Bible. I enjoyed watching kids grow through the years and watch them progress in their understanding of the scriptures. My two kids had to endure my teaching and ramblings every Sunday for years. But as my hair greyed, I decided to step down and hand it over to someone younger and more relatable to kids. I realized that it would be better to step down from Sunday school and soon thereafter the new opportunity with the board opened up. The timing was perfect.

I was still on the hunt for full-time work and decided to attend ASCO, the American Society of Clinical Oncology, meeting held each year in the spring. I had attended this symposium almost every spring for the last sixteen years attending meetings, manning the exhibit booth, and meeting with customers. I now used this opportunity to network with former colleagues and follow-up on some job opportunities. The fruit of that endeavor resulted in meeting employees at Cell Therapeutics, a biotech company based out of Seattle, WA, which led to a job offer later that summer.

During one of the meeting breaks at ASCO, I had the opportunity to chat with a former colleague I worked with when I was promoting Zevalin. After catching up on our activities over the last few years he introduced me to two gentlemen from Cell Therapeutics, the VP of Sales, and the VP of Marketing. As they were sharing information about a chemotherapy product, they expected the FDA to approve and discussed the type of cancer it would be indicated for; they asked about my experience. After some banter about my background in selling in the lymphoma space, the conversation shifted to talk about some oncologists that I worked with and my interactions with them. Just as I mentioned Dr. John Leonard's name, a hematological oncologist from The New York Hospital, I turned to my right, and he was standing ten feet away from me navigating through the round tables and chairs in the lounge area of the exhibit hall.

Hey, Dr. Leonard, how are you? I was just mentioning you and I wanted to introduce you to a couple of gentlemen.

Was this pure serendipity or a divine set up? Either way, the two gentlemen from the Seattle based company started to laugh over the unlikely happenstance of these introductions.

We kept in touch, and I was told that when they were ready to hire, they would reach out to me and schedule a formal interview. A mid-August interview was scheduled and in between a lot of laughs and serious conversation I left the interview feeling positive about my prospects for a job offer. As I dined outside with my wife on a warm summer evening in Piermont, NY, my phone rang. She eyed me with distain as I looked at the phone number light up on the display. This phone call, like every other phone call during dinner, was an unwelcome interruption of her date night. Her eyes told me:

Don't pick up the phone, don't do it, let it ring!

I noticed the 206 area code and knew it was from Seattle. My dinner could either evolve into a celebration of a new job or a determined resolve to press forward. I spaced the sidewalk in front of the restaurant as I spoke with the human resource staff. I hung up after a short exchange. Not pleased with being left alone at the table while I answered the call, Adriane sharply remarked that I better have a good reason for picking up that phone. Her countenance immediately changed as I giggled and shared that I just received a job offer as Regional Sales Director.

I travelled back and forth to Seattle and various other cities for nine months in preparation of a new product launch which included building a sales team, marketing, market access, sales training, and administrative infrastructure. I loved the biotech industry and working with oncology products. I have seen the benefits of chemotherapy and biologic agents personally with my mom, and professionally with the many patients I had been introduced to. Building a biotech commercial team from scratch was exhilarating. And I hoped to continue with this new company for a long time.

Nine months later it all came crashing down. The new sales force and managers were in Seattle for a training meeting. As we listened to ODAC, the oncology drug advisory committee, deliberate the merits of the data it became obvious that the doubts raised were problematic. The level of evidence presented to the committee was insufficient. The clinical trial had planned to enroll 320 patients but only 140 patients were enrolled. The FDA drug advisory panel voted nine to zero against the drug's approval and I found myself unemployed three weeks later. It was the spring of 2010. I was very disappointed, but that was the risk of joining a startup biotech, and while not happy, I accepted the risk.

I returned to ASCO a few weeks later. Once anew I embarked on a job search. I was frustrated with the unfortunate turn of events but that is the risk I accepted. I could have opted for the stability of a larger pharmaceutical company with a robust product pipeline and job security but that was a false promise as well. I had known many friends and colleagues over the years who lost jobs due to downsizing, or through mergers. The pharmaceutical career path I embarked on entailed risk, perseverance, and sacrifice. My experience, success, and relationships were instrumental in me landing many jobs over the years but there had been several unforeseen circumstances that had derailed my employment. Employment uncertainty would continue for a while.

I remember going on an interview in Chicago with a start-up biotech company. I thought the panel interview went well, but afterwards the hiring manager looked through my resume, made some observations about the frequent job changes over the last year and a half, and sarcastically commented:

You have a great resume, but your career seems to be spiraling out of control.

Nothing I could say would alter his preconceived opinion that the frequent job moves were somehow due to a character flaw. Not that I disagree with his questioning my frequent job changes.

As someone who has interviewed hundreds of candidates, I fully understand all the misgivings of a candidate who is a job hopper. But a skillful interviewer needs to parse the real reasons for the frequent changes in employment. Nothing I said was going to alter his opinion. It didn't help that this interviewer was the twin brother of someone I used to manage. He went on medical leave for mental distress, and he accused me of contributing to his wretchedness. I knew from the line of questioning and from his family ties that this interview was going nowhere. I tried to keep focus, and I spent all summer in the basement looking for job leads and kept contacting former colleagues for references and updates to help me along. In the afternoon I lay on the hammock resting, thinking and praying for something positive to shake me out of my doldrums. I wasn't bitter at the situation, although when you are in your mid-fifties with two kids about to enter college, and you have no income other than your wife's part-time job at the library, it is easy to get discouraged and depressed. Prayer and hope sustained me. The contact I made at ASCO that spring turned into a contract position with Eisai Pharmaceutical in their sales training department. This was not ideal since I had no health insurance, but I was able to negotiate an hourly wage that matched my previous salary. I lasted three months before I found a full-time job with a cancer research company. When I announced my resignation, I was still scheduled to lead a sales training class for the next two weeks. The head of sales training and head of learning and development were nervous that I would not honor my obligations, but I allayed their anxiety when I promised to fulfill my commitments. At the end of the two weeks, we met in one of their offices and they both gave me cards and gifts thanking me for not reneging on my promises.

Champions Oncology Inc., focused on cancer research, individualized cancer care, and facilitating expert provider review of a patient's disease and treatment plan. The origin of company names usually has a unique story behind its inspiration. Adria Laboratories took its name after Adriamycin, a chemotherapy drug discovered on the banks of the Adriatic Sea. Upjohn was named its founder, Dr. William Upjohn. IDEC was an acronym for anti-idiotype engineering company. The uniqueness of Champions name was no different. Champions came from Champions sports bars. The owner of this sports bar franchise had successfully integrated restaurant bars on the ground floors of Marriott hotels throughout the country, and now the owner was sought a new venture. He decided to get into the biotech space and started a new company specializing in attracting high net worth customers. The business model was to provide cancer patients with concierge consultations. Academic centers usually attracted nationally renowned experts to conduct research and act as department heads. The Champions' model was to conduct tumor boards with experts from every field: pathology, radiology, oncology, nuclear medicine, surgery, infectious disease, etc. Wealthy cancer patients were more than willing to pay a hefty fee to cover the expense of flying experts from around the country to attend a live meeting to review their medical history and offer advice for disease management. This was an expensive endeavor and attracted many international patients displeased with socialized medicine.

Champions' other business model was called in vivo tumor testing. They partnered with a researcher from John Hopkins University to explore an individual patient's tumor tissue responsiveness to drug therapy. Pieces of tumors removed through surgery were transported to a specialized laboratory in Baltimore, MD. The tumor was implanted into hybridized mice; bioengineered mice that had no natural immune system. It became a living laboratory where the tumor tissue grew and was further implanted in additional mice. Different chemotherapy agents were injected into the mice to observe if the tumors disappeared, shrunk, remained the same, or grew. This information was then shared with the patient's oncologist who would be better informed of which chemotherapy drugs to use if the patient relapsed.

This was extremely interesting in that I was not selling a product but was selling a research service. I had to interact with medical oncologists, surgical oncologists, pathologists, patients, and their family members. My role was to convince doctors that this research could provide them with valuable information, motivate the doctor to introduce me to interested patients, and if they all agreed, I would coordinate the procurement of the tumor tissue from the surgeon or pathologist and arrange for the tumor tissue to be flown by helicopter to the labs in Baltimore. This research did not have insurance coverage, so I had to convince patients to sign a contract promising payment of forty-thousand dollars. It was fascinating, innovative science and no other company was doing this type of research commercially.

I collected tumor tissue such glioblastoma, mesothelioma, colorectal carcinoma, and sarcoma from the pathology departments at NYU, Memorial Sloan Kettering Cancer Center, and Mount Sinai Medical Center. Unfortunately, a problem was encountered when a pathologist from Mount Sinai asked to see the company's CLIA certificate. This essential document, clinical laboratory improvement amendment, was a certification that the laboratory director met specific education, training, and experience requirements and that the facility itself adheres to federal requirements for testing of human specimens. I soon discovered the company did not have a CLIA certificate. I learned from the company laboratory manager that Champions had not even applied for one, and that it could take up to nine months to get it. I realized that I was working for the wrong firm. Part of my compensation was to be paid on the procurement of tumor tissue. Without a CLIA certificate, hospitals refused to hand over cancer tissue and soon my income would shrivel. Disappointed, I knew that this was not a viable entity for long term growth and longed to get back into a legitimate pharmaceutical company.

Is this Jim Fabio, The *Jim Fabio?*

It was mid-morning, and I was sitting on a stoop on E 97th St. between Madison and 5th Aves. when I received call from a former colleague. Her voice was instantly recognizable. I answered with a mix of curiosity and excitement. I had known this colleague for a long time, and we crossed paths over the years. We had been employed at mutual companies and often saw each other at various scientific symposiums. She said to me that my name has been floating around her new employer, Regeneron.

Have you applied for a job? And what do you want to do?

The question was personal, and it cut through the clutter. Equally curious, I answered that I recently applied for a position as sales trainer. I was confused as she started to quiz me:

What do you really want to do?

I told her:

I want in.

A colleague told me about a biotech start-up based out of Tarrytown, NY called Regeneron. Regeneron had no commercially available products at the time, but they were planning on launching a drug for a retinal disease called age related macular degeneration, a common retinal disease that, if left untreated, could cause blindness. I did not have any experience in the ophthalmology space, and initially did not find it very exciting. However, when I researched the treatment, I discovered the product was a monoclonal antibody injected intra-ocularly. The product was similar a drug called Avastin, an anti-VEGF, commonly used to treat colorectal cancer, and that prompted me to explore the opportunity further. I saw a job posting as a sales trainer and within days I was granted a job interview. Wow, that was quick, I thought. They must really be desperate. Unfortunately, two days later I was informed by the talent acquisition secretary that I was not qualified.

Not qualified? Are you kidding me, I thought.

All my years of oncology sales training experience, coordinating with vendors, writing training modules, and facilitating training classes, must count for something. Apparently, it did not. Disappointed yet resolved I put this set back behind me. A few days later I found myself contemplating my professional journey yet again, as I sat across from the medical offices of Mount Sinai Hospital.

As Andrea and I went back and forth I told her the only job posted on the company website was for a sales training position. She explained that some of the folks from commercial leadership asked if she knew me and what she thought about me as a sales trainer. Without missing a beat, she told them that she knew me as a regional director, and that they needed to hire me. We ended the conversation with her telling me the talent acquisition secretary would contact me about applying for the regional director role. Within minutes I received a call, and an interview was scheduled the following week. I could not believe the turn of events. But the whole process became even stranger as circumstances were conspiring against me. Three times I had to cancel the interview with Regeneron. Within days of an interview being scheduled, I was informed by my boss at Champions that I had tumor tissue to collect at one of the local hospitals. I called and cancelled the interview with Regeneron, hoping it could be rescheduled. And it was. This happened two more times. An interview was scheduled, I found out I had tumor tissue to pick up and was unavailable for the interview. Finally, after the third cancellation I called the secretary back and informed them that I was withdrawing my candidacy. I reasoned that my chances of being hired after cancelling an interview three times was very low. I should have heeded the advice of scripture.

Trust in the Lord with all your heart, and do not lean on your own understanding. In all your ways acknowledge him, and he will make straight your paths.

PROVERBS 3:5–6

I left the recruiter a message and said I was withdrawing my candidacy. To my surprise, the recruiter called me back and said,

Mr. Fabio, you don't understand, they really want to speak with you!

I couldn't believe it. That had never happened to me in my career. A company was chasing me down. I apologized for the repeated cancellations and explained to the recruiter that the only sure time I would not have to cancel an interview was on a Friday. Fridays were the only days tumor tissue could not be delivered to the lab in Baltimore. I interviewed with four different people on a Friday afternoon in late June. I started my new job three weeks later.

I was with Regeneron for thirteen years. I launched two products, and each had four indications. Four indications for retinal diseases and four indications for different types of cancer. I learned a lot about the disease states and treatment modalities from the promotion of the company's products. VEGF-trap and checkpoint inhibitors were terms that described the different biologic mechanisms of action that these products had. These were complex medicines that were administered intravenously or intravitreally, literally a needle was inserted into an eyeball. The general public hardly had any knowledge of the products or diseases, but patients and caregivers quickly became experts as they sought to manage these respective ailments. I am so happy to be a resource to my dear mother who now suffers from some of the same illnesses my products were used for, wet-related macular degeneration and cutaneous squamous cell carcinoma. Her quality of life has improved, and I am grateful I had the opportunity to help her navigate through the many diagnostic tests, providers, and treatment modalities.

In my role as Regional Director, I had a hand in the professional development and promotion of many colleagues that reported to me. It had been a privilege to have a role in helping to relieve a patient's suffering. It was also very satisfying to coach, mentor, and advocate for individuals who reported to me and were dedicated to improving their craft. I am extremely thankful for my colleagues and the professional and personal growth I experienced during my time there.

But all things must come to pass. There was a sudden end to a great career. I was informed one Friday afternoon that I was being terminated and that in two hours I would lose electronic access to all my work. I protested. How could I be terminated after thirteen years of faithful service. But I wasn't naïve. I had witnessed several other colleagues lose their jobs due to departmental restructuring resulting in their positions being eliminated. And I had seen other colleagues fired for gross negligence. But my dismissal seemed different. I had no written warning, no notice, and no recourse. A decision was made, and that decision was final.

There had been signs that the corporate culture had changed. Several directors that had started the oncology division were fired, demoted or resigned in disgust to take other positions in different departments. New management with little commercial oncology experience was now ruling the roost. That inexperience, coupled with toxic arrogance, crossed my path when I was turned down for a promotion. Age discrimination was written all over my denial for this new position. A female colleague twenty years my junior with no relevant managerial experience or knowledge of the disease state was offered the job. I had hired her, mentored her, and encouraged her to seek a director level role. I was infuriated. I consulted a lawyer. He described the turn of events as,

Intriguing.

But he ultimately concluded:

Mr. Fabio, you are a successful white male in New York State, you have no legal standing.

I thought to myself,

How could all my work and experience be summarily dismissed? How could I have no legal recourse?

My lawyer stated that he could easily refer me to another attorney who would happily take my case, and money, but the likelihood of success was null. Pissed off and disappointed, I had to move on. I did move on and resolved myself to put my head down and lead my sales region as I had been doing. Six months later I was dismissed. I sought out another lawyer to pursue wrongful termination or perhaps age discrimination. She thought the circumstances I described could have legal merit, but the problem was where I lived. I could not believe what I heard when she said the exact same thing as my previous lawyer did six months earlier:

Mr. Fabio, you are a successful white male in New York State, you have no legal standing.

This is difficult to comprehend and understand. It would be one thing if my lawyers did not think I had a legitimate case to bring before a judge. It is something completely different when my lawyers explained that the merits of my complaint would be prejudiced because of my demographic. The lawyers shared their opinions based on experience. I would likely have paid thousands of dollars in attorney and court fees over a two-year period and the probability for a positive outcome would be minimal. This was a bitter pill to swallow, but I had to accept the realities. I have accepted my lawyer's counsel. I now move on to the next chapter. Not knowing the path forward, I trust in the Lord's direction.

Commit your works to the Lord, and your plans will be established.

PROVERBS 16:3

The heart of man plans his way, but the Lord establishes his steps.

PROVERBS 16:9

Chapter 25

You go, and do likewise.

—Jesus

I'm a bacteria! I'm the devil! You shouldn't hang around me!

Robert screamed. He was writhing in pain from an infection, shaking in anticipation of more agony from the dreaded needle, and overwhelmed by the despondency that befell him. I had never seen my cousin, the tough guy, who pompously proclaimed that he feared no man, so utterly helpless, vulnerable, and miserable. I had never heard him express his own assessment. He was in physical pain but also in mental anguish. And in his mental anguish there was an epiphany. He cried out to warn me not to be like him, not to be influenced by his contemptuous attitude and behavior. I sought to ease his burden and provide a respite from his misfortune but now found myself traversing a web of suffering that entangled him. This was the beginning of a two-year journey of me deciphering, comprehending, and chronicling how and why he ended up in this predicament. Why was I here with him in the dentist's office, and why now?

The last time I saw my cousin fully healthy was at our other cousin's home in Yonkers three years earlier. Fifteen of us sat around the dinner table catching up, laughing, debating, and teasing each other as cousin Linda served a delicious meal of Cornish hens. Robert was invited but no one really knew if he would show up. As everyone was craving the post meal caffeine and sugar rush that would come from the espresso and dessert, Robert blew in like a hurricane in search of a landing spot. He made a grand entrance, loudly greeting everyone followed with kisses, hugs, and smiles all around.

Robert was an enigma. Tales of his adventures made some of us cringe, some laugh, and left everyone wondering how he came to embrace the lifestyle choice he often inferred. We all heard rumors of his card dealing and gambling. We all had seen his Rolex watches, gold rings, new cars, and penthouse apartment. It seemed unlikely that a painting foreman could afford such things. But what did we know?

Robert looked good. His closely cropped salt and pepper hair stood out in contrast to his black sweater. Sitting at the head of the long wooden dining room table with a demitasse and biscotti he seemed energized and carefree. Many of us had not seen him in ten years. We laughed and remarked how he was just like his father, Jack. Loud, animated, and always had a story to tell. He appealed to the listener like a skilled orator. He made eye contact with everyone and nodded with the expectation that you would nod back as an unspoken sign of you following his narration. He would swing his arms wildly above his head or with his arms stretched out, palms up, pointed directly in your face as his excitement boiled over. And he would tap the nearest person's body part within his reach; a hand, an arm, a leg, or a shoulder, to make sure you had his undivided attention.

It was Thanksgiving morning 2019 when I received the call. I rarely heard from my cousin Jackie and when I did it was usually bad news; about a death of an aunt, uncle, or cousin, followed with dates and times for the wake and funeral.

Jimmy, it's Jackie, Robert had a stroke. He fell on the floor and couldn't get up, he knew something was wrong and managed to call 911. It's bad, Jimmy, he's paralyzed.

I was shocked. Jackie cried. I was in Arizona getting ready with my wife and kids to have dinner at my brother-in-law's house. Robert was in Mount Vernon, NY getting ready to take Jackie and his nephews out to dinner. He had been playing horses on his OTB app and was up a few thousand dollars. Happy with a few extra dollars, he was just about to leave when he noticed a spot on the rug near his bed. With a cigarette in his mouth, he bent down and applied the cleaning powder, rubbed it in, and attempted to get up and vacuum the powder. Suddenly he collapsed on the floor and could not move. He thought that the heavy hand of God was holding him down. He spoke to himself:

Rob, get the fuck up.

He could not. He struggled to lift his head, but it was frozen, embedded in the rug. He heard his phone ring. It was a lifeline. He managed to pull the sheet off his bed and grab it. It was Jackie calling him asking where he was.

Jackie, call 911, I'm having a stroke!

How do you know?

I CAN'T MOVE, CALL 911!

Robert managed to crawl on his right side to the refrigerator and drink some orange juice. He couldn't even swallow it as the left side of his esophagus failed to contract. He laid there helpless. Within minutes the EMTs broke down his second-floor apartment door. His Thanksgiving was spent at Montefiore Medical Center. Jackie's baby brother was forever handicapped. The stroke resulted in his left side, arms, hand, face, and leg with no feeling and limited movement. He would have to relearn how to walk, talk, and care for himself. The doctors said it was a miracle he was alive.

Three years passed from that jovial family gathering in 2017. Robert was now a shadow of his former self. I had not seen Robert in three years and not since he suffered that catastrophic stoke. I had contacted him after his sister assured me that he was stabilized and well enough to be on his own and back into his apartment. I called him and proposed we met at a restaurant in Elmsford, NY. My brother Greg and I took him out, feeling confident that the worst of the COVID-19 pandemic was behind us; all of us having been vaccinated months earlier. I was waiting at the restaurant when Greg and Robert walked in together.

Hey, Cuz, glad to see you. How are you?

I said as I embraced him.

He replied,

I'm hanging tough.

My cousin looked gaunt, thin, and unsteady. His gray button-down shirt grimly reflected off his face making him look sullen and intense. As the evening wore on, it became evident that he had aged and was unwell. He repeated the same stories, as Greg and I looked at each other, unsure why he was rambling about a painting job he did at some wealthy customer's house in NYC over five years ago. Robert was confrontational with the wait staff and sarcastically mocked the tall, twenty something year old server for being Albanian, as if the poor waiter could help it. Robert was still talkative as ever but slightly paranoid. As we listened to his stories he started to poke at my mid-section with his right hand. He didn't say anything, and I assumed he was just gesturing as he normally did to make sure he had my undivided attention. I thought nothing of it but when he jabbed his finger into my ribs two other times, he abruptly stopped talking and blankly stared at me. I confronted him:

What the hell are you doing?

He mumbled something and then aggressively said:

Are you wearing a wire?

He was accusing me of clandestinely wiretapping him for the police. I laughed.

What? Are you out of your mind? You're talking and I'm listening. You're just like Uncle Jack, no one gets a word in edgewise. The only difference is that Jack talked about the marines and World War II, and all you talk about is gambling and the racetrack!

Greg laughed while Robert said nothing. When the steak arrived, Robert struggled to hold the fork in his left hand in order to cut the glistening NY strip with the knife in his right hand. He stubbornly would have continued to struggle until I called the Albanian waiter over and told him to take it back and cut in up in smaller pieces. Robert stared at the waiter apprehensively. In between the steak and Pino Noir we had some laughs, talked about the extended family, and enjoyed a good meal. After dessert and coffee, we parted ways and Greg and I offered to help him out with anything he needed. Not one to ask for anything he replied,

I'm fine, hanging tough, love you guys.

Robert thought he was hanging tough, but he was really struggling with this unexpected curve ball life threw in his direction.

A year and half passed, and I had no contact with my cousin Robert. Jackie was handling his doctors' appointments. But his mental struggles of coping with the loss of independence was even more problematic as he took out his frustrations on the person closest to him. Robert reached out to me via text wishing me a happy birthday. It caught me by surprise, but I was happy that he made the effort. I offered to take him out to dinner again and he mentioned something about that his dentures broke and to contact him at the end of the summer. When I did call him, he said he never did get his dentures fixed. I pressed him, telling him to forget the steak, we'll just go get some lunch. It was early September 2022, and I couldn't believe his condition. He was having trouble with his living arrangements, had no car, no income, no driver's license, and now was under immense pressure to find a new apartment. He owed $40,000 in back rent to his landlord. The NYS COVID inspired emergency law that allowed renters to stay in their housing regardless of one' s ability to pay rent was ending. The landlord was willing to forgive the back rent, but repeatedly took him to court and wanted him out.

Robert's physical conditioned mirrored his apartment. This one-bedroom apartment in Mount Vernon was disgusting. It was nothing like his apartment in New Rochelle that sported a balcony with gorgeous views of the Manhattan skyline. The view out his window was drab. The red brick façade on the other side of his apartment building looked dank and sickly; crumbling and coated with algae and moss. The kitchen area had a buzzing, circular fluorescent light with no covering, glaring down, cold, sterile, and unwelcoming. The carpet was a dingy tan and had black wear from lack of cleaning. The bathroom, not upgraded since I don't know when, used to be white but was now a combination of stains, mold, and filth. He offered me to sit and relax. I declined to go near his worn, brown couch, preferring to pace the floor waiting for him to get ready. A brown calico marble table was situated against the windows and scattered with prescription bottles, a pipe for smoking weed, cigarette ashes, unopened mail, and brass knuckles. He claimed he made this perfectly machined weapon in shop class when he was in high school. I looked at him incredulously. He pulled out an eight-inch hunting knife that he kept in a shoe box while he looked for something else. It was an Original Bowie Hunting knife. He said it was a gift from his friend Dave Stefanik. I only later discovered that Dave stole it with the Ruggiero brothers when they robbed an upstate NY hunting supply store.

When we finally went outside into the bright light, I noticed how bad his teeth were. While he puffed on a cigarette it became clear he was missing several teeth. Others were crooked and he even grabbed one and wiggled it around. It was a miracle he could eat. He spat when he spoke, drooled when he ate, and held a napkin in his hand to prevent food from flying out. I didn't know why he was not proactive with his health, but I soon discovered it had everything to do with him not understanding the consequences for his actions. I convinced him to meet my dentist and get a treatment plan. My original intent was to meet him for dinner, but I soon realized I was getting sucked into a whirlpool of problems. Little did I know.

A few weeks later I picked him up and brought him back to Nanuet, NY to meet with my dentist. We were both in shock as we learned what was required to get new dentures. Nine teeth would need to be pulled, and two root canals would need to be performed before dentures could even be considered. After the appointment, he paced around my kitchen asking me point blank,

Why are you helping me? Why are you doing this?

Robert seemed suspicious, as if I had an ulterior motive. Without hesitation I responded,

Because you are a Fabio, we're family, I can't stand by and watch you struggle like this. My father instilled in me a devotion to look out for family, and you're family.

Robert seemed doubtful and mumbled something under his breath. The next day I thought more about why I was going to help him and texted him back:

I'm helping you because I'm loyal to family, I want to demonstrate Christ's love, I want to give you hope and help ease your burden.

His only affirmation was a text that read *Thank God* and a prayer emoji.

Anyone who interacted with my cousin outside of immediate family stayed clear of him. In his current state he looked like trouble. The stroke left him paralyzed on his left side. He walked with a limp that others could easily interpret as a person who was under the influence of alcohol or drugs. His disheveled hair and wrinkled shirt advertised his lack of care. His left arm was permanently contracted, giving the appearance that he was ready to throw a punch. When he glanced in someone's direction, he usually stared a little too long. I could sense their discomfort. People make quick decisions of strangers and with one look at Robert people knew to steer clear. He looked like he had a chip on his shoulder. He could be as nasty as an angry Doberman pincher, aggressively barking and willing to bite at the slightest provocation. He mocked and verbally challenged a six-foot-six pizza maker stretching out pizza dough because Robert thought he looked at him wrong way. When he spoke to waiters or convenience store clerks, he barked out his demands in loud, short, outbursts. He was not approachable, and most people made no effort at small talk, even avoiding eye contact. The only time Robert proactively spoke with someone was when he wanted to flirt. Too often he put his hands in the wrong place. On several occasions he inappropriately put his hands on a cute medical technician or receptionists' hair, shoulder, or waist which made them visibly uncomfortable. In his mind he was still the mobbed up, street-wise, man of power and influence, that party girls wanted to be with. Now, three years after his stroke, with no job, soon to be homeless, no car, no driver's license, no bank account, no savings, no companion, and in poor health. He was more akin to a sick dog kicked to the curb. His physical, mental, and financial troubles conspired against him. Pitifully, almost all of his misfortunes were self-inflicted.

Robert's choices caught up with him. His decades of unhealthy choices led him down this path and there was no escape route. Gambling was the core of his being. He was a degenerate gambler. Everything in his life took a back seat to his one true obsession. Gambling and the desire for free money surpassed any other occupation and pursuit. His formal education ceased in high school. He navigated the unpredictable disruption of police raids, arrests, incarceration, and the wrath of ruthless mobsters and common criminals by his own wits and bravado. Gambling supported his drug habit. Weed, alcohol, and coke were his daily companions. They mellowed his racing mind, dulled his senses, and stimulated his nerves. They also obscured any desire and preparation for long term plans. Drugs fueled his vices and became a magnetic device that attracted his cadre of likeminded friends and associates. His stints with boxing, painting, and restaurant ownership all collapsed because of his lack of discipline and his debts. His family suffered from his constant lawlessness and succumbed to indifference as they were powerless to influence him. Every relationship collapsed. He admitted he never truly loved any of his wives or girlfriends. His relationships were transactional. They all benefitted from the money that came from gambling winnings or large sums of cash provided by a loan shark. His lifestyle of hand to mouth survival and paying everything by cash, was not sustainable. His choice to be paid in cash eliminated any chance of getting employer healthcare. He refused to pay any insurance himself. By not having insurance he was forced to pay out of pocket for doctors' services and prescription medicines. And the costs would be astronomical. He refused to get checkups, and his health suffered. His incessant smoking contributed to his health decline in energy, to lose rotten teeth, and have a sullen, pale complexion. Months before the stroke, he accompanied his boss at his doctor's appointment. The doctor looked at Robert and offered to evaluate him as well. Robert waved him off, said he wasn't going to pay cash, it was too much to lay out. For decades he forfeited hundreds of thousands of dollars in gambling losses. His faulty logic would not allow him to pay out large sums of cash with no immediate return of value. Robert had no problem with paying for meals, drinks, drugs, clothes, travel, car leases, rent, and utility bills. He valued what his senses could perceive, he valued the tangible benefits that he could taste, touch, smell, and see. The idea of preventative medicine was a foreign concept. Robert was a gambler to the core and unknowingly gambled with his health.

Gambling is often referred to as a disease. It is really a psychological phenomenon giving an illusion of control and many times guided by superstition. It is an addictive disorder that effects the brain. Young people are particularly susceptible to the reward mechanism high risk gambling provides. High risk, high reward was Robert's mantra. Bet large, win large. In reality Robert spent most of his life winning just enough to sustain a modem of comfort while mostly chasing his losses. The reward of winning was reinforced by his own beliefs in his mastery of the games. In his mind, he was smarter than everyone else. He had a system: Robert believed in patterns that if he won, he would continue to win, an unlikely possibility, but if he lost, he would not quit because luck was bound to change. If a dealer busted, lost their hands, he believed that fortune favored the gambler. Robert did not gamble for entertainment. This was not a leisure sport for him. Gambling was his lifestyle.

None of his rationales for gambling was based on logic and reason. None of it was guided by any moral principle or spiritual code.

I'm an atheist. I believe in myself.

he proclaimed when I asked him about what he believed in. Robert thrived on the attention, respect, and perks he received from his frequent wins. Party girls love men with money and Robert flashed his façade of wealth through the stack of chips or wads of cash he would lay out on a blackjack table. His business partners valued his ability to attract customers and keep threats from organized members of the mob at bay. And he loved the fantasy of wealth he had through comped drinks, meals, entertainment, and hotel rooms. For most of his life Robert was guided by his belief of using force to gain power; power to beget money, money to satisfy his vices. He gambled to win money. Free money.

Robert is now penniless, totally dependent of government entitlement, social security, disability, and food subsidies. He spends most of his time texting imaginary scam artists posing as beautiful celebrities. He has a winning smile with his new dentures and his health has improved dramatically although he refuses to quit smoking cigarettes.

Robert is more reflective, a bit more somber. He often shares with me that he wished he had obtained an education, a wife and children, and a house and car. He still commands an audience at summer get-togethers with my brothers and cousins and has become a welcome guest at the Christmas dinner table. He is remorseful about his choices but does not dwell of his failures. He is a survivor. His knowledge or interest in anything spiritual is minimal. On our trips to the doctors' office or just hanging out in his apartment he often wonders why God punished him.

I want my life back. I loved my life.

Other days he wonders why God spared him. I don't have any answers that could satisfy his dilemma. I and many others have sought to ease his burden and help him navigate through this next season of life. I avoid quoting Bible passages, preferring to demonstrate Christ's love through action. Robert is most appreciative and often calls me his brother.

As I was flipping through cable TV one Saturday morning I stopped for a while to hear a Rabbi discuss a passage from Genesis. It caught my interest because it addressed man's first question to God in the Bible. In all the Sunday morning sermons I have heard over the years I don't recall ever hearing this being discussed. Rabbi David Wolpe was being interviewed and explained his interpretation of Genesis 4:9.

Then the LORD said to Cain "Where is Abel your brother? He said "I don't know; am I my brother's keeper?"

I immediately thought of my brother Greg's smart aleck response to Mr. Fornabio, our next-door neighbor. I was eager to hear what the Rabbi would say about man's first question to God. He explained that the message of the Old Testament could be summed up by learning from Cain's question to God; all the books of the Bible reveal a clear message.

Am I my brother's keeper?

The Rabbi asserted,

The answer is yes.

Epilogue

"You must take another path,"
he replied, when he saw me weeping,
"if you wish to escape from this savage place;

for this beast, for which you cry,
does not allow others to pass on its path,
but so impedes it that it kills it;

and its nature is so wicked and evil,
that it never satisfies its greedy desire,
and after the meal it is hungrier than before.

Many are the animals with which it marries,
and there will be more still, until the hound
comes, who will make it die in pain.

-Dante Alighieri

The soul's journey toward God is a lifelong endeavor. Obstacles to holiness are boundless where feral beasts obstruct the way in a gloomy forest. We deceive ourselves and are deceived.

> *The heart is deceitful above all things, and desperately sick; who can understand it? "I the Lord search the heart and test the*

mind, to give every man according to his ways, according to the fruit of his deeds."

JEREMIAH 17:9–10

Spiritual enslavement is manifested through thoughts and deeds. These shackles come in many forms. The lack of mental strength or will power to act with good judgement, violence in all its forms; physical, sexual, psychological, and through deprivation, or the intentional deception to deprive someone of a legal right or to unjustly gain from a victim. These chains so vividly described by Dante in the *Divine Comedy* are not novelties, but are evinced in our flawed human nature. The three beasts: lonza, leone, and lupa representing akrasia, violence, and fraud, and block our way. Feral and uncontrolled they turned the pilgrim astray from the straight path to salvation. On his path through the Inferno, Purgatorio, and toward Paradiso, Dante, the pilgrim, is confronted with the consequences of sin. Souls were tormented from their own devic-es. They lie imprisoned by unrepentant pride, envy, rage, spiritual laziness, greed, gluttony, and lust. They all faced eternal damnation, forever separated from God.

I too was lost in the wilderness of sin. It enslaved my being. Inwardly, I was alone and without the presence of God. Outwardly my behavior reflected my chosen vices. Smoking marijuana was one of my vices that I was freed from. I toked to get high. But the thrill and high failed to satisfy. Marijuana and drugs clouded my thinking, inhibited my social development, negatively affected my health, and stagnated my personal and professional growth. I lacked the will to quit and was blinded to opportunities that lay before me. I lacked self-control, a fruit of the spirit, because I did not have the indwelling of the Holy Spirit. I made a trip through my own Inferno. But I was cleansed of the grime of my thoughts and deeds. I came out cleansed, anew. All my waywardness was covered with a balm of forgiveness. I am forgiven through repentance and faith in Jesus. Not through penance, but instantaneously through repentance. My life gained faith where there was none. My heart was pierced by the promise of hope through the word of God. There was hope, after all.

> *... and hope does not disappoint, because the love of God has been poured out within our hearts through the Holy Spirit who was given to us.*
>
> ROMANS 5:5

The source of my entrapment was pride. The idea that my way of living is superior to that of how God would have me live. And how sad it is that one of the vehicles of my entrapment, marijuana, and Robert's, gambling, is now so pervasive and socially acceptable. The smell of weed is everywhere due to recent laws allowing the recreational use of marijuana. No longer a reflection of counterculture rebellion, marijuana in all its forms is celebrated and promoted. The poison that entrapped me for years is now legalized. Gambling is no longer perceived as a seedy endeavor to make quick money. It is no longer restricted to Las Vegas, Atlantic City, or Native American run casinos; it is promoted and celebrated by celebrities and sports heroes through online apps. It is presented as fun, enticing, and exciting. The power of these vices to entrap and enslave is real. These pursuits promise escape and fortune from the drudgery of the daily grind of work, and life's difficulties. Let the buyer beware. These desires are feral beasts that always want more. The Lord warned Cain about sin crouching at his door, desiring him. But Cain failed to heed His counsel.

> *... If you do well [believing Me and doing what is acceptable and pleasing to Me], will you not be accepted? And if you do*

not do well [but ignore My instruction], sin crouches at your door; its desire is for you [to overpower you], but you must master it."

GENESIS 4:7 (AMPC)

It is wise to heed God's counsel.

I often reflect on my spiritual purpose. What should be my priorities in life? How can I be used for the greater good? On one of the many visits my parents made back north to visit their family, I was often given a plant from his garden as a gift. My father had dropped off some tomato plants to me. He knew I would enjoy the fresh tomatoes, Roma and Beefsteak, that were carefully nurtured in his greenhouse, when they fully ripened on the vine at the end of the summer. His expectation was that I would plant them right away. I could not believe how angry he became when I told him I would plant them the next morning. I had other things planned that afternoon and evening. He was quite displeased with my response to which he proceeded to berate me saying:

You need to get your priorities straight!

I laughed at his insistence. But realized if I waited too long to plant them, they may wither in the hot sun. I planted them soon thereafter and enjoyed the fruitful harvest later that summer. Not acting on wise counsel has ramifications. And while I was not always in synch with my dad's priorities, I have sought guidance from scripture about heavenly priorities. There is a straight path and the direction is clear.

And you shall love the Lord God with all your heart and with all your soul and with all your mind and all your strength. The second is this "You shall love your neighbor as yourself." "There is no other commandment greater than these."

MARK 12:30–33

I know that I cannot do these in my own strength and power. But scripture tells me I always had a helper.

> *But the Helper, the Holy Spirit, whom the Father will send in my name, he will teach you all things and bring to your remembrance all that I have said to you.*
>
> John 14:26

> *Nevertheless, I tell you the truth: it is to your advantage that I go away, for if I do not go away, the Helper will not come to you. But if I go, I will send him to you.*
>
> John 16:7

Thanks be to the Lord!

Chapter Notes

Chapter 1

1. Brian Kates, "Cops Hit New Joint & Find Posh Casino." *Daily News*, 25 Feb. 1977, pp. 17, https://www.newspapers.com/image/481934403
2. Don Gentile, "Despite cops, casinos are still winners." *Daily News*, 20 Aug. 1980, pp. 5+, https://www.newspapers.com/article/daily-news/130164025/

Chapter 2

1. "Stevens Confers Graduate Degrees." *The Journal News*, 17 Jun. 1958, pp. 9.
2. "Our History." *Ourladymtcarmelbx.org*, accessed 30 Jul. 2024.
3. "History of the Founding of the ARS and Major Awards." *arsoffice.org*, accessed 30 Jul. 2024.
4. "Crosbie–Fabio Wedding at St. Margaret's Church." *The Journal News*, 14 Aug. 1958, pp. 6.

Chapter 3

1. Rebecca Schetterer, "Flaming Car Crash Kills Fleeing Youth." *The Reporter Dispatch*, 7 Oct. 1971, pp. 4.

Chapter 4

1. "Death Notices." *The Herald Statesman*, 12 Jun 1968, pp. 2.
2. "Who Ate the Aid Money Received by Moris-Şinasi Children's Hospital from Outside?" https://avrupapress-com.translate.goog/main/2019/06/18/moris-sinasi-cocuk-hastanesinin-disardan-gelen-yardim-paralarini-kimler, yedi/?, accessed 17 Mar. 2025.
3. G. Lincoln McCurdy, "A Chronicle of Turkish American Relations." https://www.ataa.org/pdf/Chronicle_of_Turkish_American_Relations_1923-2023.pdf, pp. 53.
4. "Schinasi—The Cigarette King." *The Morning News*, 14 Oct. 14,1919, pp. 4.
5. "Schinasi Was Real Tobacco King." *The Index-Journal*, 24 Oct.1919, pp. 3.
6. "Mrs. Semple Acquires Schinasi Mansion in New York." *The Montgomery Advertiser*, 21 Aug. 1930, pp. 6.
7. "Man Drowns as Brother Fails Rescue." *The Herald Statesman*, 11 Aug. 1969, pp. 2.
8. Bryan Thomas, "The Mello-Kings Biography." *allmusic.com*, accessed 2 Jun. 2024.
9. "Yonkers and area obituaries." *The Herald Statesman*, 17 Jul. 1972, pp. 16.
10. "Wrestling." Lincoln Log 1973, Lincoln High School Yearbook, *classmates.com*, pp. 188.
11. "The Avengers." Lincoln Log 1973, Lincoln High School Yearbook, *classmates.com*, pp. 33.
12. "Football." Lincoln Log 1973, Lincoln High School Yearbook, *classmates.com*, pp. 170.
13. "Son of PBA president arrested in gambling." *The Herald Statesman*, 3 Sept. 1976, pp. 28.
14. Peter Johnson and M.J. Zuckerman, "D.A.: Arrests will put crimp in syndicate." *The Reporter Dispatch*, 3 Apr. 1981, pp. 7.

15. "Yonkers man shot in dispute." *Mount Vernon Argus*, 6 Sept. 1980, pp. 6.

CHAPTER 5

1. "Spring '60." Red and White, Lowell High School Yearbook, *classmates.com*, pp. 19.
2. Philip Wechsler, "Charge Bankers, Biz Execs Looted Union Pension Fund." *Daily News*, 4 Feb. 1975, pp. JL5.
3. "To Honor Joseph Tonelli with Investiture Dinner." *The Post-Star*, 3 Dec. 1969, pp. 21.
4. "John Toomey, Joseph Tonelli Inducted in Knights of Malta." *The Post-Star*, 18 Jan. 1974, pp. 11.
5. "Paperworkers 'Chief' accused of embezzling, racketeering." *The Daily Sentinel*, 30 Jul. 1978, pp.13.
6. "Union President Is Indicted." *Richmond Times-Dispatch*, 20 Jul. 1978, pp. 8.
7. "Lawyer says Carter call not influence." *The Orlando Sentinel*, 20 Jul. 1978, pp. 3-A.
8. "Check Kiting in the Digital Age." *White Paper*, NICE Actimize, https://www.niceactimize.com/Documents/fraud_white_paper_check_kiting_in_the_digital_age.pdf, accessed 23 Aug 2024.
9. "Labor veteran with many friends." *The Reporter Dispatch*, 17 Dec. 1979, pp. 11.
10. "2 LI Bankers Indicted in Pension Theft." *Newsday* (Suffolk Edition), 4 Feb. 1975, pp. 25.
11. "N.Y. Woman Admits Guilt in Pension Fund Theft." *The News*, 28 Aug. 1975, pp 11.
12. "United States of America v. James R. Tonelli, Appellant, 577 F.2nd 194 (3rd Cir. 1978)." *law.justia.com*, accessed 6 Oct. 2018.

13. "Produce broker sentenced." *The Record*, 22 Apr. 1976, pp. 6.
14. "Woman charged with loan defraud." *The Eunice News*, 5 Nov. 1986, pp. 3.
15. First National Bank of Louisville, Plaintiff-appellant, v. Loretta Lustig, et al., Defendants, fidelity & Deposit Co. of Maryland, Defendant-appellee, 975 F.2nd 1165 (5th Cir. 1992), *law.justia.com*, accessed 7 Oct. 2018.
16. First National Bank of Columbus, Columbus, Georgia, Plaintiff, v. Pelican Homestead and Savings Association, Formerly First financial Louisiana Savings & Loan Association, defendant-third Party Plaintiff-appellee, v. Robert F. Farmigoni, Third Party Defendant-appellant, 869 F.2nd 896 (5th Cir. 1989), *law.justia.com*, accessed 7 Oct. 2018.
17. "Labor veteran with many friends." *The Reporter Dispatch*, 17 Dec. 1979, pp. 11.

Chapter 6

1. "Gloves Results." *Daily News*, 11 Feb. 1976, pp. 105.
2. "Gloves Results." *Daily News*, 18 Feb. 1976, pp. 89.
3. "Robbery attempt." *The Herald Statesman*, 5 May 1976, pp. 31.

Chapter 7

1. "Stolen goods case leads to arrest." *The Herald Statesman*, 26 Mar. 1976, pp. 3.
2. "Judge Sentences New Yorker in Stamford Case." *The Hartford Courant*, 5 Jun. 1965, pp. 6.
3. "Masiello faces bribe count." *The Journal News*, 7 Oct. 1972, pp. 8
4. "Mafia-Linked Insurance Frauds Under Study." *Corpus Christi Times*, 7 Jun. 1969, pp. 2A.

5. "Indictments Paint Bloody Picture of Mob Takeover." *Press of Atlantic City*, 27 Aug. 1977, pp. 6.
6. Lincoln Log 1962, Lincoln High School Yearbook, *classmates.com*, pp. 6.
7. "Masiello faces bribe count." *The Journal News*, 7 Oct. 1972, pp. 8.
8. "Fleetwood Bank Suspect Pleads Guilty." *Mount Vernon Argus*, 16 Sep. 1966, pp. 1.
9. "Painter Guilty of Killing Wife." *Daily News*, 29 May 1958, pp. 34.
10. William Federici, "A Hoodlet Arrested in Bribery." *Daily News*, 6 Oct. 1972, pp. 5.
11. Peter Johnson and M.J. Zuckerman, "Rockland man arrested in crime-syndicate bust." *The Journal News*, 3 Apr. 1981, pp. B5.
12. Neil S. Martin, "Bootleggers gain in area." *The Journal News*, 8 Oct. 1973, pp. 25.
13. Peter Hardin, "City man dies in 1-alarm fire." *The Herald Statesman*, 8 Jul. 1976, pp. 1.
14. Peter Hardin, "Police probe 'gangland' city slaying." *The Herald Statesman*, 17 Nov. 1976, pp. 1+.
15. Lynn Mulvaney, "Slaying Leads to Stolen Guns." *The Kingston Daily Freeman*, 17 Feb. 1977, pp. 1+.
16. Tara Connell, "Suspects had skull 'souvenir.'" *The Standard-Star*, 16 Feb. 1977, pp. 6.
17. Tara Connell, "DeRuggieros plead guilty." *The Reporter Dispatch*, 17 Nov. 1978, pp. 2.

Chapter 8

1. Brian Kates, "Cops Hit New Joint & Find Posh Casino." *Daily News*, 25 Feb. 1977, pp. 19.

2. "14 indicted for driver's license scam." *The Standard-Star*, 27 Jan. 1983, pp. 5.
3. "Gibbins KO'd, In Hospital." *Daily News*, 28 Sat. 1976, pp. 33.
4. Michael Daly, "Down for the count, Ex-boxer vanished on visit to guard." *Daily News*, 5 Jan. 1997, pp. 3+.
5. Gary Craig, "Cops hot on trail of two local cold cases." *Democrat and Chronicle*, 3 Jun. 2003, pp. 1+.
6. Gary Craig, "Gibbons disappearance appears tied to robbery." *Democrat and Chronicle*, 13 Dec. 2011, pp. 6A.
7. Mary Ann Giordano, "Police nab duo; bounty recovered." *The Herald Statesman*, 8 May 1978, pp. 12.

Chapter 9

1. "Criminal Disposition Information." New York State Unified Court System, accessed 26 May 2023.
2. Don Gentile, "Despite cops, casinos are still winners." *Daily News,* 20 Aug. 1980, pp. 5+.
3. "29 charged in DOB-mob corruption sting." *https://abc7ny.com/archive/7043142/*, accessed 1 Aug. 2024.
4. "Testimony links Gotti to mob actions." *The Daily Times,* 4 Apr. 1998, pp. 9.

Chapter 10

1. "Experts." Institute for New Economic Thinking, *https://www.ineteconomics.org/research/experts/gschinasi,* accessed 30 Jul. 2024.
2. Barbara Gribbon, "Let's Get Acquainted: 'Farm House' Residents Have Varied Interests." *The Journal News,* 23 Aug. 1962, pp. 15.

CHAPTER 11

1. Hal Lindsay, *The Late Great Planet Earth*, Zondervan, 1970.
2. "Our History." *Maranthanj.org*, accessed 4 Jun. 2024.
3. Nina Wood, "Church of Nazarene Offers New Approach." *The Record*, 25 Jan. 1971, pp. B-1+.
4. Peggy Parke, "'Jesus Thing' Crowds Small Church." *The Sunday News*, 14 Mar. 1971, pp. 92.
5. Ken Bookman and David Corcoran, "1,000 Youths 'Turn On' to Christ." *The Record*, 12 Apr. 1971, pp. B-1+.
6. "The Maranatha Coffeehouse photo." *The Record*, 7 Oct. 1970, pp. 1.
7. "Maranatha-Soon." *Psychedelic-rocknroll.blogspot.com*, accessed 4 Jun. 2024.
8. Patrick Clark, "Kids Returning to 'Old-Time Religion.'" *Daily News*, 19 Mar. 1972, pp. 1+.
9. William Reel, "Hooray for Jesus as Kids Tout Big Garden Rally." *Daily News*, 19 Aug. 1972, pp. 16.

CHAPTER 12

1. Freddie Francis, director. *Dr. Terror's House of Horror's* Amicus Productions, 1965.
2. Jon Cahn, Your View, "Power for Living" Message." *The Journal News*, 14 Feb. 1984, pp. 14.
3. "Directory of Religious Services, Messianic." *The Record*, 15 Apr. 1988, pp. D-5.
4. Jonathan Cahn, *https://www.facebook.com/jonathancahn.official*, accessed 31 Jul. 2024.
5. Jonathan Cahn, *https://www.youtube.com/jonathancahn.official*, accessed 31 Jul. 2024.

Chapter 13

1. "Manhattan's Invisible Korean Power." *nypress.com,* accessed 4 Jun. 2024.
2. Edward O. Thorp, *Beat the Dealer, A Winning Strategy for the Game of Twenty-One*, Penguin Random House, 1966.
3. Helen Brown, interviewer, "Chip Taylor: 'Playing in maximum security prisons is one of my favorite things to do.'" *Independent.co.uk,* accessed 4 Jun. 2024.
4. Bill McGarvey, "Busted: Chip Taylor." *bustedhalo.com*, accessed 4 Jun. 2024.
5. Brett Berns and Bob Sarles, directors, *BANG, The Bert Berns Story.* Abramorama, 2016.
6. Ryan Walsh, *Astral Weeks: A Secret History of 1968,* Penguin Press, 2018.
7. "Suffern Man Arrested in '81 Queens Slaying." *Newsday*, 24 Nov. 1998.
8. Jonathan Bandler and Timothy O'Connor, "19 held in gambling ring." *The Journal News*, 2 Oct. 2009, pp. 1+.
9. "The Heat's on for 'Lights Out' Parking Parties." *The Herald Statesman*, 13 Sep. 1960, pp. 12.
10. "3 Dice Game Participants Plead Guilty." *The Herald Statesman,* 23 Sep. 1959, pp. 17.

Chapter 14

1. John Dalmos, "Their gospel is to spread the 'good news.'" *The Journal News,* 12 Jan. 1984. pp. 37.
2. Frank Leonard, "Hearing on gambling charge." *The Journal News*, 21 Jun. 1984, pp. 14.
3. "NYC man pays fine after admitting charges." *The Journal News*, 29 Jun. 1984, pp. 16.
4. Stan Zagorski, "Jesus Revolution." *Time*, 1971.

5. Belinda Luscombe, "The Story Behind TIME's 'Jesus Revolution' Cover-And Where the Movement Stands a Half-Century Later." *time.com*, accessed 4 Jun. 2024.
6. Kings Garden (1984, Dec.). [Advertisement for Kings Garden] *Battle Creek Enquirer*, pp. B-4.
7. King's Garden (1985, Jul.). [Advertisement for King's Garden] *Battle Creek Enquirer*, pp. 2B.
8. King's Garden (1985, Oct.). [Advertisement for King's Garden] *Battle Creek Enquirer*, pp. 2B.
9. King's Garden (1985, Nov.). [Advertisement for King's Garden] *Battle Creek Enquirer*, pp. 2B.

CHAPTER 16

1. *harvestnyc.org*
2. *calverychapel.com*
3. Jay E. Adams, *Competent to Counsel.* Zondervan, 1986.
4. *noutheticmedia.com*

CHAPTER 18

1. Lederle Laboratories, *nyheritage.contentdm.oclc.org*, accessed 5 Jun. 2024.
2. "Thank You." Denny Vivolo, *https://youtu.be/DmN80epAF2o*, accessed 7 Oct 2025.
3. Pastor Chuck Corradino, *https://www.bconlove.org/pastor-chuck*, accessed 6 Oct. 2025.
4. KC Murdock et al. "Antitumor agents. 1. 1,4-Bis[(aminoalkyl) amino]-9,10-anthracenediones," *Journal of Medicinal Chemistry*, 1979 Sep;22(9):1024-30.
5. "Adria Labs to market Adriamycin in pre-filled vials under licensing accord." *The Pink Sheet*, 6 Jul. 1992.

6. Larry Norton, MD, *mskcc.org*
7. Robert Berkow, M.D., editor-in-chief, *The Merck Manual of Diagnosis and Therapy,* Merck Sharp & Dohme Research Laboratories, 1987.
8. Bruce G. Raphael, MD, *nyulangone.org*
9. Rituxan (rituximab) FDA Approval History, *drugs.com,* accessed 5 Jun. 2024.
10. Paul Kirby, "3 are charged after 6-week police probe of drugs in Yonkers." *The Reporter Dispatch,* 2 Oct. 1994, pp. 7.
11. "List of deaths." *The Herald Statesman,* 13 Sep. 1998, pp. 6A

CHAPTER 19

1. Robert Celestino, director, *Mr. Vincent,* Vanguard Cinema, 1997.
2. "Mr. Vincent." Schermi d'Amore – Verona Film Festival, *imdb.com,* 1997.
3. Today's Screening — "Mr. Vincent." Montreal World Film Festival, *The Gazette*, 24 Aug. 1997.
4. Robert Celestino, director, "Mr. Vincent." *pro-www.tcm.com,* accessed 5 Jun. 2024.

CHAPTER 22

1. Obituaries, *The Journal News,* 23 Jul. 2007, pp. 5B.
2. Obituaries, *The Journal News*, 28 Jul. 2007, pp. 5B.

CHAPTER 23

1. Alvin Roth, "The Roth-Stone System: Al Roth on bridge." *Melville,* 1953.
2. Alvin Roth, "Modern Bridge Bidding Compete." *Funk & Wagnalls,* 1968.

3. Jack Altshul, "It's Neither Chess Nor Bridge." *Newsday*, 18 Aug. 1972.
4. Hello Gorgeous (1996, Dec.). [Advertisement for Hello Gorgeous] *Daily News*, pp. 7CN.
5. Anthony M. DeStefano, "AG seeks death for gangster." *Newsday*, 23 Apr. 2007, pp. A22.

www.ingramcontent.com/pod-product-compliance
Lightning Source LLC
Chambersburg PA
CBHW051504120626
46551CB00012B/776

* 9 7 9 8 9 9 3 2 6 6 0 2 2 *